Computer
C Programming

V. RAJARAMAN

Honorary Professor
Supercomputer Education and Research Centre
Indian Institute of Science, Bangalore

PHI Learning Private Limited

Delhi-110092
2020

₹ 695.00

COMPUTER BASICS AND C PROGRAMMING
V. Rajaraman

© 2008 by PHI Learning Private Limited, Delhi. All rights reserved. No part of this book may be reproduced in any form, by mimeograph or any other means, without permission in writing from the publisher.

ISBN-978-81-203-3343-7

The export rights of this book are vested solely with the publisher.

Fifth Printing . . . . **April, 2020**

Published by Asoke K. Ghosh, PHI Learning Private Limited, Rimjhim House, 111 Patparganj Industrial Estate, Delhi-110092 and Printed by Syndicate Binders, A-20, Hosiery Complex, Noida, Phase-II Extension, Noida-201305 (N.C.R. Delhi).

CONTENTS

Preface   *ix*

Part I COMPUTER BASICS
---

1. Information Technology and Computer Basics   **3–22**

Learning Objectives   *3*
1.1   Introduction   *3*
1.2   Types of Data   *5*
    1.2.1   Numeric Data   *6*
    1.2.2   Internal Representation of Numeric Data   *6*
    1.2.3   Encoding of Decimal Numbers   *7*
    1.2.4   Counting in Binary System   *8*
    1.2.5   Representing Powers of 2   *9*
    1.2.6   Hexadecimal Representation of Numbers   *9*
1.3   Representation of Characters in Computers   *10*
1.4   Some Examples of Processing Textual Data   *13*
1.5   A Simple Model of a Computer   *15*
1.6   Data Processing Using a Computer   *17*
1.7   Desktop Computer   *18*
Exercises   *21*

2. Computer Software   **23–36**

Learning Objectives   *23*
2.1   Introduction   *23*
2.2   Operating System   *24*
    2.2.1   Basic Input–Output System (BIOS)   *25*
    2.2.2   Functions of an Operating System   *26*
    2.2.3   Types of Operating Systems   *27*
2.3   Programming Languages   *30*
    2.3.1   Assembly Language   *30*
    2.3.2   High Level Languages   *31*
2.4   A Classification of Programming Languages   *33*
Exercises   *35*

3. Internet and the World Wide Web   **37–62**

Learning Objectives   *37*
3.1   Introduction   *37*
3.2   Local Area Network (LAN)   *38*
    3.2.1   Technology Used in LAN   *40*
3.3   Wide Area Network (WAN)   *41*
3.4   Internet   *43*
    3.4.1   IP Address   *43*
    3.4.2   Connecting PCs/LANs to Telephone Lines   *44*
3.5   Naming Computers Connected to Internet   *45*
3.6   Some Internet Applications   *47*
3.7   E-mail   *48*
3.8   The World Wide Web   *51*
    3.8.1   Hypertext   *52*
    3.8.2   Universal Resource Locator   *52*
3.9   Information Retrieval from the World Wide Web   *55*
    3.9.1   Resource Directories   *55*
    3.9.2   Search Engine-based Retrieval   *56*
3.10 Other Facilities Provided by Browsers   *58*
    3.10.1 File Transfer   *59*
    3.10.2 Telnet   *60*
3.11 Conclusions   *60*
Exercises   *61*

Part II   PROGRAMMING USING C

4. Computer Algorithms   **65–69**

Learning Objectives   *65*
4.1   Algorithms   *65*
4.2   Characteristics of Computers   *68*
4.3   An Illustrative Computer Algorithm   *68*

5. Developing Algorithms   **70–85**

Learning Objectives   *70*
5.1   Flow Charts   *70*
5.2   A Simple Model of a Computer   *72*
5.3   More Flow Charting Examples   *74*
Exercises   *84*

6. Programming Preliminaries   **86–90**

Learning Objectives   *86*
6.1   High Level Programming Languages for Computers   *86*
6.2   C Language   *88*
6.3   On the Description of a Programming Language   *90*

7. Simple Computer Programs   **91–102**

Learning Objectives   *91*
7.1   Writing a Program   *91*
7.2   Input Statement   *96*
7.3   Some C Program Examples   *97*
Exercises   *102*

8. Numeric Constants and Variables   **103–111**

Learning Objectives   *103*
8.1   Constants   *103*
8.2   Scalar Variables   *107*
8.3   Declaring Variable Names   *108*
8.4   Defining Constants   *109*
Exercises   *110*

9. Arithmetic Expressions   **112–128**

Learning Objectives   *112*
9.1   Arithmetic Operators and Modes of Expressions   *112*
9.2   Integer Expressions   *113*
9.3   Floating Point Expressions   *113*
9.4   Operator Precedence in Expressions   *114*
9.5   Examples of Arithmetic Expressions   *116*
9.6   Assignment Statements   *118*
9.7   Defining Variables   *119*
9.8   Arithmetic Conversion   *120*
9.9   Assignment Expressions   *121*
9.10   Increment and Decrement Operators   *122*
9.11   Multiple Assignments   *123*
9.12   Summary   *125*
Exercises   *127*

10. Input and Output in C Programs   **129–137**

Learning Objectives   *129*
10.1   Output Function   *129*
10.2   Input Function   *133*
Exercises   *136*

11. Conditional Statements   **138–151**

Learning Objectives   *138*
11.1   Relational Operators   *139*
11.2   Compound Statement   *140*
11.3   Conditional Statements   *141*
11.4   Example Programs Using Conditional Statements   *145*
11.5   Style Notes   *149*
Exercises   *150*

12. Implementing Loops in Programs   152–167

Learning Objectives   152
12.1 The *while* Loop   *154*
12.2 The *for* Loop   *159*
12.3 The *do while* Loop   *164*
Exercises   166

13. Defining and Manipulating Arrays   168–184

Learning Objectives   168
13.1 Array Variable   *168*
13.2 Syntax Rules for Arrays   *171*
13.3 Use of Multiple Subscripts in Arrays   *173*
13.4 Reading and Writing Multidimensional Arrays   *174*
13.5 Examples of for Loop with Arrays   *178*
Exercises   183

14. Logical Expressions and More Control Statements   185–207

Learning Objectives   185
14.1 Introduction   *185*
14.2 Logical Operators and Expressions   *187*
14.3 Precedence Rules for Logical Operators   *189*
14.4 Some Examples of Use of Logical Expressions   *191*
14.5 The *switch* Statement   *193*
14.6 The *break* Statement   *201*
14.7 The *continue* Statement . *203*
Exercises   205

15. C Program Examples   208–228

Learning Objectives   208
15.1 Description of a Small Computer   *208*
15.2 A Machine Language Program   *211*
15.3 An Algorithm to Simulate the Small Computer   *212*
15.4 A Simulation Program for the Small Computer   *213*
15.5 A Statistical Data Processing Program   *216*
15.6 Processing Survey Data with Computers   *221*
Exercises   227

16. Functions   229–256

Learning Objectives   229
16.1 Introduction   *229*
16.2 Defining and Using Functions   *230*
16.3 Syntax Rules for Function Declaration   *237*
16.4 Arrays in Functions   *240*
16.5 Global, Local and Static Variables   *250*
Exercises   255

17. Processing Character Strings 257–278

Learning Objectives 257
17.1 The Character Data Type *257*
17.2 Manipulating Strings of Characters *259*
17.3 Some String Processing Examples *268*
17.4 Input and Output of Strings *275*
Exercises 277

18. Enumerated Data Types and Stacks 279–292

Learning Objectives 279
18.1 Enumerated Data Type *279*
18.2 Creating New Data Type Names *284*
18.3 A Stack *288*
18.4 Simulation of a Stack *289*
Exercises 291

19. Structures 293–304

Learning Objectives 293
19.1 Using Structures *295*
19.2 Use of Structures in Arrays and Arrays in Structures *299*
Exercises 303

20. Pointer Data Type and Its Applications 305–314

Learning Objectives 305
20.1 Pointer Data Type *305*
20.2 Pointers and Arrays *308*
20.3 Pointers and Functions *310*
Exercises 313

21. Lists and Trees 315–337

Learning Objectives 315
21.1 List Data Structure *315*
21.2 Manipulation of a Linearly Linked List *320*
21.3 Circular and Doubly Linked Lists *324*
21.4 A Doubly Linked Circular List *329*
21.5 Binary Trees *332*
Exercises 336

22. Recursion 338–351

Learning Objectives 338
22.1 Recursive Functions *338*
22.2 Recursion versus Iteration *340*
22.3 Some Recursive Algorithms *341*
22.4 Tree Traversal Algorithms *347*
Exercises 350

23. Bit Level Operations and Applications   **352–360**

Learning Objectives   352
23.1 Bit Operators   *352*
23.2 Some Applications of Bit Operations   *353*
23.3 Bit Fields   *357*
Exercises   360

24. Files in C   **361–382**

Learning Objectives   361
24.1 Creating and Storing Data in a File   *361*
24.2 Sequential Files   *366*
24.3 Unformatted Files   *374*
24.4 Text Files   *379*
Exercises   381

25. Miscellaneous Features of C   **383–394**

Learning Objectives   383
25.1 Conditional Operator   *383*
25.2 Comma Operator   *384*
25.3 Macro Definition   *385*
25.4 Union   *386*
25.5 Combining C Programs in Different Files   *387*
25.6 Command Line Arguments and Their Use   *389*
25.7 Conditional Compilation   *392*
Exercises   394

Appendix I   *Compiling and Running C Programs under UNIX*   *395–396*

Appendix II   *Reserved Words in C*   *397*

Appendix III   *Mathematical Functions*   *398*

Appendix IV   *String Functions*   *399–400*

Appendix V   *Character Class Tests*   *401*

Appendix VI   *File Manipulation Functions*   *402–405*

Appendix VII   *Utility Functions*   *406–407*

Appendix VIII   *Applications of MS Office Software*   *408–423*

Bibliography   *425*

Index   *427–431*

PREFACE

This book consists of two parts. The first part is on Basics of Computers and the second on Programming a Computer using the C language. Many universities have a first course on computers and computing for all entering engineering students to enable them to become conversant with computers in general and also how to program computers to solve interesting problems. The author has earlier written books titled: *Computer Programming in C, Fundamentals of Computers* and *Introduction to Information Technology*. Each of them is a full-fledged book on those topics. It was felt that it would be useful for students to have a single book which includes both the basics of computers and programming computers using C. This book attempts to cater to this need.

This book has been written assuming that the reader would have acquired some knowledge of computers during high school days. This knowledge, even though useful, is not a must to follow this book since we proceed from the first principles. The first part called "Computer Basics" has three chapters. We cover three aspects of computers which we feel are important for all engineers to know. The first chapter deals with the binary representation of numeric and character data in computers. It then describes the various units of a computer and how they cooperate in solving problems. The second chapter is a general introduction to computer software. It discusses the various computer languages and their role in computing and why an operating system is needed. In the current world it is essential for every student to know how to use the Internet. It is a basic information infrastructure and all engineers should know how this is organized, how it works and how to use it effectively. Thus the technology of the Internet and the organization of the World Wide Web are discussed in the third chapter. It is also essential for students to know how to use a PC to do simple tasks such as word processing, spreadsheet calculations and PowerPoint presentations. Thus, an Appendix illustrating these applications of MS Office software suite is included in the book. It will allow students to quickly use these applications as exercises in a computing laboratory before they start writing programs.

The second part of the book (Chapters 4–25) introduces computer programming to a beginner using the programming language C. The version of C is the one standardized by the American National Standards Institute (ANSI). The book begins with an introduction to algorithms and computers. It is followed by a chapter on the methodology of evolving algorithms. A number of algorithms are developed in this chapter from first principles. A simplified model of the computer is introduced and used to illustrate how algorithms are executed by computers. The next chapter introduces the concept of high level languages and their translation. We start discussion of C language by encouraging a student to read and understand C programs.

A formal discussion of the rules of syntax of the language follows. The rules for writing variable names, arithmetic expressions, statements and input/output functions are given. Two chapters, following this, present the branching control statements and loop control statements. A number of example programs are used to motivate and illustrate the use of these statements. The need to adopt a good style in writing programs is stressed and illustrated in all the example programs. A chapter on *array* data structure and its use and a chapter on logical operations on data follow this. At this juncture, a student would be ready to write relatively large programs to do some significant jobs. A chapter is therefore written, at this stage, in which are illustrated three complete programs—one to simulate a small computer, another to process students' result data and a third one to analyse responses to a questionnaire. The concept of functions in C and their application in program development and modularization is taken up next in Chapter 16. The rest of the book (Chapters 17–25) is devoted to a discussion on the use of C in solving non-numerical problems. This part of the book presents the rich data structures and their applications which are supported by C. The distinctive features of C and the power of the language to solve a variety of interesting problems are brought out in these chapters. This part of the book starts with Chapter 17 on processing *character strings*, their representation, manipulation and applications. Following this is a chapter which illustrates the use of *enumerated data types*. The next chapter describes the data structure known as structures. A data type known as *pointer type* is available in C which distinguishes it from many other popular languages such as FORTRAN and COBOL. This data type and how it can be manipulated is described in Chapter 20. The freedom allowed by C to manipulate pointers makes C very powerful. At the same time this facility can lead to subtle errors which are difficult to detect. The use of pointers in creating and manipulating interesting data structures such as *lists* and *trees* is illustrated with examples in Chapter 21. The next chapter is devoted primarily to a discussion of *recursion*. The concept of recursion is defined first. The problems in which it can be profitably used and where it should not be used are explained. The power and elegance of recursive formulation of algorithms is brought out with some examples. C provides instructions to manipulate bits in words stored in memory. This is a powerful facility. We illustrate its use in Chapter 23.

Chapter 24 contains a discussion on how files are created, edited, searched, updated and merged. This chapter also introduces a feature in C which allows direct accessing of structures stored in a file. All the concepts are illustrated with well chosen examples. The book concludes with a discussion on some miscellaneous features of C enumerated in Chapter 25.

In the author's view, the most important feature of this book is the illustration of all important language features of C through carefully selected examples. Besides illustrating the correct use of C, the book also shows how algorithms are formulated to solve problems. All programs in the book were executed on a workstation using ANSI C and the programs are reproduced by photo-offset to eliminate printing errors. The methodology adopted in the book makes it eminently suitable for self-study. A teacher's manual with additional laboratory exercises in C is available with the publisher for use by teachers.

The author would like to thank his students, who were expert C programmers, for their valuable suggestions. Thanks are due to Mr. Karthikeyan for keying in the C programs and testing them and to Mr. Roshan Joy for assistance with Appendix VIII and teacher's manual.

Thanks are also due to Ms. T. Mallika for secretarial assistance. The author is indebted to the Chairman, Supercomputer Education and Research Centre, and the Director, Indian Institute of Science, Bangalore, for the facilities provided which enabled him to write the book.

Finally, the author wishes to express his heartfelt appreciation to his wife Dharma who corrected the manuscript and proofs and cheerfully devoted herself to this arduous task.

V. RAJARAMAN

Part I
COMPUTER BASICS

1

Information Technology and Computer Basics

LEARNING OBJECTIVES

In this chapter we will learn:
1. The difference between data and information.
2. The different types of data which are processed by computers.
3. Why binary numbers are used in computers.
4. Representation of numeric and text data in binary form.
5. About the different units required by a computer to process data.
6. How data is processed by a computer.
7. About various parts of a desktop computer.

1.1 INTRODUCTION

Information Technology (IT) may be defined as the technology which is used to acquire, store, organize, and process data to a form which can be used in specified applications, and disseminate the processed data. Information is *processed data*, based on which decisions can be taken and appropriate actions initiated. Information is also processed data which improves our knowledge, enabling us to do our work better.

EXAMPLE 1.1 Let us take a very simple example. A home-maker who buys vegetables, provisions, milk, etc. everyday would write in a diary the money spent on each of these articles (see Table 1.1). At the end of each day she adds up the data on money spent for these items. The total obtained is the information which she uses to adjust expenses to spend within her budget. This is illustrated in the block diagram of Fig. 1.1.

3

Table 1.1 Daily expenses

Date	Expenses in rupees				
	Vegetables	Milk	Provisions	Miscellaneous	Daily total
1.1.2001	25.50	20.00	95.00	150.00	290.50
2.1.2001	30.40	20.00	85.40	250.50	386.30
3.1.2001	15.50	25.00	128.00	80.00	248.50
⋮	⋮	⋮	⋮	⋮	⋮
⋮	⋮	⋮	⋮	⋮	⋮
31.1.2001	19.50	20.00	25.00	15.00	79.50
Total	750.50	650.00	2800.50	2852.50	7053.50

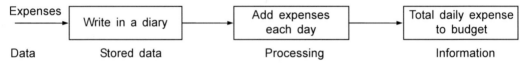

Fig. 1.1 Data and information.

Observe that data is the raw material with which she started, and information is processed data which allows her to initiate action to balance her budget.

The data entered in the diary each day may be processed in other ways too to obtain different information. For example, if the total amount of monthly expenses on milk is divided by the monthly income, it gives information on the proportion of the budget spent on milk. This is shown in Fig. 1.2.

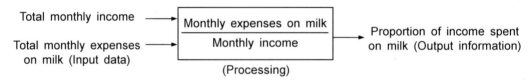

Fig. 1.2 Information as input data.

This information may be useful to manage the family income in a more efficient manner. Observe that the information obtained in Fig. 1.1 is used as data in Fig. 1.2. This illustrates that the distinction between data and information is not always clear. The point to be emphasized is that mere facts and figures about activities do not enable one to take decisions or to initiate actions. Only when they are processed and presented in an effective manner, they become useful. While data is used by computers, information is used by people in their day-to-day activities.

EXAMPLE 1.2 As an example of how organizing data enhances our understanding, let us consider marks obtained by students in an examination. The marks by themselves do not give any immediate idea about the performance of the class. By processing this data, a bar chart may be obtained, which gives the number of students with marks between 100 and 90, 90 and 80, 80 and 70, and so on. This chart (Fig. 1.3) gives the teacher of the class information on the performance of the class, which would enable him or her to initiate appropriate action.

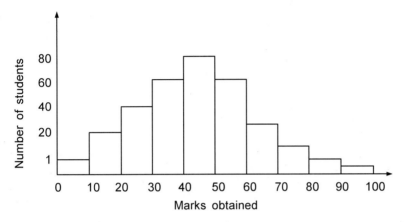

Fig. 1.3 Bar chart giving performance of students in a class.

1.2 TYPES OF DATA

In Examples 1.1 and 1.2, the data was numeric. This is the simplest data type and historically the earliest data type to be processed. The versatility of IT comes from the ability to process a variety of data types (Fig. 1.4).

Fig. 1.4 Types of data.

The variety of data types, besides numbers, are:

1. *Text.* For example, a paragraph in this book is textual data.
2. *Picture or image.* For example, your photograph (both black and white and colour). Other types of pictures are a map of India, a fingerprint, a line drawing as in Fig. 1.3, an image transmitted by a satellite, and an X-ray of your chest. Their main characteristic is that they are two-dimensional images, and static (i.e. they do not move). In the literature the terms picture and image are used interchangeably.
3. *Audio* or *sound.* For example, speeches, songs, telephone conversations, street noise, etc. Their main property is that they are continuous (i.e. vary with time) and cause pressure waves in the air which enter our ears and we hear the sound.

4. *Video or moving pictures.* When a number of images (each one slightly different from the other) are shown one after another at a rate of about 30 to 60 pictures per second, due to persistence of vision, we have an illusion of movement. An example is silent movies starring Charlie Chaplin in the 1930s. Another example is animations used in computer games. Video is usually combined with audio to give a better effect, for example, computer games with background noises synchronized with the images or current cinemas (called "talkies" in early days when sound was introduced in movies).

In modern information technology all these types of data are required to be processed. All these data types taken together are called *multimedia*. We will be concerned with only numeric and character data in this book. Those interested in other data types may refer to (Rajaraman, 2007) given in the list of references.

1.2.1 Numeric Data

This is the most important data type used by engineers and scientists. The two basic types of numbers are *integers* and *reals*. Integers are primarily used for counting whereas reals are numbers with fractional parts which are more often used in calculations. An ordered set of numbers is called a *vector* or an *array*. Multidimensional arrays are called matrices. In this book we will be using these extensively. Examples 1.1 and 1.2 illustrate numeric data processing.

1.2.2 Internal Representation of Numeric Data

Once a data is fed to a computer it is converted to a form which is efficient to store and easy to interpret by the hardware of the machine. This is called the *internal representation* of data. This should be contrasted with the *external representation* which is the form that is easy for humans to read and understand. For example, we use the decimal system to represent numbers for our use. This is the external representation. A decimal number is represented in another form called binary for storing in the memory of a computer. This is the internal representation.

At this point we would like to point out that even though we briefly described five varieties of data, there is a unifying aspect when we examine their internal representation. All these data types are represented by a string of *binary digits* (zeros and ones). They are all processed by a computer which can process only data represented as zeros and ones. The results obtained after processing are also zeros and ones but in a rearranged form based on the processing rules used. This result is converted back to numbers, text, audio, etc. which can be understood by us. In other words, even though the processing is on binary data and the results are also binary, they are converted back to numbers, text, audio, image or video data as appropriate.

The question that will now be foremost in your minds is: Why should all data be converted to zeros and ones? The answer is simple. Physical devices used to store and process data in computers (as of today) are *two-state* devices. A switch, for example, is a two-state device. It can be either ON or OFF. Very reliable recording or reading on a magnetic surface (such as the one used in floppy disks) is achieved when the surface is magnetized in either one of two opposite directions. The two states in this case are magnetic field aligned left to right

$(S \rightarrow N)$ or right to left $(N \leftarrow S)$. Electronic devices such as transistors used in computers function most reliably when operated as switches, that is, either in conducting mode or in non-conducting mode. Thus, all data to be stored and processed using computers are transformed or coded as strings of two symbols, one symbol to represent each state. The two symbols normally used are 0 and 1. They are known as *bits*, an abbreviation for *binary digits*.

1.2.3 Encoding of Decimal Numbers

The next question is: How do we represent numbers using bits? The simplest way is to represent each digit in a number by a unique string of bits. There are 4 (2×2) unique combinations of 2 bits, namely:

00   01   10   11

This is because each bit can be either 0 or 1. There are 2 bits giving $2 \times 2 = 4$ possible unique strings of 2 bits each. There are $2 \times 2 \times 2 = 8$ unique strings of three bits each, i.e.

000   001   010   011   100   101   110   111

There are ten decimal digits 0, 1, 2, 3, 4, 5, 6, 7, 8, 9. Thus 3-bits strings are not sufficient to represent 10 digits. We need at least 4 bits. The number of unique 4-bit strings are $2 \times 2 \times 2 \times 2 = 16$ and they are:

0000   0001   0010   0011   0100   0101   0110   0111

1000   1001   1010   1011   1100   1101   1110   1111

We can arbitrarily pick any 10 of these 16 strings and assign each of them to represent 0, 1, 2, ..., 9. This is known as *binary encoding* of decimal digits. One of these assignments is shown in Table 1.2. This assignment is called *natural binary coded decimal digits* (NBCD).

Table 1.2 Representaton of decimal digits by binary strings

0000	0001	0010	0011	0100	0101	0110	0111	1000	1001
0	1	2	3	4	5	6	7	8	9

Observe that out of the 16 possible combinations of 4 bits, only 10 are used. It is thus not very efficient. It is, however, very easy to do the encoding. If we want to store a 4-digit number 2358 using this encoding scheme, the representation is obtained by looking up Table 1.2 and replacing each digit by its 4-bit equivalent as shown below:

2	3	5	8
0010	0011	0101	1000

EXAMPLE 1.3 (BINARY ENCODING OF DECIMAL NUMBERS). What is the binary encoding of the decimal number 589048?

Solution. Replace each digit by its 4-digit binary code by looking up Table 1.2. The encoded binary string is

$$0101100010010000001001000$$

In this method of representing, we ignore the fact that a decimal number has a *value.* The fact that a decimal number has a value is irrelevant in some applications. For example, a telephone number such as 23445781 is used to uniquely represent a subscriber's name. A code is used instead of a subscriber name as a name may not be unique. If we want to perform arithmetic operations, for example, add two decimal numbers, then value is important. In such a case, instead of *encoding* a decimal number in binary, we *convert* its value to an equivalent binary string which also has a value. For example, in Example 1.1, an expense has a value. We have to add the expenses to find the total. Value is important for performing arithmetic operations. Thus, an expense should be converted to binary and stored in the memory.

Decimal-to-binary conversion and vice versa are nowadays taught in high schools. We will thus not discuss it in this book but those who want to revise it may read section 2.3.2 (pp. 27–34) of (Rajaraman, 2007) given in the list of references.

1.2.4 Counting in Binary System

Counting in the binary system is similar to that in the decimal system. In the decimal system, we start from 0, add a 1, obtain a 1, and continue adding 1 successively till we reach 9. As the base of the system is 10, there are no further symbols. Thus when we add 1 to 9, we get 10. The 1 becomes the *carry* to the 10's position in the decimal system. Similarly, we get 100 after reaching 99. Counting in the binary system is similar and proceeds as follows:

$$0, 1, 10, 11, 100, 101, 110, 111, 1000, 1001, \ldots .$$

Table 1.3 shows the binary counting sequence. Observe that we require 3 bits to represent decimal numbers 4 to 7 and 4 bits to represent 8 and 9.

Table 1.3 Binary counting sequence

Binary number	*Decimal equivalent*	*Binary number*	*Decimal equivalent*
0	0	1001	9
1	1	1010	10
10	2	1011	11
11	3	1100	12
100	4	1101	13
101	5	1110	14
110	6	1111	15
111	7	10000	16
1000	8	10001	17

1.2.5 Representing Powers of 2

Just as powers of 10 are important in the decimal system of enumeration, powers of 2 are important in the binary system. We give in Table 1.4 the powers of 2 and their decimal equivalents. The abbreviation K in Table 1.4 stands for 1024 which is approximately 1000, a kilo. Thus the notation 16K means $16 \times 1024 = 16384$. The abbreviation M (mega) stands for $1024 \times 1024 = 1048576$, which is nearly a million. The abbreviation G (giga) is used to represent $1024 \times 1024 \times 1024$, which is nearly a billion, and T (tera) for $1024 \times 1024 \times 1024 \times 1024$, a trillion.

EXAMPLE 1.4   What is the value of 3M?

Solution. $M = 2^{20} = 1048576$ from Table 1.4.

Thus, $3M = 3 \times 1048576 = 3145728$

Table 1.4   Powers of 2

Power of 2	Decimal equivalent	Power of 2	Decimal equivalent	Abbreviation
2^0	1	2^{10}	1024	1K
2^1	2	2^{11}	2048	2K
2^2	4	2^{12}	4096	4K
2^3	8	2^{20}	1048576	1M
2^4	16	2^{21}	2097152	2M
2^5	32	2^{22}	4194304	4M
2^6	64	2^{30}	1073741824	1G
2^7	128	2^{31}	2147483648	2G
2^8	256	2^{40}	1099511627776	1T
2^9	512	2^{41}	2199023255532	2T

1.2.6 Hexadecimal Representation of Numbers

The binary equivalent of a 10 digit number will be approximately 32 bits long. It is difficult to write such long strings of 1s and 0s and convert them to equivalent decimal numbers without making mistakes. The *hexadecimal* system, which uses 16 as base, is a convenient notation to express binary numbers. This system, by definition, uses 16 symbols, viz. 0, 1, 2, 3, 4, 5, 6, 7, 8, 9, A, B, C, D, E, F. Note that the symbols A, B, etc. now represent numbers in hexadecimal. As 16 is fourth power of 2, namely 2^4, there is a one-to-one correspondence between a hexadecimal digit and its binary equivalent. We need only 4 bits to represent a hexadecimal digit. Table 1.5 gives a table of hexadecimal digits and their binary and decimal equivalents.

Table 1.5 Binary, hexadecimal and decimal equivalents

Binary number	Hexadecimal equivalent	Decimal equivalent	Binary number	Hexadecimal equivalent	Decimal equivalent
0000	0	0	1000	8	8
0001	1	1	1001	9	9
0010	2	2	1010	A	10
0011	3	3	1011	B	11
0100	4	4	1100	C	12
0101	5	5	1101	D	13
0110	6	6	1110	E	14
0111	7	7	1111	F	15

A binary number can be quickly converted to its hexadecimal equivalent by grouping together successively 4 bits of the binary number, starting with the least significant bit and replacing each 4-bit group with its hexadecimal equivalent given in Table 1.5. The following examples illustrate this conversion process.

EXAMPLE 1.5

Binary number	0111	1100	1101	1110	0011
Hexadecimal equivalent	7	C	D	E	3

EXAMPLE 1.6

Binary number	001000111110000·0010110						
Grouped binary number	0001	0001	1111	0000	·	0010	1100
Hexadecimal equivalent	1	1	F	0	·	2	C

1.3 REPRESENTATION OF CHARACTERS IN COMPUTERS

In the last section we saw how numbers are represented as binary strings in order to store and process them using a computer. In this section we will see how text is represented. A text consists of letters of a language such as English, punctuation marks, e.g. comma (,), semicolon (;), special characters like −, +, *, etc. The set of characters which is valid for a computer is called its *character set*. Nowadays, the number of valid characters is quite large, including characters of many languages like Hindi, Tamil, Chinese, etc. The external representation of text is for catering to humans. For example, this paragraph you are reading is text and it is in a printed form suitable for you to read. For storing this in a computer (suitable for processing) it is necessary to *encode* the characters using strings of bits. What do we mean by processing? One type of processing may be to find the number of vowels in this page you are reading. Another may be to sort a set of names of students in a class and arrange them in alphabetical order. Encoding is representing each character using a unique string of bits. We saw that there are $2 \times 2 \times 2 \times 2 = 16$ unique strings of 4 bits, and we use 10 out of these 16 to code decimals. If we want to encode the 26 capital (or uppercase) letters of English alphabet, 4 bits are not sufficient as they can represent only 16 symbols. Five bits, however, are sufficient as there are 32 ($2 \times 2 \times 2 \times 2 \times 2 = 32$) strings of 5 bits each. Twenty-six out of these 32 strings of 5 bits may be picked to code the 26 letters as illustrated in Table 1.6.

Table 1.6 Illustrating the coding of English letters

Bit string	Letter	Bit string	Letter
00000	A	10000	Q
00001	B	10001	R
00010	C	10010	S
00011	D	10011	T
00100	E	10100	U
00101	F	10101	V
00110	G	10110	W
00111	H	10111	X
01000	I	11000	Y
01001	J	11001	Z
01010	K	11010	
01011	L	11011	
01100	M	11100	
01101	N	11101	Not used
01110	O	11110	
01111	P	11111	

Data processing using computers requires processing of not only the 26 capital (or upper case) English letters but also the 26 small (or lower case) English letters, 10 digits and around 32 other characters, such as punctuation marks, arithmetic operator symbols, parentheses, etc. The total number of characters to be coded is thus: $26 + 26 + 10 + 32 = 94$. With strings of 6 bits each, it is possible to code only $2^6 = 64$ characters. Thus, 6 bits are insufficient for coding. If we use strings of 7 bits each we will have $2^7 = 128$ unique strings and can thus code up to 128 characters. Strings of 7 bits each are thus quite sufficient to code 94 characters.

Coding of characters has been standardized to facilitate exchange of recorded data between computers. The most popular standard is known as ASCII (American Standard Code for Information Interchange). This uses 7 bits to code each character. Besides codes for characters, in this standard, codes are defined to convey information such as end of line, end of page, etc. to the computer. These codes are said to be for *non-printable control characters*.

Table 1.7 gives the ASCII code for both printable and non-printable control characters. Columns 1 and 2 are non-printable codes. The entry CR, for example, indicates carriage return (or end of line) control character. The most significant bits of the code are given in Table 1.7 as column headings and the least significant bits of the code are given as row headings. Thus the code for A, for example, is identified from the table by finding the column and row bits. The column gives bits 100 as bits b_6, b_5, b_4, and the row gives bits 0001 for b_3, b_2, b_1, b_0.

Table 1.7 ASCII code for characters

Least significant bits b_3 b_2 b_1 b_0	Most significant bits b_6 b_5 b_4							
	000	001	010	011	100	101	110	111
0000	NUL	DLE	SPACE	0	@	P	`	p
0001	SOH	DC1	!	1	A	Q	a	q
0010	STX	DC2	"	2	B	R	b	r
0011	ETX	DC3	#	3	C	S	c	s
0100	EOT	DC4	$	4	D	T	d	t
0101	ENQ	NAK	%	5	E	U	e	u
0110	ACK	SYN	&	6	F	V	f	v
0111	BEL	ETB	'	7	G	W	g	w
1000	BS	CAN	(	8	H	X	h	x
1001	HT	EM	)	9	I	Y	i	y
1010	LF	SUB	*	:	J	Z	j	z
1011	VT	ESC	+	;	K	[	k	{
1100	FF	FS	'	<	L	\	l	|
1101	CR	GS	–	=	M	]	m	}
1110	SO	RS	.	>	N	^	n	~
1111	SI	US	/	?	O	–	o	DEL

Thus the code for A is

$$b_6 \quad b_5 \quad b_4 \quad b_3 \quad b_2 \quad b_1 \quad b_0$$
$$1 \quad \ 0 \quad \ 0 \quad \ 0 \quad \ 0 \quad \ 0 \quad \ 1$$

The internal representation of the string RAMA J is

1010010	1000001	1001101	1000001	0100000	1001010
R	A	M	A	SPACE	J

Observe that the space between RAMA and J also needs a code. This code is essential to leave a space between RAMA and J when the string is printed.

Observe that in ASCII code, digits are encoded using 7 bit codes. Thus if an item code, say, is a combination of letters and digits we use the 7 bit equivalent of each character to encode it. In ASCII code, digits are considered as printable characters rather than numbers with value.

EXAMPLE 1.7 The licence number of a car is KA02M47. What is its ASCII code?

Solution

1001011	1000001	0110000	0110010	1001101	0110100	0110111
K	A	0	2	M	4	7

In addition to ASCII, another code known as ISCII (Indian Standard Code for Information Interchange) has been standardized by the Bureau of Indian Standards. The full description of this code is available in the document IS:13194-91 published by the Bureau of Indian Standards. It is an 8-bit code which allows English and Indian script alphabets to be used simultaneously. It retains the standard ASCII code for English. It extends Table 1.7 by adding columns 1010, 1011, up to 1111. (Observe that Table 1.7 as shown has columns 0000 to 0111 only.) With this addition, it is possible to define 96 more characters.

A common code for all Indian languages is feasible as all Indian scripts originated from the Brahmi script. The phonetic nature of Indian languages is used to design the code. All consonants have an implicit vowel. For example, क = क् + अ. Thus a consonant such as की is split into क् and इ. Using this idea the consonants and vowels are separated. Two character codes are therefore needed for a consonant.

A string of bits used to represent a character is known as a *byte*. Characters coded in ISCII need 8 bits for each character. Thus a byte, in this case, is a string of 8 bits. A character coded in ASCII will need only 7 bits. The need to accommodate characters of languages other than English was foreseen while designing ASCII and therefore 8 bits were specified to represent characters. Thus a byte is commonly understood as a string of 8 bits.

Recently, a new coding scheme for characters, called *unicode*, has been standardized specifically to accommodate a large number of special symbols such as Greek characters α, β, v, etc. mathematical symbols such as $\Rightarrow$, and non-English characters. It uses 16 bits (2 bytes) to represent each character. As $2^{16} = 65536$, the number of different characters which can be coded using unicode is very large. Unicode has, however, defined codes from $(0000)_{16}$ to $(FFFD)_{16}$ hexadecimal which is 65534 codes, 2 less than 65536. Thus any character of any language in the world can be represented with this large number. It is important to note that the first 128 characters of unicode are identical to ASCII codes. Thus unicode is compatible with the existing ASCII and ISCII coded data stored in computers.

In order to process character data, we should be able to read or enter it into a computer, process it, and display and distribute (on request) the results of processing to the outside world. We will now consider textual data.

1.4 SOME EXAMPLES OF PROCESSING TEXTUAL DATA

EXAMPLE 1.8 (WORD PROCESSING) One of the most important applications of IT now is *word processing*. In this application a rough draft of a text (may be an essay) is typed using the keyboard of a computer. A number of commands are also given along with the text to format it, i.e. right-justify the text, arrange the text as paragraphs, italicise some words, check spelling etc. The data type in this example is a string of characters or a text. The output is a formatted text which has a neat appearance and is thus easy to read, as illustrated in Fig. 1.5.

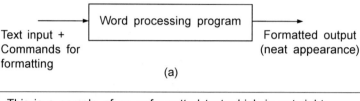

Text input +
Commands for
formatting

Formatted output
(neat appearance)

(a)

This is a sample of an unformatted text which is not right justified. It also has speling errors. This text has no spcial fonts such as italics and boldface. In Fig. 1.4(b) ths text is formated, high-lighted, right justified and correted.

(b)
Unformatted text with errors

This is a sample of an *unformatted text* which is not right justified. It also has spelling errors. This text has no special fonts such as italics and boldface. In Fig. 1.5(c) this text is **formatted**, highlighted, right justified and corrected.

(c)
Text formatted and spell checked using word processor

Fig. 1.5 Text processing, unformatted and formatted text.

A word processor also does many other interesting tasks. For example, it detects any spelling errors made and (if you command it) corrects them. Some word processors also examine the construction of sentences and give suggestions to improve the style of presentation. It should now be clear to you that a word processor available with a computer is not a mere typewriter but does more complex tasks such as checking spelling, checking style, etc. (See Appendix VIII which tells you how to use a word processor.)

EXAMPLE 1.9 (DICTIONARY) Another interesting aspect of IT is the way it is able to enhance our ability to perform many other day-to-day tasks. For example, if you do not know the meaning of a word you refer to a printed dictionary. Words in a dictionary are arranged alphabetically to enable you to search the word quickly. Nowadays, dictionaries are published not only in printed form but also in computer readable form using a Compact Disk Read Only Memory (CDROM), which is similar to the music CDs you buy in the audio shops. The words are now arranged not only in an alphabetical order but each word is also linked with words with similar meaning. Thus, if you want to find the meaning of a word, you type it using the keyboard of a computer and its meaning is displayed. No manual searching is needed. Not only do you *get* the meaning but also a list of other words which have the same or similar meaning. This will allow you to pick the right word which meets your requirements.

There are also other interesting things which are done by the designers of the computer readable dictionary. Every word is linked not only with words having a similar meaning but also with those which have an opposite meaning. For example, the word "early" is linked with words such as "punctual", "prompt", etc. which have a similar meaning. It is also linked with words such as "late", "tardy", "delay" which have an opposite meaning. Given a word, this linking will allow you to search for words with opposite meaning. Besides this, very complex processing rules may be programmed.

1.5 A SIMPLE MODEL OF A COMPUTER

In Section 1.2 we have seen that computers process not only numerical data but also text, images, audio and video data. Information technology is concerned with:

1. Acquisition of data
2. Storage of data
3. Organization of data
4. Processing of data
5. Output of processed data, i.e. information for application/use
6. Dissemination or distribution of information.

If a machine is to be a versatile data processing machine, it should

- be able to acquire or read data of all the five types, i.e. numbers, text, images, audio and video and also be able to read instructions to process the data.
- have the facility to store and organize data. The amount of data storage required is quite large—trillions of characters nowadays. It should also be able to store the instructions to be processed.
- be able to process data. Data is processed by interpreting and executing a set of instructions called a *program*, stored in the machine's primary memory unit.
- have devices to output the processed data. Remember that output data can be numeric, textual, audio, image or video. Sometimes the results may also be stored in the storage unit for future use.
- also be easily connectable to other computers using communication networks for widely disseminating information (see Fig. 1.6).

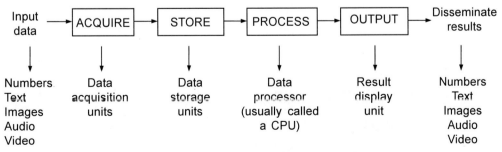

Fig. 1.6 Various steps in data processing.

Such a machine has a structure shown in the block diagram of Fig. 1.7. It has an *input system* which is used to acquire data from the external world and convert it into a form which can be stored in its storage system. There are a variety of input units ranging from a keyboard to specialized data acquisition systems such as video cameras, microphones and scanners. The collection of input units constitutes the input system.

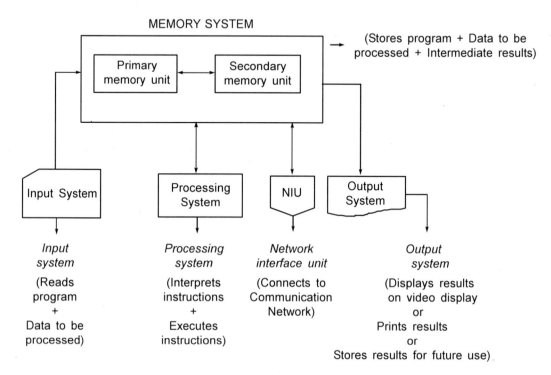

MEMORY SYSTEM

(Stores program + Data to be processed + Intermediate results)

Primary memory unit

Secondary memory unit

Input System

Processing System

NIU

Output System

Input system

(Reads program + Data to be processed)

Processing system

(Interprets instructions + Executes instructions)

Network interface unit

(Connects to Communication Network)

Output system

(Displays results on video display or Prints results or Stores results for future use)

Fig. 1.7 Block diagram of a data processing system (or computer system).

The machine has a *memory system* where the program for processing data and the data to be processed are stored. The memory system also consists of a variety of units, the most important one being a fast Random Access Memory (RAM), which is the primary memory used to store instructions and data to be processed. As the amount of data to be stored is usually very large and the stored data is used for many purposes, the storage system has, besides a RAM, a variety of interconnected units such as floppy disks, hard disks, CDROMs, DVDROMs, flash memory and magnetic tape drives. The collection of this storage is called *secondary memory*.

The third important system is the *processing system*. The processing system is the heart of the machine and is designed to interpret and execute instructions of a program stored in memory. There are a variety of processing systems. The simplest ones are used to control microwave ovens, washing machines, etc. Faster powerful processors are used for complex mathematical calculations. Some others process audio and video data and are known as Digital Signal Processors (DSPs). Many computing systems now have several processing units.

The next important part of a computer is the *output system*. The output system prints or displays the results of data processing. Sometimes the results of processing may not be immediately printed. They may be stored for printing later. Sometimes data may be printed or displayed and also stored for future reference. There are several types of output devices such as video displays, inkjet printers, loudspeakers and laser printers.

The last important part of all recent computers is a Network Interface Unit (NIU) to connect it to a communication system and through this to other computers. Nowadays it is rare to find an isolated computer not connected to a communication system. Such a connection is essential to widely disseminate data processed by the computer.

1.6 DATA PROCESSING USING A COMPUTER

To fix our ideas we will take an example to show how data is processed to obtain information. The steps followed are:

1. Analyse the given data processing task and understand what is to be done.
2. Having understood the task to be performed, find a method to do it.
3. Express the method to be followed as a step-by-step procedure which is called *algorithm*.
4. Express the algorithm using a precise notation called a *programming language* obtaining what is called *computer program. Programs* can be interpreted and executed by a computer's processing system.
5. Input the program to be executed and store it in the memory of the computer. Keep the data to be processed ready and waiting at the input unit.
6. Order the computer to start executing the program.
7. The computer interprets the program stored in its memory. When a command to "READ" data is encountered (which is normally at the beginning of the program) it reads the data waiting at the input unit and stores it in the memory. It then continues following the program step by step and carries out the data processing task which has been programmed.
8. At the end of the program being executed (or during the execution of a program), an instruction(s) will be found to write the result(s) via the output unit. This is the processed data, that is, the information which is required. It may also send the results to another computer connected to it.

We will now illustrate the steps given above with an example.

EXAMPLE 1.10 (FINDING VOWELS IN A TEXT) Find the number of vowels in a given text.

Method
Read the text character by character. If the character is a vowel, that is, if it is a, e, i, o, u or A, E, I, O, U, count it as a vowel. When the end of the text is reached, output the count as the number of vowels.

Algorithm

Step 1: Create a counter to count the number of vowels and store 0 in it.
count-vowels = 0

Step 2: Call vowel = a, e, i, o, u or A, E, I, O, U

Repeat Step 3 to Step 5 until the end of input text is reached. Go to Step 6 when no more characters are left in the text.

Step 3: Read a character from the string of characters (or text) waiting at the input unit. Store it in input-character.

Step 4: *If* input-character = vowel
          then Add 1 to count-vowels and continue
          else continue

Step 5: Move to next character. *Remark*: We now go back to Step 3

Step 6: Output count-vowels. *Remark*: This step is reached when the end of input text is reached.

Step 7: Stop

Observe that the algorithm is independent of the length of text and what is contained in the text. Given *any* text, the algorithm will find the number of vowels in it. In other words, the method is general and not dependent on specific data input. This is what gives the power to a computer. Once an algorithm is written, it may be used for all tasks of the same type. This property of an algorithm which makes it independent of input data, is called *data independence of algorithm*.

The model of computer used in this section was first proposed by John von Neumann, a computer scientist, in 1945. The major contribution of von Neumann is the idea of storing the program in the memory and executing it by taking one instruction at a time from it to the processor which interprets and executes it. Storing a program in memory is essential if a series of instructions are to be executed repeatedly. In the algorithm given in this section, Steps 3 to 5 are repeated again and again until no more characters are left in the input text. These steps cannot be carried out unless they are stored in a memory and are thus available for repeated reference and interpretation.

Storing a program in memory also makes the operation of computers *automatic*. Unlike a simple pocket calculator where one has to press buttons after each operation is carried out, the instructions stored in the memory of a computer are taken one by one automatically to the processing system, interpreted and executed without any human intervention.

1.7 DESKTOP COMPUTER

The best way of learning IT is to start using a computer as early as possible. To enable you to do it we will describe in this section various parts of a desktop computer (commonly known as IBM PC compatible). A picture of a desktop PC is given in Fig. 1.8. The major parts of a PC are:

1. **A keyboard** which is very similar to a typewriter keyboard with some extra keys called control keys and function keys. This is used to enter program and data for storage in the computer's memory. It is called *input unit*.

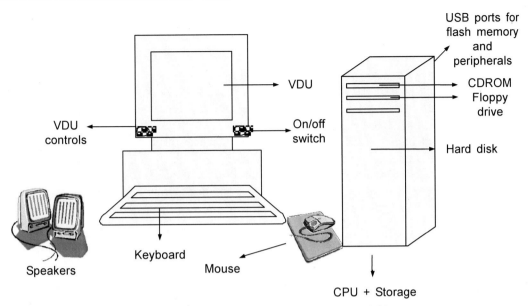

Fig. 1.8 A desktop personal computer (PC).

2. **A video display unit** (VDU) which is similar to a TV screen. The screen size is normally 15″ (diagonal). It is normally a colour screen and is used to primarily display strings of characters you input. It, however, can display pictures with reasonably good resolution. It is also used to display small graphics symbols called *icons* which assist you to give commands to the computer. This is called a Graphical User Interface (GUI, pronounced Gooyee). The VDU is the most common *output unit* of a computer. To effectively give commands using GUI, every PC has a small hand-held unit called *mouse* which normally has three buttons that can be pressed (called *clicking*). The mouse is moved on a rubber pad. As the mouse is moved, a small picture of an arrow moves on the VDU screen. The arrow can be placed over a graphical icon and the mouse button clicked to initiate an action by the computer. The mouse is also an input unit as it is used to initiate commands to a computer.

3. A separate box is used in most recent PCs to accommodate the *CPU,* the *main memory*, the *secondary memory* and the *power supply.* This box also has a number of sockets called ports to *connect external devices* such as a printer, loudspeaker, flash memory (which is also popularly known as memory stick) etc. and also to connect a communication system such as a local network or a telephone. The CPU is a microprocessor, mounted on what is known as *motherboard*. Besides the microprocessor, the motherboard also accommodates electronic circuits to interface the microprocessor with other units such as a network interface unit (NIU) to connect the PC to a communication system. The main memory is also mounted on the motherboard. PCs have very large main memory with capacity to store 256 million characters, specified as 256 MB.

The secondary memory consists of a large hard disk which is in a sealed unit and is connected to the main memory (with circuits inside the box), a floppy disk and a CDROM. A disk is used to store several programs required to use the computer. In modern PCs a disk can store hundred billion characters (specified as 100 GB). The disk store is essential for the functioning of a PC. A floppy disk is pushed into a slot on the box and is used to store small files and is a removable store. Other removable stores are a CDROM (similar to audio CD) which has a capacity of around half a billion characters (500 MB), flash memory whose capacity ranges between 32 KB and 4 GB and DVD with capacity up to 17 GB.

4. Most PCs today are called multimedia PCs as they are capable of acquiring and processing pictures, audio and video data besides textual and numeric data. In order to acquire and process multimedia data PCs are equipped with:

   (i) A box called a *scanner* external to PC and connected to it by a connecting cable. The scanner is used to convert pictures placed on it to digital form for storage in the memory of the computer.

   (ii) A *printer* which can print pictures besides text and numbers.

   (iii) A *microphone* and an audio jack to accept audio data.

   (iv) A pair of *loudspeakers* to provide audio output obtained from a PC.

   (v) An electronic circuit called a *sound card* which is connected to the CPU board (in the box).

   (vi) An electronic circuit called a *graphics card* to display pictures and video. This card is mounted on the motherboard.

   (vii) A small electronic video camera external to the PC to take pictures.

All the above constitute what is known as *hardware.* A computer is useless unless it has a number of ready-made programs to enable easy use of the hardware. This is provided by *software.* The most important software required to use a computer is what is known as *operating system* (OS). It is also essential to have a set of *application programs.* An OS coordinates the activities of various parts of a computer, namely CPU and input/output units, manages memory, organizes data and allows you to control the activities of the PC. The most popular OS for PCs is the Windows OS made by Microsoft Corpn. Another OS gaining ground is called LINUX which is a free software.

The most important set of application software consists of a program for word processing, a program to send/receive e-mails and search for information, a program to organize data, and a program for doing calculations such as finding instalment payment on hire purchase, etc. Such a set of programs is known as an *office suite* of programs. The most popular office suit today is Microsoft's Office XP. A software called open office for PC is a free software and is becoming popular.

EXERCISES

1.1 Define Information Technology.

1.2 What is the difference between data and information? Give an example of organizing data which allows human decision-making.

1.3 What are the different types of data? Give an example of each of these data types.

1.4 What is the difference between internal and external representation of data?

1.5 In what internal form are data stored in a computer? Why is this form used?

1.6 How many symbols can be encoded with 5 bits?

1.7 Encode in binary the decimal number 842369.

1.8 What is the difference between encoding a decimal number in binary and converting it to binary? Encode the number 47. Convert 47 to binary.

1.9 How many symbols are used in hexadecimal? What is the hexadecimal equivalent of (a) 1011 (b) 111001011111 (c) 101.110101

1.10 Find the decimal equivalents of the following hexadecimal numbers:

(a) AE.6FC (b) D123.AB (c) EFF.3DA

1.11 Give the ASCII codes of the following:

(a) aADd (b) HE CAME (c) $623.40

1.12 What is ISCII code? How is it different from the ASCII code?

1.13 What is Unicode? What is the advantage of Unicode compared to ASCII? What is the disadvantage?

1.14 What is word processing? What are the facilities provided by a word processor?

1.15 What special facilities are provided by a computer readable and processable dictionary as compared to a text-based dictionary?

1.16 Give the block diagram of a machine capable of processing data and disseminating it. Explain the functions of each of the blocks.

1.17 What is the difference between primary memory and secondary memory?

1.18 What are the steps followed in processing data using a computer?

1.19 What is an algorithm? Write an algorithm to count all punctuation marks in a text.

1.20 Write an algorithm to find whether a given number is odd or even.

1.21 Develop an algorithm to count the number of capital letters in a text.

1.22 What is the main advantage of storing a program in the main memory of a computer?

1.23 What do you understand by data independence of an algorithm? Illustrate the idea of data independence with an example.

1.24 What are the parts of a desktop computer such as an IBM PC? Draw a block diagram of such a computer.

1.25 What is a keyboard used for? Is it an input unit or an output unit?

1.26 What is a VDU? What is its application?

1.27 What is an icon? How is it used?

1.28 What is a mouse? What is its use? Is it an input or an output unit?

1.29 What is a motherboard? What parts of a computer are accommodated on a motherboard?

1.30 What are the storage devices included in the secondary storage unit?

1.31 Which are the removable secondary storage units of a PC?

1.32 What is a scanner? What is its use?

1.33 In order to process audio data what units should be provided in a PC?

1.34 What is the application of a graphics card in a PC?

1.35 What software is essential to use a PC?

1.36 What is the main use of an operating system (OS)? Name two OSs for PCs.

1.37 What is the most important set of application software in a PC? What applications does it include?

2

Computer Software

```
╭─────────────────────────────────────────────────────────────────────────╮
              LEARNING OBJECTIVES

In this chapter we will learn:
    1. What is computer software and why it is necessary to make a computer a useful tool.
    2. Why different types of software, namely the system software, the packaged and application software,
       are needed and their role in a computer system.
    3. Why do we need operating systems for computers.
    4. Why do we need programming languages and how they differ from each other.
╰─────────────────────────────────────────────────────────────────────────╯
```

2.1 INTRODUCTION

We learnt in Chapter 1 that in order to solve a problem on a computer, we should first evolve a detailed and precise step-by-step method of solving it. Such a method is called *algorithm* if the instructions are precise and unambiguous and take a finite time to carry out. An algorithm expressed using a precise notation is called *program*. The precise notation itself is called *programming language*. Thus a program is needed to solve a problem on a computer. The general terminology *software* is used to describe all programs. This is to be contrasted with the terminology *hardware* which is used to describe the electronic circuits, I/O devices, memory, etc. which are required to execute software. The terms 'hardware' and 'software' are also used nowadays to describe many other systems. For example, the television set you buy from a shop is the hardware whereas the entertainment programs you watch on the TV is the software. It is immediately clear that hardware is necessary but not sufficient to make a TV a useful appliance. In fact, software is vital to make TV useful. What is the use of buying an expensive TV if all the programs shown on it are boring! Another important point brought out by this analogy is that hardware is a one-time expense whereas software is a continuous expense. You have to make new programs daily to make TV useful. Further, software production is time consuming and expensive whereas hardware can be built to specifications and, if there is a mass market, its cost will keep coming down continuously.
   You would have seen newspaper advertisements for computers which specify all the hardware details such as CPU type, memory size, disk size, etc. Besides, the advertisement

may say, "Microsoft Windows XP operating system preloaded" or "Linux operating system", and you may be wondering what it is all about. It is a software known as *operating system* which is essential to make the computer you buy a useful device. If there is no operating system, the computer will not work.

You would also have seen advertisements by computer education companies which say "Become a computer expert—learn C++ and Visual Basic". C++ and Visual Basic are programming languages. Of course, there is more to becoming a computer expert than knowing two programming languages. As we pointed out at the beginning of this chapter, a programming language is nothing but a precise notation to express algorithms. It is useful to know a language, but it is not essential knowledge to use a computer. Operating system and programming languages are part of what is known as *system software*. We will learn more about these later in this chapter. Besides these types of advertisements, you probably would have seen advertisements saying, "Buy Microsoft Office XP-Home to make the PC in your home or office assist you in all your office work". Microsoft Office XP-Home is what is known as *packaged software*.

You would have reserved accommodation either in a train or a bus. The clerk uses a keyboard of a computer to enter your request, and the reservation status, ticket, etc. are displayed on the video screen. The entire process of reservation is written as a program which is stored in the computer's memory. Such programs written for specific applications are known as *application programs*.

In this section we have learnt that there are three broad classes of programs, namely:

- System software
- Packaged software
- Applications software.

We will begin our discussion by examining system software which provides the environment to develop applications software. There are three types of system software: They are:

- Operating system
- Programming languages and their translators
- Utility programs.

2.2 OPERATING SYSTEM

A bare computer hardware is similar to a scooter without a clutch, brakes and an accelerator. A computer needs an OS to control its operation and make it usable. An OS consists of two parts: one part is called the BIOS (Basic Input Output System) which is stored in a non-erasable ROM. The other part which provides most of the services is stored on the hard disk. A user interacts with a computer using the OS as it provides many important facilities. An OS may be defined as a set of system programs that control and coordinate the operation of a computer system. Some of the major facilities provided by an operating system are:

1. Starting the operation of a computer when the power is first turned on.
2. Storing users' programs in memory and scheduling them in an orderly fashion.
3. Invoking programming language translator programs when necessary.

4. Controlling input and output operations.
5. Managing the use of main memory.
6. Managing and manipulating (i.e. editing) of users' files.
7. Easy interaction between users and computers.
8. Providing security to users' jobs and files.
9. Keeping accounts of resource usage.

Thus, a user of a modern computer uses a machine whose hardware is hidden by layers of software with features which include, besides those provided by its processor (e.g. arithmetic and logic circuits, memory, etc.), a number of functions provided by the OS listed above (see Fig. 2.1).

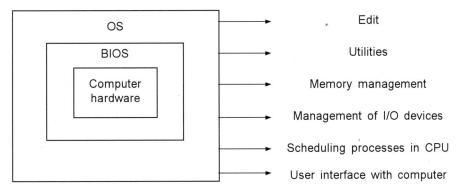

Fig. 2.1 Functions provided by an OS to a user.

Let us now begin our discussion by examining the functions of BIOS.

2.2.1 Basic Input–Output System (BIOS)

As already pointed out, BIOS is a small program to start and control a computer. It is stored in a ROM (non-erasable memory). When a computer is switched on, BIOS instructions are retrieved and start executing. BIOS first tests the memory and displays on the screen the available memory. Now it prepares the computer to start interpreting and executing users' programs. This process is called *booting* of the system.

The major functions of the BIOS are:

- Interpreting your keystrokes on the keyboard and storing data typed by you in the main memory
- Controlling of display and printer
- Making it possible to input/output data via other ports.

One of the advantages of BIOS is that when new I/O devices come in the market, they can be easily made to work with an existing computer by adding new programs known as *device driver programs* to the BIOS. Device drivers control the operation of I/O devices.

Software, which is permanently stored in a ROM and cannot be modified by a user is called *firmware* in the literature. Thus BIOS is a firmware.

2.2.2 Functions of an Operating System

An OS is a program which is permanently stored in a part of the main memory and is protected from accidental or intentional intrusion by users' programs. The non-changing part of OS is called *kernel*. The main function of an OS is to control and optimally use the resources of a computer system. It is similar to the functions of the captain of a cricket team. The captain decides who will bowl and when, who will bat and the batting order and also controls the placement of fielders. He tries to optimally use the resources under his command such as bowlers, fielders, batsmen, etc. Similarly, an OS allocates and controls the use of resources of a computer, namely, main memory, CPU and I/O units. It allocates memory to different programs being executed in a computer, monitors their progress and schedules the use of CPU to different programs.

Besides resource management, the other major functions of an OS are:

1. *Command processing*, that is, interpreting users' commands and executing these commands. Typical commands are: copy a file, close a file.
2. *Detection of errors*, if any, in the functioning of hardware or system software and gracefully shutting down the system if it is a fatal error. If the error is not serious, it will report it, and if possible, correct the error and continue processing.
3. *Managing power consumption*. For example, in a PC if there is no activity on the keyboard/mouse for a specified time, the CPU is taken to a "sleep mode", shutting many of its functions.
4. *Managing files*. For example, users of Microsoft's OS place related files in what is known as a folder. The file itself is given a name and there is an extension stating the type of file. For example, the identifier of a file is: biodata.doc. The *file name* is *biodata*, and the *extension* is doc which specifies that it is a document prepared using a word processor. Another example is myphoto.bmp specifying that the file myphoto is a bit mapped file. Various storage devices connected to the PC are given single letter codes to indicate to the Microsoft OS where the file is stored. For example, in Microsoft OS, A and B indicate floppy drive, C hard disk, D CDROM and E may represent a tape drive. Files are organized in folders. For example, the file myphoto.bmp may be stored in hard disk in a folder named photos. The path to the file is specified by the notation C:\photos\myphoto.bmp. OS manages directories of files and retrieves the specified files when the path is defined. Another function is keeping a "ghost" copy of a file after it is deleted by a user. This file is kept in what is known as *recycle bin* so that a user may get it back if someone has accidentally erased it.
5. Besides these, OS supports many commonly used programs called *utilities* which simplify the use of a computer. Some of these utilities are disk formatting, defragging and disk scanner:

    (a) *Disk formatting:* When a hard disk is supplied by a vendor, it is said to be in unformatted form. Formatting is done to allocate addresses to sectors which can be used to allocate space for files. Formatting creates a directory of the locations of each file stored in the disk. This is called a *File Allocation Table* (FAT). When a file is saved by you on a disk, the OS stores it in a group of sectors called *clusters* which is the smallest storage unit which is addressable by a computer. Before saving a file, the OS examines the FAT to find empty clusters. Having found one, the file is stored there. FAT is updated giving the beginning and end addresses of the stored file. Thus, when a file is opened, the OS is able to find where it is stored by referring to FAT.

(b) *Defragging:* As new files are added to the disk, clusters are progressively occupied. If adjacent clusters are available to store the file, storing as well as retrieval is fast. But as a disk gets progressively full and new files are added, neighbouring clusters may be fully occupied, leaving only the clusters that are far apart. A file may thus end up scattered all over the disk. Scattering of a file on a disk is similar to a situation which arises when you reserve accommodation for a group of persons very late in a sleeper coach on a long distance train. If you book early, the members of a group would get adjacent berths. If you are late, you may get only odd berths available in various bogies of the train. Thus the members of your family may be scattered all over the train. Sometimes it may be possible to adjust with fellow passengers to reduce scattering. It is possible to use a similar idea when the OS finds some fragments of files scattered all over a disk. It tries to rearrange fragments to reduce scattering. This is called *defragging*. Defragging is done by a utility program. A user can invoke this utility when he finds that some applications run very slowly and suspects that it may be due to fragmentation of files used by the application.

(c) *Disk scanner:* Another utility related to disk files is called *disk scanner*. When a disk is manufactured, there may be defects in some parts thereby making some sectors unusable. The manufacturer will scan the disk and mark the defective sectors electronically as bad. Usually, the physical storage available would be larger than the advertised size to allow for defective sectors. When a file is stored, the sectors marked defective are left vacant. Sectors may become bad with continuous use of a disk. A disk scanner utility is run to detect such sectors and if a part of a file is stored in such a sector, it is retrieved and stored in a good sector.

2.2.3 Types of Operating Systems

A variety of operating systems are available in the market and they are designed for different types of users and systems. We will first consider OS for different types of systems and their characteristics. The smallest OS is used by embedded computers such as the ones used in washing machines, and medical instruments. These have limited functions, are small, and can be stored in a ROM. They have limited functions of providing a simple interface to the outside world.

The next in complexity is the OS used in hand-held computers. Hand-held computers such as a machine called *Palm pilot* also have built-in OS stored in a ROM. They are similar to BIOS but provide a better graphical user interface. An OS marketed by Microsoft for such small machines is called Windows CE and provides a good graphical user interface.

An OS of higher complexity is used by desktop PCs. It is assumed that a PC will be used by a single user or at most by a small group of users such as members of one family. It thus provides very little security. The earliest single user OS was MSDOS (Microsoft Disk Operating

System) intended for the PC. It has been the most popular OS. It is now on the way out. The later versions of Microsoft single-user OS for PCs used it as the base to built more powerful and user friendly operating systems. The greatest advance was the provision of a very good graphical user interface (GUI pronounced Gooyee) which made it easy for any one to use the system. Later versions called Windows operating system used a technique called *multitasking* to utilize the increased CPU power of newer models of Intel processors, namely Pentium. Multitasking allows a user to invoke multiple processes simultaneously. For example, while editing a document, another process may be invoked to download a file from the disk. These two tasks may be viewed in two different parts of a VDU screen and are called *windows*. The CPU can execute only one process at a time, but the user has the illusion that both the tasks are being executed simultaneously as the OS makes the CPU switch between the two jobs and allocates to each a slice of time. As the user's reaction time on a keyboard is slow, he does not observe this switching between tasks. Complex scheduling algorithms to schedule CPU are often used.

The next more complex OS is called a multiuser system. This type of OS allows many users to simultaneously use a single computer. Such a computer used by several persons is also called a *server*. The individual user's computer connected to it is called *client*. Normally, several clients and a server are connected to an electronic communication network, called a Local Area Network (LAN). Two popular multiuser OS are Microsoft Windows NT and UNIX. The major requirements of a multiuser system are:

- Each of the user's program has to be protected from the other's program and run independently on the computer.
- As the server is accessible to many users, good security should be provided to the files of users. In other words, unauthorized access to data should be prevented.
- The OS must allow multiprogramming. In multiprogramming, programs of many users are stored on a disk by the server. At a time one of the users' program is loaded in the main memory and given CPU time to execute. When this program needs data to be read from the input unit, it is suspended as reading data from the input is slow and CPU will be idle. The suspended program is stored back on the disk and another program which is ready to execute is placed in the main memory and given the CPU to execute. Thus the OS optimizes the use of CPU.

The most complex OS is the one used with large mainframe computers. It is highly secure, very reliable and efficient. It is normally multiprogrammed and has time sharing. In a time sharing system the computer is available to a number of users simultaneously. Each user is given memory space in main memory and a time slice on CPU during which his program is executed. At the expiry of this time slice, the next user's program is taken up for execution. As human reaction time is slow compared to CPU speed, each user feels that he has all the resources available to him exclusively and does not experience delay.

Mainframes are also used as *batch systems*. In a batch system, a batch of users' programs is fed to the computer which processes them using multiprogramming and optimally uses the computer's resources and completes processing the batch of programs in minimum time. The throughput of the computer is thus maximized.

Another way of classifying OS is to examine if it is machine independent or machine dependent. A machine dependent OS is one which is designed to run only on a specific manufacturer's computers. For example, Apple Computers has an OS which will only run on Apple machines. Linux is an example of a machine-independent OS. It can be run on a variety of computers. Microsoft OS can also be run on a variety of PCs using Intel's processors.

Lastly, an OS may be classified as proprietary or open source. A proprietary OS is owned by a company which distributes only the binary (or object) code of the OS. The binary program may be used only on a specified computer for which the OS is licensed. The OS distributed by Microsoft is a proprietary OS. An open source OS, on other hand, is written in a high level language such as C and distributed free on the internet. Any one can download it and use it on his/her machine. No licence is needed. It is also portable to many systems. The main problem with open source software is that it is not guaranteed or supported by an organization. Some vendors distribute open source software such as Linux (a variation of the powerful multiuser OS is known as UNIX) and support it. A popular vendor of Linux is Red Hat. This vendor distributes Linux on a CD and supports it. By support we mean providing help whenever there is a problem in using the OS on your machine. Nowadays there is a strong move towards using open source OS as it is inexpensive and often much more reliable than some proprietary operating systems. In Tables 2.1 and 2.2 we summarize the discussions of this sub-section.

Table 2.1 Classification of operating systems based on type of computer

Type of computer	*OS type*	*Remarks/Examples*
Embedded computer	ROM based, small size, simple functions	More like a BIOS
Hand-held computer	Simple I/O, use of touch screen	Palm OS, Windows CE
Desktop PC	Good GUI, windows based, Multitasking, accommodates a variety of I/O by modifying BIOS	MS Windows, Vista Linux
Server	Multiuser client/server, multiprogrammed	Good security, Windows Server 2003 Linux, Unix
Mainframe	Multiuser, multiprogrammed, time shared, reliable and very efficient	Good security, AIX 5L of IBM, Z/VM of IBM

Table 2.2 Classification of operating systems based on its intrinsic characteristics

Type of computer	OS type	Examples
Desktop PC or server	Machine independent and open source	Linux
Desktop PC or server	Machine dependent and proprietary	MS Windows XP Windows VISTA Apple MAC OS,
Server	Machine dependent and proprietary	HP UXIIi, IBM AIX 5L, SUN SOLARIS
Mainframe	Machine dependent and proprietary	IBM AZ/VM

Having discussed the operating systems we will now describe in Section 2.3 the programming languages in some detail.

2.3 PROGRAMMING LANGUAGES

Programming languages for computers are developed with the primary objective of making it easy for a large number of persons to use computers without the need to know in detail the internal structure of a computer. Languages are matched to the type of applications which are to be programmed using the language. The ideal language would be one which is able to express precisely the specification of a problem to be solved. The specification must be unambiguous so that it can be converted to a series of instructions for a computer. It is not possible to achieve this ideal as a clear specification of a problem is often not available and developing an algorithm from specifications requires subject knowledge and expertise. In actual practice, a detailed algorithm to solve a problem is the starting point and it is expressed as a program in a programming language. A large number of languages exist, over a 1000, each catering to a different class of applications. All modern programming languages (with the exception of assembly language) are designed to be *machine independent*. In other words, the structure of the programming language would not depend upon the internal structure of a specified computer; one should be able to execute a program written in the programming language on any computer regardless of who manufactured it or what model it is. Such languages are known as *high level machine independent programming languages*.

In this section we will briefly review various programming languages which are currently used. We will look at a classification of programming languages based on their characteristics and another classification based on their applications. We will also point out some of the recent developments in programming languages.

2.3.1 Assembly Language

The first step in the evolution of programming languages was the development of what is known as *assembly language*. In an assembly language, mnemonics are used to represent operations to be performed by the computer and strings of characters to represent addresses of locations in the computer's memory where the operands will be stored. Thus the language is matched to a particular computer's processor structure and is thus *machine dependent*. A translator called an *assembler* translates a program written in assembly language to a set of machine instructions which can be executed by a computer. Each assembly language instruction is translated to one machine language instruction. Thus programs written in assembly language are normally very efficient. In other words, the number of instructions is minimal and hence the execution time is also reduced. Writing programs in assembly language is difficult and requires a person to know hardware details of a computer. Thus programs are written in assembly language only in applications which are cost sensitive or time critical as the efficiency of machine code is of paramount importance in these types of applications. A cost sensitive application is one in which microprocessors are used to enhance the functionalities of consumer items such as washing machines or music systems. In these cases the computer is an embedded processor and the program is stored in a Read Only Memory. Its size should therefore be small. Thus code optimization is important. A time-critical application is the use of microprocessors in aircraft controls where real-time operation of the system is required. Here again, the number of machine instructions executed should be minimized.

2.3.2 High Level Languages

During the evolution of computers, till about 1955, computers were slow and had a small memory. Thus programming efficiency was very important and assembly language was dominant. With improvements in technology, computers were designed with larger memory capacity, higher speed and improved reliability. The tremendous potential of computer applications in diverse areas was foreseen. It was evident that this potential could be realized only if a non-expert user could effectively use the computer to solve problems. It was thus clear that a user should be concerned primarily with the development of appropriate algorithms to solve problems and not with the internal logical structure of a computer. Consequently, a good notation to express algorithms became an essential requirement. For algorithms to be executed by computers, the notation to express them should be simple, concise, precise and unambiguous. The notation should also match the type of algorithm. For example, the notation required to solve science and engineering problems should support arithmetic using wide ranging, high precision numbers and complex numbers and should have features to express operations with arrays and matrices. On the other hand, the notation for processing business data would have operations to be performed on massive amounts of organized data known as files. The notation, in this case, must facilitate describing files and formatting and printing intricate reports. Such notations to express algorithms are known as *high level, machine independent, programming languages*. High level programming languages are further classified as *procedural* and *non-procedural*. Languages which express step-by-step algorithms written to solve a problem are known as procedural languages whereas those which express specifications of a program to be solved are known as non-procedural. The difference between procedural and non-procedural languages may be illustrated with the following example. If you want to go to the railway station from your home, one way of doing is to hire an autorickshaw and tell the driver which roads to take, where to turn, etc. and guide him in detail the way to the station. This is called procedural method. Another method would be to get into the autorickshaw and tell the driver to go to the railway station by the fastest route. In this case you assume that the driver knows the route well and takes you using your specification, namely the fastest route to the railway station. This is non-procedural as you did not give detailed instructions on *how to solve the problem* of going to the station but told him only *what problem was to be solved.* We will discuss first the common features of procedural languages.

Procedural languages have:

(i) Facilities to specify data elements such as real number, integers, logical, characters and data structures such as arrays, matrices, stacks, records, sets, strings of characters, lists, and trees.

(ii) Control structures to sequence operations to be performed. An *if then else* structure is necessary to allow programs to follow different sequences of statements based on testing a condition. For example, the statement:

$$\textbf{\textit{if}} \ (a > b) \ \textbf{\textit{then}}$$
$$x = y + z;$$
$$p = q + t$$
$$\textbf{\textit{else}}$$
$$x = y - z;$$
$$p = q * t$$
$$\textbf{\textit{endif}}$$

commands that the statements $x = y + z$ and $p = q + t$ are to be executed if $(a > b)$ is *true*. If $(a > b)$ is *false* $x = y - z$ and $p = q * t$ are executed.

(iii) Repetition structures carry out a group of statements again and again while a condition is *true* as shown below.

$$\textbf{\textit{while}} \ (a > b) \ \textbf{\textit{do}}$$
$$x = y - z;$$
$$p = q * r$$
$$\textbf{\textit{end while}}$$

(iv) Statements to input and output data.

Besides rules of syntax, each language has *semantic rules,* namely the rules on how to understand and interpret statements of a language. Each syntactically correct structure should have one and only one semantic interpretation.

Associated with each high level language is an elaborate computer program which translates it into the machine language of the computer in which it is to be executed. There are two types of translators. One of them takes each statement of the high level language, translates it and immediately executes it. This type of translator is called *interpreter.* Interpreters are easy to write but the translated programs' execution is slow. The other approach is to scan the whole program and translate it into an equivalent machine language program. Such a translator is called *compiler.* A compiler is a complex program, but the compiled machine code takes much less time to execute compared to an interpreted program.

2.4 A CLASSIFICATION OF PROGRAMMING LANGUAGES

We give in Fig. 2.2 a classification of programming languages. We have classified high level machine independent languages into three groups, namely, procedural, non-procedural, and problem-oriented. Procedural languages have as their starting point, an algorithm to solve the problem. Languages such as FORTRAN, COBOL and C are procedural. These languages provide a methodology to break up a large job into a number of tasks and program the tasks independently as functions or subroutines. These functions or subroutines are then combined to form a program. The general idea is to simplify debugging a program and to reuse the procedures in other programs which may need them. Over the years it was realized that this was not sufficient to enable reuse of programs. Subroutines and functions are too rigid in requiring a specific data type to be used and data to be passed to them in a rigid order. As the cost of programming continually increased, it was realized that "building" programs using a library of reusable "components" was imperative. This led to the emergence of the so-called *object-oriented languages*. In these languages the concept of subroutine/functions is extended to that of an object. An object models a complex real world or abstract object. A real-world object, for example, is a student, whereas an abstract object is a course taken by a student. In an object oriented program (OOP), an object is modelled by a collection of data structures and a set of procedures that use these data structures. A program consists of a collection of objects, each object providing a service when it is invoked and all the objects cooperating to get the job done. Objects are invoked by sending messages to them and they return messages when the job is done.

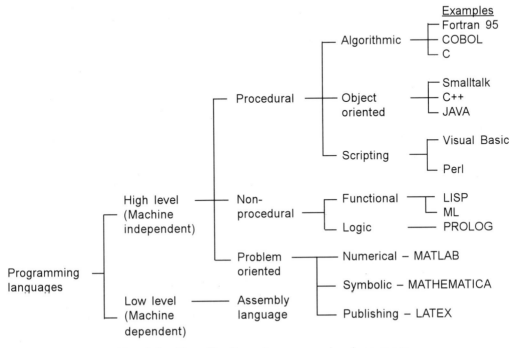

Fig. 2.2   Classification of programming languages.

The advantages of object oriented programming (OOP) accrue only when a large software project is undertaken—also known as "programming in the large". The methodology of OOP enables a programmer to remain close to the conceptual higher level model of the real world problem. One of the earliest OOP languages which was developed was Smalltalk. It, however, did not become popular. Currently an object oriented version of C, known as C++, is the most popular OOP language.

Another development which has taken place in the last few years is the *Internet*—an international network of a very large number of national computer networks. The Internet will be described in greater detail in the next chapter. The technology developed in creating the Internet has been adapted for networking computers within an organization. A computer network within an organization using TCP/IP protocol and providing services similar to the Internet is called an *Intranet*. In both internet and intranet, small application programs (agents or objects to perform some services—known as *applets*) may be developed and stored in any one of the computers connected to the network. One would like to create a new application by using these applets by either importing them to one's own computer or using them via the network. This is achieved by a language known as Java, which is an object-oriented language. This language achieves machine independence by defining a Java virtual machine for which the compiler is written. The Java code compiled for the virtual machine is then executed on any machine by an interpreter which generates the machine code from the compiled code. This technique makes it easy to port Java language to any machine quickly (see Fig. 2.3). Java is gaining wide acceptance now as a programming language to write applications for a network of heterogeneous computers. (By heterogeneous computers we mean computers whose CPU architectures are not identical.)

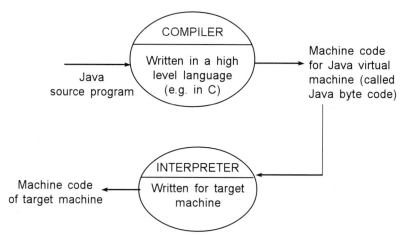

Fig. 2.3   Illustrating portability of Java.

The area of programming languages is dynamic. As more sophisticated hardware systems appear in the market new computer applications emerge, which spawn new languages for such applications.

Another trend is the continuous increase in complexity of applications as hardware becomes more sophisticated and cheaper. The increase in size of programs needs new methods of tackling complexity while keeping the cost of program development low and ensuring correctness of program. This leads to many innovations.

EXERCISES

2.1 What do you understand by the terms computer hardware and computer software? How do you distinguish between the two?

2.2 Define the terms: algorithm, programming language and computer program.

2.3 What is system software? Give an example.

2.4 What is packaged software? Cite an example.

2.5 What is application software? Give an example.

2.6 What are the three types of system software?

2.7 What is an operating system? Why is it required?

2.8 What are the different facilities provided by an operating system?

2.9 What is BIOS? What are its functions?

2.10 What is a device driver? Why is it required?

2.11 Where is BIOS normally stored? Why?

2.12 What is firmware? How is it different from software?

2.13 What is a file allocation table (FAT)? Why is it required?

2.14 What is file fragmentation? What is defragging?

2.15 Enumerate the different types of OS.

2.16 What is multitasking? What are its advantages? Which OS provides multitasking?

2.17 What is a multiuser OS? Which OS provides multiuser facility?

2.18 What is multiprogramming? What is the advantage of multiprogramming?

2.19 What is the difference between a machine dependent and machine independent OS? Give an example of a machine independent OS?

2.20 What is an open source OS? Give an example.

2.21 What is a high level machine independent programming language? Give an example of such a language.

2.22 What is assembly language? Is assembly language machine independent?

2.23 What are the advantages of assembly language? What are its disadvantages?

2.24 Give some applications of assembly language.

2.25 What is a procedural language? Give an example.

2.26 What is an interpreter? When are interpreters used?

2.27 What is a compiler? What is the difference between an interpreter and a compiler?

2.28 What is an object-oriented language? Give an example.

2.29 What is Java? What are the advantages of using Java?

3

Internet and the World Wide Web

```
                    LEARNING OBJECTIVES
```

In this chapter we will learn:
1. What are computer networks and various types of computer networks.
2. Why are computers networked and the advantages of doing so.
3. How computers are connected to form computer networks.
4. The evolution of internet and how it works.
5. Internet applications.
6. The world wide web and how to search for information using the web.

3.1   INTRODUCTION

A transformation in computer technology occurred in 1982 with the introduction of personal computers (PCs) by IBM. Computers of power much more than the early mainframes were available for Rs. 1 lakh. Thus it became possible for many departments to install a computer in their own departments for their students and staff. The price of computers went down rapidly and their power increased. By about 1988 it was possible for many users to have a computer on their desktop for their exclusive use as their price went down to Rs. 50,000. Whereas the price of computers came down the same was not the case with the price of peripherals such as laser printers and plotters. Besides this, there was need to communicate with one another within each academic department of a college and also with those in other departments. Communication consisted of sending data files, messages, etc. A similar development was taking place in commercial organizations. Big single mainframe computers were being replaced by smaller desktop computers in each department. Accounts department, purchase department, sales department, each had its own computers. In order to coordinate the activities of all the departments it was essential to exchange data on sales, payments, receipts, purchases, etc. In fact, it was becoming increasingly clear that database common to all the departments was to be shared. Thus it became evident that the smaller desktop computers required to communicate with one another. They had to be interconnected. A number of computers connected to one another, is called a *computer network*. In fact, today it is understood that an isolated computer is not very useful. A computer in one's home is connected to the *internet*, a world wide computer network. Computers in organizations are connected together to form a *local area network* and if a company has branches dispersed all over the country, they are connected to a *wide area network*. An important point is that the value of a computer (in terms of its utility) increases manyfolds if it is connected to other computers. It is like your telephone. If all your friends have telephones then the use of your own telephone goes up as you can call anyone of them and they can also call you. If you are the only one with a telephone then it is almost useless as you cannot call any of your friends. Thus being connected is an important requirement for computers nowadays. In this chapter we will examine various methods used to connect computers together to form computer networks and then study their uses.

3.2 LOCAL AREA NETWORK (LAN)

When computers which are connected together normally belong to one organization and all computers are situated within a radius of about 1 km, the network is called a *Local Area Network* (LAN). Nowadays all computers are so designed that it is easy to connect them to a LAN without buying any extra equipment. All computers have a unit called a Network Interface Unit (NIU). Referring to Fig. 3.1, whenever a computer wants to send data to another computer, it places the data in its NIU. It also specifies where the data is to be delivered. Thus if the computer p wants to send data to the computer q, it puts the data in its NIU with the address of computer q. After placing the data in NIU, computer p is free to do any other work it wants to do. It is the job of NIU to deliver the data safely to computer q. Thus NIU is like a post office box. Its job is to deliver safely whatever data is placed in it for the intended receiver. Similarly, when data is received by computer p, the data is placed in its NIU by the

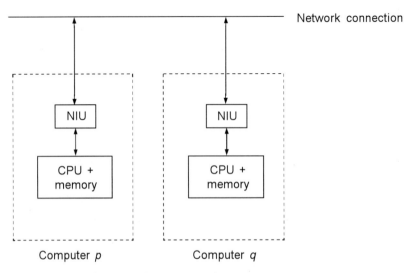

Fig. 3.1   Interconnecting computers.

sender. NIU intimates CPU of the arrival of data and CPU suspends its current task and takes the data from the NIU into its memory. It then proceeds with the task it was doing earlier. After completing the task, it attends to the data received from its NIU.

In Fig. 3.1 we showed only two computers connected together. In general, in a LAN there will be many computers. The NIUs of these computers are connected to an electronic circuit called HUB as shown in Fig. 3.2. Normally up to 16 computers are connected to a HUB.

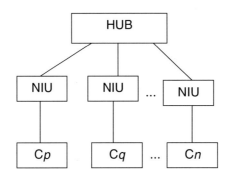

Fig. 3.2   Computers connected to a HUB.

The number of computers in a LAN is not necessarily limited to 16. It can be any number. The design must be such as to avoid "traffic jams". In other words, the time taken to deliver data between any two computers in the LAN must be reasonable, of the order of tens or hundreds of milliseconds and not minutes. This is achieved by connecting individual HUBs, to what is known as a backbone HUB as shown in Fig. 3.3. Thus, if C2 wants to send data to C18, HUB1 sends it to the backbone HUB which forwards it to HUB2, which in turn sends it to NIU of C18.

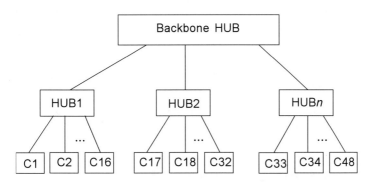

Fig. 3.3   A LAN connecting 48 computers.

Any data to be exchanged between computers connected to, say, HUB2 (e.g. C17 and C32), need not go to the backbone HUB. It will be handled by HUB2 itself. The arrangement is like that in post offices. Any letter posted within a city is sorted and handled locally. If it is to be sent to another state, it is sent to the appropriate post office of that state by the sorting system using the PIN code. It is the responsibility of the receiving office to handle that letter and deliver it to the correct address. For applications of LAN and the technology used in LAN you may refer to (Rajaraman, 2007) given in the list of references.

3.2.1 Technology Used in LAN

We have seen what LANs are. You may wonder how computers in a LAN are connected and communicate with one another. There are three broad methods used. They are known as *Ethernet connection, Token ring* and *Star connection.* The Ethernet connection is the most popular one and we will describe it here and not the other two.

Ethernet connection

We illustrate the Ethernet connection in Fig. 3.4. As can be seen from this figure, 16 computers C1, C2, ..., C16 are connected as a LAN using a HUB. If C1 wants to send data to C4, it will attach the data to some other fields, the most important ones being the sender's address and the receiver's address as shown in Fig. 3.5. We will call this a *message.*

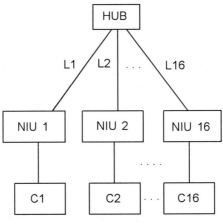

F . 3. Ethernet connection.

Preamble	Sender's address	Receiver's address	Data	Error detection bits

Fig. 3. Ethernet message format.

This message will be placed in NIU1 which will in turn send it via link L1 to the HUB. The HUB is an inexpensive electronic circuit which examines the message, finds the address of the receiver (which is in this case C4) and forwards it to NIU4. This method will work provided it is the only message being sent at that time. It may not be, so as all 16 computers are connected to the HUB, and some other computer, say, C8 may also be trying to send a message to another computer, say, C12. If both messages are being sent simultaneously, HUB will detect that a collision has taken place. It will broadcast a jamming signal to all NIUs connected to it, informing that a collision has taken place and the messages have got corrupted. On receiving this jamming signal, C1 and C8 which were trying to send messages will both wait for different random intervals (a few microseconds) and resend their respective messages. The probability of a collision happening again is lower as the two computers which were trying to send messages back off by different random times. One of them, say C1, will send the message and after this message is delivered to C4, C8 will send its message to C12. This procedure adopted by the network to share the communications system is called CSMA/CD (Carrier Sense Multiple Access with Collision Detection). This method used by Ethernet works quite well in practice as long as the number of computers in the LAN is less than 16. Technically, this technology is known as 10 Base T Ethernet. In this, 10 Base is used to indicate the bandwidth which will be supported by this system, namely 10 megabits/s. T stands for the fact that a twisted pair of copper wires (similar to the ones used in telephones) is used to connect NIUs to the HUB. Recently, 100 Base T (100 megabits/s bandwidth) and gigabit Ethernet have been introduced. Gigabit Ethernet uses fibre optics network and allows a bandwidth of 1 gigabit/s. Currently, 10 Base T is the most inexpensive LAN technology, and hence popular.

3.3 WIDE AREA NETWORK (WAN)

When a geographical area to be spanned by a computer network is a few 100 sq. km (such as Mumbai, Bangalore, Delhi, etc.), it is called the Metropolitan Area Network (MAN). The connection between computers in a MAN is usually through the local telephone network. Usually, dedicated lines are leased from the telephone company to connect organizations. In India the telephone company in major metros is the Mahanagar Telephone Nigam Ltd (MTNL). Leased lines are not shared with other telephone users.

If an organization has multiple sales offices in a city it can exchange information using a MAN. When the geographical area to be spanned by the network is a whole country, then it is called *Wide Area Network* (WAN). The world-wide connection of computers may also be called a Wide Area Network. There are two types of WANs; private and public. Private WANs use dedicated private communication infrastructure provided by telephone companies such as Bharat Sanchar Nigam Ltd. (BSNL), Reliance Infocomm, etc. to interconnect computers. In fact, in India many companies will soon provide country-wide telephone networks using optical fibre cables which will be used for data transmission. Private WANs are expensive to create and maintain but they provide high data rates and are secure as no one from outside this network can gain access to the network. Private WANs are maintained by some big banks such as State Bank of India as they are secure. Railways also maintain their own wide area network for the reservation system. Most organizations, however, use the public telephone network. Public networks use a number of different technologies such as multicore copper cables, fibre optic lines, coaxial cables, microwave networks, and communication satellites. We will not discuss these technologies in detail in this book. These technologies are described in the book *Fundamentals of Computers* written by the author (see references at the end of the book).

When an organization's network is connected to a public network, a filter (which may be a dedicated computer with specially designed software or a server in the organization with special software) is placed between the organization's LAN and a device called a router which connects it to the public switched network (see Fig. 3.6). This filter is called a *firewall*. In fact, a firewall is needed at each location of the organization which is connected to the public network as shown in Fig. 3.6.

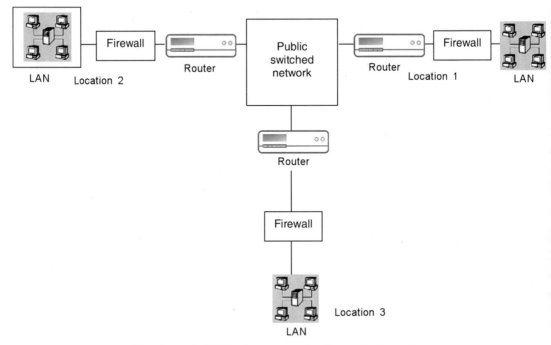

Fig. 3.   A WAN of an organization with firewalls.

Firewalls can be programmed to perform one or more of the following actions depending on the management policies of the organization:

• Prevent unauthorized persons from accessing the data resource of the company such as sensitive databases. Authorized users have legal passwords to login to the network which are used by the firewall to permit access.
• Block access to certain undesirable sites such as pornography, games, etc. by employees.
• Filter e-mails which are suspected to be advertisements or from suspect sources.
• Scan e-mails and e-mail attachments and delete files which have suspected viruses.
• Prevent remote logging into a computer in the organization.

An organization may like to allow free access to their web site and allow access to certain files. These may be stored in a server called a web server and this server is placed between the router and the firewall as shown in Fig. 3.7. Special precautions should be taken to protect web information from being altered by vandals.

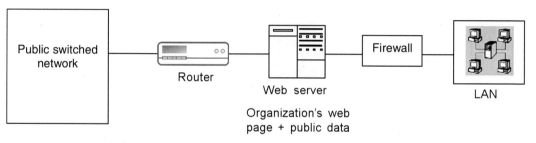

Fig. 3.   Placement of firewall.

3.4   INTERNET

We saw in the last section that LANs which are geographically dispersed are connected using public switched networks to create a WAN. In fact, WAN is a network of many LANs. In Section 3.3, we confined our discussions to LANs belonging to a single organization. This need not be so. If there is an agreement to use a common set of rules to exchange messages between computers of diverse organizations connected to a world wide public switched network, then any computer can communicate with any other computer in the world. Such an infrastructure is called the *Internet*. Technically, we may define the internet as a world-wide computer network whose constituents are computer networks located in organizations. All these individual networks are interconnected using *routers* and public switched telephone networks. (We will explain the functions of a router later.) All computers connected to the internet communicate with one another using a common set of rules. The common set of rules is called a protocol. TCP/IP (Transmission Control Protocol/Internet Protocol) is the protocol used by the internet. An important point to note is that the individual computer networks may use any technology provided the set of rules of communications among computers is standardized such as TCP/IP. We will now describe in greater detail how individual computers connected to the internet communicate with one another.

3.4.1   IP Address

The Network Interface Unit (NIU) of every computer/device which wants to send or receive messages must have an address. This is similar to the need for you to have a unique address to receive mail. Such an address is called an IP address. It should be noted that routers which interconnect local networks are special purpose computers and will require IP addresses. The IP address is 4 bytes long. It is difficult for people to remember a string of 32 bits. Thus the IP address is expressed in the so-called dotted decimal format. For example, an IP address is

144.16.79.48

where each number is the decimal equivalent of a byte (remember that with 8 bits we can represent 0 to 255). Fortunately, in day-to-day use, it is not necessary to remember the IP address of your machine in numerical form. A character string which is easy to remember is usually assigned as your address. The actual assignment of IP addresses follows a systematic process to make it easy to route messages between networks. Each internet service provider (called ISP) is assigned a set of IP addresses by an international agency. The ISP in turn assigns a subset of addresses to each organization from this set.

3.4.2 Connecting PCs/LANs to Telephone Lines

The next question which arises is, how can an individual in a home or an organization be connected to the internet? As we saw, connection to the internet is provided by internet service providers (ISPs). In India there are a large number of ISPs. Educational institutions mostly use ERNET (Education and Research Network), an internet service provided by the Ministry of Information Technology, Govt. of India. Other major internet service providers are: Videsh Sanchar Nigam Ltd. (VSNL), Satyam Infoway (SIFY) and BSWL.

Having identified an ISP, how do you connect your home computer to the internet? It is done using your telephone line. The telephone line is connected to the server at the ISP's location via your telephone exchange. Usually, you dial a telephone number given by the ISP to access their server. Telephone lines are designed to efficiently transmit your conversations with the person at the other end, i.e. they are designed to transmit and receive voice data— an analog audio signal. Data input and output to computers are however digital. Thus the digital output of a computer has to be converted to an analog audio signal before it is transmitted using the telephone line. This is done by an electronic circuit known as *modem*. Nowadays modems are built-in as part of any PC. Older PCs require a small box called an external modem to connect them to a telephone line. The expansion of modem is modulator demodulator. As shown in Fig. 3.8, the modulator part of modem accepts a string of 1s and 0s from the PC and converts each 1 to a continuous audio signal of a low frequency and each 0 to another continuous audio signal of a higher frequency.

Typically, the low frequency will be around 800 oscillations per second and the high frequency around 1200 oscillations per second. (Technically, the SI unit used to represent oscillations per second is called hertz.) The output of the modem is thus an analog signal. This signal is fed to the telephone line as shown in Fig. 3.8. The other end of the telephone line is connected to the ISP's server as shown in Fig. 3.9 through a modem. The analog signals received by the ISP's modem are converted back to digital signals, namely a string of 0s and 1s, by the demodulator part of the modem as shown in Fig. 3.8(b). Similarly, the ISP's server will convert the bit strings to continuous analog signals using its modem and send them to your PC's modem. This modem will convert these signals back to bit strings and store it in PC's memory.

Usually dial-up telephone lines connected between home PC and ISP's server allow you to transmit and receive data at a maximum rate of 56.6 kilobits/s. In reality you will get speeds of the order of only 20 kilobits/s. Such a low speed is generally sufficient for home PC users for getting e-mail and small files, but not good enough if you want to receive video signals. A high speed modem called ADSL modem can be connected to your telephone line if you want to receive video signals via the internet. Such a connection is popularly known as broad band connection. For details of how the data sent by you on the internet reaches the specified destination, you may refer to (Rajaraman, 2007) given in the list of references.

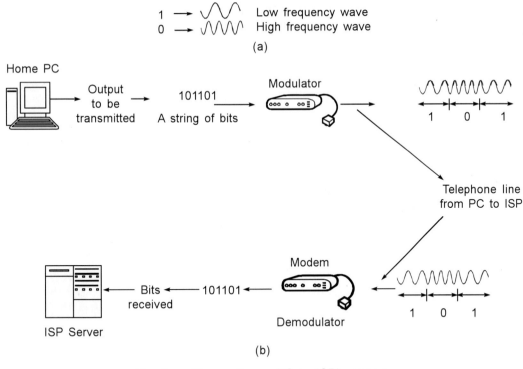

Fig. 3.   Connecting a PC to ISP's server.

Fig. 3.   Connecting a PC to ISP using telephone line.

3.5   NAMING COMPUTERS CONNECTED TO INTERNET

We saw in Section 3.4.1 that each NIU connected to the internet has a unique IP address expressed in a dotted decimal format. As an example we saw that 144.16.79.48 is an IP address. It is difficult for people to remember such a long sequence of digits. Thus it is a common practice to assign easy-to-remember names to computers connected to the internet. For example, you may name your computer "*leela*", which may also be a name chosen by someone else who does not know that you have chosen this name. Thus the name is normally qualified by the department, the organization, ISP and the country code to make it unique. If your department is Chemistry at IISc., Bangalore and your ISP is ernet, then the unique IP address assigned (see Fig. 3.10) may be leela.chem.iisc.ernet.in

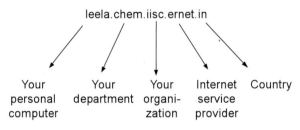

Fig. 3.1   Internet (IP) address.

There should, of course, be a method of uniquely assigning names for each IP address. This is done by keeping a directory similar to a telephone directory. This directory is called *Domain Name System*. If the directory for the entire internet is kept in one computer, it will be too large with hundreds of millions of entries and will be difficult to search for an IP address. It is thus decentralized. One method of decentralizing is for each organization to keep a server which has a directory of all computers connected to its network and their IP addresses. For example, IISc, Bangalore may have a domain name server which can keep a directory of names of computers in each department and their respective IP addresses. The ISP of IISc, namely, ernet, will have a domain name server which will store the address of IISc's domain name server. Such a hierarchical organization will make the directory system manageable, both from the point of view of size and for keeping it up-to-date.

The overall Domain Name Service of the internet has been hierarchically organized as illustrated in Fig. 3.11. You may observe that USA is conspicuous by its absence in this figure. As the internet was started in the USA, the computers in the USA do not have a

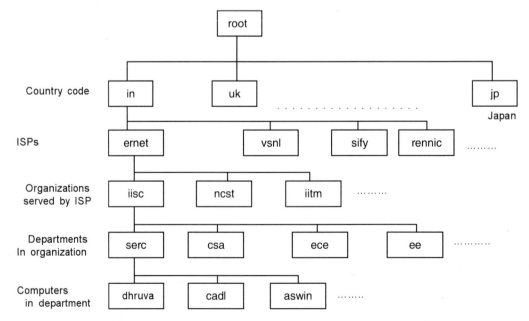

Fig. 3.11   Hierarchy of domains for domain name service.

country name as they thought at that time that the internet will be confined to the USA only. The domain names in the USA are given in Fig. 3.12 (see also Table 3.1).

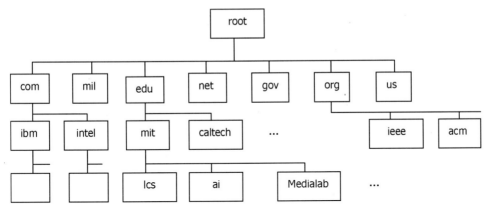

Fig. 3.12   Domain names in the USA (explanation of top level domains given in Table 3.1).

Table 3.1   Top level domain names in the USA

Domain	Nature of organization
com	Commercial organizations
edu	Educational institutions
gov	US Federal government agencies
mil	US Military sites
org	Nonprofit organizations
net	Network support centres
us	Local bodies, State governments, local public libraries

3.6   SOME INTERNET APPLICATIONS

One of the earliest applications of computer networks was exchanging messages and files among users of the network. When networks expanded into internet, a logical step was to exchange messages among persons spread out all over the world. It soon became one of the most popular applications of the internet and was called electronic mail or e-mail, for short. E-mail allows almost instant communication at a very low cost among people spread out all over the world. Whereas airmail letters from India take at least 10 days to reach the USA, e-mail reaches almost instantly and you may get a reply within a few minutes if the person to whom you sent the mail has his computer on. It is even possible to exchange short messages and carry on an e-chat! This is one of those applications called "killer application" (abbreviated killer app in computer jargon) as it is almost universally used and has made the internet highly popular. E-mail system is so reliable today that people use it for important communications and do not send the so-called postal copy for confirmation. As e-mail is so fast, the normal postal mail is often called 'snail mail' by e-mail users! The use of e-mail has expanded with provisions available to attach pictures and audio files to the text.

Another major application of the internet is known as the *world wide web* or *web*, for short. The web has become the most important information infrastructure in the world and has a user base of billions. At the touch of a terminal button, you can now get information from all corners of the globe. It has also enabled many other services such as e-commerce, e-governance, e-publishing, etc. We will describe what a web is, and how it is created and used. The web became useful with the creation of a software called *browser*. A browser is used for many purposes: to search for information desired by you, to access any web site using a unique address called its URL (Universal Resource Locator), download files, login and use remote computers and for sending and receiving e-mail. The internet can also be used for downloading music files and for sending and receiving what is known as voice mail. Recently, we also have services in the USA which are emerging, called *internet radio*. We will describe how it works. Finally, we will examine how images, animation and video can be transmitted.

3.7 E-MAIL

Current e-mail systems provide the following facilities:

- Send a message to a specified recipient or a group of recipients.
- Send a message that includes as an attachment a text, audio, images or video file.
- Send a message along with a program which can be executed at the recipient's computer and send a response.

In order to be able to send or receive e-mail, you need a unique address. It is similar to the need to have a postal address if you want to receive letters. The e-mail address has the form:

`yourname@name of your e-mail server assigned by domain name server`

For example, my e-mail address is:

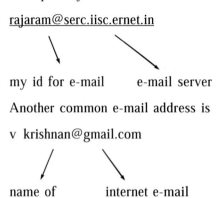

rajaram@serc.iisc.ernet.in

my id for e-mail   e-mail server

Another common e-mail address is

v krishnan@gmail.com

name of   internet e-mail
a person   service provider's server name

In order to send/receive e-mail, you need an application program which should be installed in your computer. It allows you to compose a message, edit a message, specify the recipient or recipients by giving their e-mail addresses and specify the names of attachment files (if any). It also provides a mail inbox for you to receive mail and an outbox to store mail to be dispatched from your machine.

A typical e-mail looks as shown in Fig. 3.13.

```
From    :      ramu6@ee.iitk.ac.in
To      :      rajaram@serc.iisc.ernet.in
Date    :      10 Jan 2003   11.02.04 IST
Subject:       Thank you

Dear sir,

Thank you for responding to my mail and answering
my question.

Kind regards

                              Sincerely
                              Ramu
```

Fig. 3.13   A typical e-mail format.

If you want to send e-mail from your home, you require the following:

1. A telephone connection.
2. A modem in your computer. Most recent computers have a built-in modem which can transmit/receive data at the rate of 56.6 Kbps. If your computer does not have a built-in modem, you need an external modem which is usually connected to a serial port (called USB port) of your computer (see Fig. 3.14).

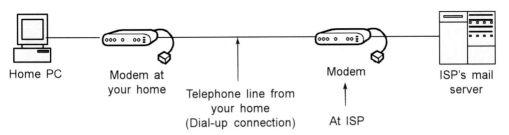

Fig. 3.1   A dial-up line from a home PC to ISP.

3. An account with an Internet Service Provider (ISP) who will maintain for you in his server a mail box to receive your mail (called inbox) and another box for the mail you send (called outbox). His server will be kept on 24 hours a day and 7 days a week as mails may come from any part of the world at any time. There are many ISPs in India and they have a variety of subscription terms.

4. The ISP will provide you an e-mail id and allow you to use a secret password of your own to access your mail boxes.
5. The ISP will also normally provide you with a telephone number to connect to his server for sending/receiving mail. This telephone number is usually stored by the e-mail application program in your computer. Thus, when you want to send mail, you connect to ISP's server by dialling the ISP's telephone number. You now click an icon marked *send* in your application program and it will automatically download your mail to your outbox in the server.
6. It is possible to have files attached to your mail (just like enclosures in a typed letter). These could be any file such as ASCII, jpeg, tif, mp3, etc.
7. Each call to ISP will cost you one local call charge which BSNL will charge you. Thus it is preferable to compose a number of mails you want to send, keep them ready and send all of them once a day. At the same time, you can also receive the mails stored in your mailbox at your ISP.
8. If you have a broadband connection it is permanently connected to ISP and there is no need to dial. Telephone calls can go on while you are using the internet as the ADSL modem virtually splits the telephone line into two parts.

If you are connected to a LAN in your office (or college), then there will be a mail server in the LAN and your mail boxes will normally be in that server. There is no need to dial up ISP. The organization's LAN will be connected to the ISP through a router and possibly a leased line of high bandwidth. The mail server will be kept on 24 hours, 7 days a week, and will send any mail almost immediately to the destination address (see Fig. 3.15).

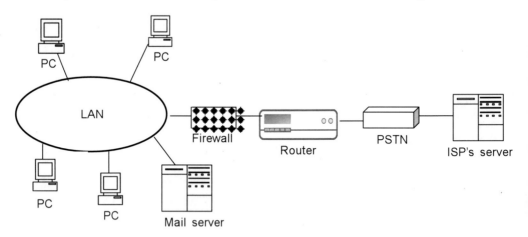

Fig. 3.1   E-mail via a LAN.

If you are logged on and the server receives a mail, it will immediately forward it to you and a message will normally flash in your PC.

The e-mail system on the internet is normally very reliable. When an e-mail is sent from the outbox of the server, it is not immediately erased. The server waits for an acknowledgement from the intended receiver. If there is no acknowledgement for a specified period, the mail is resent. If there is no response again, the ISP informs the sender that the mail could not be delivered (it is normally said that the mail has bounced).

Mail systems also allow you to keep a directory of nicknames (or shorter names) for frequently used e-mail addresses. This reduces your typing effort. There are a number of other facilities available with e-mail systems. Some of these are:

- You can send the same mail to many recipients by specifying all their e-mail addresses in the To field. For example, you can write

  To: ramu@vsnl.com,kichu@sify.com,balu@sancharnet.in,seenu@iitm.ac.in
  and the same mail will go to ramu, kichu, balu and seenu.

- The same message can be broadcast by the ISP providing the e-mail service to all the subscribers.
- A message can be multicast, that is, broadcast to a restricted pre-specified group.
- e-mail can be forwarded to another e-mail address if it is specified.
- You can type the reply to the sender and send it by clicking on "reply". It is not necessary to retype the sender's address.

To summarize, e-mail has become a very important service provided by the internet infrastructure and has proved extremely fast, reliable and flexible.

3.8 THE WORLD WIDE WEB

The idea of the world wide web originated in the high energy particle physics laboratory where the physicist Tim Berners-Lee was trying to find a convenient method of exchanging documents among researchers in particle physics, spread all over the world. This was in 1989 when the internet was becoming a reliable information exchange infrastructure. His purpose was to build a software which would use this infrastructure effectively to retrieve documents stored in various servers spread across laboratories. He designed a new set of rules for computers to retrieve textual data from remote servers. This was called Hypertext Transfer Protocol (HTTP). The next step was to describe a notation to mark keywords in documents for ease of search and retrieval. This was called Hypertext Markup Language (HTML). The final step was to assign a unique address specifying the server connected to the internet in which the document resided and how to access it. It was called a Universal Resource Locator (URL). These were the basic steps necessary to facilitate easy retrieval of desired documents from a distributed interlinked set of computers.

These steps and the relevant software were essential but not sufficient to allow easy retrieval of documents on a variety of subjects. The next crucial step was the development of *hypertext browser* by Marc Andersen and his team of programmers at the National Centre for Supercomputer Applications at the University of Illinois. This was called Mosaic Web Browser and was the software which really opened up the world wide web as we know it today. Mosaic provided a good graphical user interface and made the web accessible to the general public who do not know any special programming knowledge. The browser technology has continuously improved, and the currently popular web browsers are the Internet Explorer designed by Microsoft and integrated with Window OS, Netscape Communicator which is the successor of Mosaic and Mozilla firefox. These browsers are freely available and easy to use.

3.8.1 Hypertext

Assume a text such as that given in Fig. 3.16. This text gives a brief write-up about Bangalore in which a number of *keywords* are shown in a differnt font. These keywords are linked to other pages which give information in more detail about the keywords.

---

b   a gal   e

Bangalore is the capital of Karnataka. It is called the Silicon Valley of India as it has a large number of InfoTech industries. Leading among them are INFOSYS, WIPRO, TCS and SONATA. It is also the home of the Indian Institute of Science, a pioneering educational and research institution which was founded in 1907 by Sir J.N. Tata. It also has many engineering colleges. It is also called the garden city as it has one of the largest and oldest botanical gardens of India called Lalbagh. Lalbagh has several flowering trees and some rare birds with wonderful chirping sounds.

Fig. 3.1   A document with keywords linking it to other documents (keywords are shown in a different font).

This idea of embedding a selectable keyword in a text, which links it to other documents, is called *hypertext*. The hypertext facilitates what may be called nonlinear reading, i.e. while reading a document stored in a computer if some topic interests you, it is possible for you to click on the keyword corresponding to that topic. After reading the document, you could return to the original document to the same point where you left it. In the computer's memory (normally the disk) the documents are linked as shown in Fig. 3.17. This figure is given just to satisfy your curiosity.

Given an ordinary text, a language to format the document and mark the keywords in the text is called *hypertext markup language*. This language has become popular to create documents called web pages which are linkable to other web pages in the world wide web.

3.8.2 Universal Resource Locator

We stated in the last section that a hypertext is organized by specifying a number of keywords and the links from these keywords to other relevant documents. The major innovation in world wide web browser is that it specifies the address of the server where the document, also called a web page, is kept, and this address is displayed.

The world wide web is organized using web pages. Web pages use hypertext with a set of clickable (i.e. selectable) keywords which are normally highlighted in a different colour. Web pages are stored in servers (also called hosts) in various organizations with the primary intention of allowing free access to this page to any person, anywhere in the world. The host

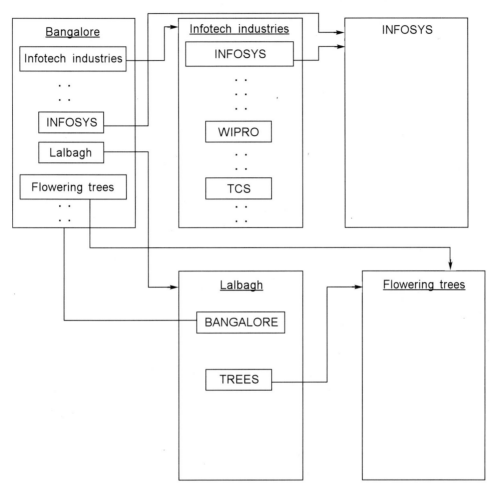

Fig. 3.1   Hypertext links between documents.

is normally given the name www by every organization which wants to be a participant in the world wide web of documents. A web page in the world wide web is accessed by specifying what is called a Universal Resource Locator (URL). A typical URL has the form shown in Fig. 3.18.

In the URL of Fig. 3.18, **http** specifies the rules agreed on between a client and a server to transfer messages and documents. This protocol is now a universal standard and is often omitted while entering URL. The second part following ://, namely, www.xcollege.ernet.in is the domain name of the server where the web pages are stored. Following this is /ydept/ admissions.html which gives the path to the file you want. It says that a folder named admissions.html has the file required by you and it is an html document.

As we have seen, a software called browser is used to access web pages. When you activate a browser, a web page is displayed with the URL. A sample page is shown as Fig. 3.19. In many cases you may not know the explicit path to a specific file. Usually, all

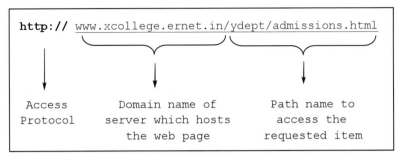

Fig. 3.1   A Universal Resource Locator (URL) of a hypothetical web site.

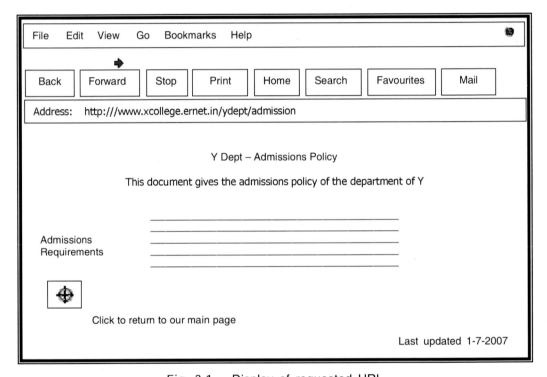

Fig. 3.1   Display of requested URL.
(We have shown a typical screen you will see. It is not that of any particular browser.)

sites have a top page which contains a table of contents. You can click on any of the items you are interested in and the browser will automatically go to the relevant document, display it and also show the URL in the address field of the page. This is illustrated in Fig. 3.20. If you click on Departments on this page, it will take you to a page with all the departments listed. You can click on the specific department you are interested in and it will display information on that department.

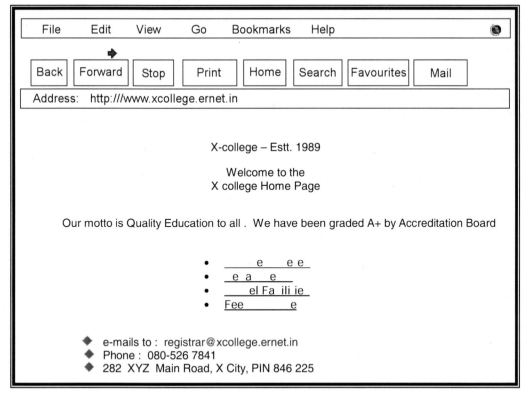

File   Edit   View   Go   Bookmarks   Help

Back | Forward | Stop | Print | Home | Search | Favourites | Mail

Address: http:///www.xcollege.ernet.in

X-college – Estt. 1989

Welcome to the
X college Home Page

Our motto is Quality Education to all . We have been graded A+ by Accreditation Board

- _____ e   e e _
- _ e a _ e __
- _____ el Fa ili ie_
- Fee_____ e_

◆ e-mails to : registrar@xcollege.ernet.in
◆ Phone : 080-526 7841
◆ 282 XYZ Main Road, X City, PIN 846 225

Fig. 3.2   Display of main web page of X college. Any of the underlined items may be clicked to go to the relevant page.

3.9 INFORMATION RETRIEVAL FROM THE WORLD WIDE WEB

As of today, there are over 200 million hosts on the world wide web serving over a billion users all over the world. The web is thus a vast mine of useful information. It is so huge (over a peta byte, i.e. a million gigabytes) that looking for specific information you require, may be like looking for a needle in a haystack unless you use a systematic method of searching for information. Many tools are available in the internet to assist you to obtain the information you require and you must know how to use them. In addition, if you know the principles these tools use to search for information, it will be an added advantage.

One of the best ways of searching for information on the web is to start with a known web site (i.e. known URL) which will lead you to other similar sites via hypertext links. One link may lead to another and you may forget which intermediate pages interested you. Thus it is advisable to store these URLs with what is known as bookmarks. Bookmarking tool is available with all browsers.

3.9.1 Resource Directories

If you do not know any URL, it is a good idea to use what are known as *internet resource directories*. These directories normally categorize resources by subjects and resource type (e.g. institutions, patents, etc.). Many of these employ human experts for indexing and classification by subjects. There are two types of resource directories: those that cover all subjects and those that are subject specific. Some examples of general purpose directories are *yahoo.com* and *einet.com*. Several professional societies have co-operated to produce scitopia.org which provides journal articles in Physics, Electronics, Electrical, Civil and Mechanical engineering. Another good general purpose information source is wikipedia.org which is an encyclopaedia written and edited by volunteers.

A good general purpose subject directory is maintained by yahoo.com. This site uses many methods to create subject directories and keep them updated. Some of the methods are:

- Submissions of their URLs by developers of websites with subject key words.
- Human indexers to search the web and add important keywords to the subject index.
- Use of websites of special interest groups who gather information on the area of their interest.
- Use of programs called web crawlers which systematically and automatically visit many websites and add URLs to the subject index.

The subject index maintained by this site (yahoo.com) can be used by you to obtain the information you seek on the subject. Queries called *Boolean queries* are allowed to search the index. By Boolean query we mean a query of the type: [keyword1 (AND) keyword2]. We interpret this as pick all websites which deal with *both* keyword 1 *and* keyword 2. Either one is not sufficient, both should occur. For example, if you are interested in seventeenth century history of South India, you can pose the Boolean query:

Seventeenth century AND History AND South India

If you wrote either just History or South India, a lot of irrelevant information will be retrieved. You should formulate your query so that *only* the relevant information is retrieved and *all* the relevant information is retrieved. In other words, *no* relevant information should be missed and the information retrieved are *all* relevant and useful. This is not always easy. Even if your query is well formulated, the tool you use may not be very good. Thus it is also important to pick good tools.

Boolean queries allow what is known as NOT operation. For example, if you want a list of hotels in Bangalore which are not very expensive, you may write:

(Bangalore *AND* Hotels) *AND NOT* (Five Star Hotel). This will remove all five star hotels from the list.

The search using a Boolean query in yahoo will display documents subjectwise with the first few lines of the document. This will enable you to decide whether or not to get the full document.

3.9.2 Search Engine-based Retrieval

Currently the most popular method of retrieving documents from the world wide web is to use what are known as search engines. The following sites provide search engines:

- Google.com
- Altavista.com
- Yahoo.com

India-specific search engine sites are:

- Searchindia.com
- Khoj.com

We will consider the currently popular search engine google.com as an example and examine the facilities available in it for information retrieval. It is important to know that newer search engines appear periodically, which are superior to existing ones for certain purposes. The following site gives a continuously updated information on available search engines and their good and bad qualities. http://www.searchenginewatch.com. Google allows search queries using phrases, i.e. combination of words. For example, "Computer Network" is a phrase which can be used in a query. It is quite different from the term: "Computer" *AND* "Network" which will retrieve too many irrelevant documents. It allows search within the results of earlier searches. It automatically inserts AND as a Boolean operator between search terms. For example if you write:

"Seventeenth Century" "History" "South India" the AND connective is inserted between phrases. For example, "in URL" will limit the search to the specified URL only. Other qualifiers can be "in title", meaning the phrase must appear in the title of an article.

AltaVista search engine is similar to Google except that it allows Boolean Operators AND, OR, NOT, and also an operator called NEAR which is not really a binary operator. It uses a closeness index to retrieve documents similar to the ones you specify.

The following tips are useful to retrieve information from the web:

- If you know the URL of a site where the topic you want is there, start the search from there and follow the links.
- If you only know a broad subject category, use a directory-based tool such as yahoo.com
- Use narrow search terms rather than broad terms. A term such as "computer network" will retrieve too many documents. If you are interested in *local area network design,* use it as a search phrase.
- Use specific and somewhat unusual words in your query which will narrow down the search. General terms will flood you with documents.
- Use as many synonyms as you know of the keyword in your search query.
- Some search tools are sensitive to word order and take the first word as the most important. So use the most important keyword first in your query.
- If the search allows NOT operator, use it to exclude information you do not want.
- Some search engines rank order retrieved documents, giving the most relevant ones first and irrelevant ones later. This may not always be the correct order. So see at least the first four or five pages retrieved to choose what you want.
- Create bookmarks of useful sites so that you can use them later if you need them.

Before we conclude this section, we will briefly explain how search engines function. Unlike directories, search engines such as google do not use humans to index documents. Documents are automatically indexed by the web crawler programs. These programs systematically visit web pages and pick those containing the specified keyword(s) and create an index. Web crawling can get out of control. So crawlers use some methods of limiting the number of branches taken. They also rank web pages by their importance and relevance and give them as first few items when you search. Importance is normally determined by how many URLs refer to the web page in their hypertext link, the number of words in the web page which match those used in the search query, the number of times the web page has been referred to, etc. The design of search engines and relevance ranking has been a research area for many years. Continuous improvements are taking place based on experimentation and in a few years excellent search tools are bound to appear. This will make it easy for lay users to retrieve all the relevant documents satisfying their query from the world wide web.

3.10   OTHER FACILITIES PROVIDED BY BROWSERS

We primarily emphasized the http protocol provided by a browser program interface and how it is used to search for documents and retrieve them from the web. In Fig. 3.21 we give a conceptual organization of a browser which provides a uniform user interface to use other services available on the internet.

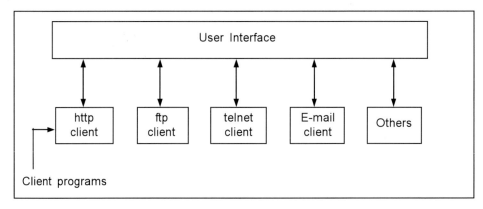

Fig. 3.21   Various client programs allowed when you invoke a browser program.

The most important services are:

- ftp—a program to transfer files from any computer connected to the internet, provided free access to the file is allowed.
- Telnet—a program that allows you to login to a remote computer (may be a computer server or a database server) from your desktop or mobile computer provided, of course, you have access privileges. Telnet is very useful when you travel. You can log on to your computer from anywhere in the world using the internet, read your mail, download any files you may need, and also run programs remotely.
- E-mail—Sending/receiving mail on your client.

We will now describe how these programs are used.

3.10.1 File Transfer

When you transfer a file from a server to your computer, it is called *downloading* a file. On the other hand, if you send a file from your computer to another computer connected to the network, you are said to *upload* a file. Ftp is an application that allows you to access any computer connected to the internet and download file(s) from it. If you want to download a file named admission-rules from the web site of *x* college, you enter in your browser the information given in Fig. 3.22.

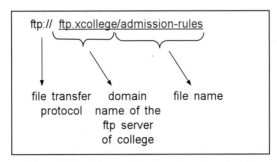

Fig. 3.22   Use of ftp to download a file.

The remote file server (in this case *ftp.xcollege*) will send back a message asking for login id and password. If it is a publicly accessible file server, you normally write **anonymous** as user id and your e-mail id as password. Some systems will accept **guest** as password. It will also ask a filename to which the downloaded file should be transferred. Normally, it is better to receive a binary file image rather than a text file (in ASCII) unless you are certain that the text file can be opened as is on your computer. In windows environment the usual file extensions are *.zip* (for compressed binary file) or *.txt* (for ASCII text file).

Apart from files containing information which you download from websites, a large number of computer programs are available in the internet for you to download and use. Normally there are four types of programs. They are explained in Table 3.2.

Table 3.2   Downloadable software from the internet

Type of software	Mode of use
Freeware	Free programs which you can use for personal use and give copies to friends. You cannot sell them.
Shareware	Free programs given for a trial period (about a month) after which you may buy it or return it. You cannot keep copies.
Beta programs	Programs being tested. They are free but may have many bugs. If you find bugs report them to the developer so that they can be corrected.
Open source	Source programs available free. Can use and distribute.

When you download programs, they are usually executable files and you should use .exe as file extension. Source files can be obtained as binaries.

3.10.2 Telnet

As we saw, by telnet we mean logging on to a computer from a remote computer and using facilities provided by it. If you type:

telnet: <domain name of the remote computer> or IP address (if you know it)

an application program in your browser will connect you to the remote computer and get ready to accept messages from it. The remote machine will send a message asking for your login id and password, exactly as though you are using that computer. You now give your login id and your password and it will admit you as an authorized user. You can have all the facilities such as running a program, accessing your files stored there, and modifying them if you so desire. You can even develop programs from a remote location, compile and execute them. If the internet connection is via a high bandwidth line, you will not even know you are remotely located.

Telnet is routinely used by software companies in India for the so-called "off shore software development". In this model, these companies often use the network of computers of the client remotely from India, upload programs, test and run them with live data. Errors are remotely corrected and any fault reports are attended to from India. This is highly economical compared to sending software engineers to foreign countries to work on client sites. In fact, many software companies maintain the existing systems from India for clients abroad. Remote telnet is also used in some call centre operations. When a client complains about a problem in a software product, a call centre technical person can remotely log in and find out the problem and solve it.

3.11   CONCLUSIONS

In this chapter we learnt about the internet and the most important application supported by the internet, namely the world wide web. The world wide web is one of the most useful and widely used systems and has become an essential facility nowadays. Using it you can search for information; it is like having a huge library at home. Besides this, the internet allows you to use e-mail, download useful files, remotely use your computer, chat with your friends on-line and book tickets by train, bus or by air. It also allows you to download music, send photographs, download video and even have telephone conversation using what is known as internet telephony. The details of how multimedia information can be sent is given in [1] and we have not discussed it here. Thus it is important to know how to use the internet and the world wide web. With this chapter we conclude Part I of the book. Part II of the book teaches you how to program a computer using the C Languge.

EXERCISES

3.1 What is a computer network? Why is a network useful?

3.2 What is a LAN? How are computers connected to a LAN?

3.3 Explain the functions of a NIU.

3.4 What is a HUB? What are its functions? How many computers can normally be connected to a HUB?

3.5 When is a backbone hub required? What are its functions?

3.6 What is Ethernet? Explain how ethernet works. Give the ethernet message format.

3.7 What is CSMA/CD. How does it function?

3.8 What is 10 Base T?

3.9 What is a wide area network? How is a WAN formed?

3.10 What is a Metropolitan Area Network? Give an example of a MAN and its application.

3.11 What is the difference between private WAN and a public WAN? When are private WANs deployed?

3.12 What is a firewall? Why is it needed in computer networks?

3.13 Describe the functions of a firewall.

3.14 What is internet? What protocol do computers connected to the internet use?

3.15 What is an IP address? Why is it needed?

3.16 What is a modem? Why is it needed?

3.17 Explain how your home computer can be connected to the internet.

3.18 What is an ISP? What services are provided by ISP?

3.19 What is DNS? Why is it necessary?

3.20 Who assigns names to internet addresses? Give a typical address and explain the different parts in it.

3.21 How is DNS organized? Why is this organization chosen? How does it ensure flexibility in assigning e-mail ids?

3.22 What do you understand by the term "killer-application"? Why is e-mail called a killer-application?

3.23 What facilities does an e-mail system provide?

3.24 What are the different parts of an e-mail address?

3.25 What are the facilities required if you want to send e-mail from your home?

3.26 What do you understand by the term ISP? What services does an ISP provide?

3.27 What are the components of cost for sending/receiving e-mail?

3.28 How does sending an e-mail from your college differ from sending an e-mail from your home?

3.29 When you send an e-mail, do you receive an acknowledgement? How do you know that the e-mail has been delivered to the intended recipient?

3.30 Define information browsing using the internet. What facilities does a browser provide?

3.31 What is hypertext? What is hypertext-based browsing? Give an example of a hypertext-based browsing.

3.32 What is the main advantage of hypertext?

3.33 Who first came up with the idea of world wide web? Where was this done?

3.34 What do you understand by world wide web? What are the different steps needed to create the world wide web?

3.35 What is URL? Why is it an essential part of the world wide web?

3.36 What are the different parts of a URL? Explain the purpose of each part.

3.37 What is a web browser? Name two popular web browsers.

3.38 What is a web page? How is a web page accessed?

3.39 What is a bookmark in a browser? Why is it useful?

3.40 What is a search engine? What are the main principles used by a search engine to retrieve information from the web? Give the names of some popular search engines.

3.41 Enumerate some useful tips to search for the information required by you from the world wide web.

3.42 What are the various client programs which can normally be invoked from a browser program?

3.43 What is ftp? How do you use ftp?

3.44 How do you download files using ftp?

3.45 What is telnet? How is it used?

Part II
PROGRAMMING USING C

4

Computer Algorithms

LEARNING OBJECTIVES

In this chapter we will learn:
1. The properties of an algorithm.
2. The basic structure of a computer necessary to carry out algorithms.
3. Steps followed to solve a problem using a computer.

4.1 ALGORITHMS

The fundamental knowledge necessary to solve problems using a computer is the notion of *an algorithm*. An algorithm is a precise specification of a sequence of instructions to be carried out in order to solve a given problem. Each instruction tells what task is to be performed. Specification of a sequence of instructions to do a job is used in many fields. One such specification taken from a popular magazine is given as Example 4.1.

EXAMPLE 4.1   Recipe for Bournvita Cake

Ingredients
Bengal gram flour 2 cups, sugar 2 cups, ghee 3 cups, milk 1/2 cup, Bournvita 6 teaspoons, vanilla essence 5 drops, 1/2 cup water.

Method

Step 1:   Warm 1 cup ghee. Put gram flour and fry for 2 minutes on low flame.
Step 2:   Separately dissolve Bournvita in warm milk and add vanilla essence.
Step 3:   Add 2 cups sugar in 1/2 cup water in a pan and warm it till sugar dissolves. Boil syrup till it become sticky.
Step 4:   Pour the prepared Bournvita in syrup and stir continuously.
Step 5:   Add fried gram flour to the syrup and continue stirring 15 to 20 minutes adding the remaining melted ghee until the mixture does not stick to the pan.

Step 6: Pour the mixture on a plate smeared with melted ghee shaking while pouring to ensure uniform spreading.

Step 7: After 10 to 15 minutes cut into 40 pieces.

Result

40 pieces of Bournvita cake.

The recipe given above is similar to an algorithm but it does not technically qualify as one. It is similar to an algorithm in the following respects:

1. It is a sequence of instructions to be carried out to solve the problem of making Bournvita cake.
2. It begins with a list of ingredients which is the *input.*
3. The sequence of instructions specify the actions to be carried out with the input to produce the cake which is the *output.*
4. It takes a finite time to execute the instructions and stop.

It does not technically qualify as an algorithm as the instructions given to make the cake are not precise. For example, in Step 3, the instruction to be carried out is to boil syrup until sticky. The interpretation of degrees of stickiness is subjective and would vary from person to person. In Step 5 the exact time to cook is not specified. In fact the instructions are meant for a reasonably experienced cook with "common sense".

We will now examine another sequence of instructions (taken again from a popular magazine).

EXAMPLE 4.2   Instructions to knit a sweater

Input

Needles No. 12 = 2

Wool 4 ply = 9 balls

Method

Step 1:   Cast on 133 stitches

Step 2:   Repeat Steps 3 and 4, 11 times

Step 3:   Knit 2, *Purl 1, Knit 1, Repeat from * to last stitch, Knit 1.

Step 4:   Knit, *Purl 1, Knit 1, Repeat from * to End

....

....

(Similar Steps)

Result

A Sweater

The above example illustrates the following points:

1. The instructions are much more precise and unambiguous when compared to the recipe for Bournvita cake. There is very little chance for misinterpretation.
2. The number of different types of actions to be carried out are very few. If we know how to knit, how to purl, cast stitches on or off needles and count then any sweater can be knit.
3. By a proper permutation and combination of this elementary set of actions, virtually an infinite number of patterns may be created.

The preciseness of the instructions combined with the small variety of tasks to be performed to carry out each instruction facilitates design of a machine to automate knitting. In fact a machine similar to the modern computer was a loom designed by a French engineer Jacquard in 1801 which could be 'programmed' to create a large number of patterns. The program consisted of cards with specific patterns of holes in them which would control the loom.

We have illustrated two sequences of instructions for solving problems and stated that they are similar to algorithms but do not possess all the necessary attributes of algorithms.

What are the attributes which characterize an algorithm? What is the origin of this word?

The origin of this word has been hotly debated. It is, however, generally accepted among mathematicians that it comes from the name of a famous Arab mathematician Abu Jafar Mohammed ibn Musa al-Khowarizmi (literally meaning father of Jafar Mohammad, son of Moses, native of al-Khowarzm) who wrote the celebrated book "Kitab al jabr Walmuqabla" (Rules of restoration and reduction) around A.D. 825. The last part of his name al-Khowarizmi got corrupted into algorithm.

An algorithm may be defined as a finite sequence of instructions which has the following five basic properties:

1. A number of quantities are provided to an algorithm initially before the algorithm begins. These quantities are the *inputs* which are processed by the algorithm.
2. The *processing rules* specified in the algorithm must be precise, unambiguous and lead to a specific action. In other words the instructions must not be vague. It should be possible to carry out the given instruction. For example, the instruction: "add 15 to 20" can be carried out. On the other hand it is not possible to carry out the instruction 'Find the square root of –5'. An instruction which can be carried out is called an *effective* instruction.
3. Each *instruction* must be sufficiently *basic* such that it can, in principle, be carried out in a finite time by a person with paper and pencil.
4. The total time to carry out all the steps in the algorithm must be finite. An algorithm may contain instructions to repetitively carry out a group of instructions. This requirement implies that the number of repetitions must be finite.
5. An algorithm must have one or more *output*.

Based on the above definition we see that a recipe does not qualify as an algorithm as it is not precise. The knitting pattern, on the other hand, does qualify. Just as a machine may be built to knit sweaters using the knitting algorithm it is possible to build a machine to process data fed to it provided the data processing rules are specified as an algorithm. Further, the basic instructions used by the algorithm should be elementary such as add, subtract, read a character, write a character, compare numbers and find out which is larger, etc., so that these can be carried out by a machine. In the example on knitting we saw that even though the basic types of instructions are few it is possible to develop an enormous number of different interesting patterns by permuting and combining these. The same principle is used in building computers. Thus with a machine which can carry out as few as ten different operations it is possible to carry out a large variety of data processing tasks by designing appropriate algorithms.

4.2   CHARACTERISTICS OF COMPUTERS

The interesting features of a computer are as follows:

1. Computers are built to carry out a small variety of elementary instructions. It is not necessary to have more than fifty types of instructions even for a very versatile machine.
2. Each instruction is carried out in less than a millionth of a second.
3. Each instruction is carried out obediently with no questions asked.
4. Each instruction is carried out without making a mistake.

A computer may thus be thought of as a servant who would carry out instructions at a very high speed obediently, uncritically and without exhibiting any emotions. Giving instructions to an obedient servant who has no common sense is difficult. Take the instance of a colonel who sent his obedient orderly to a post office with the order "Buy ten 25 paise stamps". The orderly went with the money to the post office and did not return for a long time. The colonel got worried and went in search of him to the post office and found the orderly standing there with the stamps in his hands. When the colonel became angry and asked the orderly why he was standing there, pat came the reply that he was ordered to buy ten 25 paise stamps but not ordered to return with them!

A consequence of the uncritical acceptance of orders by the computer is the need to give extensive, detailed, and correct instructions for solving problems. This is quite challenging. If you wish to give correct instructions to an idiot to do a job, you better know how to do the job correctly yourself!

4.3   AN ILLUSTRATIVE COMPUTER ALGORITHM

In order to carry out a task using a computer the following steps are followed:

1. The given task is analysed.
2. Based on the analysis an algorithm to carry out the task is formulated. The algorithm has to be precise, concise and unambiguous. Based on our discussions we recognize that this task is difficult and time consuming.
3. The algorithm is expressed in a precise notation. This can be interpreted and executed by a computing machine and is called a *computer program.* The notation is called a *computer programming language.*
4. The computer program is fed to a computer.
5. The computer interprets the program, carries out the instructions given in the program and computes the results.

We will now consider an example of formulating an algorithm.

EXAMPLE 4.3   A procedure to pick the highest tender from a set of tenders

We first decide the format in which the tenders would be presented. We assume that each tender will have an identification number and the tender value.

Method

Having decided the data format we formulate the steps needed in a procedure to pick the highest tender.

Step 1: Read the first tender and note down its value as the maximum tender value so far encountered. Note down the tender identification number.

Step 2: As long as tenders are not exhausted do Steps 3 and 4. Go to Step 5 when tenders are exhausted.

Step 3: Read the next tender and compare this tender with the current maximum tender value.

Step 4: If this tender value is greater than that previously noted down as maximum tender then erase the previous maximum value noted and replace it by this new value. Replace the previously noted tender identification number by this identification number. Else do not do anything.

Step 5: Print the final value of maximum tender and its identification noted down in Step 4.

Observe that Example 4.3 qualifies as an algorithm as:

1. It has inputs. The inputs in this case are the set of tenders each with an identification number and value.
2. Each step in the algorithm is precise, has a unique interpretation and can be effectively carried out.
3. Each instruction is basic. If we sit with paper and pencil, and follow the instruction literally, we would be able to perform the job and do it in a finite length of time.
4. Observe that the algorithm is repetitive. In other words Steps 3 and 4 are repeated until all tenders are exhausted. The number of repetitions are finite as the number of tenders are finite. Thus the algorithm will terminate in a finite length of time.
5. The algorithm has an output, namely, the identification number of the maximum tender and the value of the maximum tender.

Other interesting features illustrated by this algorithm are:

1. The structure of the algorithm does not change when the input data change. In other words we can use as input one set of tenders and it will pick the highest tender in this set. If another set of tenders is used as input (after the completion of the previous job) then the highest tender in this new set will be picked by the same algorithm. It is thus a good idea to generalise an algorithm and write it so that it can work with a class of input data.
2. The number of instructions in an algorithm is finite and fixed. The number of *executions* of instructions, however, is not constant. It depends on the input data. For instance, the number of times Steps 3 and 4 in the algorithm of Example 4.3 are executed depends on the number of tenders input to the algorithm.
3. The output obtained by executing an algorithm depends on the input used by it. If the input data has errors then the output will also be wrong. If for example, in Example 4.3, the tender identity of the maximum tender is incorrectly entered in the input, the same mistake will be found in the output.

5

Developing Algorithms

LEARNING OBJECTIVES

In this chapter we will learn:

1. The broad strategy to solve a problem using a computer.
2. Flow charts and their use.
3. How to trace the execution of an algorithm by a computer.

In this chapter we will explain, with a number of examples, how a broad strategy for solving a problem may be developed into a detailed sequence of elementary instructions. This process of development is aided by *flow charts*. A flow chart depicts pictorially the sequence in which instructions are carried out in an algorithm. Flow charts are used not only as aids in developing algorithms but also to document algorithms.

Another algorithm development and documentation tool is the *decision table*. A decision table depicts in a tabular form the set of conditions to be tested and the sequence of actions to be performed for solving a problem. This tool is useful in solving problems which require a large number of decisions.

In this chapter we will also introduce a simple model of a computer which will enable us to understand how an algorithm is executed by a computer. We will also see how the "correctness" of an algorithm can be checked by using test data on this simple model of a computer.

5.1 FLOW CHARTS

EXAMPLE 5.1   The problem is to pick the largest of three numbers.

Broad Strategy
Read the three numbers A, B and C. Compare A with B. If A is larger compare it with C. If A is found larger than C then A is the largest number; otherwise C is the largest number. If in the first step A is smaller than or equal to B, then B is compared with C. If B is larger than C then B is the largest number else C is the largest number.

The strategy given above is not concise. It may be expressed much more clearly and concisely as a flow chart. The flow chart is given in Fig. 5.1.

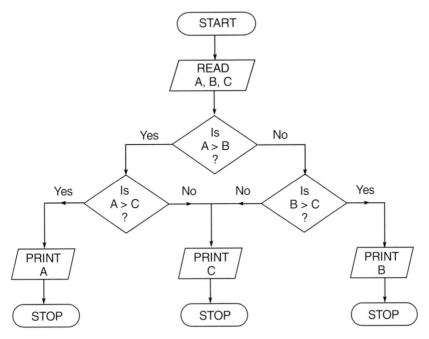

Fig. .1   A flow chart to pick the largest of three numbers.

The arrows in this flow chart represent the direction of flow of control in the procedure (to solve the problem), that is, having completed one task the direction of the arrow is to be followed to go to the next task.

For easy visual recognition a standard convention is used in drawing flow charts. This convention has been standardized by the International Standards Organization and we will use this standard.

In this standard convention:

(i)   Parallelograms are used to represent input and output operations.
(ii) Rectangles are used to indicate any processing operation such as storage and arithmetic.
(iii) Diamond-shaped boxes are used to indicate the questions asked or the conditions tested, based on whose answers appropriate exits are taken by a procedure. The exits from the diamond-shaped box are labelled with the answers to the questions.
(iv) Rectangles with rounded ends are used to indicate the beginning or the end points of a procedure.
(v)   A circle is used to join the different parts of a flow chart. This is called *a connector*. The use of connectors gives a neat appearance to a flow chart. Further, they are necessary if a flow chart extends over more than one page and the different parts are to be joined together. The fact that two points are to be joined is indicated by placing

connectors at these points and by writing the same identifying letter or digit inside both the connectors.

(vi) Arrows indicate the direction to be followed in a flow chart.

Every line in a flow chart must have an arrow on it.

All the flow chart symbols and conventions are illustrated in Fig. 5.2. The use of connectors may also be seen in Fig. 5.2. The circles with 'A' written inside are to be joined together.

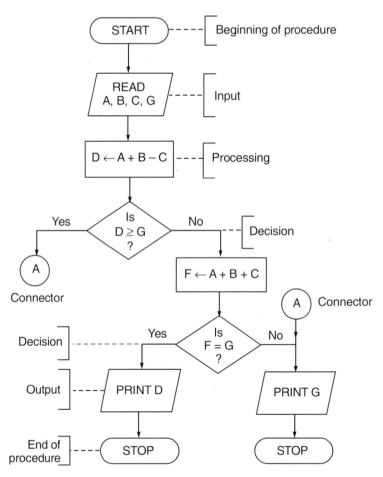

Fig. .2 Illustrating flow chart symbols and conventions.

5.2 A SIMPLE MODEL OF A COMPUTER

In this section we will use a simplified model of a computer to understand how algorithms are executed by a computer. This model consists of four blocks and is shown in Fig. 5.3. The four blocks are:

1. Input unit
2. Memory unit

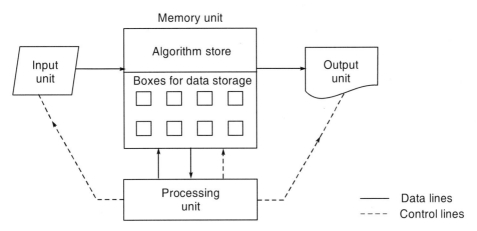

Fig. .3 A simple model of a computer.

3. Processing unit
4. Output unit

The *input unit* is used to read the data to be processed and to read the program which processes the data.

The *memory unit* is a store used to store the data, intermediate results and the program. We can imagine the memory to be partitioned into two parts. One part consists of a large number of labelled boxes—one box per data item. The other part stores the algorithm.

A data item in a box in the memory may be retrieved by referring to the label or name of the box. When a data item is read from a box, a copy of the data item is used; the original data item is not destroyed. When a data item is written in the memory, this data item is stored in the specified box in the memory and the old contents of the box are destroyed.

The *processing unit* interprets the instructions given in an algorithm and carries them out obediently and accurately. It has subunits to do arithmetic and logic.

The *output unit* is used to print the results of computation.

We will now use this model to explain how the algorithm given by the flow chart of Fig. 5.1 is executed. First an appropriately coded version of the flow chart is "stored" in the memory. The data required to solve the problem are kept ready at the input unit and arranged in the order in which they will be read by the input instruction in the flow chart.

In the example being considered if the values of A, B and C are −7, 10, 6 then these three numbers are kept queued up and ready at the input unit.

The processing unit now starts from the START block in the flow chart. It gets all the units of the computer ready to follow the instructions stored in the memory. The next block is an instruction to READ A, B, C. This command is interpreted as follows:

> "Name three boxes in memory as A, B and C. Read the first number queued up at the input unit and place it in the box named A. Advance the queue at the input unit by one place. Take the number at the top of the queue and place it in the box named B. Repeat this procedure and place the number presently at the top of the queue in the box named C". The procedure is illustrated in Fig. 5.4.

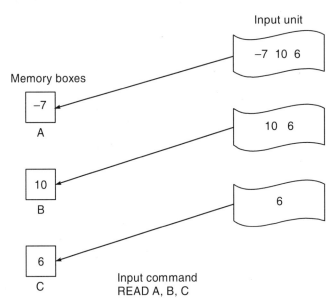

Fig. . Reading numbers from an input unit and storing in memory.

The next block in the flow chart is the question "Is A > B?". This is interpreted as:

Read the numbers stored in boxes named A and B in memory; compare these two numbers and return an answer "yes" if the number in A 'is greater' than that in B and "no" otherwise. If the answer is "'yes" then the processing unit follows the path labelled "yes" in the flow chart and if it is "no" then the path labelled "no" is followed.

With –7, 10 and 6 stored in boxes named A, B and C respectively the answer to the question "Is A > B ?" is "no" as –7 is not greater than 10.

The processing unit now follows the "no" path in the flow chart and reaches the question "Is B > C?". The processor compares the numbers stored in memory in boxes named B and C. Comparing 10 and 6 the processor answers "yes", follows the "yes" path and reaches the command PRINT B. This is interpreted as "ask the output unit to print the number stored in the memory box named B". Thus 10 is printed. After doing this the processor reaches the next command STOP and stops.

5.3 MORE FLOW CHARTING EXAMPLES

EXAMPLE 5.2 In Example 5.1 we developed a flow chart to find the largest of three numbers. Suppose we want to pick the largest of four numbers instead of three numbers. We can, of course, use the same strategy and obtain the flow chart, shown in Fig. 5.5. This flow chart is bigger than the one of Fig. 5.1 but it is still not too large. If we, however, try to find the largest of five numbers using the same strategy the flow chart will become too large. The strategy used in Example 5.1 is thus not good enough to be generalised. We need an alternate

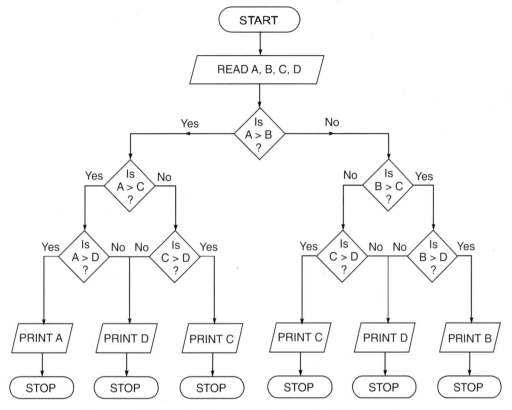

Fig. .   A flow chart to pick the largest of four numbers.

strategy to pick the largest of a set of numbers assuming that we do not know how many numbers are there in the set.

Broad Strategy
The strategy is to read the first number and call it the largest number encountered so far. (If there is only one number in the list then that number would be the largest.) The second number (if present) is compared with the current largest number. If it is larger, then it replaces the current largest. These steps are repeated till all the numbers are exhausted. This strategy is expressed more precisely by the following algorithm written in English.

PROCEDURE 5.1:   Procedure to pick the largest of a set of numbers

Step 1: Read Number
Step 2: Largest ← Number
Step 3: As long as numbers are there in the input repeat Steps 4 and 5
Step 4: Read Number
Step 5: If Number > Largest then Largest ← Number
Step 6: Write Largest
Step 7: Stop

This procedure is expressed pictorially by the flow chart of Fig. 5.6.

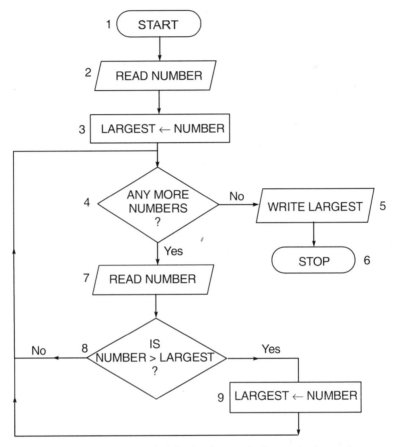

Fig. .   A flow chart to pick the largest of a set of numbers.

We will now carry out the instructions given in the flow chart as would be done by the processing unit. This methodology is adopted to make sure that the logic of solving the problem given by the flow chart is correct and that the correct results which we expect would indeed be obtained when the flow chart is faithfully followed. The method of carrying out the instructions given by the flow chart with paper and pencil is called *tracing a flow chart.* Tracing is carried out with sample data. "Memory boxes" are identified and named and their contents changed as instructed by the flow chart instruction. The flow chart of Fig. 5.6 is traced in Table 5.2 with the data of Table 5.1. The table depicts the contents of each memory box at each step during the execution of the flow chart.

Referring to Table 5.2 the first row corresponds to executing instruction 2 of the flow chart. The first data item in the input queue is read and stored in memory box named Number. The next instruction commands that the contents of the memory box named Number should replace the contents of the memory box named Largest. (The symbol ← is to be interpreted as "is replaced by"). The old contents of the memory box to the right of ← are not changed.

Table .1   List of numbers used as input

Item 1	9600 → Top of input queue
Item 2	8900
Item 3	9800
Item 4	8900
End of input list	

Table .2   Tracing the flow chart of Fig. 5.6

Box in flow chart executed	Instruction in flow chart executed	Contents of memory boxes	
		Number	Largest
2	Read Number	9600	
3	Largest ← Number	9600	9600
4	Any more Numbers? Answer: Yes		
7	Read Number	8900	9600
8	Is Number > Largest? Answer: No		
4	Any more Numbers? Answer: Yes		
7	Read Number	9800	9600
8	Is Number > Largest? Answer: Yes		
9	Largest ← Number	9800	9800
4	Any more Numbers? Answer: Yes		
7	Read Number	8900	9800
8	Is Number > Largest? Answer: No		
4	Any more Numbers? Answer: No		
5	Write Largest	(Largest written = 9800)	
6	STOP		

This is shown in row 2 of Table 5.2. The fourth instruction in the flow chart asks the question "any more numbers in the input?" It is necessary to ask this question at this stage because if the input has only one number it should be declared as the largest number. For the data of Table 5.1 the answer to this question is "yes". The processor thus proceeds to the instruction in box 7 of Fig. 5.6 which commands that the data item presently waiting at the top of the input data queue is to be read. This is item 2 as item 1 has already been read into the memory in Step 1. Thus the number 8900 is read and stored in the memory box named Number. The old contents of this box are overwritten by this new value. After this, a question is asked in box 8 of the flow chart. The answer to this question is "no". Following the arrow the flow chart returns to box 4 which again commands that the input queue is to be checked to see if more data are there. The answer is "yes". Thus item 3 which is on top of the queue is read into the memory box named Number replacing the old value. Executing box 8 of the flow chart we get a "yes" answer. Executing the command in box 9 of the flow chart the previous contents of Largest is replaced by the current contents of Number. This is shown in Table 5.2. Following the flow chart obediently the rest of the rows in Table 5.2 are obtained. Execution is finally stopped when no more numbers are left in the input. As seen from Table 5.2 execution stops after writing the largest number in the given list.

This example illustrates an important idea in procedure formulation intended for execution by a computer. It is the idea of repetitively performing a set of instructions. In this procedure the basic idea is to pick up a number and check if it is greater than the current largest number. If it is greater, then replace the old largest by this and continue. This action is repetitively performed till the end of the input list is reached. The set of actions performed for each new number read is invariant. The actions are implemented in the flow chart (Fig. 5.6) by the Steps 4, 7, 8, (9); 4, 7, 8, (9);... till no numbers are left. The Steps 4, 7, 8, (9) constitute a *loop* in the flow chart.

EXAMPLE 5.3   It is required to develop a procedure to find the average height of boys and that of girls in a class.

Broad Strategy
Add the heights of all boys and count the number of boys. Divide the sum of heights by the number of boys. Do the same for girls.

Detailed Procedure Development
Assume that for each student in the class one slip is filled up which has the Roll No. of the student, a code identifying the sex of the student (1 is used to indicate boy and 2 for girl), and the height of the student in centimetres. Table 5.3 illustrates the data organization.

The procedure is to pick up a slip and find the sex code. If it is 1 then the height is added to total boys height. The number of boys is also incremented by 1. If the sex code is 2 then the height is added to total girls height. The girl count is incremented by 1. This procedure is repeated till the end of slips is reached. When this is reached then boy and girl height totals and total numbers of boys and girls are separately available and the separate averages can be computed. The detailed procedure needs accumulators to be set up which have to be cleared to zero before actual accumulation of totals begins. The procedure is given as Procedure 5.2.

Table .3 Student height data organization

Slip no.	Roll no.	Sex code	Height
1	4234	1	95
2	4682	2	105
3	4762	2	100
4	4784	1	100

PROCEDURE 5.2: Procedure to find average heights of boys and girls

Step 1: Initialize counters to accumulate totals and store zeros in them.
Step 2: Repeat Steps 3 and 4 until end of slips is reached.
Step 3: Read a slip.
Step 4: If sex code = 1

        Total boy height ← Total boy height + height
        Total boys ← Total boys + 1

    Else

        Total girl height ← Total girl height + height
        Total girls ← Total girls + 1

Step 5: Av. boy height ← Total boy height/Total boys
        Av. girl height ← Total girl height/Total girls
Step 6: Print Total boys, Av. boy height,
        Total girls, Av. girl height
Step 7: Stop.

This procedure is depicted as a flow chart in Fig. 5.7 and traced in Table 5.4 with the data in Table 5.3.

This example illustrates what is known as *initialization*. In this procedure zeros are stored in a number of memory boxes which are later used to accumulate sums. Memory boxes named Total boy height, Total boys, Total girl height and Total girls are set to zero in Step 1 of the flow chart. In Step 5 (see Fig. 5.7) is written:

$$\text{Total girl height} \leftarrow \text{Total girl height} + \text{height}$$

This is to be interpreted as "take the contents of the memory box labelled Total girl height and add to it the contents of the memory box labelled height and replace the previous contents of memory box Total girl height by this "sum". The arrow ← is thus to be interpreted as *replaced by*. Similarly, we interpret

$$\text{Total girls} \leftarrow \text{Total girls} + 1$$

as "contents of the memory box Total girls is *replaced by* (the previous contents of) Total girls + 1".

This example also uses a loop.

EXAMPLE 5.4 It is required to develop a procedure to count the number of non-zero data in a list of 100 data.

Broad Strategy
The strategy is to read a data value. Check if it is non-zero and increment a counter. The reading is continued till 100 data values are read.

Detailed Procedure
The detailed procedure is given as Procedure 5.3.

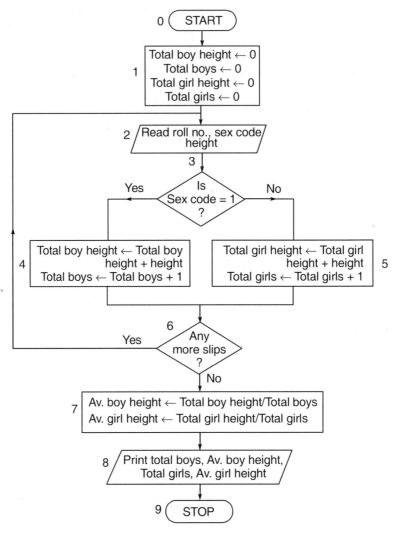

Fig. .   Flow chart to find the average height of boys and girls.

PROCEDURE 5.3:   To count the number of non-zero data

Step 1:   Initialize the non-zero data counter nzdcount to 0
Step 2:   Repeat 100 times all steps up to Step 4
Step 3:   Read d
Step 4:   If $d \neq 0$ then

nzdcount $\leftarrow$ nzdcount + 1

Step 5:   Print nzdcount
Step 6:   Stop

Procedure 5.3 is depicted as a flow chart in Fig. 5.8.

Table . Tracing the flow chart of Fig. 5.7

Box in flow chart executed	Nature of box	Contents of memory boxes								
		Total boy height	Total boys	Total girl height	Total girls	Roll no.	Sex code	Height	Av. boy height	Av. girl height
1	Process	0	0	0	0					
2	Read	0	0	0	0	4234	1	95		
3	Decision 'Yes'	0	0	0	0	4234	1	95		
4	Add	95	1	0	0	4234	1	95		
6	Decision 'Yes'	95	1	0	0	4234	1	95		
2	Read	95	1	0	0	4682	2	105		
3	Decision 'No'	95	1	0	0	4682	2	105		
5	Add	95	1	105	1	4682	2	105		
6	Decision 'Yes'	95	1	105	1	4682	2	105		
2	Read	95	1	105	1	4762	2	100		
3	Decision 'No'	95	1	105	1	4762	2	100		
5	Add	95	1	205	2	4762	2	100		
6	Decision 'Yes'	95	1	205	2	4762	2	100		
2	Read	95	1	205	2	4784	1	100		
3	Decision 'Yes'	95	1	205	2	4784	1	100		
4	Add	195	2	205	2	4784	1	100		
6	Decision 'No'	195	2	205	2	4784	1	100		
7	Arithmetic	195	2	205	2	4784	1	100	97.5	102.5
8	Print	PRINTS		Total boys = 2,			Av. boy height = 97.5				
				Total girls = 2,			Av. girl height = 102.5				
9	STOP									

An important new notation used in this chart is the symbol to depict repetition of a group of instructions for a fixed number of times. The symbol is an elongated hexagon in which the number of repetitions to be performed and the last step to be repeated are given. The group of instructions to be executed repeatedly is said to be in *a loop*. The end of the loop is indicated in the flow chart by a small hexagon inscribed with a digit.

EXAMPLE 5.5 Students' examination results are declared using the following rules

There are two subjects in the examination called main and ancillary. If a student gets 50 percent or more in the main subject and 40 percent or more in the ancillary, he passes. If he gets less than 50 percent in the main he must get 50 percent or more in the ancillary to pass. However, the minimum passing marks are 40 percent in the main subject. If a student

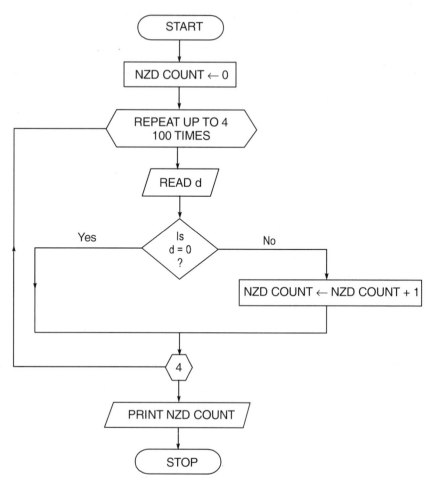

Fig. . Flow chart to count non-zero digits in a set of 100 digits.

gets 60 percent or more in the main subject, he is allowed to repeat the ancillary subject if the ancillary marks fall below 40 percent. However, there is a group of students in the class, which is granted a special consideration. For students in this group the pass percentage is 40 percent in the main and 40 percent in the ancillary. If a student in this group gets less than 40 percent in the ancillary he is allowed to repeat that subject if he obtains 40 percent or more in the main subject.

The above complex set of rules is translated into a flow chart in Fig. 5.9.

Observe the complexity of the chart and the appearance of the same test in more than one place in the chart.

Flow charts are not suitable for problems with complex decision logic as they become clumsy when the number of conditions to be tested is large. Another technique of representing complex decision logic is by using *decision tables*.

The procedure for Example 5.5 which was given as the flow chart of Fig. 5.9 can be

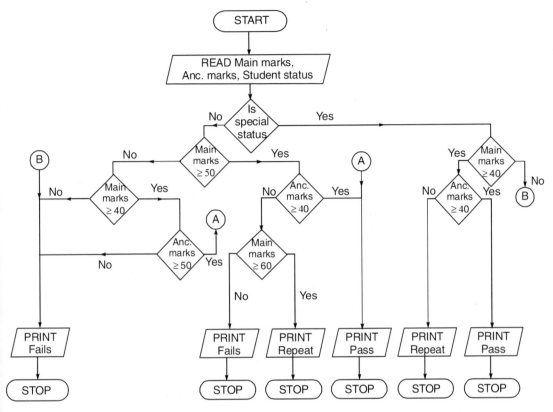

Fig. . Flow chart depicting the processing of examination results.

equivalently represented by the decision table of Table 5.5. In this table a 'x' against an action means perform the action and '–' against an action means do not perform the action. The table is self-explanatory. The reader is urged to compare the flow chart of Fig. 5.9 with the table (Table 5.5).

We will discuss the use of decision tables at greater length later in this book.

Table . A decision table corresponding to flow chart of Fig. 5.9

Conditions	Rule 1	Rule 2	Rule 3	Rule 4	Rule 5	E
Main marks percentage	≥ 50	≥ 40	≥ 60	≥ 40	≥ 40	L
Anc. marks percentage	≥ 40	≥ 50	≥ 40	≥ 40	< 40	S
Special status	No	No	No	Yes	Yes	E
Actions						
Pass	x	x	–	x	–	–
Repeat ancillary	–	–	x	–	x	–
Fail	–	–	–	–	–	x

EXERCISES

5.1 (i) Extend Procedure 5.1 to pick the highest of a set of tenders. Assume that each tender is represented by a tender identification number and the amount of the tender.

(ii) Draw a flow chart using standard symbols to represent this procedure.

5.2 (i) If you assumed in evolving the procedure for Exercise 5.1 that there is only one tender which has the highest value then extend the procedure to account for the case when more than one tender amount is highest. In such a case all the tender codes which have the same highest value should be given as output.

(ii) Draw a flow chart corresponding to this procedure.

(iii) Check the flow chart by tracing it with sample data.

5.3 Extend Procedure 5.1 to pick the highest tender and the second highest tender.

5.4 (i) Obtain a procedure to find the minimum quotation from a set of quotations. The procedure should account for the case when more than one quotation has the least value.

(ii) Check your procedure by tracing it with sample data.

5.5 Given a set of hundred integers, evolve a procedure which will find:

(i) The total number of even integers in the set.

(ii) The total number of odd integers in the set.

(iii) The sum of all even integers.

(iv) The sum of all odd integers.

5.6 A Fibonnacci sequence is defined as follows:

The first and second terms in the sequence are 0 and 1. The subsequent terms are found by adding the preceding two terms in the sequence. A part of the sequence is: 0, 1, 1, 2, 3, 5, 8, 13, 21, 34, 55, 89, ... Obtain a flow chart to find all numbers in the Fibonnacci sequence less than 200.

5.7 Fifteen pairs of coordinates of points in a plane are given. Obtain a procedure to find the number of points in each of the 4 quadrants in a plane (For example the pair (–3, 6) is in the second quadrant).

5.8 (i) Given one hundred pairs of length and breadth of rectangles, obtain a procedure to find all the rectangles whose area is greater than their perimeters. (For example the area of the rectangle with length = 5 and breadth = 4 is greater than its perimeter.)

(ii) Extend the procedure to find the average area of the rectangles found in part (i).

5.9 (i) 100 student records are given, each with the roll number of the student and his or her marks in three subjects. Obtain a procedure which will read the 100 records one after another and find the total marks, the average marks and the division of each student. A student with average marks of 60 percent or above is placed in first division, those with average marks less than 60 but 50 or above are placed in second division, those with less than 50 are declared fail.

(ii) Extend the procedure of part (i) to find the average marks of all 100 students and the number of students passing in first division and second division.

5.10 Given ten sequences each consisting of six digits, evolve a procedure to print those sequences which are in strict ascending order. For example the sequence (5, 6, 7, 9, 11, 14) is in strict ascending order whereas the sequence (5, 5, 6, 7, 9, 11) is not in strict ascending order.

5.11 Given three points (x_1, y_1), (x_2, y_2) and (x_3, y_3) obtain a flow chart to check if they are collinear.

5.12 Obtain algorithms to find the sum of the following series:

(i) $\Sigma\ x^r$ with r varying from 0 to 100
(ii) $-x + x^2/2! - x^3/3! + x^4/4! - x^5/5! + ... - x^{13}/13!$

5.13 An insurance company uses the following rules to calculate premium:

(i) If a person's health is excellent and the person is between 25 and 35 years of age *and* lives in a city *and* is a male *then* the premium is Rs. 2 per thousand and his policy may not be written for more than Rs. 2 lakhs.

(ii) If a person satisfies all the above conditions except that the sex is female *then* the premium is Rs. 1.50 per thousand and her policy may not be written for more than Rs. 1 lakh.

(iii) If a person's health is poor and the age is between 25 and 35 *and* the person lives in a village and is a male *then* the premium is Rs. 9 per thousand and his policy may not be written for more than Rs. 10,000.

(iv) In all other cases the person is not insured.

Obtain a flow chart to give the eligibility of a person to be insured, his or her premium rate and maximum amount of insurance. Obtain a decision table and compare with the flow chart.

5.14 Given the coordinates (x, y) of ten points, obtain a procedure which will output the coordinates of all points which lie inside or on the circle with unit radius with its centre at (0, 0).

5.15 A company manufactures three products: engines, pumps and fans. It gives a discount of 10 percent on orders for engines if the order is for Rs. 5000 or more. The same discount of 10 percent is given on pump orders of value Rs. 2000 or more and on fan orders for Rs. 1000 or more. On all other orders they do not give any discount. Obtain a decision table corresponding to this word statement.

6
Programming Preliminaries

LEARNING OBJECTIVES

In this chapter we will learn:
1. The need for a high level programming language and a compiler.
2. The difference between source and object programs.
3. The difference between syntax rules and semantics of a programming language.
4. The history of development of C language.

6.1 HIGH LEVEL PROGRAMMING LANGUAGES FOR COMPUTERS

We saw in Chapter 5 how a flow chart is evolved to solve a problem. The flow chart is an aid to the programmer to plan his strategy to solve a problem. It cannot be directly interpreted by a computer. A computer can interpret and execute a set of coded instructions called *machine language instructions.* For instance a set of three instructions to add two numbers and store the answer in a (hypothetical computer) is given below:

Operation code	Memory location
0110	10001110
0111	10001111
1000	01110001

In the first instruction 0110 is an operation code to load into a storage register in CPU an operand from location 10001110 in memory. The operation code 0111 (of the second instruction) instructs the computer to add the contents of memory location 10001111 to the contents of the storage register (where the first operand has been stored by the previous instruction). The third operation code 1000 instructs that the result which is in the storage register is to be copied into location 01110001 of memory. It is evident that we should memorise all the binary operation codes and keep track of the contents of each and every location in memory to be able to write a machine language program. This is difficult as there would be more than 100 different machine instruction codes and hundreds of thousands of locations in memory. Errors will be made so often that it will be difficult to get the correct answers. Secondly, the operation codes will differ from one machine model to another. Thus we have to rewrite a program for an application again and again as new computers are introduced.

Fortunately, it is not necessary to write programs in machine language any more. Computer programs may be written in a host of *high level programming languages.* The instructions in a high level programming language are not coded numbers. They resemble ordinary English statements. Further, it is not necessary to refer to numerical memory addresses. Symbolic names may be used to label memory locations. Thus high level programming languages are easy to learn and use.

Associated with each high level programming language is an elaborate computer program which translates it into machine language. This translating program is called a *compiler* or a *language processor.* The resulting machine language program is called the *object program* and the original program written in the high level programming language is called the *source program.* These terms are explained pictorially in Fig. 6.1.

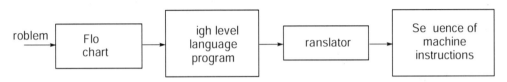

Fig. .1   erms used in high level language translation.

Compilers are written by professional programmers. A high level programming language may be used in different computers. The translators are different leading to different machine language equivalents of the source program. This is illustrated in Fig. 6.2.

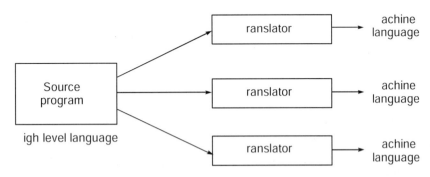

Fig. .2   Illustrating machine independence of high level language.

A high level programming language can be designed so that it can be used on any computer regardless of who manufactured it or what model it is. Such a language is also known as a *machine independent language.*

As a high level machine independent programming language has to be translated by a computer program it is essential to define precisely the rules for writing instructions in that language. These are the *syntax rules* of the language. When a source program in a high level language is fed to a computer, the compiler analyses each instruction and determines if any syntax rules are violated. If any syntax rules are violated by the programmer in writing his source program, these errors are printed out as messages to the programmer to enable him to correct his program. These error messages are called *compile time diagnostic error messages.* A source program which has no syntax errors is translated to an equivalent machine language object program. The object program is now executed by the computer. During execution too, errors can occur. These mostly relate to improper data or improper sequence of instructions. Such errors, if they occur, may stop a computation abruptly. Appropriate *execution time error messages* are printed for the information of the programmer. Programs which have neither syntax errors nor execution errors are successfully executed and answers are printed out.

A flow chart showing the steps in compilation of a high level language program is shown in Fig. 6.3.

It is essential to emphasize that compilers *cannot* diagnose errors in logic. They can diagnose only grammatical errors in writing the source program. For example, if a programmer (by mistake) writes an instruction to divide, instead of to multiply, this error cannot be detected by a compiler. Programs containing such errors will be successfully executed and give incorrect answers. To avoid such errors it is essential to be careful and precise in writing programs and attend to the smallest detail. It is also necessary to choose test cases which are manually computed and compared with computer solutions. The test cases must be chosen so that they test thoroughly all aspects of the program.

6.2 C LANGUAGE

In this book we will discuss in detail the high level programming language known as C. Our primary aim will be to discuss how to solve problems using C as the programming language.

C was developed by Dennis Ritchie in 1972 at the Bell Telephone Laboratories in U.S.A. C was derived from a language known as BCPL which was evolved at the Massachusetts Institute of Technology in the late 60s. BCPL was used to develop an operating system known as MULTICS for early multi-user time shared computers. One of the aims of BCPL was to achieve efficiency in compiled code. Thus BCPL was defined such that a translator could produce efficient machine language code. C being a successor of BCPL has a similar philosophy. C language has been defined so that it has the advantages of a high level language, namely machine independence. At the same time it is concise, providing only the bare essentials required in a language so that a translator can translate it into an efficient machine language code. The first major use of the C language was to write an operating system known as UNIX.

UNIX turned out to be a good efficient multi-user operating system and became very popular. Currently it is the most widely used operating system for all varieties of computers. The fact that UNIX was written in C demonstrated the effectiveness of C for writing large system programs. The current popularity of C is due to its efficiency and its connection with UNIX. Many ready-made programs used by UNIX which are written in C can be easily borrowed by a C programmer in writing application programs.

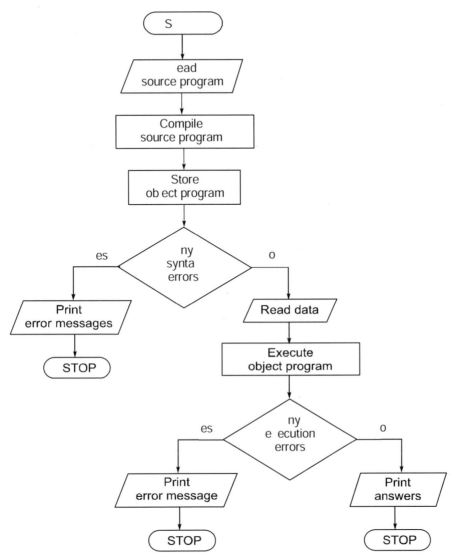

Fig. .3   flo   chart sho ing the steps in compilation of a high level language.

An aspect of C which makes it a powerful system programming language is the access it provides to the addresses where variables are stored. These addresses are known as pointers. The access to pointers and the operations which can be performed with pointers is what distinguishes C from other high level languages such as FORTRAN and COBOL. Pascal does provide pointers but restricts their use. C has minimal restrictions on the use of pointers.

C has been standardized by the American National Standards Institute (ANSI). In this book we will use this standard. We will discuss all the important features available in C. Over a hundred programs will be written in C to illustrate how to solve problems using this language.

The main disadvantage of C, particularly for a beginner, is its conciseness and extensive use of pointers. Brief statements may be written to carry out complex computations. This is a disadvantage as it is difficult to read C programs. In other words it often becomes difficult to understand C programs written by professional programmers as they tend to use tricks with pointers and other C features to make the program small.

A program which cannot be read and understood cannot be maintained (i.e. cannot be modified or improved). As program maintenance is a very important activity of programmers it is a good programming practice to write programs which are easy to read and understand. Tricks available in C to write concise programs should not be used. In this book our attempt will be to write programs which are easy to read and understand and thereby teach good programming style.

6.3   ON THE DESCRIPTION OF A PROGRAMMING LANGUAGE

The classical method of learning a language is to first learn the alphabets or characters used in the language. The next step is to learn how to combine these alphabets to form words, words to form sentences and sentences to express a thought. Modern language teaching is somewhat different. It lets a student read sentences and paragraphs and understand their meanings. By illustrating many such examples a student finds it easier to learn formal rules of grammar. It is more important to express a thought precisely in a language rather than be an expert in grammar. We follow a similar route in this book. We illustrate the need for certain structures to solve problems and then define rules of grammar.

Any language has two distinct parts. These are the *syntax* and *semantics*. By syntax we mean rules which are to be followed to form structures which are grammatically correct. Semantics assigns meanings to syntactic structures. A sentence which is syntactically correct need not be semantically correct. For instance, the sentence "Sita plays the violin" is both syntactically and semantically correct whereas the sentence "Violin plays Sita" is syntactically correct as it does not violate any rules of grammar. It is, however, semantically incorrect. In a similar manner we have to learn both syntax and semantics of programming languages. Syntax is easily checked mechanically and is mostly done by the language translator. Checking semantic correctness is the responsibility of the programmer.

We re-emphasize that it is not sufficient to design programs which are syntactically and semantically correct. Programs should also be simple to understand and easy to modify and improve. Thus it is essential to develop a good *style* in programming which would lead to not only correct programs but understandable and maintainable programs.

7

Simple Computer Programs

LEARNING OBJECTIVES

In this chapter we will learn:

1. The structure of a C program.
2. How to develop small programs in C.
3. How to input data and print the results obtained from a C program.

In this chapter we will write some programs in C and as we proceed learn the syntax and semantic rules of the language.

7.1 WRITING A PROGRAM

We will consider as the first example a program to find the area and perimeter of a rectangle whose sides are p and q. The area is given by

$$area = pq$$

and the perimeter by

$$perimeter = 2(p + q)$$

We have written the formulae above as we would normally do in algebra. In algebra, when we write pq where p and q are variables it is implied that p is multiplied by q. When we write an instruction for a computer, however, we have to explicitly specify that multiplication is to be performed. The formula is thus written in the C language as

$$area = p * q$$

which is called a *statement*. p, q and area are called the *variable* names. The symbol $*$ is the *multiplication operator*. p $*$ q is an *arithmetic expression*. The symbol = is the *assignment operator*. The semantics or meaning of the above statement in C is interpreted as follows:

"Read the contents of the memory box whose label or name is p and multiply it by the contents of another memory box named q. Store the result in a memory box named area".

Figure 7.1 illustrates this. Observe that the contents of p and q are *copied* and used. They are not destroyed.

Before Executing Statement

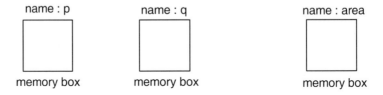

Execution of Statement

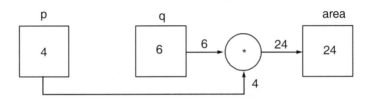

After Executing Statement

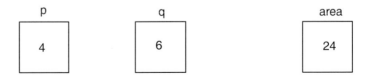

Fig. 7.1 Execution of statement: area = p * q.

The formula for the perimeter is written in C as

perimeter = 2 * (p + q)

In the above C statement, 2 is an *integer constant*. As before p, q and perimeter are the variable names. 2 * (p + q) is an arithmetic expression. The semantics of the statement is as given below:

"Add the contents of the memory box named p to the contents of the memory box named q. Store the result temporarily in the CPU. Multiply this result by 2. Store the answer in memory box named perimeter".

Figure 7.2 illustrates this. We have seen in this simple example the need for constants, variable names and operators. Example Program 7.1 is a C program to solve this problem.

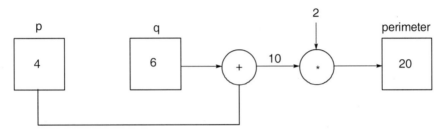

Fig. .2 Calculation of perimeter. Observe that the constant 2 is supplied by the compiler.

```
/* Example Program 7.1 */
/* This program finds the area and perimeter of a rectangle */
#include <stdio.h>

main()
{
    int p, q, area, perimeter;
    p = 4;
    q = 6;
    area = p * q;
    perimeter = 2 * (p+q);
    printf("area = %d\n", area);
    printf("perimeter = %d\n", perimeter);
} /* End of main */
```

g a   .1 Area and perimeter of a rectangle.

We will now explain this program. The first line in the program starts with /* and ends with */. Anything written between /* and */ is called a *comment*. In the C language, comments are an aid to the programmer to read and understand a program. It is not a statement of the language. The compiler ignores comments. It is a good practice to include comments in a program which will help in understanding a program. Observe the line

#include < stdio.h >

after the comments.

This is called a *preprocessor directive*. It is written at the beginning of the program. It commands that the contents of the file stdio.h should be included in the compiled machine code at the place where #include appears. The file stdio.h contains the standard input/output routines. All preprocessor directives begin with the pound sign # which must be entered in the first column. The #include line *must not* end with a semicolon. Only one preprocessor directive can appear in one line.

The next line is main (). It defines what is known as a *function* in C. A C program is made up of many functions. The function main () is required in *all* C programs. It indicates the start of a C program. We will use main () at the beginning of all programs. Observe that main () is *not* followed by a comma or semicolon.

Braces { and } *enclose* the computations carried out by main ( ). Each line in the program is a *statement*. Every statement is terminated by a semicolon ;. The statement itself can be written anywhere in a line. More than one statement can be on a line as a semicolon separates them. However, it is a good practice to write one statement per line.

In this program the first statement is:

int p, q, area, perimeter;

This statement is called a *declaration*. It informs the compiler that p, q, area and perimeter are the variable names and that the individual boxes must be reserved for them in the memory of the computer. Further it tells that the data to be stored in the memory boxes named p, q, area and perimeter are integers, namely, whole numbers without a fractional part (e.g. 0, 1, 2, ...). These can be either positive or negative. The statement is said to *declare* p, q, area and perimeter as of type *integer*. The statement ends with a semicolon. The effect of this statement is shown in Fig. 7.3. Observe that 4 locations are reserved and named as: p, q, area and perimeter respectively.

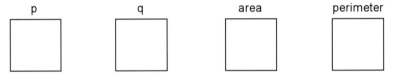

Fig.   .3   Effect of defining p, q, area and perimeter as integer variable names.

The statement p = 4; is an *assignment statement.* It commands that the integer 4 be stored in the memory box named p. When the statement is executed the integer 4 will be stored in the memory box named p as shown in Fig. 7.4.

Fig.   .   Effect of statement p = 4.

More briefly we can state that this statement *assigns* a value 4 to the variable name p. The next statement q = 6; assigns 6 to q. Following this is the statement:

area = p * q;

This is an *arithmetic statement*. It commands that the numbers stored in memory boxes p and q should be *copied* into the CPU. The original contents of p and q remain in their respective boxes. These numbers are multiplied by the CPU and the product is stored in the box named area. After executing this statement the box named area will contain 24 as shown in Fig. 7.1.

area = p * q;

The next statement perimeter = 2 * (p + q); is also an arithmetic statement. We have already explained how this statement is interpreted. After this statement is executed the number stored in memory box named perimeter should be 20.

The next two statements in the program are commands to display the contents of memory box named area and perimeter respectively. C language does not provide any statements for reading data into memory or displaying the contents of memory. Instead a set of standard *library functions* provided by the UNIX operating system for input and output are borrowed and used. The library functions for input and output are contained in the file stdio.h which we included using a preprocessor directive. Unless otherwise specified C assumes that the input of data is from the keyboard of a video terminal and the output is displayed on the screen of the video terminal. The library function used for display is printf( ). The general form of this function is:

$$printf(format\text{-}string, variable\ 1, variable\ 2, ..., variable\ n)$$

The format-string is enclosed in quotes. It specifies any message to be printed, and the manner in which the contents of variables are to be displayed for each of the variables in the list of variables.

In the statement

$$printf(\text{“area} = \%d\backslash n\text{”}, area)$$

the format-string is

$$\text{“area} = \%d\backslash n\text{”}$$

and the variable is area. This format-string specifies that area is to be displayed as it is. The special symbol %d says: "interpret the variable area occurring after the comma in the printf statement as an integer and display its value". The symbol \n causes the display to advance to the next line. Thus when this statement is carried out we will see on the screen

$$area = 24$$

After the statement

$$printf(\text{“perimeter} = \%d\backslash n\text{”}, perimeter)$$

is carried out, we will have on the screen

$$area = 24$$

$$perimeter = 20$$

Observe that perimeter = 20 is displayed on the next line as /n in the previous printf statement advanced the display by one line. Many compilers require return 0; to be placed just before closing the braces of main. If it is not put the compiler gives a warning message. In this book we have not used this convention as our compiler did not require return 0. The statement return 0 returns 0 to the operating system.

7.2 INPUT STATEMENT

In Example Program 7.1 the variables p and q are assigned values. If we want to find the area and perimeter of another rectangle with sides 8 and 10, for instance, we have to replace the statements p = 4 and q = 6 by p = 8 and q = 10 respectively. We have to then recompile the program and run it again. This is not a good idea. We should actually have a facility to assign any desired values to p and q by feeding the data through an input unit (usually the keyboard of a video display unit). This is possible if we can use an *input statement*. The input statement in C uses the library function scanf. To read an integer from the keyboard and assign it to variable p the statement is

scanf("%d", &p);

The format-string is %d. It states that the value to be stored in the specified variable name is an integer. Following this string we write &p which states that the variable name to which the integer is assigned is p. The symbol & in front of p is essential. This symbol gives the address of the variable name p so that data can be stored in it. We can similarly write another statement to read a value into a variable name q. It is

scanf("%d", &q);

There should be no blank space between the quote sign " and %, % and d and d and ". No blank should separate & and q. We can combine the two statements into one and write:

scanf("%d %d", &p, &q);

In this case the values of p and q input on a terminal should be separated by a blank space. If 8 and 10 are to be stored in p and q then the values input through the keyboard are

8   10

The integer 8 is followed by one or more blanks after which the integer 10 is typed on the keyboard.

We can now rewrite Example Program 7.1. Using this input statement by replacing the statements

p = 4; q = 6; with

scanf("%d %d", &p, &q);

At the end of the program we type a line containing the data. This program is written as Example Program 7.2. To compile and execute the program we have to use the commands appropriate to the operating system of the computer being used. The student should get this information from the appropriate manuals. In Appendix I we give the method which is used when a UNIX operating system is used. We will write some more simple programs in the next section.

```
/* Example Program 7.2 */
/* Use of Input/Output statements */
#include <stdio.h>

main()
{
    int p, q, area, perimeter;
    scanf("%d %d", &p, &q);
    /* Reads values of p and q from terminal
    & before p and q is essential */
    printf("p = %d, q = %d\n", p, q);
    /* The printf statement above is used to check if scanf has read the values
       of p and q correctly */
    area = p * q;
    perimeter = 2 * (p+q);
    printf("area = %d\n", area);
    printf("perimeter = %d\n", perimeter);
}   /* End of main */
```

g a   .2 Area and perimeter—use of input/output statements.

7.3   SOME C PROGRAM EXAMPLES

In this section we will write a few simple programs in C. This is intended to let a student start programming quickly. Detailed rules of syntax of the language will be given later.

EXAMPLE 7.1   As the first example we will write a program to convert a temperature given in Celsius to Fahrenheit. The formula for conversion is

$$F = 1.8C + 32 \qquad (7.1)$$

where C is the temperature in Celsius and F that in Fahrenheit. The program is given as Example Program 7.3. Observe that we have used more descriptive names for variable names rather than just F and C. Using such variable names makes the program more readable. Also observe that when we write the term 1.8C in Equation (7.1) the multiplication operator is implied. In a computer program such operators should be explicitly specified.

```
/* Example Program 7.3 */
/* This program converts a Celsius temperature to Fahrenheit */
#include <stdio.h>

main()
{
    float fahrenheit, celsius;
    scanf("%f", &celsius);
    printf("Celsius = %f\n", celsius);
    fahrenheit = 1.8 * celsius + 32.0;
    printf("Fahrenheit = %f\n", fahrenheit);
} /* End of main */
```

g a   .3 Celsius to Fahrenheit conversion.

After #include line we define the main function. Observe the statement:

$$\text{float fahrenheit, celsius;}$$

This is a declaration which informs the compiler that fahrenheit and celsius are variable names in which *floating point* numbers will be stored. By a floating point number we mean a number with a fractional part, for example, 14.456. (We will describe later in detail the representation of floating point numbers in a computer.) The following statement

$$\text{scanf(“%f”, &celsius)}$$

is a command to read a floating point number and store it in variable name celsius. The format-string %f indicates that a floating point number is to be read. We follow this with a statement to print the value read. The next statement is an arithmetic statement. Contents of celsius is multiplied by 1.8 and added to 32.0 and stored in fahrenheit. Observe that the number 32 is written with a decimal point to indicate that it is a floating point number. The last statement is to print the answer.

We will now consider an example of summing a small series. The use of intermediate variables simplifies the program and reduces the number of arithmetic operations performed by a computer.

EXAMPLE 7.2 Required to calculate

$$\text{sum} = 1 - x^2/2! + x^4/4! - x^6/6! + x^8/8! - x^{10}/10!$$

A program to calculate the sum is given as Example Program 7.4. We will present a more concise program later in the book. Observe that after calculating x^2 and storing it in x^2 it is used to calculate x^4, x^6, etc. See also that we have written the statement

$$\text{printf(“x = %f\textbackslash n”, x)}$$

```
/* Example Program 7.4 */
/* Program to sum a series */
#include <stdio.h>

main()
{
    float x, x2, x3, x4, x6, x8, x10, sum;
    scanf("%f", &x);
    printf("x = %f\n", x);
    x2 = x * x;
    x4 = x2 * x2/24.0;
    x6 = x4 * x2/30.0;
    x8 = x6 * x2/56.0;
    x10 = x8 * x2/90.0;
    sum = 1.0 - 0.5 * x2 + x4 - x6 + x8 - x10;
    printf("value of x = %f, sum = %f\n", x, sum);
}   /* End of main */
```

g a . Summing a series.

immediately after scanf. The printf statement displays on the screen the value of x read by scanf. This enables the programmer to make sure what has been read into x. Such a check is important, particularly for a beginner. This is called the echo check, as we are printing the value read immediately after reading it.

EXAMPLE 7.3 Mangoes cost Rs. 52.80 per dozen. It is required to find the cost of 28 mangoes to the nearest paisa and to print the answer as Rupees and Paise. A program to do this is given as Example Program 7.5.

```
/* Example Program 7.5*/
/* This program calculates the price of 28 mangoes given the price of a dozen
      mangoes */
#include <stdio.h>

main()
{
    int rupees, paise, cost_of_28;
    float cost_dozen, rcost_28;
    /* read cost of 12 mangoes */
    scanf("%f", &cost_dozen);
    printf("Cost of dozen = %f\n", cost_dozen);
    rcost_28 = ((cost_dozen * 100.0 / 12.0) * 28.0 + 0.5);
    cost_of_28 = rcost_28;
    rupees = cost_of_28 / 100;
    paise = cost_of_28 % 100;
    printf("Cost of 28 mangoes\n");
    printf("Rs.%d ps.%d\n", rupees, paise);
}   /* End of main */
```
g a   .   Price of 28 mangoes.

In Example Program 7.5 in the main () function we first define the variables. The scanf statement reads the price of a dozen mangoes. The next statement prints the values read by scanf. This printf statement is used to assure oneself that the correct data has been read. The next statement calculates the cost of 28 mangoes to the nearest integral paisa. Adding 0.5 ensures that the integral part is rounded correctly. The cost of 28 is declared an integer whereas rcost 28 is a floating point number. When we assign rcost 28 to cost of 28 the fractional part of rcost 28 is removed and the integral part is stored in cost of 28. In the next statement the operator / is a division operator. Thus cost of 28 is divided by 100. As both numerator and denominator are integers the result obtained when / operator is used as an integer. For example, 438/100 = 4 and not 4.38. The quotient obtained when cost of 28 is divided by 100 is stored in rupees.

Observe that in the next statement

$$\text{paise} = \text{cost of 28 \% 100};$$

we have introduced an operator %. This operator is the *mod* operator which gives the remainder obtained after dividing. For example 438 % 100 = 38. The *mod* operator is specifically used when the operands are integers. The rest of the program is self-explanatory.

Example Program 7.5 is correct and will work for the given problem. It is, however, not general. If we want to calculate the price of 29 mangoes instead of 28 the program should be re-written. When a program is written it should be made as general as possible. We can easily generalize the program by keeping the quantity to be bought and cost per dozen as variables. This will enable us to use the same program for different quantities of mangoes and varying costs by changing only the data entered on a terminal. This generalized program is given as Example Program 7.6.

```
/* Example Program 7.6 */
/* This program calculates the price of x mangoes given the price of a dozen
      mangoes */
#include <stdio.h>

main()
{
    int rupees, paise, cost, quantity;
    float cost_dozen;

    scanf("%f %d", &cost_dozen, &quantity);
    printf("Cost of dozen = %f, quantity = %d\n", cost_dozen, quantity);
    cost = ((cost_dozen * 100.0/12.0) * quantity + 0.5);
    rupees = cost/100;
    palse = cost % 100;
    printf("Number of mangoes = %d\n", quantity);
    printf("cost = Rs.%d ps.%d\n", rupees, paise);
}   /* end of main */
```

g a   .   Price of x mangoes.

Observe the statement:

$$\text{cost} = ((\text{cost of dozen} * 100.0 / 12.0) * \text{quantity} + 0.5)$$

In this statement cost of dozen on the right-hand side is a floating point number. The calculation will thus give a floating point number as the result. The left-hand side, however, is an integer variable name in which only an integer can be stored. Thus the fractional part of the floating point number obtained as the result on the right hand side is removed and the integral part is stored in cost.

EXAMPLE 7.4   A five digit positive integer is given. It is required to find the sum of the individual digits. For example, if the given number is 96785 the required sum is 9 + 6 + 7 + 8 + 5 = 35. Finding the sum of digits of a number is used in data processing to validate the numbers read in as data. A program to find the sum of digits of an integer is given as Example Program 7.7.

```
/* Example Program 7.7 */
/* This program reads a positive integer which is 5 digits long and sums the
     digits in it */
#include <stdio.h>

main()
{
    int digit_1, digit_2, digit_3, digit_4, digit_5, sum, number, n;
    scanf("%d", &number);
    printf("number = %d\n", number);
    n = number;
    digit_1 = n % 10;
    n = n / 10;
    digit_2 = n % 10;
    n = n / 10;
    digit_3 = n % 10;
    n = n / 10;
    digit_4 = n % 10;
    n = n / 10;
    digit_5 = n;
    sum = digit_1 + digit_2 + digit_3 + digit_4 + digit_5;
    printf("sum of digits = %d\n", sum);
}   /* End of main */
```

g a . Adding digits of an integer.

One method of checking whether the program is correct is to act as though we are a computer and execute each instruction as it is given in the program. This is known as tracing the program. Assume that the number read in is 96785. We now follow the instructions in the program.

After reading the number the program prints it. The values stored in the variables in each step are shown below:

n = 96785
digit 1 = n % 10 = 96785 % 10 = 5
n = n / 10 = 96785 / 10 = 9678
digit 2 = n % 10 = 9678 % 10 = 8
n = n / 10 = 9678 / 10 = 967
digit 3 = n % 10 = 967 % 10 = 7
n = n / 10 = 967 / 10 = 96
digit 4 = n % 10 = 96 % 10 = 6
n = n / 10 = 96 / 10 = 9
digit 5 = 9
sum − digit 1 ɪ digit 2 ɪ digit 3 ɪ digit 4 ɪ digit 5
       = 5 + 8 + 7 + 6 + 9 = 35

At the end of the program the data read into the variable name number is preserved.

Observe that there is a simple repetitive pattern in this program. A concise program may be written which employs this pattern. In order to do this we need some more instructions which we will learn in later chapters.

EXERCISES

7.1 Write a program to convert fahrenheit temperature to celsius.

7.2 Read the following program and explain what it does. Trace it with yard = 20

```
#include < stdio.h >
main ( )
{ int yard, feet, inch;
    scanf("%d", &yard);
    feet = 3 * yard;
    inch = 12 * feet;
    printf("feet=%d inch =%d", feet, inch);
}
```

7.3 Write a program to convert pounds to kilograms.

7.4 Given a 5 digit integer write a program to print it in reverse order (for example given 92674 the result should be 47629).

7.5 Write a program to read the radius of a circle and compute its area and circumference.

7.6 Given a number = d_5 d_4 d_3 d_2 d_1, find Σ i d_i mod 11 where i varies from 1 to 5.

7.7 Write a program to find the rupee equivalent of x US dollars using the exchange rate to the nearest ten paise. For example if x = 42.25 and the exchange rate is Rs. 41.16 per dollar the answer should be Rupees 1739 Paise 01. (You should allow any arbitrary exchange rate and read it in as data in your program.)

7.8 Write a program to express a length x given in millimetres in metres, centimetres and millimetres.

8

Numeric Constants and Variables

```
┌─────────────────────────────────────────────────────────────┐
│                    LEARNING OBJECTIVES                        │
│  In this chapter we will learn:                              │
│    1. Different types of numeric constants which may be used in C. │
│    2. Types of numeric variables in C and how they are declared and initialized. │
│    3. How constants may be given symbolic names.            │
│    4. Specification of syntax rules for numeric constants and variables. │
└─────────────────────────────────────────────────────────────┘
```

In Chapter 7 we saw how small programs are written in C. Before we write larger programs it is necessary to learn the rules of syntax of the language in some detail. We will give the rules for specifying constants and variable names in this chapter.

8.1 CONSTANTS

The term constant means that it does not change during the execution of a program. Constants may be classified as

   (i) integer constants
  (ii) floating point constants.

Integer Constants
Integer constants are whole numbers without any fractional part. Floating point constants (also known as real constants), on the other hand, may have fractional parts. There are three types of integers which are allowed in C. They are:

   (i) Decimal constants (base 10)
   (ii) Octal constants (base 8)
  (iii) Hexadecimal constants (base 16)

The allowed digits in a *decimal* constant are 0, 1, 2, 3, 4, 5, 6, 7, 8, 9. The digits of an *octal* constant can be 0, 1, 2, 3, 4, 5, 6, 7 and those in a hexadecimal constant can be 0, 1, 2, 3, 4, 5, 6, 7, 8, 9, A, B, C, D, E, F.

Rule

A decimal integer constant must have at least one digit and must be written without a decimal point. The first digit in the constant should not be 0. It may have either of the signs, i.e. + or – . If either of these signs does not precede the constant it is assumed to be positive.

EXAMPLES The following are valid decimal integer constants:

(i) 12345
(ii) 3468
(iii) –9746

The following are invalid decimal integer constants:

(i) 11.   (Decimal point not allowed)
(ii) 45,256   (Comma not allowed)
(iii) $ 125   (Currency symbol not allowed)
(iv) 025   (First digit should not be 0 for a decimal integer)
(v) x248   (First symbol is not a digit)

C also provides *short* and *long* integers. The integer size depends on the word size of a machine. In a 32-bit machine it has a range from $+(2^{31} – 1)$ to $–2^{31}$; the short integer declaration means it is a 16-bit integer in such a machine with a range from $(2^{15} – 1)$ to $–2^{16}$. The size of long integer depends on the machine and the C language implementation.

The qualifier *signed* or *unsigned* may be applied to any integer. The unsigned integers are 0 or positive. Arithmetic operations with unsigned integers are modulo n where n is the number of bits used to store the integer. Suppose we have two short unsigned integers a and b.

Let a = 1024 and b = 65035

then d = a + b = 523 (66059 *mod* 65536 = 523)

(The maximum number that can be stored in a 16-bit unsigned short integer = $2^{16} – 1 = 65535$).

A long integer constant is written with a L or lowercase *l* at the end of the number, for example, 67894676L. An unsigned integer is written with the letter U at the end of the integer. For example, 4578U is an unsigned integer. 14678946UL is an unsigned long integer. A declaration int implies that it is a signed integer.

EXAMPLES

–246876   (an integer)
–267896789L   (a long integer)
–28   (A short integer)
26789U   (An unsigned integer)
36794267UL   (unsigned long integer)

The rule to write an octal constant is:

Rule

An octal constant must have at least one digit and start with the digit 0. It must be written without a decimal point. It may have either of the signs, i.e. + or –. A constant which has no sign is taken as positive.

EXAMPLES The following are valid octal constants:

  (i) 0245
  (ii) – 0467
  (iii) + 04013

The following are invalid octal constants:

  (i) 25   (Does not begin with 0)
  (ii) 0387   (8 is not an octal digit)
  (iii) 04.32   (Decimal point is not allowed)

The rule to write a hexademical constant is:

Rule
A hexadecimal constant must have at least one hexadecimal digit and start with 0x or 0X. It may have either of the signs, i.e. + or –.

EXAMPLES The following are valid hexadecimal constants:

  (i) 0x14AF
  (ii) 0X34680
  (iii) – 0x2673E

The following are invalid hexadecimal constants:

  (i) 0345   (Must start with 0x)
  (ii) 0x45H3   (H is not a hexadecimal digit)
  (iii) Hex2345   (0x defines a hexadecimal number, not Hex)

Floating Point Constants
A floating point constant may be written in one or two forms called the *fractional form* or the *exponent form.* The rule for writing a floating point constant in these two forms is given below.

Rule
A floating point constant in a fractional form must have at least one digit to the right of the decimal point. It may have either the + or the – sign preceding it. If a sign does not precede it then it is assumed to be positive.

EXAMPLES The following are valid floating point constants:

  (i) 1.0
  (ii) –0.5678
  (iii) 5800000.0
  (iv) –0.0000156

The following are invalid floating point constants:

  (i) 1   (Decimal point missing)
  (ii) 1.   (No digit following the decimal point)
  (iii) –1/2.   (The symbol / is illegal)

(iv) .5   (No digit to the left of the decimal point)
(v) 58,678.94   (Comma not allowed)

In the examples above even though 5800000.0 and -0.0000156 are valid floating point constants it is more convenient to write them as 0.58×10^7 and 0.156×10^{-4} respectively. ($\times$ is the multiplication symbol). The exponent notation for writing floating point constants provides this facility. In this notation these two numbers may be written as

(i) 0.58E7   or   0.58e7
(ii) -0.156E–4   or -0.156e–4

In the above examples E7 and E–4 are used to represent 10^7 and 10^{-4} respectively (E or e may be used).

In this notation a floating point constant is represented in two parts: a mantissa part (the part appearing before E) and an exponent part (the part following E). Thus 0.58 and -0.156 are the respective mantissas and 7 and -4 the exponents. We will now give the formal rule for writing floating point constants in the exponent form.

Rule
A floating point constant in the exponent form consists of a mantissa and an exponent. The mantissa must have at least one digit. It may have a sign. The mantissa is followed by the letter E or e and the exponent. The exponent must be an integer (without a decimal point) and must have at least one digit. A sign for the exponent is optional.

The actual number of digits in the mantissa and the exponent depends on the computer being used, for example, the mantissa may have up to seven digits and the exponent may be between –38 and +38 in IBM PC. For details of other machines one may refer to the appropriate manufacturer's manual.

EXAMPLES   The following are valid floating point constants in the exponent form:

(i) (a) 152E08   (b) 152.0E8   (c) 152e+8
     (d) 152E+08   (e) 15.2e9   (f) 1520E7
(ii) -0.148E–5
(iii) 152.859E25
(iv)   0.01540e05

Observe that in (i) above six equivalent ways of writing the same constant are given.
The following are invalid floating point constants in the exponent form:

(i)   152.AE8   (Mantissa must have a digit following the decimal point)
(ii) 125*e9   (* not allowed)
(iii) +145.8E   (No digit specified for the exponent)
(iv) –125.9E5.5   (Exponent cannot be a fraction)
(v)   0.158E+954   (Exponent too large)
(vi) 125,458.25 e–5   (Comma not allowed in mantissa)
(vii) .2E8   (A digit must precede the decimal point in mantissa)

8.2 SCALAR VARIABLES

A quantity which may vary during program execution is called a variable. Each variable has a specific storage location in memory where its numerical value is stored. The variable is given a name and the variable name is the "name tag" for the storage location. The value of the variable at any instant during the execution of a program is equal to the number stored in the storage location identified by the name of the variable. Figure 8.1 illustrates this. The variable name in Fig. 8.1 is total and its content is 2.8.

total

Fig. .1   Illustrating a variable name and its content.

When a variable name can contain only one number it is called a *scalar variable*. In C the word *identifier* is used as the general terminology for names given to variables, functions, constants, structures, etc.

As variable names are name tags of memory locations where numbers are stored, and numbers are of two types, integer and floating point, one has to declare a variable name as being of type floating point or type integer. A number stored in a memory location with variable name of type integer is an integer (with the restrictions given while discussing the integer constants) and one stored in a location with a variable name of type float may have a fractional part (with the restrictions discussed in the preceding section). We will now give the rules for forming identifiers used as variable names.

Rule
An identifier is any combination of one or more letters (uppercase or lowercase) or digits. The first character in the identifier must be a letter. It must not contain any character other than letters or digits.

The underscore   is taken as a letter. Identifiers may have any number of letters and digits. Even though the C syntax rule allows identifiers of any length, in practice, the number of characters in an identifier which are significant is dependent on the specific translator.

ANSI standard specifies at least 31 characters in an identifier as significant. Both uppercase and lowercase letters (i.e. capital and small letters) may be used for writing an identifier.

The uppercase and lowercase letters are treated as distinct. In other words, temp and Temp are two different identifiers. The convention in C is to use only the lowercase letters for variable names.

EXAMPLES   The following are valid identifiers which may be used to name variables:

  (i) nA
  (ii) theta

(iii) amin
(iv) min50
(v) temp X
(vi) absolute

The following are invalid identifiers:

(i) $count   (First character $ invalid)
(ii) roll#   (Character # not allowed)
(iii) no.   (Character . invalid)
(iv) 2nd   (First character as digit not allowed)
(v) ROLL NO   (No blanks allowed in a name)
(vi) case   (It is a reserved word)

We stated above that case is an illegal variable name as it is a *reserved word*. A set of keywords are used in C for special purposes and may not be used for any other purpose. They are known as reserved words. A list of reserved words in C is given in Appendix II.

8.3 DECLARING VARIABLE NAMES

Identifiers used as variable names are explicitly typed as float or integer by the following *declaration* which should appear at the beginning of a program before the variable names are used.

type-name variable name, ..., variable name;

We have used italics for type-name to emphasize that it is a reserved word. The *type_name* available for variable names storing numbers are *int* for integers and *float* for floating point numbers. An example of valid declaration is given below:

int n, height, count, digit;

float average, x coordinate, p;

When a variable name is declared then a memory location is identified and given this name. The following declarations of variables are invalid:

float, a, b, c; (comma after float not valid)

int:x; (: after int invalid)

real x, y; (real is not the correct type-name)

Note that an enormous number of variable names may be defined using the rules to form identifiers. It is a good practice to exploit this enormous choice in naming variables in programs by using meaningful identifiers. Thus for example if one is calculating a temperature, pressure and the life of a catalyst in a chemical process the corresponding variables in programs may be named temperature, pressure and catalyst life. Contrast this with the names t, p and cl, which one may have given. These latter names are not meaningful and thus provide no help in understanding the role of a variable name.

Double Precision Floating Point Numbers
When a variable name is declared float the number of mantissa digits stored and the exponent size depend on the computer on which the C program runs. For machines with 32-bit words such as IBM PCs, it is 7 digit mantissa and an exponent range of ±38. In some calculations the mantissa length may not be sufficient. Thus C provides a type-name called *double*. The use of double in declaring a floating point variable provides 16 mantissa digits storage for the variable name. Arithmetic with variable names declared double carries out all arithmetic operations using the 16-digit mantissa. (The exponent size is normally not affected. It is, however, implementation dependent.)

If we want variable names theta, lambda and iota to store 16-digit mantissa floating point numbers, we use the declaration:

double theta lambda iota;

All floating point constants are normally taken as double precision. If we want to specify a constant as requiring only 7 digit precision, then we use the suffix f or F.
For example,

4.35678F,　　3.4678e–15F,　　–4.96789e–16f

are all taken as constants needing the 7-digit mantissa 436.87492L as a long double precision constant.

8.4 DEFINING CONSTANTS

In C a value can be assigned to a variable name when it is declared. If no value is assigned it is undefined. For example, we can write:

int x = 2, p = –2842, val = 3492;

float y, z = 2.5678e–5, q = –3.8469e3;

In the above declaration y is undefined. The other variables are assigned initial values specified. (Some compilers assign 0 to a variable when declared but it is a good practice to explicitly initialize the variable values.) Unless a variable is defined it cannot be used in an arithmetic expression.

A constant appearing as it is in a program does not convey any meaning regarding its purpose or role to a programmer. Frequently it is attractive to associate an identifier or a name with the constant and use this name instead of the actual number, everywhere the number occurs in a program. C allows defining an identifier as having constant value using the #define directive. This is called a *pre-processor directive* as it is not part of a C program. This directive is placed at the beginning of a C program. # occurs in the first column. No semicolon follows #define.

For example the following pre-processor directive gives names to three different constants.

#define PI 3.1415927
#define MINIMUMBAL 500.0
#define MAXSPEED 200

The name in a #define line is formed using the syntax rules given for the identifier. In addition to giving a meaningful name to a constant, #define makes it easier to modify programs. Suppose a constant occurs a dozen times in a program and its value is to be changed. If the constant is declared using #define, the change is done in only one place, namely, where it is defined and not in all twelve places.

We use the #define line to specify a constant when:

(i) the constant is used at many places in a program
(ii) the constant is subject to frequent change
(iii) a meaningful name for a constant would aid in understanding a program.

Even though an identifier of a constant can be composed of both uppercase and lowercase letters the convention used in C is to use capital letters to specify constants in order to distinguish them from variables which are formed using lowercase letters only.

Table 8.1 gives examples of various types of variables and constants described in this chapter.

Table .1 Summary of variable declarations and constants

Data types	Example
int	int i, j ;
unsigned int	unsigned int k = 5 ;
long int	long int p, q ;
float	float value = 32.5602, x ;
double	double y, temp;
decimal integer	2468
octal integer	– 02357
Hexadecimal integer	0xAFF2
long integer	267894346
integer	37842
short integer	– 46
unsigned integer	3625
floating point number	–34.46e–5
double precision number	0.6734679423e+4

EXERCISES

8.1 Pick the incorrect decimal integer constants from the following list. Explain why they are incorrect.

(i) – 4689
(ii) + – 785
(iii) 4.25,325

    (iv) 1/4
    (v) 62 – 34 – 86
    (vi) 0234
    (vii) 2A45
    (viii) Ox234

8.2 Pick the incorrect type declarations from the following list. Explain why they are incorrect.

    (i) float, servo, mass, iota;
    (ii) int servo, digit, count;
    (iii) int rs.ps, unsigned;
    (iv) float real, root, big;

8.3 Pick the incorrect floating point constants from the following list. Explain why they are incorrect.

    (i) 40,943.65
    (ii) 428.58
    (iii) 46 + E2
    (iv) 46E2
    (v) 485. + 6
    (vi) 462XE – 2
    (vii) 425E2.5
    (viii) .0045E + 6
    (ix) 1/2.2
    (x) 465.
    (xi) 43

8.4 Pick the incorrect identifiers from the following list. Explain why they are incorrect.

    (i) constant
    (ii) variable
    (iii) double
    (iv) Rs-ps
    (v) roll.no
    (vi) lambda
    (vii) lab man
    (viii) int result

8.5 Classify the following constants as decimal, octal or hexadecimal:

    (i) 0234
    (ii) – 0456
    (iii) 0xAB56
    (iv) – 468734689
    (v) – 0x38
    (vi) 22

9

Arithmetic Expressions

LEARNING OBJECTIVES

In this chapter we will learn:

1. How to form arithmetic expressions using integer, float and/or double variables and constants.
2. Various arithmetic operators, their precedence when they operate on variables and rules of associativity among operators of equal precedence.
3. The assignment operator, the assignment expressions and their use.

An arithmetic expression is a series of variable names and constants connected by arithmetic operation symbols, namely, addition, subtraction, multiplication and division. During the execution of the object program the actual numerical values stored in variable names are used, together with the operation symbols, to calculate the value of the expression. In this chapter we will discuss the syntax rules for writing arithmetic expressions and the rules followed by C to evaluate them.

9.1 ARITHMETIC OPERATORS AND MODES OF EXPRESSIONS

The arithmetic operation symbols used in C and their meanings are given in Table 9.1. In Table 9.1 the symbol – is used for both *unary minus* and *subtraction*. In the expression –A + B the – symbol is a unary minus, that is, it indicates that the negative of A is to be taken. In the expression A – B, however, the – symbol indicates a binary – or subtraction. Thus in this case B is to be subtracted from A.

The / operation for integer gives the quotient after division. Thus if we write 7 / 3 the answer would be 2. The % operation gives the remainder obtained in integer division. Thus 7 % 3 is 1. The symbol used for division of floating point numbers is /. Thus 7.0 / 3.0 would give 2.3333333. Observe that C does not have an operator to raise a variable to a power. Integer powers may be obtained by repeated multiplication. Thus x^4 may be written as x * x * x * x. Fractional powers have to be obtained by using a mathematical library function pow(x, y) which gives x^y. We will describe the mathematical functions available in C later in the book.

Table .1   rithmetic operator symbols

Operation	Arithmetic operator	
	For float	*For integers*
Unary minus	–	–
Division	/	/
Remainder obtained in integer division		%
Multiplication	*	*
Addition	+	+
Subtraction	–	–

9.2 INTEGER EXPRESSIONS

Integer expressions are formed by connecting (using integer arithmetic operators) constants or variable names declared as integer or integer constant identifiers with similar quantities. For example, the following are integer expressions:

```
#define P 20
int a, b, c, d, k, p, m;
```

(i)   –a + b
(ii) p / m + P
(iii) –a + b * m
(iv) (a / b – p) * (k % m * 8)
(v)   –a * c + 4 – p / m * a % c * 6 + P
(Remember that p and P are different quantities)

The following are incorrect integer expressions:

$$\text{int a, b, c, d, k, p, m;}$$

(i) a – b + j	(j not declared integer)
(ii) a – 4.0	(4.0 not an integer)
(iii) a + + b + c	(+ + occur together)
(iv) a / b * % c	(Two operator symbols, namely, * and % occur together)
(v) –a (% b + c)	(Incorrect left parenthesis)
(vi) a ** b + m	(Two operator symbols, namely * and * occur together)
(vii) (p * (m + k)	(One right parenthesis missing)
(viii) k /* m	(Two operators / and * occur next to one another)

9.3 FLOATING POINT EXPRESSIONS

Floating point expressions are formed by connecting (using arithmetic operators) variable names declared as float or double with floating point (or double precision) constants or floating point variables or floating point constant identifiers. The following is a list of real expressions:

```
#define A 3.145
float x, y, z, n;
double p, j;
```

  (i) −x + y
 (ii) n / z + A
(iii) −z + p + n * z
(iv) (x / y − j) * (p / j * 6.0)
 (v) x * p − 8.5 + p / 0.8435e−2 / j + A

The following are incorrect real expressions: float x, y, z, n, p, j;

(i)	x − z + d	(d not declared float)
(ii)	(x + y)(p + z)	(Missing operator. Should be written as (x + y) * (p + z) if that is intended)
(iii)	z ** n	(* follows another operator *)
(iv)	n . j	(. not an arithmetic operator)
(v)	x / + p	(Two operators / and + occur together)
(vi)	(x + (j − p)	(Right parenthesis missing)
(vii)	z p * n	(Missing operator between variables z and p)

9.4 OPERATOR PRECEDENCE IN EXPRESSIONS

In a program the value of any expression is calculated by executing one arithmetic operation at a time. The order in which the arithmetic operations are executed in an expression is based on the rules of *precedence* of operators. The precedence of operators is: unary − FIRST, multiplication (*) division (/) and %, SECOND, addition (+) and subtraction (−) LAST.

For example, in the integer expression −a * b / c + d the unary − is done first, the result −a is multiplied by b, the product is divided by c (integer division) and d is added to this last result. The answer is thus:

$$\frac{-ab}{c} + d$$

All expressions are evaluated from *left* to *right*. All the unary negations are done *first*. After completing this the expression is scanned again from left to right; now all *, / and % operations are executed in the order of their appearance. Finally all the additions and subtractions are done startmg agaIn from the left of the expression.

For example, in the expression

$$-a * b / c + d \% k - m / d * k + c$$

the computer would evaluate −a in the first left-to-right scan. In the second scan

$$\frac{-ab}{c}, \, d \% k \quad \text{and} \quad \frac{m}{d} \, k$$

would be evaluated. In the last scan the expression evaluated would be

$$\frac{-ab}{c} + d \% k - \frac{m}{d} \, k + c$$

In the float expression

$$x * y + z / n + p + j / z$$

in the first scan

$$xy, \, z / n \text{ and } j / z$$

are evaluated. In the second scan the expression evaluated is

$$xy + \frac{z}{n} + p + \frac{j}{z}$$

Use of Parentheses

Parentheses are used if the order of operations governed by the precedence rules is to be overridden.

In the expression with a single pair of parentheses the expression inside the parentheses is evaluated FIRST. Within the parentheses the evaluation is governed by the precedence rules.

For example, in the expression

$$a * b / (c + d * k/m + k) + a$$

the expression within the parentheses is evaluated first giving

$$c + \frac{dk}{m} + k$$

After this the expression is evaluated from left to right using again the rules of precedence giving

$$\frac{ab}{c + \dfrac{dk}{m} + k} + a$$

If an expression has many pairs of parentheses then the expression in the innermost pair is evaluated first, followed by the next innermost parentheses, and so on till all the parentheses are removed. After this the operator precedence rules are used in evaluating the rest of the expression.

For example, in the real expression

$$((x * y) + z / (n * p + j) + x) / y + z$$

xy, $np + j$ will be evaluated first.

In the next scan

$$xy + \frac{z}{np + j} + x$$

will be evaluated. In the final scan the expression evaluated would be

$$\frac{xy + \dfrac{z}{np + j} + x}{y} + z$$

9.5 EXAMPLES OF ARITHMETIC EXPRESSIONS

In this section we will consider some expressions which occur frequently in practice and are improperly translated into C expressions by beginners.

EXAMPLE 9.1 Consider the expression

$$\frac{1}{1 + x}$$

where x is a floating point variable.

A beginner might write the expression as $1 / 1 + x$. This expression is syntactically correct. It does not, however, mean what the programmer intended it to mean. The computer will evaluate it using the precedence rules as $(1 / 1) + x$. Observe that this mistake in writing is an error in logic rather than in syntax and the computer cannot detect this error. It will go ahead and compute the wrong answer. The correct way (logically and syntactically) of translating the expression is $1 / (1 + x)$. The parentheses enclosing the denominator expression are essential.

In the expression $(1 + x)$ the constant 1 is an integer and x is the declared float. An expression such as this which mixes an integer with a float is called a mixed mode expression. C allows the mixed mode expressions. It automatically converts the integer to float before adding. In general, a "narrower type" is converted to "broader type" to avoid losing information. Beginners should avoid mixing types as the "automatic conversion" may lead to errors which are difficult to locate. We will discuss this in greater detail later in the chapter.

EXAMPLE 9.2 Consider the expression

$$\frac{a + b}{a - b}$$

where a and b are real. A translation of this which is syntactically correct, might be $a + b / a - b$

This will be evaluated as

$$a + \frac{b}{a} - b$$

which is not what the programmer intended. The expression a + b / (a – b) is also a wrong translation as the expression evaluated would be

$$a + \frac{b}{a - b}$$

The correct expression is (a + b) / (a – b)

The above examples illustrate the need for parentheses. In practice a good rule to follow is: "if in doubt use parentheses".

EXAMPLE 9.3 Consider the expression $a^2 + b^2 - 2ab$. A careless programmer might translate this into a * a + b * b – 2a * b. This has a syntax error. The expression 2a * b has no meaning syntactically. It is to be written as 2 * a * b. An operator is required, it is not implied. After this correction the expression is syntactically correct and does what the programmer intended it to do. The expression is

$$a * a + b * b - 2 * a * b$$

EXAMPLE 9.4 Consider a polynomial expression: $5x^4 + 3x^3 + 2x^2 + x + 10$. A correct syntactic translation of this expression is:

$$5 * x * x * x * x + 3 * x * x * x + 2 * x * x + x + 10$$

This however, is an inefficient way of writing a polynomial for computer evaluation as it involves a total of 4 addition operations and 9 multiplication operations (verify this). Another technique of writing the polynomial requires a far lesser number of arithmetic operations and is given below:

$$
\begin{aligned}
5x^4 + 3x^3 + 2x^2 + x + 10 &= 10 + x + 2x^2 + 3x^3 + 5x^4 \\
&= 10 + x(1 + 2x + 3x^2 + 5x^3) \\
&= 10 + x(1 + x(2 + 3x + 5x^2)) \\
&= 10 + x(1 + x(2 + x(3 + 5x)))
\end{aligned}
$$

Translated into C this is

$$10 + x * (1 + x * (2 + x * (3 + 5 * x)))$$

The above expression requires only four multiplications and four additions. Even though this expression is efficient it is less readable. Further, errors could be made in parenthesising. Whenever there are a large number of parentheses in an expression one check is to separately count the number of left and right parentheses. These counts should be equal.

EXAMPLE 9.5   Consider the following expression

$$\frac{mv^2}{2.5} + \frac{gh}{4d}$$

A careless programmer may translate this as

m * v * v / 2.5 + gh / 4.d

In the second term gh is written as it appears in the formula and is wrong. 4d is translated as 4.d which is also wrong. They should be written as g*h and 4*d respectively. After making these corrections the expression is

m * v * v / 2.5 + g * h / 4 * d

which is syntactically correct. There is still one error left.

g * h / 4 * d will be evaluated as

$$\frac{gh}{4} * d$$

The correct way of writing this would be

(m * v * v / 2.5) + (g * h) / (4 * d)

EXAMPLE 9.6   (A NOTE ON INTEGER DIVISION)   When an integer is divided by another integer the answer may have a fractional part. All fractions are, however, discarded during calculation with the / operator. Thus 3 / 4 will give an answer 0 and 5 / 4 an answer 1. When expressions are evaluated using the precedence rules, whenever division is performed, the truncated numbers are the ones which are used in the final evaluation. Thus i / 10 * 10 and 10 * i / 10, even though they seem equivalent, give different answers. If i = 35, the first expression gives

35 / 10 * 10 = 3 * 10 = 30

The second expression gives

10 * 35 / 10 = 350 / 10 = 35

9.6   ASSIGNMENT STATEMENTS

An assignment statement has the following form:

Variable name = expression

For example,

total pay = gross pay – deduction + allowances   and

rate = gross rate – discount

are assignment statements.

Total pay + deduction = gross pay + allowances

is *not* an assignment statement as this has expressions on both sides of the assignment operator =

When an assignment statement is executed, the expression on the right of the assignment operator is *evaluated* first and the *number* obtained is stored in the storage location named by the variable name appearmg on the left of the assignment operator.

Thus when an expression is assigned to a variable the previous value of the variable is *replaced* by the value calculated using the expression. For example, in the assignment statement b = b + 3 the integer 3 is added to the number stored in variable name b and this new value replaces the old value stored in b.

The equal sign must thus be interpreted as "is to be replaced by" rather than "is equal to" (A more appropriate symbol would have been ← instead of =)

Type Conversion in Statements
In the examples given in the last section the variable types used in the expression on the right hand side of the = sign were the same as the variable type on the left. This need not be so.

Rule
A variable declared float or double can be set equal to an integer expression and vice-versa.

If an integer expression is assigned to a float variable name then the value of the integer expression is converted to a floating point number and is stored in the float variable name.

For example, consider the following statements:

int j , k ;
float a ;
a = j / k ;

If j = 3 and k = 2 then j / k = 1. The variable a will be assigned the value 1.0

If a floating expression is assigned to an integer variable the value of the float expression is "truncated" and stored in the integer variable name. In other words the *fractional part* of the floating point number obtained by evaluating the expression is chopped off (not rounded!) and the integer part is stored in the integer variable name.

For example, consider the following statements:

float a, b ;
int p ;
p = a / b ;

If a = 7.2 and b = 2.0 then a / b = 3.6. When 3.6 is assigned to p it will be truncated to 3 (as p is the declared int) and stored in p.

9.7   DEFINING VARIABLES

A variable is said to be *defined* if a value has been assigned to it. In other words, a variable is defined if a number has been stored in the storage location corresponding to its name.

Unless a variable is defined it cannot be used in an arithmetic expression. Values may be assigned to variables when they are declared in main ().

They may also be defined by the statement

Variable name = Constant

For example x = 4.5 defines the variable x by storing 4.5 in the memory location corresponding to x.

If all the variables appearing on the right of the assignment operator in an assignment statement are defined then the variable on the left is also defined. It follows from the fact that when an assignment statement is executed the numerical value of the expression on the right of the assignment operator is evaluated and stored in a memory location corresponding to the variable on the left.

For example the statement b = a $*$ d + e $-$ f defines the variable b if a, d, e and f are already defined.

9.8 ARITHMETIC CONVERSION

C allows mixing of float with integers in expressions. In such a case integers are converted to float before computation. However, if there is an integer sub-expression in the expression, it is computed using integer arithmetic. This feature is often overlooked by programmers and leads to unexpected errors. Consider the expression:

$$(1 + x) / (1 - x)$$

In the above expression 1 is converted to float and the expression is correctly computed. If we want to write an expression for i $x^2/2$ where i is an integer and x is float and write (i / 2) $*$ x $*$ x then (i / 2) is computed using integer arithmetic. Thus if i = 1 the expression will be zero which is wrong.

Consider the expression:

> int k ;
> float x, y ;
> y = x $*$ k / 4 with x = 8, k = 3

If we write y = x $*$ (k / 4) then y will equal 8. $*$ (3 / 4) = 8. $*$ 0 = 0. If we write y = (x $*$ k) / 4 then k is converted to float first giving 24.0 for the numerator. The denominator integer 4 is converted to float and 24.0 is divided by 4.0 giving 6.0.

Thus whenever integer division is seen in a sub-expression one should re-examine the expression carefully.

It has been observed in practice that mixing integers with float can lead to mistakes which are difficult to locate. The conversion is so automatic that it is easy to overlook a problem. Thus it is better not to use this facility.

C provides *explicit type conversion* functions using which a programmer can intentionally change the type of expressions in an arithmetic statement. This is done by a unary operator called a *cast* which may be either (float) or (int). If we write a (type-name) expression the expression is converted to the *type-name*. For example, if we write:

(float) (integer expression or variable name)

then the integer expression or variable name is converted to float. If we write

$$\text{(int) (float expression or variable name)}$$

then the float expression or variable name is converted to integer. These functions are safer to use as the programmer intentionally uses them. Using this we can write the expression

$$i / 2x^2$$

as $$\text{(float) } i / 2 * x * x$$

The expression xk / 4 may be written as

$$x * \text{(float) } k / 4$$

Conversion with Float and Double
If in an expression real variables declared as float and double appear together, all variables are converted to double. For example, in the statement

$$\text{float x, y, s ;}$$
$$\text{double p, q, z ;}$$
$$z = y * p / q + s ;$$
$$x = q / (y + s) ;$$

the variable names y and s are assumed to be double. The result is double as z is double. In the second statement (y + s) is calculated using single precision. As q is double, (y + s) is converted to double before division. As x is single precision, the answer is made single precision and stored in x.

9.9 ASSIGNMENT EXPRESSIONS

We have already defined the assignment operator = which assigns the value calculated for the expression on the right-hand side of the operator to the variable name on the left-hand side of the operator. For example, in

$$a = x + y * z;$$

the assignment operator is = .

  C unlike most other languages provides a new assignment operator. For example, if we write

$$\text{float x ;}$$
$$x + = y;$$

the expression is taken as

$$x = x + y$$

In general, if we write

$$\textit{<variable name><operator>} = \textit{<expression>}$$

it is interpreted as

$$\textit{variable name} = (\textit{variable name}) (\textit{operator}) (\textit{expression})$$

Example 9.7 illustrates the result of applying this operator.

EXAMPLE 9.7

    float x = 4.0, y = 12.0, z = 3.5 ;
    int p = 6, q = 4, r = 8 ;
    x + = 3.0 ; x * = y ;
    x / = y + z;
    p % = q;
    q - = p + 2 * r + 4;
    q / = p% r + 4 ;

We get as results:

    x = x + 3.0 = 7.0
    x = x * y = 7.0 * 12.0 = 84.0
    x = x / (y + z) = 84.0 / (12.0 + 3.5) = 5.4193548
    p = p % q = 6 % 4 = 2
    q = q - (p + 2 * r + 4) = 4 - (2 + 16 + 4) = -18
    q = q / (p % r + 4)
      = -18 / (2 % 8 + 4) = -18 / (2 + 4) = -3

The assignment operator is particularly useful when a long variable name appears on the left-hand side of the expression. For example,

                sum of height of students + = height;

is much more concise than writing

        sum of height of students = sum of height of students + height;

9.10   INCREMENT AND DECREMENT OPERATORS

C has two useful operators for incrementing and decrementing the values stored in variable names.

Thus if we write ++x then 1 is added to the contents of the variable name x. This is called incrementing x. If we write

                            y = ++x ;

then x is incremented by 1 and the result is stored in y. It is equivalent to the statements,

                            x = x + 1 ;

                            y = x ;

If we write – – z then 1 is subtracted from the contents of the variable z. If we write

                            p = --z ;

it is equivalent to the statement

                            z = z - 1 ;

                            p = z ;

This is mainly a shorthand notation to make it easy to write shorter programs.

There is another way in which increment and decrement can be used in C. If we write

$$y = x++ ;$$

it means first assign x to y and *then* increment x. In other words this statement is equivalent to statements:

$$y = x ;$$
$$x = x + 1 ;$$

Similarly

$$p = z -- ; \text{ is equivalent to}$$
$$p = z ;$$
$$z = z - 1 ;$$

The methods of incrementing and decrementing as given above are confusing to a beginner and should be used carefully.

EXAMPLE 9.8   The following example illustrates the use of increment and decrement operators.

```
int x = 6, y = 8, z, w, p = 10, q ;
y = x++ ;
z = ++x ;
w = p-- ;
q = ++p ;
```

The values obtained by calculating the above expressions are

$$y = 6$$
$$x = 6 + 1 = 7$$
$$x = x + 1 = 8$$
$$z = 8$$
$$p = p - 1 = 9$$
$$w = p = 9$$
$$p = p + 1 = 10$$
$$q = 10$$

In fact the unary operators ++ and – – can change the values of operands on which they operate without the need for an assignment statement. For example, if x = 8 and we write ++x then 8 + 1 = 9 is stored in x. In other words, x gets incremented.

9.11   MULTIPLE ASSIGNMENTS

C also has the provision to do multiple assignments. For example, if we write

$$a = b = c = 1$$

1 will be assigned to c. The value of c will be assigned to b and the value of b to a. Thus a = 1, b = 1, c = 1.

In the statement

$$a = b = c + d - e$$

C language will first calculate c + d − e. This will be assigned to b. The value stored in b will be assigned to a. Thus an assignment b = (c + d − e) can be *thought to have a value* which is the value of b. The = operator is said to be *right associative* as we scan the statement from right to left. + and − operators in c + d − e are *left associative* as we scan the expression from left to right. We can also write

$$a = x = b = c + d - e$$

which will be interpreted as

$$a = (x = (b = c + d - e))$$

If we write: a + = b * = c + d − e
it is equivalent to

$$a = a + b = a + (b * (c + d - e))$$

Observe that when we use the operator + = or * = the right-hand side is assumed to be enclosed in parentheses.

Thus

$$x * = y + 1$$

is $x = x * (y + 1)$ and *not* x = x * y + 1

The right-to-left associativity of = , * = operators is clarified by the following example. Suppose we write

$$a = (b = d * = c)$$

with c = 3, d = 4. The operators = and * = have equal precedence but are right associative. As (b = d * = c) is enclosed in parentheses and parentheses have higher precedence, it will be done first. Within the parantheses = and * = have equal precedence but due to right associativity of = and * =, the operation * = will be done before =. Thus d will be evaluated as d = d * c = 12. The = operator will next assign 12 to b. Thus a = b = d = 12 at the end of execution. The expression

$$a = b = d * = c$$

will be interpreted as

$$a = (b = (d * = c))$$

Observe that we have put parentheses from right to left to illustrate the right associativity of = and * = operators which have the same precedence. In this case d = d * c = 12. Thus, a = 12 and b = 12 at the end of execution.

9.12 SUMMARY

We have introduced many concepts in this chapter. We will summarize them now.

1. Arithmetic expressions are formed by variable names and or constants operated on by arithmetic operators.
2. In Table 9.2 we have given all arithmetic operators and their meanings.

Table .2 nary and binary arithmetic operators

Operation	Operator	Operands		Example	Effect
		Number	Type of both		
Unary					
minus	–	1	int or float*	– x	x ← – x
increment	++	1	int or float	++x or x++	x ← x + 1
decrement	– –	1	int or float	– –x or x– –	x ← x – 1
Binary					
add	+	2	int or float	x + y	Add y to x
subtract	–	2	int or float	x – y	Subtract y from x
multiply	*	2	int or float	x * y	Multiply x by y
divide	/	2	int	x / y	Integer quotient
divide	/	2	float	x / y	Divide x by y
modulus	%	2	int	x % y	Integer remainder

*Wherever *float* is mentioned *double* may also be used.

3. An expression is evaluated by scanning it from left to right. The order of application of operators is determined by hierarchy rules. In Table 9.3 we summarize these rules.

Table .3 ules of hierarchy of operators

Rank	Symbol	Evaluation rule
First	()	Evaluation expressions enclosed by parentheses, innermost parentheses first.
Second	Unary operators – –, ++, and cast, namely, (int), (float) or (double)	Right-to-left associativity among these unary operators.
Third	/, *, %	Division, multiplication and modulus are applied in the order in which they appear during left-to-right scan of expression.
Fourth	– , +	Binary – and + are done next in their order of appearance during left-to-right scan of expression.
Last	= , + =, * = – =, / =, % =	Right-to-left associativity among these operators.

4. An assignment expression is: x = (expression) the symbol = is an assignment operator. The expression is calculated and the result is stored in x. The assignment expression x = (expression) has a value equal to that assigned to x.
5. Assignment operators of the type <operator>= where <operator> is a binary operator, are available in C. The statement: x + = (expression), is equivalent to x = x + (expression) and x /= (expression) is equivalent to x = x / (expression). In general x <operator> = (expression) is interpreted as x = x<operator>(expression).
6. The type of variable on the left-hand side of an assignment operator need not match that of the expression on the right-hand side. Table 9.4 summarizes the rules when the types do not match.

Table . ype conversion in assignment statement e p

Type of x	Type of (exp)	Effect
float	float or double	x ← float (exp)
double	float or double	x ← double (exp)
int	float, double	x ← int (exp)
int	int	x ← int (exp)
float	int	x ← float (exp)
double	int	x ← double (exp)

7. C allows mixing of float and integers in arithmetic expressions. In such a case integers are converted to float before computation. Integer sub-expressions are computed using integer arithmetic rules, It is not a good practice to mix integers and float. Explicit type conversion using cast operator is a better solution. If float and double variables are found in an expression then all float variables are converted to double.
8. Increment and decrement operators ++ and – – respectively are convenient to use. The effect of using these operators is shown in Table 9.5.

Table . Increment and decrement

Operator	Example	Effect	Remarks
++	++x	x ← x + 1	Increment
– –	– –x	x ← x – 1	Decrement
++	x++	x ← x + 1	Increment
– –	x– –	x ← x – 1	Decrement
++	p = ++x	x ← x + 1 p ← x	Increment and store
– –	p = – –x	x ← x – 1 p ← x	Decrement and store
++	p = x++	p ← x x ← x + 1	Store and increment
– –	p = x– –	p ← x x ← x – 1	Store and decrement

EXERCISES

9.1 Write C expressions corresponding to the following:
Assume that all quantities are of type float.

(i) $\dfrac{ax + b}{ax - b}$

(ii) $\dfrac{2x + 3y}{x - 6}$

(iii) $x^5 + 10x^4 + 8x^3 + 4x + 2$

(iv) $(4x + 3)(2y + 2z - 4)$

(v) $\dfrac{ax + b}{c} + \dfrac{dy + e}{2f} - \dfrac{a}{bd}$

(vi) $\dfrac{a}{b(b - a)}$

9.2 What is the final value of b in the following sequence of statements?

```
float b ;
int i ;
b = 2.56 ;
b = (b + 0.05) * 10 ;
i = b ;
b = i;
b = b / 10.0 ;
```

If b = 2.56 is replaced by b = 2.54 above, what is the final value of b?

9.3 What is the value of i calculated by each of the following statements?

```
int i, j = 3, k = 6 ;
```

(i) i = j * 2 / 3 + k / 4 + 6 - j * j * j / 8 ;

(ii) float a = 1.5, b = 3.0 ;
    i = b / 2.0 + b * 4.0 / a - 8.0

(iii) int i, j = 3 ;
    i = j / 2 * 4 + 3 / 8 + j * j * j % 4 ;

9.4 Write the final value of k in the following program:

```
int k = 5, i = 3, j = 252, m ;
m = i * 1000 + j * 10 ;
k - m / 1000 + k ;
k = m % k++;
```

9.5 Evaluate the following expressions:

float a = 2.5, b = 2.5 ;

  (i) a + 2.5 / b + 4.5
  (ii) (a + 2.5) / b + 4.5
  (iii) (a + 2.5) / (b + 4.5)
  (iv) a / 2.5 / b
  (v) b++ / a + b--

9.6 Evaluate each of the following expressions. (The expressions are to be evaluated independent of one another.):

int i = 3, j = 4, k = 2 ;

  (i) i++ - j--
  (ii) i-- % j++
  (iii) j++ / i--
  (iv) ++k % --j
  (v) k++ * --i
  (vi) j + 1 / i - 1
  (vii) i - 1 % j + 1
  (viii) i = j * = k = 4
  (ix) i * = k = ++j + i
  (x) i = j /= k + 4

9.7 Find the value of i, j k at the end of the execution of each of the following statements:

i int k = 3, i = 4, z = 6 ;

k + = i % j++ ;
k % = ++i * j / 2 ;
k * = k++ * j - i-- ;

9.8 Find the value of a in each of the following statements:

int i = 5, j = 5, k = 7;
float a = 3.5, b = 5.5, c = 2.5 ;

  (i) a = b - i / j + c / j
  (ii) a = (b - i) / (j + c) / j
  (iii) a = b - ((i + j) / (k + i)) * c
  (iv) a = b - i + j / k + i * c
  (v) a = b + 1 % 1 + c
  (vi) a = (b + 1) % (1 + c)

10

Input and Output in C Programs

LEARNING OBJECTIVES

In this chapter we will learn:
1. How to input data to C program and display the results.
2. The need for format string and how to specify a format string for a given requirement.
3. How to display messages using printf statement.

We have seen that any program requires data to be read into variable names. Data stored in variable names need to be displayed. As a programming language, C does not provide any input–output (I/O) statements. Instead, a set of standard library functions provided by the operating system UNIX for input and output are borrowed and used by C. Compilers using other operating systems such as MS-DOS have also emulated the same idea. Some minor differences may be there which a programmer should find out from the system staff.

If no I/O device is specified, C assumes that the keyboard of a video terminal is the input device and the video screen, the output device. There are a pair of I/O functions which we will discuss in this chapter. These are: scanf () for input and printf () for output. These are used for data to be read in a specific format and written in a specific format.

10.1 OUTPUT FUNCTION

The general form of an output function is

$$\text{printf (format-string, var}_1, \text{var}_2, \dots, \text{var}_n)$$

where format-string gives information on how many variables to expect, what type of arguments they are, how many columns are to be reserved for displaying them and any character string to be printed. The printf () function may sometimes display only a message and not any variable value. In the following example

printf ("Answers are given below") ;

the format-string is

Answers are given below

and there are no variables. This statement displays the format-string on the video display device. After displaying, the cursor on the screen will remain at the end of the string. If we want it to move to the next line to display information on the next line, we should have the format-string

printf ("Answers are given below \n") ;

In this string the symbol \n commands that the cursor should advance to the beginning of the next line.

In the following example

printf ("Answer x = %d \n", x) ;

%d specifies how the value of x is to be displayed. It indicates that x is to be displayed as a decimal integer. The variable x is of type int. The %d is called the *conversion specification* and d the *conversion character*. In the example

printf (" a = %d, b = %f \n", a, b) ;

the variable a is of type int and b of type float or double. %d specifies that a is to be displayed as an integer and %f specifies that b is to be displayed as a decimal fraction. In this example, %d and %f are conversion specifications and d, f are conversion characters.

If a = 248 and b = – 468.8643, they will be displayed as

a = 248, b = – 468.8643

If the approximate value of b is not known it is preferable to display it in mantissa, exponent form. For this the specification is %e. When this specification is used the answer will be displayed in the form

+m. m m m m m m e   pp

Example Program 10.1 illustrates how printf () displays answers. Observe that there is a discrepancy between the values assigned to x and y in the program and those printed by the printf statement. This is due to the fact that decimal floating point numbers are stored in the machine in binary mantissa, exponent form. The number of bits used for mantissa in single precision mode in 32-bit computers is usually 22 bits. This limits the number of significant decimal digits to 6. Thus only the first 6 significant digits will be guaranteed to be correct when the number is printed. More digits will be printed depending on the format specification but they may be meaningless.

```
/* Example Program 10.1 */
/* Program illustrating printf() */
#include <stdio.h>

main()
{
    int a = 2567, b = -467;
    float x = -123.4567, y = 12345.67;
    double z = -123.4567891234, w = 123456789.1234;
    printf("Output:\n");
    printf("123456789012345678901234567890\n");
    printf("\n");
    printf("%d, %d, %f, %f\n", a, b, x, f);
    printf("\n");
    printf("%d, %d, %e, %e\n", a, b, x, y);
    printf("%f, %f\n", z, w);
    printf("%e, %e\n", z, w);
}

Output:
123456789012345678901234567890

2567, -467, -123.456703, 12345.669922

2567, -467, -1.234567e+02, 1.234567e+04
-123.456789,123456789.123400
-1.234568e+02, 1.234568e+08
```

g a   1 .1   Illustrating the use of printf statement.

So far we specified that the variable values to be printed should be integers, decimal fractions or decimal fractions in exponent notation. We have not specified the number of columns to be reserved to display a variable. The function decides, based on the value to be displayed, the number of columns to be reserved on the display unit. We can explicitly specify the number of columns to be reserved by using the conversion specification

%w conversion character

Here *w* is an integer which specifies the width of the field to be displayed. Example Program 10.2 illustrates the use of width specification.

```
/* Example Program 10.2 */
/* Program illustrating the use of width specification */
#include <stdio.h>

main()
{
    int a = 2567, b = -467;
    float x = -123.4567, y = 45645.6;
    double z = -789.4567891234, p = 3456789.1234;
    printf("Output:\n");
    printf("123456789012345678901234567890123456789\n");
    printf("a =%6d, b =%8d, x =%8f\n", a, b, x);
```

```
    printf("x =%18e, y =%18e\n", x, y);
    printf("z =%18f, p =%13e\n", z, p);
    printf("a =%-6d, b =%-8d\n", a, b);
    printf("x =%-15f, y =%-18e\n", x, y);
}   /* End of main */
```

Output:
```
12345678901234567890123456789012345678901234567890123456789
a =    2567, b =     -467, x =-123.456703
x =        -1.234567e+02, y =        4.564560e+04
z =           -789.456789, p = 3.456789e+06
a = 2567   , b = -467
x = -123.456703   , y = 4.564560e+04
```
/* Comment; Observe that x = %8f gives more than 8 column width of output. printf
    seems to use a default 6 digits after the decimal point. It is implementation
    dependent */

g a   1 .2   Use of width specification in printf.

Observe the conversion specification %–6d where the sign precedes the width specifier. This specification left justifies the number printed.

A more general specification is

%w.p conversion character

In this specification *w* is the width of the field to be reserved and *p* is the precision, that is, the number of digits to be displayed after the decimal point in a fraction. Example Program 10.3 illustrates the printing of double precision numbers.

```
/* Example Program 10.3 */
#include <stdio.h>

main()
{
    float x = -123.456789, y = 45745678.9;
    double z = -789.4567801234, w = 567456789.1234;
    printf("Output: \n");
    printf("12345678901234567890123456789012345678901234567890\n");
    printf("x =%12.6f, y =%12.1f\n", x, y);
    printf("z =%19.5e, w =%23.16e\n", z, w);
    printf("x =%30.20f\n", x);
    printf("z =%30.15e\n", z);
}   /* End of main */
```

Output:
```
12345678901234567890123456789012345678901234567890
x = -123.456787, y = 45745680.0
z =        -7.89457e+02, w = 5.6745678912340000e+08
x =        -123.45678710937500000000
z =        -7.894567801234000e+02
```

g a   1 .3   Printing double precision numbers.

In Tables 10.1 and 10.2 we summarize the various conversion specifications and their meanings.

Table 1 .1 Conversion specifications

Type of variable	Conversion character	Quantity to be displayed	Conversion specification	Displayed quantity
integer	d	signed decimal integer	%d	−1239
integer	u	unsigned decimal integer	%u	1238
octal	o	unsigned octal value	%o	1302
hexadecimal	x	unsigned hexadecimal	%x	A34F
floating point or double precision	f	real decimal	%f	−345.678
floating point or double precision	e	real decimal	%e	−3.456788e5

Table 1 .2   General conversion specification: %−w.p conversion character

%	First character of specification (compulsory)
−	Minus sign for left justification (optional)
w	Digits specifying field width (optional)
.	Period separating width from precision (optional)
p	Digits specifying precision (optional)
d, u, o, x, f or e	Conversion character (compulsory)
l	The letter (ell) if the integer is a long integer

10.2   INPUT FUNCTION

The function scanf () is used to read data into variables from the standard input, namely, a keyboard attached to a video tenninal. The general format of an input statement is

$$\text{scanf (format-string, } var_1, var_2, \dots , var_n)$$

where format-string gives information to the computer on the type of data to be stored in the list of variables var_1, var_2, ..., var_n and in how many columns they will be found.

For example, in the statement

$$\text{scanf (“%d%d”, \&p, \&q) ;}$$

the two variables in which numbers are to be stored are p and q. The data to be stored are integers. The integers will be separated by a blank in the data typed on the keyboard.

A sample data line may thus be

$$456 \ 58578$$

Observe that the symbol & (called ampersand) should precede each variable name. Ampersand is used to indicate that the address of the variable name should be found to store a value in it. The manner in which data is read by a scanf statement may be explained by assuming an arrow to be positioned above the first data value. The arrow moves to the next data value after storing the first data value in the storage location corresponding to the first variable name in the list. A blank character should separate the data values. This is illustrated below:

scanf("%d%d%d%d", &p, &q, &s, &t)

Data line:

initial arrow position ↓			final arrow position ↓
258	454	682	743
p	q	s	t

The statement could also have been written as

scanf("%d%d", &p, &q);

scanf("%d%d", &s, &t);

with the data line as shown above.

The scanf statement causes data to be read from one or more lines till numbers are stored in all the specified variable names.

Observe that no blanks should be left between % and characters such as *d* in the format-string. Writing scanf("% d %d", &p, &q) is thus wrong. Another common mistake is to forget the symbol & in front of the variable name. *This symbol & is essential.*

If some of the variables in the list of variables in scanf are of type integer and some are float, appropriate descriptions should be used in the format-string. The example

scanf("%d%f%e", &a, &b, &c);

specifies that an integer is to be stored in a, a float is to be stored in b and a float written using the exponent format in c. The appropriate sample data line is

485 498.762 6.845e–12

In Table 10.3 we specify the character to be used in the format-string for various types of data.

Table 1 .3 Characters to be used in format-string for various types of data

Character after % in format-string	*Type of data to be entered via keyboard*
d	integer
u	unsigned integer
o	octal integer
x	hexadecimal integer
f	floating point with decimal point in number
e	floating point expressed in exponent notation

We give below some examples of scanf statements and the corresponding data line.

EXAMPLES

(i) scanf ("%d%u%o%e", &x, &y, &z, &p);

Data line:

−258 4578 0234 −28.65e−12

(ii) scanf ("%f%x%d%e", &p, &q, &v, &s);

Data line:

−256.42 AF06 358 −456.78e14

Example Program 10.4 illustrates how scanf and printf statements work together. Example Program 10.5 illustrates the use of printf with width specifications for the data to be displayed.

In C, both scanf and printf are functions. The name of the function scanf and printf have values assigned to them when they complete their job. The scanf function has an integer value equal to the number of data converted and stored by it. If it tries to read data after the end of data is reached then it has a value EOF (called end of file). EOF is defined in stdio.h (EOF is normally −1 but it may be implementation dependent).

```
/* Example Program 10.4 */
/* Program illustrating the use of scanf and printf statements */
#include <stdio.h>

main()
{
    int a, b, c, d;
    float x, y, z, p;
    scanf("%d %o %x %u", &a, &b, &c, &d);
    printf("The first four data displayed\n");
    printf("%d %o %x %u\n", a, b, c, d);
    scanf("%f %e %e %f", &x, &y, &z, &p);
    printf("Display of the rest of the data read\n");
    printf("%f %e %e %f\n", x, y, z, p);
    printf("End of display\n");
}
Input:
    -684 0362 abf6 3856 -26.68 2.8e-3 1.256e22 6.856

Output:

The first four data displayed
-684 362 abf6 3856
Display of the rest of the data read
-26.680000 2.800000e-03 1.256000e+22 6.856000
End of display
```

g a 1 .   Use of scanf statements.

The printf function has an integer value equal to the number of data items printed. If it encounters an error while printing it has EOF stored in it.

```
/* Example Program 10.5 */
#include <stdio.h>

main()
{
    float a, b;
    int c, d;

    scanf("%f %f %d %d", &a, &b, &c, &d);
    printf("Output displayed\n");
    Printf(" --------------\n");
    printf("a =%15f b =%16.8e\n", a, b);
    printf("c =%10d d =%d\n", c, d);
}

Input:
28.467 -62.467 8345 -248

Output displayed
-----------------
a =       28.466999 b = -6.24669991e+01
c =           8345 d =-248
```

g a   1 .   Use of scanf and printf statements.

EXERCISES

10.1 Write printf statements to output the following:
   (i) int a, b, c
   (ii) float x, y, z
   (iii) unsigned int a, b, c
   (iv) float p, q, r in exponent format
   (v) int a, b, c with integers left justified
   (vi) int a, b, c with field widths of 8 left justified
   (vii) float p, q, r with 6 decimal digits after the decimal point
   (viii) int i, j, k in octal form
   (ix) int p, q, r with 5 decimal digits after the decimal point, left justified
   (x) int p, q, r in hexadecimal form.

10.2 Write printf statements to print the following table:

Case	x	y	z
1	25.25	38.42	61.4256
2	30.25	42.856	323.468
3	725.68	734.467	854.678

10.3 Write printf statements to print the following:

$$x = 468.7e25 \quad y = 256 \quad z = -256.725$$

10.4 Write scanf statements to read:

(i) Three integers, a floating point number and an octal number.
(ii) Two floating point numbers in exponent form, a hexadecimal number and an octal number.
(iii) Two negative integers and three floating point numbers.

10.5 A table of floating point numbers with 5 numbers in each line and 5 lines is given. Write scanf statements to read them.

10.6 Write scanf and printf statements to do the following:

input elements of Pascal triangle 1, 1, 1, 1, 2, 1, 1, 3, 3, 1 in a line output: Pascal triangle in the format:

```
        1
      1   1
     1  2  1
    1  3  3  1
```

11

Conditional Statements

LEARNING OBJECTIVES

In this chapter we will learn:

1. The need for conditional statements and how they are expressed in C.
2. The concept of a compound statement also known as a block in C.
3. The need to be careful in nesting conditional statements.

The order in which the statements are written in a program is extremely important. Normally the statements are executed sequentially as written in the program. In other words when all the operations specified in a particular statement are executed, the statement appearing on the next line of the program is taken up for execution. This is known as the *normal flow of control*. If one were restricted to this normal flow of control it would not be possible to perform alternate actions based on the result of testing a condition.

EXAMPLE 11.1   Suppose we introduce in Example 7.3 a rule that a discount of 10 percent will be given on purchases of mangoes more than five dozens. To implement this rule we need a statement which will test the quantity purchased to determine if it is more than five dozens. Such a statement is called *conditional statement*. Using this statement, Example Program 7.6 is rewritten as Example Program 11.1.

The new statement introduced is:

$$if \ (quantity > 60) \ discount = 0.1;$$

The statement is interpreted as:

if quantity is *greater than* 60 *then* execute the statement discount = 0.1 (i.e. set discount = 0.1), otherwise *do not* execute the statement discount = 0.1.

Thus in Example Program 11.1 after the scanf statement, discount is set to zero. The next statement sets discount to 0.1 if the quantity of the purchase is greater than 60. The next statement computes the cost (in paise) with discount = 0.1 if quantity > 60 and discount = 0 otherwise.

In the statement:

$$if \ (quantity > 60) \ discount = 0.1;$$

we have used a *relational operator* which compares two quantities. We will discuss next the relational operators available in C.

```
/* Example Program 11.1 */
#include <stdio.h>

main()
{
    int rupees,  paise,   quantity;
    float  cost_dozen,   discount,   cost;
    scanf("%f %d", &cost_dozen, &quantity);
    printf("Cost of dozen = %f,  quantity = %d\n", cost_dozen,  quantity);
    discount = 0.0;
    if(quantity > 60)
       discount = 0.1;
    cost = ((cost_dozen * 100.0/12.0) * (float) quantity * (1.0 - discount) + 0.5);
    rupees = (int)cost/100;
    paise = (int)cost%100;
    printf("Number of mangoes = %d\n", quantity);
    printf("Cost = Rs.%d ps.%d\n", rupees, paise);
}
```

g a   11.1   Price of mangoes with discount.

11.1   RELATIONAL OPERATORS

Table 11.1 lists all the relational operators available in C.

Table 11.1   List of relational operators

Operator	Meaning
==	Equal to
>	Greater than
<	Less than
>=	Greater than or equal to
<=	Less than or equal to
!=	Not equal to

Two real or integer variables, constants or expressions connected by a relational operator return a value which can be either *true* or *false*. For example, the expression n < k can be true or false. Similarly the expression index == 4 would be true if index has a value 4, else it will be false. The symbol == is a relational operator used to compare the values of variables (or constants) whereas the symbol = is used to signify the operation of assignment. Thus a = b means replace the contents of a by the contents of b whereas a == b checks for the arithmetic equality of a and b and returns a value *true* or *false.*

An expression formed with relational operators is known as *logical expression.* Some valid logical expressions are given below:

(i) a >= b
(ii) k != b
(iii) (a + b / c) < (c + d + f)
(iv) a == x
(v) x <= 0.005

In general two integer or floating point expressions may be connected by a relational operator. Float and integers should not be mixed in a logical expression.

Some illegal logical expressions are given below:

(i) int k ; 2.5 < k (An integer cannot be compared with a real quantity)
(ii) (a + b) << (c + d) (<< not a valid relational operator)
(iii) 2.5 = A (= not legal. Should write ==)
(iv) a =< b (=< is not a valid operator; <= is the correct operator)

The value returned by a logical expression, as we have seen, can be either *true* or *false.* In C *true* is assigned a non-zero integer value and *false* a value 0. Thus we can also use in an *if* statement an arithmetic expression instead of a logical expression. If the arithmetic expression is non-zero the *true* branch is taken and if it is zero the *false* branch is taken.

11.2   COMPOUND STATEMENT

The compound statement (also known as a *block)* is a group of statements enclosed by braces, namely, {and}. The individual statements enclosed by braces are executed in the order in which they appear. The general form of the compound statement is:

$$\{ \; S1 \; ;$$
$$S2 \; ;$$
$$\vdots$$
$$Sn \; ; \}$$

Observe that no ; (semicolon) is used after right braces.
For example:

{ scanf ("%f%f", &a, &b) ;
    c = a + b ;
printf ("%f, %f, %f", a, b, c);}

is a compound statement. Observe that a semicolon separates one statement from the next. More than one statement may be placed on the same line as a semicolon is a statement separator.

11.3 CONDITIONAL STATEMENTS

The statement: *if (quantity > 60) discount = 0.1;* is known as a *conditional statement*. This is a simpler version of a general conditional statement available in C. The general conditional statement is:

> *if (logical expression)*
> {   *S1t* ;
>   *S2t* ;
>   ...
>
>   ...
>   *Snt* ; }
> *else*
> {   *S1e* ;
>   *S2e* ;
>   ...
>
>   ...
>   *Sme* ;} /* *End of if* */

In the above general form *if* the logical expression is *true* then the compound statement {S1t; S2t; ...; Snt;} is executed and the control jumps to the next statement following the *if* statement. Thus the compound statement following *else,* namely {S1e; S2e; ...; Sme;} is ignored. If the logical expression is *false* then the compound statement appearing first is ignored and the compound statement {S1e; S2e; ...; Sme;} following *else* is executed. As we pointed out earlier, C allows the use of an arithmetic expression instead of a logical expression in an *if* statement. A non-zero value of an arithmetic expression is taken as *true.*

In case only one statement is to be executed if the logical expression is *true* and another single statement if it is *false* then the statement may be written as:

$$if \ (logical \ expression) \ St \ ; \ else \ Se \ ;$$

Observe that in the above case braces are not needed as *St* and *Se* are single statements. Another particular form of the conditional statement is:

> *if (logical expression)*
> {   *S1t* ;
>   *S2t* ;
>   ...
>
>   ...
>   *Snt* ;   }

In the above case if the *logical expression* is *true* then the compound statement {*S1t*; *S2t*; ...; *Snt*;} is executed. If the *logical expression* is *false* then the control jumps to the statement following the right braces ignoring the compound statement.

These two conditional statements are illustrated by the flow charts of Fig. 11.1(a) and Fig. 11.1(b).

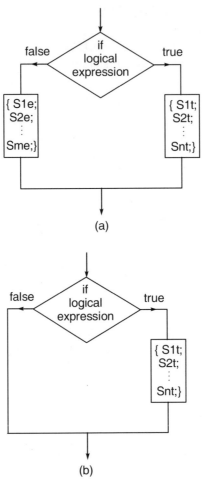

Fig. 11.1 Flow charts illustrating conditional statements.

A number of valid conditional statements are given below:

(i) if (a >= b) b = c + d * x ;
(ii) if (n == 50) x = x + 2 ; else x = x + 4 ;
(iii) if (z >= a – b + c) {x = x + 1 ; y = y + 2 ; }
(iv) if (sexcode == 1)
      {++ total boys ;
        total boy height += height ; }
   else
      {++ total girls ;
        total girl height += height ; }
(v) if (a > b)
    if (c > d)
      x = y ;
(vi) if (a > b) if (c > d) x = y ; else x = z ; else x = w ;

In the conditional statement (v) the first *if* clause has in turn another *if* clause. This is allowed. The way it is interpreted is shown in the flow chart of Fig. 11.2.

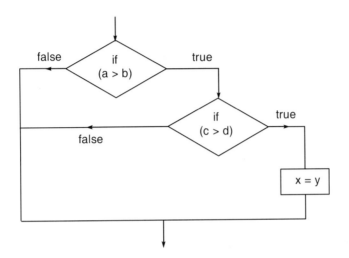

Fig. 11.2   Flow chart for the nested conditional statement of Example 11.3(v).

The conditional statement (vi) is another example of a nested *if else* clause. Such a statement is interpreted by bracketing the innermost *if* clause. Thus we would interpret the conditional statement (vi) as:

$$if\ (a > b)$$
$$if\ (c > d)$$
$$x = y\ ;$$
$$else$$
$$x = z\ ;$$
$$else$$
$$x = w\ ;$$

Such an indenting is recommended as a good style and one should make it a habit to use such an indenting which makes it easy to understand the statement. A flow chart corresponding to this statement is given in Fig. 11.3.

C allows any number of nested conditional statements. One should, however, use this facility with care as understanding many levels of nested conditional statements is not easy. We give below some illegal conditional statements.

(i) if a >= b x = y ; else x = z ;   (parentheses missing)
(ii) if (x <= z) ; { a = b + c – d ; w = b + c + d ;}   (; after if (x < = z) is wrong)
(iii) if (a != b) {x = y + z ; r = s + t ; } ;
        else {x = y – z ; y = s – t ;}   (; before else incorrect)
(iv) if (x = y) i = 1 else if (x != y) i = 2 ;   (= not a relational operator)
(v) if (x >= y) if (x <= z) else i = 4 ;   (inner if has the statement missing)

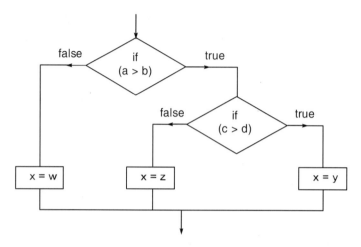

Fig. 11.3   Interpreting a nested conditional statement.

The following way of representing the flow chart of Fig. 11.4 by a C statement is incorrect:

if (a > b)
    if (c > d)
        x = y ;
else
        x = z ;

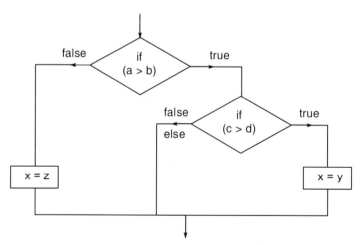

Fig. 11.   A flow chart to be converted to a C statement.

The indenting in the above statement suggests that the *else* corresponds to *if (a > b)*. This interpretation is wrong. An *else* is always paired with its logically nearest *if*. The indenting is misleading. The flow chart corresponding to this misleading statement is given as shown in Fig. 11.5.

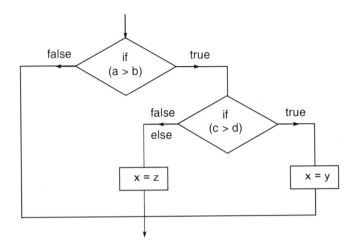

Fig. 11.   Flow chart corresponding to a wrong interpretation of a C statement.

A better style of writing the given statement is:

if(*a* > *b*)
    {*if*(*c* > *d*)
        x = *y* ;
    else
        x = *z* ; }

If the flow chart of Fig. 11.4 is to be written in C the correct statement would be:

if(*a* > *b*)
    {*if*(*c* > *d*)
        x = *y* ; }
else
    x = *z* ;

11.4   EXAMPLE PROGRAMS USING CONDITIONAL STATEMENTS

EXAMPLE 11.2   Consider the algorithm for picking the largest of three numbers developed in Chapter 5. The flow chart corresponding to this algorithm is reproduced as Fig. 11.6. A program corresponding to this flow chart is given as Example Program 11.2. Observe the indentation and the use of { } appropriately which makes the program easy to understand.

EXAMPLE 11.3   An alternate strategy for solving the same problem which can be generalized to pick the largest of an arbitrary set of numbers (not merely 3) is given in the flow chart of Fig. 11.7. A program corresponding to this is given as Example Program 11.3. Observe that this program is easy to understand. Further it can be easily generalized to pick the largest of an arbitrary set of numbers. We will do this in the next chapter.

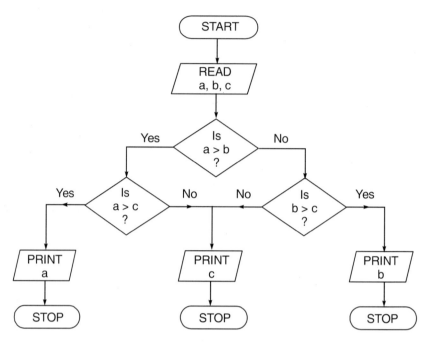

Fig. 11. Flow chart to pick the largest of three numbers.

```
/* Example Program 11.2 */
/* Picking the largest of 3 numbers */
#include <stdio.h>

main()
{
    int a,   b,   c;
    scanf("%d %d %d", &a, &b, &c);
    printf("a = %4d, b = %4d, c = %4d\n", a, b, c);
    if (a > b)
        {
        if (a > c)
            printf("a = %4d\n",   a);
        else
            printf("c = %4d\n",   c);
        }
    else
        {
        if  (b > c)
            printf("b = %4d\n", b);
        else
            printf("c = %4d\n", c);
        }
}
```

g a   11.2 Picking the largest of three numbers—method 1.

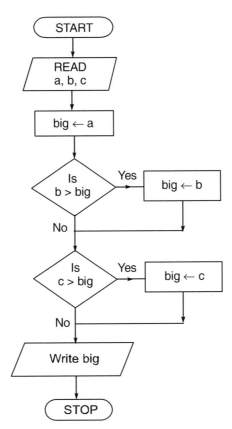

Fig. 11. Flow chart illustrating an alternate strategy to pick the largest of three numbers.

```
/* Example Program 11.3 */
/* Alternate method to pick the largest of three numbers */
#include <stdio.h>

main()
{
    int a,  b,  c,  big;
    scanf("%d %d %d", &a,  &b,  &c);
    printf("a = %4d, b = %4d, c = %4d\n", a, b, c);
    big = a;
    if (b > big)
        big = b;
    if (c > big)
        big = c;
    printf("The largest number is %4d\n", big);
}
```

g a   11.3 Picking the largest of three numbers—method 2.

EXAMPLE 11.4   A program to find the roots of a quadratic equation will now be developed. Given a quadratic equation

$$ax^2 + bx + c = 0$$

the roots are given by the formula

$$x = \{-b \quad (b^2 - 4ac)^{1/2}\} / (2a)$$

if we assume that a is not equal to zero. We should consider three cases:

(i)   The discriminant $(b^2 - 4ac) < 0$ in which case there are two complex conjugate roots.
(ii) The discriminant $(b^2 - 4ac) = 0$ in which case the two roots are real and equal. The roots are $-b / 2a$.
(iii) The discriminant $(b^2 - 4ac) > 0$ in which case both the roots are real. The algorithm may be expressed as given below:

> *Read a, b, c ;*
> *discriminant* = $(b^2 - 4ac)$;
> *if (discriminant* < 0)
>> *then*
>>> { *discriminant* = (– *discriminant*) ;
>>> *Imaginary part of root* = $(discriminant)^{1/2}/2a$
>>> *Real part of root* = $-b / 2a$;
>>> *Write out the complex conjugate roots*
>> *else*
>>> *If (discriminant* == 0)
>>>> *then*
>>>>> { *root* = – *b/2a* ;
>>>>> *Write out the repeated roots*}
>>>> *else*
>>>>> { *root1* = $-b + (discriminant)^{1/2}/2a$;
>>>>> *root2* = $-b - (discriminant)^{1/2}/2a$;
>>>>> *Write out the two real roots*}
>>> *end of algorithm.*

The above algorithm is translated to C in Example Program 11.4. Observe the ease of translating the algorithm. Note the indentation of the *if* statement to aid program understanding. Also note the placement of semicolons and curly brackets in the *if* statement. A pre-processor line #include <mathlib.h> has been placed in this program. This library is necessary to calculate the root of a number.

```
/* Example Program 11.4 */
/* Solution of quadratic equation */
#include <stdio.h>
/* math library needed for square root */
#include <math.h>
main()
{
    float a, b , c, discrmnt, x_imag_1, x_imag_2, x_real_1, x_real_2, temp;
    scanf("%f %f %f",  &a, &b, &c);
    printf("a = %f, b = %f,  c = %f\n", a, b, c);
    discrmnt = b*b - 4.0*a*c;
    if (discrmnt < 0)
       {
           discrmnt = -discrmnt;
           x_imag_1 = sqrt(discrmnt)/(2.0 * a);
           x_imag_2 = -x_imag_1;
           x_real_1 = -b/(2.0 * a);
           printf("Complex conjugate roots\n");
           printf("real part = %16.8e\n", x_real_1);
           printf("imaginary part = %16.8e\n", x_imag_1);
       }
    else
       {
           if (discrmnt == 0)
              {
                  x_real_1 = -b/(2.0 * a);
                  printf("Repeated roots\n");
                  printf("Real roots = %16.8e\n", x_real_i);
              }
           else
              {
                  temp = sqrt(discrmnt);
                  x_real_1 = (-b + temp)/(2.0 * a) ;
                  x_real_2 = (-b - temp)/(2.0 * a);
                  printf("Real roots\n");
                  printf ("real root_1 = %16.8e\n", x_real_1);
                  printf ("real root_2 = %16.8e\n", x_real_2);
              }
       }
} /* End of main */
```

g a   11.   Solution of quadratic equation.

11.5   STYLE NOTES

The most important style rule in writing conditional statements is indentation. We have illustrated the recommended indentation in all the examples in this chapter.

It is preferable to use an "open style" leaving blank spaces between the different parts of the statement to aid readability.

Even though C allows any number of levels of nested conditional statements we do not recommend more than three levels of nesting as it becomes difficult to understand.

EXERCISES

11.1 Given a point (x, y) write a program to find out if it lies on the x-axis, y-axis or at the origin, namely, (0, 0).

11.2 Extend the program of Exercise 11.1 to find whether it lies in the first, second, third or fourth quadrant in x–y plane.

11.3 Given a point (x, y) write a program to find out whether it lies inside, outside or on a circle with unit radius and centre at (0, 0).

11.4 Given a 4-digit number representing a year write a program to find out whether it is a leap year.

11.5 Given the four sides of a rectangle write a program to find out whether its area is greater than its perimeter.

11.6 Given a triangle with sides a, b, c write a program to find whether it is an isosceles triangle.

11.7 Given three points (x_1, y_1), (x_2, y_2) and (x_3, y_3) write a program to find out whether they are collinear.

11.8 Given three numbers A, B and C write a program to print their values in ascending order. For example if A = 10, B = 11 and C = 6, your program should print out:

Smallest number = 6
Next higher number =10
Highest number = 11

11.9 Write a program to round a positive number greater than 1 but less than 2 with four significant digits to one with three significant digits. For example:

1.452 rounded would give 1.45
1.458 rounded would yield 1.46
1.455 rounded would be 1.46
1.445 rounded would be 1.44

Observe that after rounding we try to keep the last digit even if the digit ignored is 5.

11.10 A bank accepts deposits for one year or more and the policy it adopts on interest rate is as follows:

(i) If a deposit is less than Rs. 1000 and for 2 or more years the interest rate is 5 percent compounded annually.

(ii) If a deposit is Rs. 1000 or more but less than Rs. 5000 and for 2 or more years the interest rate is 7 percent compounded annually.

(iii) If a deposit is more than Rs. 5000 and is for 1 year or more the interest is 8 percent compounded annually.

(iv) On all deposits for 5 years or more the interest is 10 percent compounded annually.

(v) On all other deposits not covered by the above conditions the interest is 3 percent compounded annually.

At the time of withdrawal a customer data is given with the amount deposited and the number of years the money has been with the bank. Write a program to obtain the money in the customer's account and the interest credited at the time of withdrawal. (*Hint:* Use of a decision table is recommended).

11.11 The billing policy of an electricity company is given below:

Consumption	Charges
≤ 100 units	Rs. 3.50 per unit
> 100, ≤ 300 units	Rs. 4.00 per unit for units > 100
> 300, ≤ 500 units	Rs. 4.25 per unit for units > 300
> 500 units	Rs. 4.5 per unit

Thus charges for 800 units = 350 + 800 + 900 + 1350 = Rs. 3400

Your program should use variables for the slab boundaries and charges in each slab and read the values given above as data.

Repeat when slabs and rates are changed to ≤ 100, Rs. 4.00; 101 to 400, Rs. 4.50; 401 to 600; Rs. 4.75; and above 600, Rs. 5.00.

12

Implementing Loops in Programs

LEARNING OBJECTIVES

In this chapter we will learn:

1. How to set up loops in programs.
2. How to use *while* loop, *for* loop and *do while* loop in C programming.

Consider Example Program 7.7 which is reproduced here as Example Program 12.1 for ready reference. We see a repetitive structure in this program.

```
/* Example Program 12.1 */
#include <stdio.h>

main()
{
    int digit_1, digit_2, digit_3, digit_4, digit_5;
    unsigned int sum, number, n;

    scanf("%d", &number);
    printf("number = %d\n", number);
    n = number;
    digit_1 = n % 10;
    n  = n / 10;
    digit_2 = n % 10;
    n = n / 10;
    digit_3 = n % 10;
    n = n / 10;
    digit_4 = n % 10;
    n = n / 10;
    digit_5 = n;
    sum = digit_1 + digit_2 + digit_3 + digit_4 + digit_5;
    printf("sum of digits = %d\n", sum);
}   /* End of main */
```

g a   12.1 Adding digits of a number

The statements

    digit 1 = n % 10 ;
       n = n / 10 ;

are executed again and again. The first statement finds the least significant digit of *n* and assigns it to digit 1. The second statement reduces the length of *n* by one digit by discarding its least significant digit. The same two operations are repeated four times till all the digits in *n* are exhausted. It is thus clear that if we repeatedly execute these two statements while n!= 0 (i.e. as long as n != 0) and add the digit obtained at each step to the sum of digits we would get the answer. This is shown in the flow chart of Fig. 12.1. Observe that the steps digit = n % 10, sum = sum + digit and n = n / 10 are carried out again and again using a program loop as long as n != 0. When n becomes 0 control leaves the loop and executes the steps *Print*

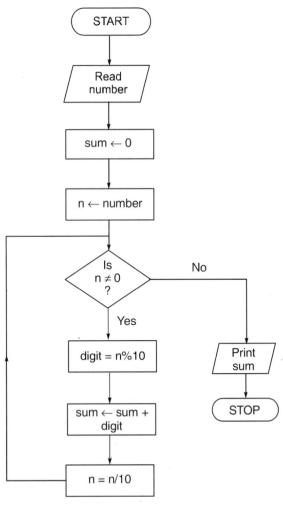

Fig. 12.1 Illustrating use of a loop in a program.

sum and *STOP*. Reformulating the strategy of finding the sum of digits using a program loop has made the program concise and at the same time it has been *generalized*. This method is general as it will add the digits of a number regardless of the number of digits in it. Contrast this with the method used in Example Program 12.1 which is valid only for a five digit number.

As such program loops are found very useful in evolving concise and generalized programs, C language provides very powerful commands for repeatedly performing a set of statements. Example Program 12.1 is rewritten as Example Program 12.2 using a C command called *while*. Example Program 12.2 is directly derived from the flow chart of Fig. 12.1.

```
/* Example Program 12.2 */
/* Summing digits of a number using a while loop */
#include <stdio.h>

main()
{
    short int d;
    unsigned int digit, number, n, sum = 0;

    scanf ("%d", &number);
    printf("Number = %d\n", number);
    n = number;
    while (n != 0)
       {
          digit = n % 10;
          sum += digit;
          n = n / 10;
       }
    printf("Number = %d, Sum of digits = %d\n", number, sum);
}   /* End of main */
```

g a   12.2   Adding digits of a number using a while loop.

The command

while (logical expression)

orders that the compound statement following it should be carried out again and again as long as the logical expression is *true*. (Remember that a set of statements enclosed in braces {} is a compound statement.) When the logical expression becomes *false* then control gets out of the loop to the statement following the compound statement. A loop set up using the *while* command is called a *while loop*.

There are two other commands in C which are also used to set up program loops. These are called *do while loop* and *for loop*. The use of these loops and the specific occasions when these should be used will also be discussed in this chapter.

12.1   THE *while* LOOP

The general form of the *while* command is:

while (logical expression)

{ s_1 ;
 s_2 ;
 s_3 ;
 ⋮
 s_n ; }
s_f ;

where s_1, s_2, s_3, ..., s_n are C statements. The *while* command orders that statements s_1, s_2, ..., s_n enclosed by braces {} are to be executed again and again as long as the *logical expression* is *true*. When the *logical expression* becomes *false* the program jumps to the statement s_f. The flow chart of Fig. 12.2 illustrates the functioning of the *while loop*. Observe that if the logical expression is false when checked first the statements are not carried out at all even once and the program jumps to the statement s_f outside the loop.

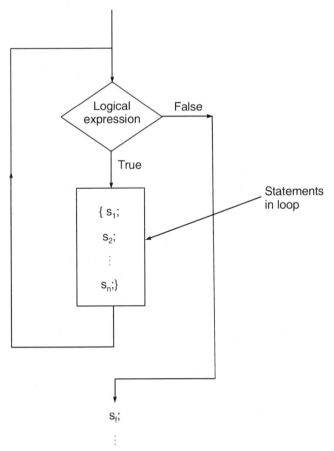

Fig. 12.2 Flow chart illustrating a *while* loop.

We will now give a few examples of using a *while* loop.

EXAMPLE 12.1 Consider Example Program 7.3 which converts Celsius to Fahrenheit temperature. In that program only one Celsius temperature is read and is converted to Fahrenheit. Assume we want to convert Celsius to Fahrenheit for Celsius = –100, –99, –98, ..., 0, 1, 2, 3, ..., 100. In other words we want to tabulate Fahrenheit equivalents of Celsius temperatures of (–100 to +100 in steps of 1 degree Celsius). Example Program 12.3 illustrates how a *while* loop may be used to do this.

```
/* Example Program 12.3 */
/* Program to convert Celsius to Fahrenheit—Illustrating while loop */
#include <stdio.h>

main()
{
    int celsius;
    float fahrenheit;
    scanf("%d", &celsius);
    printf("Celsius    Fahrenheit\n");

    while (celsius <= 100)
       {
          fahrenheit = 1.8 * (float)celsius + 32.0;
          printf("%5d %10.3f\n", celsius, fahrenheit);
          ++celsius;
       }
    printf("End of conversion\n");
}
```

g a   12.3   Celsius to Fahrenheit Conversion—use of *while* loop.

Observe in Example Program 12.3 that we declare Celsius as int as the values for which it is to be converted are integers. Fahrenheit, however, is float as it could have a fractional part. The function scanf reads the initial value of celsius (– 100 in this example). The title for the table is then printed. This is followed by the *while* loop. In this loop fahrenheit is calculated. Observe that celsius is cast into floating point. This is not essential in C language but is a good programming practice. After printing the converted values, celsius is incremented. The statements in the loop are repeatedly executed for celsius value up to and *including* 100. When the celsius value reaches 101 the program leaves the loop and prints the line: End of conversion.

The program may be slightly generalized for tabulating all values of Fahrenheit for all values of Celsius from an initial to a final value as shown in Example Program 12.4.

```
/* Example Program 12.4 */
/* Program to convert Celsius to Fahrenheit for Celsius = initial to final */
#include <stdio.h>

main()
{
    int celsius, initial_celsius, final_celsius; float fahrenheit;
    scanf("%d %d", &initial_celsius, &final_celsius);
    printf("Celsius      Fahrenheit\n");
    celsius = initial_celsius;
    while (celsius <= final_celsius)
        {
            fahrenheit = 1.8 * (float)celsius + 32.0;
            printf("%5d    %10.3f\n", celsius, fahrenheit);
            ++celsius;
        }
    printf("End of conversion\n");
}
```

g a   12.   Celsius to Fahrenheit—variable range.

EXAMPLE 12.2   A procedure to find the average height of boys and girls in a class was given in Chapter 5. It is given again as Procedure 12.1 for ready reference.

PROCEDURE 12.1:   Procedure to find the average height of boys and girls

Step 1:   Initialize counters to accumulate total number of girls and boys and their respective heights

Step 2:   While input data are left repeat Step 3 and Step 4

Step 3:   Read an input line with the data (Roll number, sex code, height)

Step 4:   *If*   sex code = 1 then
            Sum of boys height += height; ++Total boys;
        else
            Sum of girls height += height; ++Total girls;

Step 5:   Average boy height = Sum of boys height / Total boys

Step 6:   Average girl height = Sum of girls height / Total girls

Step 7:   Print Total boys, Average boy height, Total girls, Average girl height

The procedure is converted into a C program in Example Program 12.5. It is assumed that the data is presented in the following form:

Data

2345	1	115.5
2685	2	100.2
2742	1	100.8
2743	2	102.4

End of data set

The program should be general to accommodate any class size as we cannot assume a fixed number of students in a class. We should thus repeat computing total height of boys and girls as long as data remain to be read. The standard I/O library <stdio.h> in which scanf is defined provides a convenient way of detecting whether any data is left in the input data set to be read. When scanf function reaches the end of data a quantity defined as EOF (end of file) is returned to it.

```
/* Example Program 12.5 */

/* Program to find the average height of girls and boys in a class. When no more
      data is left in input a value called EOF (end of file) is returned by the
      scanf function defined in <stdio.h>*
#include <stdio.h>
main()
{
     int  sexcode,  total_girls,  total_boys,  roll_number,  float  height;
     total_girl_height, total_boy_height, av_girl_height, av_boy_height;

     total_girl_height = 0; total_boy_height = 0; total_girls = 0; total_boys = 0;

     while (scanf("%d %d %f", &roll_number, &sexcode, &height) != EOF)
        {
          if (sexcode == 1)
             {
               total_boy_height += height;
               ++total_boys;
             }
          else
             {
               total_girl_height += height;
               ++total_girl;
             }
        }  /* End of while */

     av_boy_height = total_boy_height / (float)total_boys;
     av_girl_height = total_girl_height / (float)total_girls;
     printf("total_boys = %d, av_boy_height = %f\n", total_boys, av_boy_height);
     printf("total_girls = %d, av_girl_height = %f\n", total_girls, av_girl_height);
}    /* End of main */
```

g a   12.   Average height of girls and boys.

In other words

   scanf("%d%d%f \n", &roll number, &sex code, &height)

equals EOF when end of data is reached. Thus we can check whether scanf () = EOF after reading each data line. If no data is found when scanf attempts to read data then EOF is returned to scanf. This is used in the *while* loop in Example Program 12.5.

EXAMPLE 12.3 A procedure was evolved in Chapter 1 to pick the maximum value tender among a group of tenders. The procedure is refined and reproduced as Procedure 12.2.

PROCEDURE 12.2: Procedure to pick maximum value tender among a set of tenders

Step 1: Read tender identity and tender amount
Step 2: max tender = tender amount; max tender identity = tender identity;
Step 3: Perform Steps 4 and 5 as long as the end of the list of tenders is not reached.
Step 4: Read tender identity and tender amount
Step 5: If tender amount > max tender
  then {max tender = tender amount
  max tender identity = tender identity}
Step 6: Write max tender identity and max tender

Procedure 12.2 is converted into a C program and given as Example Program 12.6.

```
/* Example Program 12.6 */
/* Program picks the maximum value tender among a set of tenders. The end of tenders
   is indicated by EOF returned to scanf when no data is left to be read */
#include <stdio.h>

main()
{
    int tender_id, max_id;
    float tender_amount, max_tender = 0;

    while(scanf("%d %f", &tender_id, &tender_amount) != EOF)
        {
        if (tender_amount > max_tender)
            {
                max_tender = tender_amount; max_id = tender_id:
            }
        }   /* End of while */
    printf("Maximum tender_id = %d\n", max_id);
    printf("Maximum amount = %f\n", max_tender);
}  /* End of main */
```

g a   12.   Picking maximum value tender.

12.2 THE *for* LOOP

The *while* loop terminates when the logical expression controlling the loop becomes false. C provides another looping structure which is more general. This structure is realized by a statement called the *for* statement. The general form of *for* statement is:

for (expression 1, expression 2, expression 3)
  { s_1 ;
  s_2 ;
  $\vdots$
  s_n ; }
s_f ;

In the above statement *expression* 1, *expression* 2 and *expression* 3 are legal C expressions. s_1, s_2, ..., s_n are statements in C. Usually *expression* 2 is a logical expression. A flow chart illustrating the execution of the *for* statement is given in Fig. 12.3. Observe that *expression* 1 is executed just before testing the logical expression. The *logical expression* 2 is then tested. If it is *true* the statements $\{s_1, s_2, s_n;\}$ in the loop are executed. After execution of these statements *expression* 3 is evaluated. Control then returns to test logical *expression* 2. As long as logical *expression* 2 is *true* the statements in the loop and *expression* 3 are executed again and again. When *expression* 2 becomes false, control leaves the loop and goes to the statement following the *for* loop.

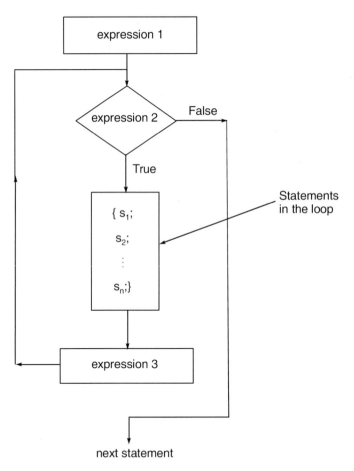

Fig. 12.3   Flow chart illustrating a *for* loop.

The syntax rules allow any one or more of these expressions to be absent. For example, if we write

> for (; expression 2 ;)

it is the same as a *while* loop!

(Observe that the semicolons are essential.)

Thus the *for* loop in C is very general. It is, however, most commonly used when the statements in a loop are to be executed a fixed number of times. For example, one common use is of the type

for (index = initial value; index <= final value; index = index + increment)

$$\{s_1 ; s_2 ; s_3 ; ... ; s_n ;\}$$

one example of this is: for (i = 1 ; i <= n ; ++i)

$$\{s_1 ; s_2 ; s_3 ; ... ; s_n ;\}$$

This is illustrated in Fig. 12.4. We will now give some examples of use of the *for* statement.

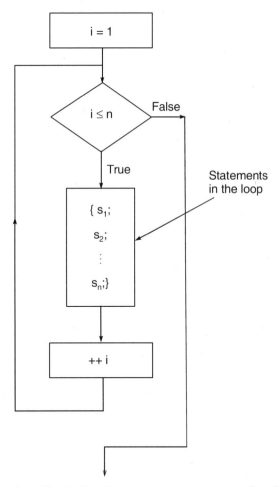

Fig. 12.   Flow chart illustrating the most common use of a *for* loop.

Example 12.3 was written to convert Celsius to Fahrenheit and tabulate it for Celsius temperatures of –100 to +100 in steps of 1 degree Celsius. Example Program 12.4 was written using a *while* statement to do this. We write Example Program 12.7 using a *for* statement to do the same job.

Compare Example Programs 12.4 and 12.7. It is quite obvious that the *for* statement is a more concise notation.

```
/* Example Program 12.7 */
/* This program is derived from Example Program 12.4. It uses a for statement */
#include <stdio.h>

main()
{
    int celsius, initial_celsius, final_celsius, float fahrenheit;

    scanf("%d %d", &initial_celsius, &final_celsius);
    printf("Celsius     Fahrenheit\n");

    for (celsius = initial_celsius;
        celsius <= final_celsius; ++celsius)
      {
         fahrenheit = 1.8 * (float)celsius + 32.0;
         printf("%5d %10.3f\n", celsius, fahrenheit);
      }
    printf("End of conversion\n");
}   /* End of main */
```

g a   12.   Use of *for* loop—Celsius to Fahrenheit conversion.

EXAMPLE 12.4   Assume that the following series is to be summed:

$$\text{Sum} = x - x^3/3! + x^5/5! - x^7/7! + \ldots + (-1)^{n-1} x^{2n-1}/(2n-1)!$$

The first step in evolving a procedure is to obtain a *recurrence relation* which gives the technique of finding a term in a series from previous terms. By inspection of the series:

$$\text{ith term} = (-1)^{i-1} x^{2i-1}/(2i-1)!$$

$$(i-1)\text{th term} = (-1)^{i-2} x^{2i-3}/(2i-3)!$$

Thus ith term $= \{(-1) x^2/(2i-2)(2i-1)\} * (i-1)$th term

Example Program 12.8 uses this recurrence relation to sum the series. Observe that in the *for* statement for *expression* 1 we have used sum = x, term = x, i = 2. This assigns the value of x to sum and term and sets the value of i = 2 before the loop begins. This concise notation is allowed in C. Observe that a comma separates the assignments.

```
/* Example Program 12.8 */
/* This program illustrates use of a for statement */
#include <stdio.h>

main()
{
    int i, n, denominator;
    float x, sum, term;
    scanf("%f %d", &x, &n);
    for (sum = x, term = x, i = 2; i <= n; ++i)
    {
        denominator = (2*i-2) * (2*i-1);
        term *= (-x * x) / (float)denominator;
        sum += term;
    }
    printf("sum = %f, x = %f, n = %d\n", sum, x, n);
}   /* End of main */
```

g a   12.   Summing a series.

EXAMPLE 12.5   Given a set of points (x_1, y_1), (x_2, y_2), ..., (x_n, y_n) it is required to fit a straight line $y = mx + c$ through these points which is the best approximation to these points. In other words, optimal values for m and c in the above equation for the straight line are to be found. A popular criterion is to find the values of m and c which minimize the sum of the squares of the error as given below:

$$(\text{Error})^2 = \Sigma \, [y_i - (mx_i + c)]^2$$

Σ is summation for $i = 1$ to n.

The values of 'm' and 'c' determined using the above criterion are derived in elementary books in statistics and are reproduced below:

$$m = \frac{n \, \Sigma x_i y_i - \Sigma x_i \Sigma y_i}{n \Sigma x_i^2 - (\Sigma x_i)^2}$$

$$c = [\Sigma y_i - m \, \Sigma x_i] / n$$

Σ is summation for $i = 1$ to n.

A computer program which reads in 'n' pairs of values (x, y) and computes m and c is easily written with *for* loops as shown in Example Program 12.9.

Observe that in each pass through the *for* loop a pair of values for x and y is read. The values of x and y are used to form Σx, Σy, Σxy and Σx^2. After all the n values are read and the totals accumulated, control passes out of the *for* loop and the values of m and c are calculated using the formulae given above.

```
/* Example Program 12.9 */
/* This program fits a straight line through n pairs of x and y coordinates.
   The straight line is y = mx + c */
#include <stdio.h>

main()
{
    float sum_x = 0, sum_y = 0, sum_xy = 0, sum_xsq = 0, x, y,
    numerator, denominator, m, c;
    int i, n;

    scanf("%d", &n);        /* number of points read */
    for (i = 1; i <= n; ++i)
      {
        scanf("%f %f", &x, &y);
        sum_x += x;
        sum_y += y;
        sum_xy += x*y;
        sum_xsq += x*x;
      }
    numerator = (float)n * sum_xy - sum_x * sum_y;
    denominator = (float)n * sum_xsq - sum_x * sum_x;
    m = numerator / denominator;
    c = (sum_y - m * sum_x) / (float)n;
    printf("slope m = %f, intercept c = %f\n", m, c);
    printf("y = %f * x + %f\n", m, c);
}   /* End of main */
```

g a   12.   Fitting a straight line through points.

12.3   THE *do while* LOOP

The C programming language provides another looping structure known as *do while*. In this structure the statements in the loop are executed and the testing is done at the end of the loop. The general form of this statement is:

do
$\quad$ { s_1 ;
$\qquad$ s_2 ;
$\qquad$ $\vdots$
$\qquad$ s_n ; }
while (logical expression) ;

The statement commands that the compound statement { s_1 ; s_2 ; ... ; s_n ; } following *do* should be executed repeatedly as long as the logical expression is *true*. When the logical expression becomes *false* the program leaves the loop and goes to the first statement following *while* (logical expression). The looping structure is illustrated in Fig. 12.5. This statement is not commonly used in C programs. There are some situations where it is useful. We give an example of the use of this statement.

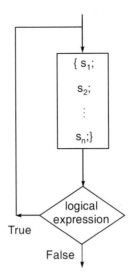

Fig. 12.   Flow chart illustrating a do while loop.

EXAMPLE 12.6   A set of integers is given. It is required to count the number of positive integers, negative integers and zeros in this set. Example Program 12.10 has been written to do this. In this program scanf ("%d", &number) reads a number. In the *do while* loop its sign

```
/* Example Program 12.10 */
/* Program to count the number of negative, zero and positive integers */
#include <stdio.h>

main()
{
    int number, no_positive = 0, no_zero = 0, no_negative = 0;
    scanf("%d", &number);
    do
        {
        if (number > 0)
            ++no_positive;
        else
            if (number == 0)
                ++no_zero;
            else
                ++no_negative;
        }
    while(scanf("%d", &number) != EOF);
    printf("no. of positive numbers = %d\n", no_positive);
    printf("no. of negative numbers = %d\n", no_negative);
    printf("no. of zeros = %d\n", no_zero);
}
```

g a   12.1   Counting negative, zero and positive integers.

is checked and the appropriate counter is incremented. Another number is read within the *while* statement. If the end of data is sensed the control leaves the loop. Observe that the statements in the loop will be executed at least once. Thus we must have at least one number in the input set for the program to work correctly.

There are not many situations when there is a requirement of the loop being executed at least once. Sometimes this may lead to unexpected error if the programmer is careless. Thus it is used rarely.

The *while* and *for* statements are the ones which are normally used.

EXERCISES

12.1 Given an integer, write a program to reverse the order of digits and print the new number. For example, if the given number is 12386 the number printed should be 68321.

12.2 Given a set of integers, write a program to find those which are palindromes. For example the number 123321 is a palindrome as it reads the same from left to right and from right to left.

12.3 Given an octal number (a number with base 8) of arbitrary length, write a program to find its decimal equivalent. For example, the decimal equivalent of the octal number 2673 is

$$2 * 8^3 + 6 * 8^2 + 7 * 8^1 + 3 * 8^0 = 1467$$

12.4 Given any decimal number, write a program to find its octal equivalent For example, the octal equivalent of 242 is 362.

12.5 Given an angle x in radians, write a program to find

$$x \% (\pi/2)$$

Remember that % is a built-in operator valid only for integers.

12.6 Given values for a, b, c and d and a set of values for the variable x, evaluate the function defined by

$$f(x) = ax^2 + bx + c \qquad \text{if } x < d$$
$$f(x) = 0 \qquad \text{if } x = d$$
$$f(x) = -ax^2 + bx - c \qquad \text{if } x > d$$

for each value of x, and print the value of x and f(x). Write a program for an arbitrary number of x values.

12.7 A machine is purchased which will produce earnings of Rs. 1000 per year while it lasts. The machine costs Rs. 6000 and will have a salvage value of Rs. 2000 when it is condemned. If 12 percent per annum can be earned on alternative investments what should be the minimum life of the machine to make it a more attractive investment compared to alternative investments?

12.8 The interest charged in an instalment purchase scheme is to be calculated by a computer program. A tape recorder costs Rs. 2000. A shopkeeper sells it for Rs. 100 down payment and Rs. 100 as a monthly instalment for 21 months. What is the monthly interest charged?

12.9 Write a program which will evaluate the following function for the set of values of x (.5, 1, 1.5, 2, 2.5, 3) and tabulate the results.

$$f = 1 + x^2 / 2! + x^4 / 4! - .50 \sin^2 x + (4 - x^2)^{1/2}$$

Caution: The answer may not be a real number.

12.10 Write a computer program to evaluate the following sum:

$$S = \Sigma (-1)^n \, x^{n/2} / n(n + 1) \qquad \text{for } n = 1 \text{ to } 10$$

12.11 Given a binary number 101101110, write a program to find its decimal equivalent and print it.

12.12 Given a decimal number 5670, write a program to find its binary equivalent and print it.

12.13 Given a decimal number 42.75, write a program to find its binary equivalent and print it.

12.14 The elements of a Pascal's triangle are found using the following formula: The outside elements are all 1s. Each interior element is the sum of the two nearest elements in the row above it, e.g. for n = 5 the elements in the rows are: row 1: 1; row 2: 1, 1; row 3: 1, 2, 1; row 4: 1, 3, 3, 1; row 5: 1, 4, 6, 4, 1. Write a program to find and print the triangle up to row 6 in the form for output given in Exercise 10.6.

13

Defining and Manipulating Arrays

LEARNING OBJECTIVES

In this chapter we will learn:

1. The use of a data structure called an array which may have one or more dimensions.
2. How an array is declared.
3. How data is read into an array.
2. How data stored in arrays is processed.

13.1 ARRAY VARIABLE

The variables considered so far were single entities, that is, each variable name stores one number. There is another type of variable called an *array* variable. An *array* variable name refers to a group of quantities by a single name. Each member in the group is referred to by its position in the group. Suppose a shop stocks different wattages of bulbs and the stock of each wattage bulbs is to be represented. One way of representing this is to make a table:

Wattage:	15 watts	25 watts	40 watts	60 watts	100 watts
Stock:	25	126	300	570	28

We can codify each wattage by a digit and represent the above table as:

Wattage code:	0	1	2	3	4
Stock:	25	126	300	570	28

where 0 represents 15 watts, 1: 25 watts, 2: 40 watts, 3: 60 watts and 4: 100 watts.

We can now represent the stock of bulbs by

$$stock = \{25\ 126\ 300\ 570\ 28\}$$

with the wattage codes not being mentioned explicitly but implied. Stock is an array variable with 5 components.

A particular component of the array is referenced by its position in the array, starting with the 0th position.

Thus   stock [0] = 25
           stock [1] = 126
           stock [2] = 300
           stock [3] = 570
           stock [4] = 28

In memory one location is reserved for each component of the array. The locations are contiguous:

Variable name:	stock[0]	stock[l]	stock[2]	stock[3]	stock[4]
Contents:	25	126	300	570	28

Assume that the cost of each wattage bulb is represented by an array *cost* as shown below:

cost[0] = 3.50 ; cost[l] = 6.50 ; cost[2] = 7.75 ; cost[3] = 8.50 ; cost[4] = 9.50

We will now write a program to find the total cost of bulbs stored in the shop. This is shown in Example Program 13.1. We will now explain this program. The declaration, int stock [5] declares that stock is an array with components 0, 1, 2, 3, 4 (i.e. 5 components) and its components store integers. In the next declaration, cost is declared as an array with 5 components where each component is a floating point number. In the *for* loop the scanf function reads an integer and a floating point number from input and assigns them to stock [0] and cost [0] respectively. In the next statement the product of stock and cost is added to total cost.

The loop is repeated with watt code = 1, 2, 3, 4 and the total cost is computed.

```
/* Example Program 13.1 */
/* Calculation of total cost of bulbs.
   Illustrating use of arrays */
#Include <stdio.h>

main()
{
    int stock[5], watt_code;
    float cost[5], total_cost = 0;

    for(watt_code = 0; watt_code <= 4; ++watt_code)
        {
            scanf("%d%f", &stock[watt_code], &cost[watt_code]);
            total_cost += (float)stock[watt_code] * cost[watt_code];
        }
}   printf("%f\n", total_cost);
```

g a   13.1   rray declaration and use.

Finally the total cost is printed. We now consider another example.

EXAMPLE 13.1   There are fifty students in a class and the marks obtained by each student in an examination are typed on one or more lines. A computer program is required which will print out the highest and the second highest marks obtained in the examination. This problem is a variation of the problem of picking the largest from a set of numbers. In this problem, after picking the largest number in the set, it should be eliminated from further consideration and the remaining numbers searched for the largest. A program to do this is given as Example Program 13.2. The new statements used in this program will be explained below:

The declaration int marks [50] provides information to the compiler that marks is an array with 50 components. Thus 50 locations in memory would be reserved for marks and its components stored in contiguous locations.

```
/* Example Program 13.2 */
/* This program uses arrays. Remember that the numbering of elements in an array
    start from 0 */
#include <stdio.h>

main()
{
    int marks[50], i, first = 0, second = 0;
    for (i = 0; i <=49; ++i)
      scanf("%d", &marks[i]);
    for (i = 0; i <= 49; ++i)
      if (marks[i] > first)
          first = marks[i];
    for (i = 0; i <= 49; ++i)
      if (marks[i] != first)
          if (marks[i] > second)
              second = marks[i];
    printf("First Marks = %4d, Second Marks = %4d\n", first, second);
}
```

g a   13.2   Finding the first and second highest mar s.

The *for* loop

$$for (i = 0 ; i <= 49, ++i)$$

$$scanf (\text{“%d”}, \&marks[i]) ;$$

reads 50 data from one or more lines. The first number is assigned to marks [0], the second number to marks [1], and the successive ones to succeeding components of marks. The next *for* loop picks the highest component of marks and stores it in first. In the third *for* loop all the components of marks equal to the first are skipped and the second highest component picked from among the rest. Instead of using two *for* loops as shown in this solution it is possible to write a program with a single *for* loop. It is also possible to solve this problem without using an array. The reader should try to solve this problem both ways and he would then appreciate the flexibility and power afforded by subscripts or array index.

13.2 SYNTAX RULES FOR ARRAYS

The general form of an array variable is

$$v[i]$$

where v is a variable name which may be of type integer or real and i is a subscript or an array index. The subscript may be any valid integer constant, integer variable name or integer expression. Subscripts may be negative, zero, or positive. Negative subscripts are allowed provided it leads to a meaningful value within the bounds of the array.

i, j, code, $i * 4 - k$, $2 * i/p$ are valid subscripts provided i, j, *code*, k, p are integer variable names. The following are invalid.

$$a[2i], \ c[2.6], \ x[i = p/4], \ p(i)$$

The following are valid.

$$a[2*i], \ b[++i], \ c[9/2], \ d[--k]$$

A declaration of a variable name as representing an array provides information to the C compiler to enable it to:

(i) identify the variable name as an array name.
(ii) reserve locations in memory to store all the components of an array.

Observe that C assumes that the subscripts evaluated during computation will never exceed the size declared in a declaration statement. If this size does exceed, wrong answers may be printed. Thus it is a programmer's responsibility to see that array bounds are not violated.

EXAMPLE 13.2 We will now write a program which interchanges the odd and even components of an array. The program is given as Example Program 13.3.

```
/* Example Program 13.3 */
/* This program interchanges the components of a vector */
#include <stdio.h>

main()
{
    int a[10], i, k, temp;
    for (i = 0; i <= 9; ++i)
       scanf ("%d", &a[i]);
    for (k = 0; k <= 8; k += 2)
       {
           temp = a[k];
           a[k] = a[k+1];
           a[k+1] = temp;
       }
    for (i = 0; i <= 9; ++i)
       printf ("%d", a[i]);
    printf ("\n");
}   /* End of main */
```

g a   13.3   Interchanging components of a vector.

EXAMPLE 13.3   We will now write a program to evaluate a polynomial

$$p(x) = a_n x^n + a_{n-1} x^{n-1} + a_{n-2} x^{n-2} + \ldots + a_1 x + a_0$$

Evaluating this polynomial by writing an arithmetic statement is simple but inefficient. It will require $n(n+1)/2$ multiplication operations and n addition operations. We will use an alternative method of writing the polynomial and write a program to evaluate the polynomial. This method requires only n multiplications and n additions.

$$p(x) = a_0 + a_1 x + a_2 x^2 + \ldots + a_{n-1} x^{n-1} + a_n x^n$$

$$= a_0 + x(a_1 + x(a_2 + x(a_3 + x(a_4 + \ldots x(a_{n-1} + xa_n)))))$$

We start evaluating the expression in the innermost parentheses and successively multiply by x in a *for* loop. The coefficients $a_0, a_1, a_2, \ldots, a_n$ are stored in an array $a[n]$. The program is written as Example Program 13.4.

```
/* Example Program 13.4 */
/* This program evaluates a polynomial upto order 20 */
#include <stdio.h>

main()
{
    int i, n;
    float x, a[20], polynomial;
    scanf("%d %f", &n, &x);
    /* n is the order of the polynomial to be evaluated and is read as input.
    n should be less than or equal to 20 */
    for (i = 0; i <= n; ++i)
      scanf("%f", &a[i]);
    /* a[0], a[1], a[2], .., a[n] typed in one or more lines */
    polynomial = a[n];
    for (i = n; i >= 1; --i)
      polynomial = a[i-1] + x * polynomial;
    printf("x = %f, polynomial value = %f\n", x, polynomial);
}
```

g a   13.   valuating a polynomial.

In Example Program 13.4 we assume that the maximum number of polynomial coefficients is 20. Thus the size of the array *a* storing the coefficients is declared a[20]. As it is desirable to write a general program to evaluate polynomials it would have been nice to declare the array as a[n] with *n* being a variable. C language, however, does not allow using a variable as array size. We thus use 20 as array size and have to state that only polynomial upto order 20 may be evaluated with this declaration. If the order of polynomial is less than 20 then this program will work. We now explain the program. The first *for* loop reads all values of the coefficients of the polynomial into the array *a*. The second *for* loop is traced in Table 13.1.

Table 13.1   racing loop in   ample rogram   .

Index i	Polynomial
Initialization	a[n]
n	a[n − 1] + x * a[n]
n − 1	a[n − 2] + x * (a[n − 1] + x * a[n])
n − 2	a[n − 3] + x * (a[n − 2] + x * (a[n − 1] + x * a[n]))
⋮	
1	a[0] + x * (a[1] + x * (a[2] + x * a[3] + ...)))

Observe that the index starts with *n* and is decremented at the end of each execution of the statement:

$$\text{polynomial} = a[\,i - 1] + x * \text{polynomial} \,;$$

which is the only statement in the *for* loop.

13.3   USE OF MULTIPLE SUBSCRIPTS IN ARRAYS

EXAMPLE 13.4   We introduced the array variable name in the beginning of this chapter by representing stock of bulbs of different wattages in a store by using a code for wattage. The stock was represented by

$$\text{stock} = [25\ 126\ 300\ 570\ 28]$$

where the first element represents the stock of 15 watt bulbs, the second element the stock of 25 watt bulbs, etc.

Assume that the store stocks several brands of bulbs and that each brand is coded by a unique integer. For example, GEC = 0, Philips = 1, Crompton = 2, Surya = 3, Mysore = 4 and Bajaj = 5. The number of bulbs of each category in stock is shown as a matrix in Table 13.2.

Table 13.2   able sho ing stoc position of bulbs

		Watts				
		15 (0)	25 (1)	40 (2)	60 (3)	100 (4)
GEC	(0)	20	15	0	25	60
Philips	(1)	0	22	34	62	0
Crompton	(2)	10	0	25	14	18
Surya	(3)	28	32	0	48	60
Mysore	(4)	43	25	25	34	68
Bajaj	(5)	22	30	41	0	25

The stock of bulbs in each category in the store may be represented by an array variable with two subscripts:

stock[brand-code][watt-code]

where brand-code and watt-code are integers. If we write stock [4][3] it means the stock of bulbs with brand-code = 4 and watt-code = 3, that is, stock of Mysore brand bulbs of wattage 60. This stock is 34 in Table 13.2. As new stocks of bulbs are received by the store, Example Program 13.5 illustrates how it would add this value to the appropriate component of stock [brand code] [watt code].

```
/* Example Program 13.5 */
/* The following small program illustrates how the number of bulbs in stock is
   updated when new stock is received */
#include <stdi0.h>

main()
{
    int stock[6][5], brand_code, watt_code, number;
    while(scanf("%d %d %d", &brand_code, &watt_code, &number)
          != EOF)
    stock[brand_code][watt_code] += number;
}   /* End of main */
```

g a   13.   pdating contents of array.

Data entered on the keyboard gives the brand code, watt code and the number of bulbs. In Example Program 13.5 if the first data indicates that 10 Surya brand 100 watt bulbs have been received, the statement

stock[brand code][watt code] += number ;

would become

stock [3][4] = stock [3][4] + 10 = 60 + 10 = 70

as brand code = 3, watt code = 4 and number = 10. Observe the declaration:

int stock [6][5]

This declaration gives information to the compiler that stock is an integer array name, has two indices or subscripts and the maximum storage required is 5 elements in each row and there are 6 such rows.

13.4   READING AND WRITING MULTIDIMENSIONAL ARRAYS

At the beginning of this chapter we used the following statement:

for(i = 0; i <= 49; ++i)

scanf ("%d", &marks [i]) ;

This statement reads 50 values typed in one or more lines and assigns them respectively to marks [0], marks [1], ..., marks [49]. In other words, the first value from the input line will be assigned to marks [0], the second to marks [1] etc. Data will be read and assigned to *all* 50 components of marks.

More than one array may be read using a scanf statement in a *for* loop. For example, the statement

$$for(i = 0 ; i <= 10 ; ++i)$$

$$scanf (``%d", \&a[i], \&b[i]) ;$$

reads numbers from the input and assigns the first number to a[0], the second number to b[0], the third number to a[1], the fourth to b[1] and so on till the last number is assigned to b[10].

The array declaration in this case must be

$$int \ a[11], \ b[11]$$

Observe that the array size of a and b are 11 as the subscript starts with 0.

We can also initialize one or more arrays in a declaration. For example,

$$int \ a[6] = \{25 \ -40 \ 0 \ 54 \ 90 \ 100\};$$

will store 25 in a[0], –40 in a[1], 0 in a[2], 54 in a[3], 90 in a[4] and 100 in a[5].

If we declare

$$int \ a[6] = \{10\};$$

then 10 will be stored in all the six array elements.

A two-dimensional array is also known as a matrix. In mathematics, a matrix is written as:

$$\text{column}$$
$$\downarrow$$
$$mat = \begin{bmatrix} 6 & -2 & 3 \\ -2 & 3 & 0 \\ 6 & 2 & -9 \\ 5 & 8 & 11 \end{bmatrix} \leftarrow \text{row}$$

This is a (4×3) matrix that is, it has 4 rows and 3 columns. If we write mat(2, 3) it means an element in the second row, third column. In this matrix mat(2, 3) = 0. In general an element in the ith row jth column is written as mat(i, j).

The row index i and the column index j both start with 1. Thus mat(1, 1) = 6 in the above matrix. In contrast C language assumes that indices start with 0. If we want to maintain the mathematical notation in writing C programs with matrices it is better not to use the zero index for row and column. The above matrix will then be declared as

$$int \ mat[5] \ [4] ;$$

This declaration will reserve 5×4 locations in memory (as indices are assumed as 0 to 4 for row and 0 to 3 for column, that is, 5 rows and 4 columns). We will not use the 0th row and the 0th column in the program. Even though this wastes memory space, quite often it leads to less confusion in writing programs involving matrices.

We will now show how values are read from input and assigned to the matrix elements. Example Program 13.6 illustrates this.

```
/* Example Program 13.6 */
/* This program reads a martix and stores in mat.
   mat[i][j] is the ith row and jth column of mat.
   Row and columns start with index 1. mat[1][1] is the element in the first
   row first column of mat */
#include <stdio.h>

main()
{
    int mat[5][4], i, j;
    /* The two for statements read the matrix row-wise */
    for (i = 1; i <= 4; ++i)
        for (j = 1; j <= 3; ++j)
            scanf ("%d", &mat[i][j]);
    /* The matrix is printed row-wise with three numbers in each row */
    printf ("Stored matrix is printed below\n");
    j = 1;
    for (i = 1; i <= 4; ++i)
        printf ("%5d %5d %5d\n",
            mat[i][j], mat[i][j + 1], mat[i][j+2]);
}   /* End of main */

/* Data read one number from each line */
/* Numbers fed from the keyboard */
```

g a   13.   eading and printing a matri

In this program two *for* statements follow one another and are said to be *nested*. The execution of the *for* statements is explained below using the flow chart of Fig. 13.1.

In this program when the first *for* statement is encountered, i is set to 1 and as $i <= 4$, the next *for* statement is taken up for execution. The second *for* statement sets $j = 1$ and as $j <= 3$ it executes the following statement which is scanf.

The scanf statement commands that a number be read from the input and assigned to mat[l][l]. After doing this j is incremented and the scanf statement is executed with $j = 2$ which reads a number from the input and assigns to mat[1][2]. The next number from the input is assigned to mat[1][3]. As $j = 3$ now, control returns to the first *for* statement. As $i <= 4$ this statement increments i which now becomes 2. The second *for* statement is now executed with $j = 1, 2$ and 3 and mat[2][1], mat [2][2] and mat [2][3] are assigned values from the input. Thus input data values should be typed in the order:

$$mat[1][1], \ mat[1][2], \ mat[1][3]$$
$$mat[2][1], \ mat[2][2], \ mat[2][3]$$
$$mat[3][1], \ mat[3][2], \ mat[3][3]$$
$$mat[4][1], \ mat[4][2], \ mat[4][3]$$

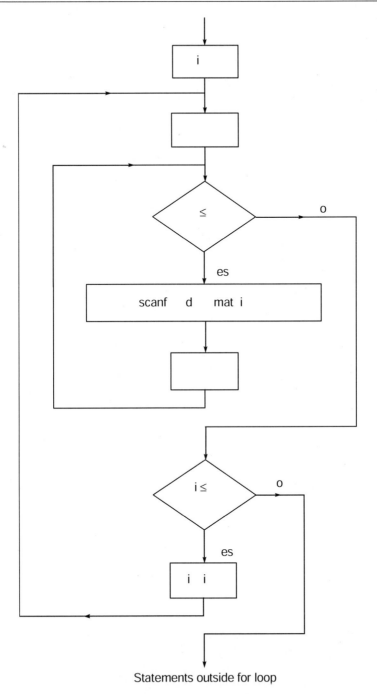

Fig. 13.1   eading a matri ro   ise.

Observe that the array is read row-wise by the above *for* loops. The inner *for* loop is executed 3 times for each value of i. Thus the inner *for* loop executes scanf, twelve times and reads 12 elements of the array. After the data is read into the matrix it is printed row-wise, 3 elements per row, in the next part of the program. Observe that in this part we have used only one *for* loop to increment the row index. The column element indices are calculated within the printf statement.

A scanf statement within two nested *for* loops may also be used to read several, two-dimensional arrays provided they have the same dimensions. For example the statements

$$int \ a[5][3], \ b[5][3] \ ;$$

```
for (j = 1 ; j <= 2 ; ++j)
    for (i = 1; i <= 4 ; ++i)
        scanf ("%d %d", &a[i][j], &b[i][j]) ;
```

will read 16 integers from input and assign them respectively to:

a[1][1], b[1][1], a[2][1], b[2][1], a[3][1], b[3][1],

a[4][1], b[4][1], a[1][2], b[1][2], a[2][2], b[2][2],

a[3][2], b[3][2], a[4][2], b[4][2]

13.5 EXAMPLES OF *for* LOOP WITH ARRAYS

EXAMPLE 13.5 Returning to Example 13.4 assume that besides the stock, the cost of bulbs of various brands is given. We will first read the value of stock and the cost into two matrices. The arrays for stock and cost are given in Table 13.3. Having read these, we will write a program which will:

1. Print out the brand and wattage codes for items out of stock
2. Calculate and print the total cost of bulbs in the inventory.

Table 13.3 Stoc and cost arrays

Brand		Watt					Watt				
		15	25	40	60	100	15	25	40	60	100
		0	1	2	3	4	0	1	2	3	4
GEC	0	20	15	0	25	60	5.5	6.0	4.5	5.0	6.0
Philips	1	0	22	34	62	0	6.0	7.0	7.5	8.0	8.5
Crompton	2	10	0	25	14	18	5.5	5.0	6.0	6.5	7.0
Surya	3	28	32	0	48	60	6.5	6.0	7.0	7.5	8.0
Mysore	4	43	25	25	34	68	5.0	7.5	8.0	7.5	8.0
Bajaj	5	22	30	41	0	25	6.0	5.0	5.5	6.5	7.5
				Stock					Cost		

A program to do this is given as Example Program 13.7. The first pair of *for* statements read data from the input unit and store it in stock [brand code][watt code]. The way data is to be presented is:

20 15 0 25 60 0 22 34 62 0 10 0 25 14 18 etc.

The second pair of *for* statements read from the input unit the cost data and store it in cost [brand code][watt code]. The data is again read starting from the row with brand code = 0 row-wise. We could have written one pair of *for* statement as shown below:

```
for (brand code = 0; brand code <= 5; ++brand code)
    for (watt code = 0; watt code <= 4; ++watt code)
        scanf ("%d%f", &stock[brand code][watt code],
                        &cost [brand code][watt code]);
```

```
/* Example Program 13.7 */
/* This program reads stock and cost arrays, prints out codes of out of stock
   items and the total cost of the inventory */
#include <stdio.h>

main()
{
    int stock[6][5], brand_code, watt_code;
    float cost[6][5], total_cost = 0;
    for (brand_code = 0; brand_code <= 5; ++brand_code)
        for (watt_code = 0; watt_code <= 4; ++watt_code)
            scanf("%d", &stock[brand_code][watt_code]);

    for (brand_code = 0; brand_code <= 5; ++brand_code)
        for (watt_code = 0; watt_code <= 4; ++watt_code)
            scanf("%f", &cost[brand_code][watt_code]);

    for (brand_code = 0; brand_code <= 5; ++brand_code)
        for (watt_code = 0; watt_code <= 4; ++watt_code)
        {
            if (stock[brand_code][watt_code] == 0)
            {
                printf("Item out of stock\n");
                printf("brand_code= %d,watt_code= %d\n", brand_code, watt_code);
            }
            total_cost += (float)(stock[brand_code][watt_code]
                        * cost[brand_code][watt_code]);
        }
    printf("Total inventory cost = %f\n", total_cost);
}
```

g a   13.   Finding the total inventory cost.

In this case the data should be presented as shown below:

$$20 \quad 5.5 \quad 15 \quad 6.0 \quad 0 \quad 4.5 \quad 25 \quad 5.0 \quad 60 \quad 6.0$$
$$0 \quad 6.0 \quad 22 \quad 7.0 \quad 34 \quad 7.5 \quad 62 \quad 8.0 \quad 0 \quad 8.5 \quad \text{etc.}$$

Observe that we have to give the stock data and cost data alternately. There is a possibility of making an error in input. Further, if either a stock data or cost data is to be altered it is difficult to do it if the data is typed as above. We thus preferred to use two pairs of *for* statements in Example Program 13.7.

Having read the data into the arrays, the next pair of *for* statements check each component of stock[brand code][watt code] to detect the components which are zero and give an "out of stock" message in such cases. It then finds the total cost of the stock.

One may have situations where more than two subscripts may be required. In the above example if each wattage bulb also comes in three varieties, say, transparent, translucent and gas filled, then a third subscript which indicates the type of bulb may be used. Thus if transparent is coded 0, translucent as 1 and gas-filled 2 then stock [4][2][2] would mean the stock of Mysore brand, 40 watt, gas-filled bulbs.

EXAMPLE 13.6 A Fibonacci number is defined as follows:

Fibonacci [0] = 0
Fibonacci [1] = 1

Given the above two

$$\text{Fibonacci}[2] = \text{Fibonacci}[1] + \text{Fibonacci}[0]$$

and in general

$$\text{Fibonacci}[i] = \text{Fibonacci}[i - 1] + \text{Fibonacci}[i - 2]$$

Example Program 13.8 generates the first 12 Fibonacci numbers and prints them.

```
/* Example Program 13.8 */
/* Generation of Fibonacci numbers */
#include <stdio.h>

main()
{
    int Fibonacci[12], i;
    /* use definition to initialize */
    Fibonacci[0] = 0; Fibonacci[1] = 1;

    for (i = 2; i <= 11; ++i)
        Fibonacci[i] = Fibonacci[i - 1] + Fibonacci[i - 2];

    for (i = 0; i <= 11; ++i)
        printf("%d\n", Fibonacci[i]);
}
```

g a 13. enerating Fibonacci numbers.

EXAMPLE 13.7   Two matrices are given:

$$[a_{ij}] = \begin{bmatrix} a_{11} & a_{12} & a_{13} \\ a_{21} & a_{22} & a_{23} \end{bmatrix}$$

$$[b_{ij}] = \begin{bmatrix} b_{11} & b_{12} \\ b_{21} & b_{22} \\ b_{31} & b_{32} \end{bmatrix}$$

It is required to multiply these matrices and get the product matrix c_{ij} which is defined as:

$$c_{ij} = \begin{bmatrix} a_{11}b_{11} + a_{12}b_{21} + a_{13}b_{31} & a_{11}b_{12} + a_{12}b_{22} + a_{13}b_{32} \\ a_{21}b_{11} + a_{22}b_{21} + a_{23}b_{31} & a_{21}b_{12} + a_{22}b_{22} + a_{23}b_{32} \end{bmatrix}$$

In general, given a matrix $[a_{ij}]$ with I rows and J columns and a matrix $[b_{ij}]$ with J rows and K columns the product matrix has I rows and K columns. The two matrices $[a_{ij}]$ and $[b_{ij}]$ cannot be multiplied if the number of columns in the first matrix $[a_{ij}]$ does not equal the number of rows of the matrix $[b_{ij}]$.

Example Program 13.9 multiplies two matrices and prints the product matrix. In this program we have declared the matrices a, b and c to have 20 rows and 20 columns each. This is the maximum size allowed in this program. The matrix c[20][20] has been initialized with zeros stored in its components. The first scanf statement reads values for the number of rows and columns of matrices a and b. After that matrices a and b are read column-wise by two pairs of *for* loops. Number of rows and columns of c are now initialized from the known values of the rows and columns of a and b respectively.

```
/* Example Program 13.9 */
/* Program to multiply two matrices. Maximum size of the two matrices is 20 x
   20 each */
#include <stdio.h>
main()
{
    int a[20][20], b[20][20], c[20][20], i, j , k,
        a_rows, a_cols, b_rows, b_cols, c_rows, c_cols;
    scanf("%d %d %d %d", &a_rows, &a_cols, &b_rows, &b_cols);
    printf("%d %d %d %d\n", a_rows, a_cols, b_rows, b_cols);
    /* Matrices a and b are read column-wise */

    for (j = 1; j <= a_cols; ++j)
        for (i = 1; i <= a_rows; ++i)
            scanf("%d", &a[i][j]);

    for (j = 1; j <= b_cols; ++j)
        for (i = 1; i <= b_rows; ++i)
            scanf("%d", &b[i][j]);
```

```
    c_rows = a_rows; c_cols = b_cols;
    /* c[20][20] assumed to be initialized to 0 */

    /* Multiplication performed by following 3 loops */
    for (k = 1; k <= c_rows; ++k)
      for (i = 1; i <= b_cols; ++i)
        for (j = 1; j <= a_cols; ++j)
          c[k][i] += a[k][j] * b[j][i];
/* Matrix c printed row-wise */
    for (k = 1; k <= c_rows; ++k)
      {
        for (i = 1; i <= c_cols; ++i)
          printf("%d", c[k][i]);
        printf("\n");
      }
}
```

g a   13.   atri multiplication.

The next set of three *for* statements perform the matrix multiplication. In Table 13.4 we trace these *for* loops to illustrate how the multiplication is performed. We use the matrices defined at the beginning of this example. Table 13.4 tabulates the values of i, j, k and c[k][i] when the three nested *for* statements are executed.

Table 13.   Illustrating ho   ample   rogram   . does matri multiplication

(max) k = c rows = a rows = 2; (max) i = b cols = 2, (max) j = a cols = 3

k	i	j	c[k][i]
1	1	1	$c_{11} = c_{11} + a_{11}b_{11}$
1	1	2	$c_{11} = a_{11}b_{11} + a_{12}b_{21}$
1	1	3	$c_{11} = a_{11}b_{11} + a_{12}b_{21} + a_{13}b_{31}$
1	2	1	$c_{12} = c_{12} + a_{11}b_{12}$
1	2	2	$c_{12} = a_{11}b_{12} + a_{12}b_{22}$
1	2	3	$c_{12} = a_{11}b_{12} + a_{12}b_{22} + a_{13}b_{32}$
2	1	1	$c_{21} = c_{21} + a_{21}b_{11}$
2	1	2	$c_{21} = a_{21}b_{11} + a_{22}b_{21}$
2	1	3	$c_{21} = a_{21}b_{11} + a_{22}b_{21} + a_{23}b_{31}$
2	2	1	$c_{22} = c_{22} + a_{21}b_{12}$
2	2	2	$c_{22} = a_{21}b_{12} + a_{22}b_{22}$
2	2	3	$c_{22} = a_{21}b_{12} + a_{22}b_{22} + a_{23}b_{32}$

EXERCISES

13.1 Write a program using a *for* loop and an array to solve Exercise 5.10.

13.2 Write a program to obtain the product of the following matrices:

$$A = \begin{bmatrix} 5 & 9 & -2 \\ 8 & 4 & 5 \\ 0 & 4 & 8 \end{bmatrix} \quad B = \begin{bmatrix} 8 & 4 \\ 0 & 5 \\ 5 & 2 \end{bmatrix}$$

13.3 Write a program to transpose the following matrix.

$$A = \begin{bmatrix} -9 & 8 & 7 & 16 & 0 \\ 4 & 13 & 2 & -1 & 5 \\ -9 & 4 & 3 & 1 & -8 \end{bmatrix}$$

13.4 Write a program to rearrange the elements of each row of the above matrix such that the elements of each row are arranged in descending order as shown below:

$$\begin{bmatrix} 16 & 8 & 7 & 0 & -9 \\ 13 & 5 & 4 & 2 & -1 \\ 4 & 3 & 1 & -8 & -9 \end{bmatrix}$$

13.5 Write a program to find the sum of squares of elements on the diagonal of a square matrix.

13.6 Write a program to find if a square matrix is symmetric.

13.7 A factory has 3 divisions and stocks 4 categories of products. An inventory table is updated for each division and for each product as they are received. There are three independent suppliers of products to the factory:

  (i) Design a data format to represent each transaction.
  (ii) Write a program to take a transaction and update the inventory.
  (iii) If the cost per item is also given write a program to calculate the total inventory value.

13.8 The data obtained from life tests of 50 electric bulbs is tabulated below. Write a program to obtain a frequency distribution table conforming to the following specifications:

992	1007	1001	1010	1001
1009	990	1003	1008	999
1014	992	991	1006	998
986	996	1010	1008	1008
998	1004	999	1000	1002
994	1002	1005	1008	1025

(*Contd.*)

1003	981	1014	982	997
1009	1001	988	1018	991
1028	1000	1011	1012	1012
1010	1017	1010	996	996

(i) Put all bulbs with life less than 985 hours in group 1.

(ii) Put all bulbs with life greater than 1024 hours in the last group.

(iii) Divide the region between 985 and 1024 hours into eight intervals such that each interval encompasses a life-time of 5 hours (e.g. 985 to 989 is one interval).

Write a general program so that you can accommodate up to 200 data and 20 class intervals. Read the following from the terminal.

N = No. of data = 50 in this specific case.
Lowlimit = Lowerlimit. All data less than Lowlimit will be put in class 1.
Hilimit = High limit. All data greater than Hilimit will be put in the last class.
Interval = Interval width, it is 5 in this example.
Do all calculations in integer mode.

13.9 Write a program to solve the following simultaneous equations by Gauss method and by Gauss Jordan method. Evaluate the determinant of the matrix of coefficients.

$$x_1 + 2x_2 + 3x_3 = 6$$
$$x_1 + 10x_2 + 4x_3 = -29$$
$$-2x_1 - 4x_2 + x_3 = 9$$

13.10 Economic order quantity may be calculated from the equation

$$Q = (2RS / I)^{0.5}$$

where R is the yearly requirement, S the setup cost and I the carrying cost per item. The values of R, S and I for 15 items in factory are given. Write a program using *for* loop and arrays to calculate the economic order quantity for each of these items.

14

Logical Expressions and More Control Statements

LEARNING OBJECTIVES

In this chapter we will learn:

1. The use of logical operators.
2. The use of *typedef* in C to create new data type names.
3. The use of switch statement when one out of a set of alternate set of statements is to be carried out.
4. The use of break statement to leave a loop if found necessary.
5. The use of continue statement in a loop if one iteration of the loop is to be skipped or partially carried out.

14.1 INTRODUCTION

We have seen in Chapter 11 that float or integer quantities may be connected by relational operators to yield an answer which is True or False. For example the expression

$$marks >= 60$$

would have an answer *true* if marks is greater than or equal to 60 and *false* if marks is less than 60. The result of the comparison (marks >= 60) is called a logical quantity. C provides a facility to combine such logical quantities by *logical operators* to yield *logical expressions*. These logical expressions are very useful in translating intricate problem statements. This is illustrated by the following example:

EXAMPLE 14.1 A university has the following rules for a student to qualify for a degree with physics as the main subject and mathematics as the subsidiary subject:

(i) He should get 50 percent or more in physics and 40 percent or more in mathematics.

(ii) If he gets less than 50 percent in physics he should get 50 percent or more in mathematics. However, he should get at least 40 percent in physics.

(iii) If he gets less than 40 percent in mathematics and 60 percent or more in physics he is allowed to reappear in an examination in mathematics to qualify.

(iv) In all other cases he is declared to have failed.

These rules may be expressed as the decision table of Table 14.1. The rules in Table 14.1 are expressed in Example Program 14.1 which uses logical expressions.

Table 1 .1   A decision table for examination results

| Physics Marks | >= 50 | >= 40 | >= 60 | Else |
Mathematics Marks	>= 40	>= 50	< 40	
Pass	X	X	–	–
Repeat Mathematics	–	–	X	–
Fail	–	–	–	X

```
/* Example Program 14.1 */
/* This program implements Decision Table 14.1 */
#include <stdio.h>

main()
{
   unsigned int roll_no, physics_marks, math_marks;
   while(scanf("%d %d %d", &roll_no, &physics_marks, &math_marks) != EOF)
/* && is logical AND operator and || the logical OR operator */
   {
      if (((physics_marks >= 50) &&
          (math_marks >= 40)) ||
          ((physics_marks >= 40) &&
          (math_marks >= 50)))
        printf("%d %d %d Pass\n", roll_no, physics_marks, math_marks);
      else
         {
            if ((physics_marks >= 60) &&
                (math-marks < 40))
              printf("%d %d %d Repeat Math\n",
                 roll_no, physics_marks, math_marks);
            else
               printf("%d %d %d Failed\n", roll_no, physics_marks, math_marks);
         }
   } /* End while */
}   /* End main */
```

g a   1 .1   Implementing Decision Table 14.1.

Observe the first *if* statement in the program. It is equivalent to the English statement:

If the physics marks is greater than or equal to 50 *and* the mathematics marks is greater than or equal to 40 *or* if the physics marks is greater than or equal to 40 *and* the mathematics marks is greater than or equal to 50 *then* write Pass. The connectives used, namely, *and*(&&), *or* (||) have a well-defined meaning when they operate on logical quantities.

We will now give the rules of syntax for forming logical expressions and the precise nature of the operations &&, ! and ||.

14.2 LOGICAL OPERATORS AND EXPRESSIONS

Programming languages such as Pascal provide a special data type called *boolean* to represent logical quantities which have only true or false values. C language, however, does not have such a data type. Data type *int* is the one which is used to represent logical quantities. In fact more strictly we could use *unsigned short int* to represent logical quantities as they have only two values 0 or 1 representing false and true. For convenience of remembering that some variables are logical quantities, C provides a facility called *typedef* for creating new data type names. Thus if we declare:

typedef unsigned short int Boolean ;

then the name Boolean becomes a synonym for *unsigned short int.* The word Boolean is used to declare logical variables which take on only values 0 or 1. An algebra using such variables was originally proposed by George Boole in the nineteenth century.

Thus if we define:

#define TRUE 1
#define FALSE 0

typedef unsigned short int Boolean ;

Boolean a, b ;

the three logical operators !, && and || which operate on variables a, b may be defined as shown in Table 14.2.

EXAMPLE 14.2   A company has three shareholders—Agarwal, Bhatia and Chamanlal. Agarwal owns 50 shares, Bhatia 30 and Chamanlal 20 shares. For a measure to pass, it must be supported by shareholders the sum of whose holdings exceeds 2/3 of the total shares. A program which will determine if a measure is successful or not and print an appropriate message will now be developed.

Let a 'yes' vote be represented by 1 and a 'No' vote by 0. Let the passage of the measure be indicated by 1 and its failure by 0. A variable name measure passes will be set = 1 by the program if the measure passes and = 0 if it fails. Example Program 14.2 is developed for this problem.

Observe in Example Program 14.2 the statement:

measure passes = (agar vote && bhat vote) || (agar vote && cham vote)

Table 1 .2   Definition of logical operators

Operator	Operation	Definition symbol		
!	Complement or negation (not)	a	!a	
		TRUE	FALSE	
		FALSE	TRUE	
&&	Logical Intersection (and)	a	b	a && b
		FALSE	FALSE	FALSE
		FALSE	TRUE	FALSE
		TRUE	FALSE	FALSE
		TRUE	TRUE	TRUE
||	Logical Union (or)	a	b	a || b
		FALSE	FALSE	FALSE
		FALSE	TRUE	TRUE
		TRUE	FALSE	TRUE
		TRUE	TRUE	TRUE

```
/* Example Program 14.2 */
/* Illustrating the use of logical operators */
#include <stdio.h>

main()
{
    typedef unsigned int Boolean;
    Boolean agar_vote, bhat_vote, cham_vote, measure_passes;

    while(scanf("%u %u %u", &agar_vote, &bhat_vote, &cham_vote) != EOF)
      {
        printf("%d %d %d\n", agar_vote, bhat_vote, cham_vote);
        measure_passes = (agar_vote && bhat_vote)
        || (agar_vote && cham_vote);
        if (measure_passes)
           printf("Measure Passes\n");
        else
           printf("Measure Fails\n");

      }  /* End while */
}  /* End main */
```

g a   1 .2   Use of logical operators.

The expression on the right of = will be TRUE (i.e. 1) if and only if agar vote = 1 and bhat vote = 1 or agar vote = 1 and cham vote = 1.

It may thus also be written as:

measure passes = agar vote && (bhat vote || cham vote)

In the statement

    if (measure passes)
        printf ("Measure Passes \n") ;
    else
        printf ("Measure Fails\n") ;

the program will print Measure Passes if measure passes is TRUE, else it will print Measure Fails.

14.3 PRECEDENCE RULES FOR LOGICAL OPERATORS

The precedence or hierarchy rules in evaluating logical expressions will be explained in this section with examples.

EXAMPLE 14.3 Consider the following expression where a, b, x, y are integers

$$a > b * 4 \text{ \&\& } x < y + 6$$

Even though syntactically the above expression is correct, it is difficult to interpret. It is better to use parentheses and write it as:

$$(a > b * 4) \text{ \&\& } (x < y + 6)$$

In the above example, the expressions within the parentheses are evaluated first. The arithmetic operations are carried out before the relational operations. Thus $b * 4$ is calculated and after that a is compared with it. Similarly $y + 6$ is evaluated first and then x is compared with it.

In general within parentheses:

1. The unary operations, namely, $-$, $++$, $- -$, ! (logical not) are performed first.
2. Arithmetic operations are performed next as per their precedence.
3. After that the relational operations in each of the subexpressions are performed, each subexpression will be either 0 or non-zero. If it is zero it is taken as *false* else it is taken as *true*.
4. These logical values are now operated on by the logical operators.
5. Next the logical operation && is performed.
6. The logical *or* operation, namely, || is performed next.
7. Lastly the evaluated expression is assigned to a variable name as per the assignment operator.

EXAMPLE 14.4

$$!(a > b / 3) \text{ || } (c != d / 3) \text{ \&\&} (d < 5)$$

Here a > b / 3, c != d / 3, and d < 5 are evaluated first !(a > b / 3) is then found. Next (c != d / 3) is *anded* with the result of (d < 5).

The result is *ored* with the result of !(a > b | 3).

If a = 8, b = 6, c = 3, d = 8 the result is:

(8 > 6 / 3) = 1 (true)
(3 != 8 / 3) = 1 (true)
(8 < 5) = 0 (false)
!(8 > 6 / 3) = !(1) = 0
(3!= 8 / 3) && (8 < 5) = (1) && (0) = 0

Finally, 0 || 0 = 0

EXAMPLE 14.5

(a – 5.5 >= 9.5) || (c < d) && (x >= y)

Given a = 15.0, c = 6.0, d = 4.0, x = 3.0 and y = 4.0

(a – 5.5) >= 9.5 is *true*
(c < d) = (6.0 < 4.0) is *false*
(x >= y) = (3.0 >= 4.0) is *false*

As per precedence we do the && operation first:

(6.0 < 4.0) && (3.0 >= 4.0) = *false* && *false* = *false*

The || operation is done next:

true || *false* = *true*

which is the result.
If the expression had been

((a – 5.5 >= 9.5) || (c < d)) && (x >= y)

then the result would be *false*.
A summary of precedence rules is given in Table 14.3.

Table 1 .3   Illustrating precedence of operators in C

Highest Precedence (Done first)	Parenthesised subexpressions – (unary negation) ++ – – !
	* / %
	+ –
	< <= > >=
	== !=
	&&
Lowest Precedence (Done last)	||
	=

14.4 SOME EXAMPLES OF USE OF LOGICAL EXPRESSIONS

EXAMPLE 14.6 We will consider again Example 5.5 for which a decision table was given in Chapter 5. It is reproduced as Table 14.4 for ready reference.

Table 1 .   A decision table for declaring results

Conditions	Rules					
Main Marks	≥ 50	≥ 40	≥ 60	≥ 40	≥ 40	Else
Anc. Marks	≥ 40	≥ 50	< 40	≥ 40	< 40	
Special Status	No	No	No	Yes	Yes	
Actions						
Pass	X	X	–	X	–	–
Repeat Anc.	–	–	X	–	X	–
Fail	–	–	–	–	–	X

A program which corresponds to Table 14.4 is given as Example Program 14.3. In this program it is assumed that each line of input has the roll number of candidate and his/her marks in the main and ancilliary subject. Status = 1 is used to indicate special status. When end of students' data is reached scanf returns EOF and this is used to terminate the *while* loop. Observe the use of logical expressions and connectives in the program.

```
/* Example Program 14.3 */
/* Illustrates the use of Decision Table */
#include <stdio.h>
main()
{
    typedef unsigned int Boolean;
    int roll_no, main_marks, anc_marks;
    Boolean pass, repeat_anc, c1, c2, c3, c4, c5, status;
    printf(    "Roll No.  Main Marks  Anc. Marks");
    printf(  "Status\n");
    while(scanf("%u %u %u %u", &roll_no, &main_marks,
        &anc_marks, &status) ! = EOF)
    {
        c1 = (main_marks >= 50);
        c2 = (main_marks >= 40);
        c3 = (main_marks >= 60);
        c4 = (anc_marks >= 50);
        c5 = (anc_marks >= 40);
        pass = (c1 && c5) || (c2 && c4) ||
                (c2 && c5 && status);
        repeat_anc = (c3 && !c5) ||
                    (c2 && !c5 && status);
```

```
        if (pass)
           printf("%10d %10d %10d %10d PASS\n",
                   roll_no, main_marks, anc_marks, status);
        else
           {
             if (repeat_anc)
                printf("%10d %10d %10d %10d REP. ANC\n",
                       roll_no, main_marks, anc_marks, status);
             else
                printf("%10d %10d %10d %10d FAIL\n",
                       roll_no, main_marks, anc_marks, status);
           }
    }  /* End while */
}  /* End main */
```

g a   1 .3 Implementing Decision Table 14.4.

EXAMPLE 14.7   A program is to be written to decide whether on a given date an employee in an organization has completed 1 year service. In order to do this a line is typed for each employee containing the data: employee number, day of joining, month of joining and year of joining. The form in which data in input is shown in Table 14.5.

Table 1 .   Data input for Example 14.7

Data	Explanation
09 08 1992	Today's date
3452 08 09 1990	
3462 09 08 1991	Employees' data
3672 08 07 1990	
3792 09 01 1992	

A decision table to decide whether an employee has completed one year's service is given in Table 14.6.

Table 1 .   Decision Table to decide completion of one year's service

	> 1	= 1	= 1	E
Diff. in year	> 1	= 1	= 1	E
Diff. in month	–	> 0	= 0	L
Diff. day	–	–	≥ 0	S
				E
One year service completed?	Yes	Yes	Yes	No

The conditions checked in Table 14.6 are:

1. Difference between today's year and the year an employee joined.
2. Difference between today's month and the month an employee joined.
3. Difference between today's day and the day an employee joined.

The reader can convince himself about the correctness of the table by fixing today's date and trying a number of cases of joining dates.

A program which implements Table 14.6 is given as Example Program 14.4. The reader would notice the simplicity of writing a program corresponding to the decision table.

```
/* Example Program 14.4 */
/* Program to check completion of one year's service */
#include <stdio.h>

main()
{
    int emp_no, day, month, year, today, tod_month,
      tod_year, dif_day, dif_month, dif_year;

    scanf("%d%d%d", &today, &tod_month, &tod_year);
    printf(" Emp.No.      Day       Month");
    printf("     Year      Eligible or not\n");
    while(scanf("%d %d %d %d", &emp_no, &day, &month, &year) != EOF)
      {
        dif_day = today - day;
        dif_month = tod_month - month;
        dif_year = tod_year - year;
        if ((dif_year > 1) || ((dif_year == 1) &&
            (dif_month > 0)) || ((dif_year == 1) &&
            (dif_month == 0) && (dif_day >= 0)))
            printf("%10d %10d %10d %10d Eligible\n",
                   emp_no, day, month, year);
        else
            printf("%10d %10d %10d %10d Not Eligible\n",
                   emp_no, day, month, year);
      }  /* End of while */
}   /* End of main */
```

g a   1 .   Completion of one year service.

14.5   THE *switch* STATEMENT

A control statement called the *switch* statement is available in C. It is useful when one out of a set of alternative actions is to be taken based on the value of an expression.

It is particularly useful when variable values are classified with codes. We will first illustrate the use of a switch statement with an example.

EXAMPLE 14.8   A company manufactures three products: engines, pumps and fans. They give a discount of 10 percent on order for engines if the order is for Rs. 5000 or more. The same discount of 10 percent is given on pump orders of value of Rs. 2000 or more and on fan orders for Rs. 1000 or more. On all other orders they do not give any discount. A program which implements this policy is given next.

Assume that the following codes are used to indicate the product:

Code 1 for engines
Code 2 for pumps
Code 3 for fans

A data is made up for each order with its serial number, the product code followed by the amount of order. For example if the order has serial number 2527 and is for pumps worth Rs. 2500 the data will be shown as:

2527 2 2500.00

A decision table showing the above discount policy is given as Table 14.7.

Table 1 .   Decision Table for discount policy

Product Code Order Amount	1 >= 5000	2 >= 2000	3 >= 1000	Else
Discount	10%	10%	10%	0%

A computer program using only *if* statements to implement the above decision table is given as Example Program 14.5.

```
/* Example Program 14.5 */
/* Discount calculation example using logical if
   The decision table of Table 14.7 is used */
#include <stdio.h>

main()
{
    int serial_no, code;
    float amount, discount, net_amount;
    printf(" Serial No.      Code      Discount");
    printf("      Net amount\n");
    while(scanf ("%d %d %f", &serial_no, &code, &amount) != EOF)
    {
        discount = 0.0;
        if (code == 1)
            if (amount >= 5000.0)
                discount = 0.1;
        if (code == 2)
            if (amount >= 2000.0)
                discount = 0.1;
        if (code == 3)
            if (amount >= 1000.0)
                discount = 0.1;
        if ((code < 1)||(code > 3))
            printf("CODE ERR, SER. NO. = %d, CODE = %d\n", serial_no, code);
        net_amount = amount * (1.0 - discount);
        printf("%10d %10d %10.2f %10.2f\n",
                serial_no, code, discount, net_amount);
    } /* End of while */
} /* End of main */
```

g a   1 .   Discount calculation.

In Example Program 14.5 observe that if (code == 1) is *true* and amount is >= 5000 discount is assigned 0.1. After this instead of reading the next data line the program will continue sequentially and execute the statement if (code == 2). This could have been avoided by using an *else*. The nesting of *ifs* with *elses* will make the program difficult to read and undetstand. The program as it is written is inefficient but somewhat easier to understand. As such nested *ifs* occur often in practice, a statement known as *switch* is available in C which is useful to write such programs. The same problem is solved with the program given as Example Program 14.6.

```
/* Example Program 14.6 */
/* Discount calculation example using switch statement */
#include <stdio.h>
main()
{
    int serial_no, code;
    float amount, discount, net_amount;
    printf(" Serial No.      Code      Discount");
    printf("      Net amount\n");
    while(scanf("%d %d %f\n", &serial_no, &code, &amount) != EOF)
        (discount = 0
            switch(code)
                {
                case 1:
                    if (amount >= 5000.0)
                        discount = 0.1;
                    break;
                case 2:
                    if (amount >= 2000.0)
                        discount = 0.1;
                    break;
                case 3:
                    if (amount >= 1000.0)
                        discount = 0.1;
                    break;
                default:
                    printf("ERR, SER. NO. = %d, CODE = %d\n", serial_no, code);
                    discount = 0.0;
                    break;
                }
            net_amount = amount * (1.0 - discount);
            printf("%10d %10d %10.2f %10.2f\n",
                    serial_no, code, discount, net_amount);
        } /* End of while */
}   /* End of main */
```

g a 1 . Implementing Decision Table 14.7.

In this program the statement

switch (code)

will transfer control to case 1 if code == 1, to case 2 if code == 2 and to case 3 if code == 3. If code is less than 1 or greater than 3 then control will go to default. If code == 2, for example, then control will go to case 2. The statements following case 2 will be executed. In this case the statement if (amount >= 2000.0) is *true* discount will be assigned the value 0.1. Observe that the next statement is *break*. This statement commands that all the statements following within the domain of the switch statement, namely, those up to closing braces } of the switch statement should not be executed. Control should go to the statement following the closing braces } of the switch statement, namely the statement:

$$\text{net amount} = \text{amount} * (1.0 - \text{discount}) ;$$

The *break* statement is very important in this problem. If *break* was not written in case 2: control would go sequentially to the following statements and perform the statements following case 3: and default: The answer will thus be incorrect.

We will now explain the syntax and semantics of the switch statement.

Syntax rules for *switch* statement

The general form of the switch statement is given below:

```
switch (expression)
  {
      case constant 1:
          S₁₁ ;
          S₁₂ ;
          ⋮
          break ;
      case constant 2:
          S₂₁ ;
          S₂₂ ;
          ⋮
          break,
          ........
          ........
      case constant n:
          Sₙ₁ ;
          Sₙ₂ ;
          ⋮
          break ;
      default:
          S_dl ;
          S_d2 ;
          S_dn ;
          break ;
  }
```

In the *switch* statement the expression can be an integer expression or a constant. It is evaluated and compared with constant 1, constant 2, ..., constant n. If it matches, say, constant 2 then the statements s_{21}; s_{22}; s_{23}; ... etc. are executed till *break* is reached. When break is encountered the program jumps to the statement following the closing braces } of the *switch* statement. If the value of the expression is not equal to any one of constant 1, constant 2, ... constant n, then control passes to *default* and the statements s_{d1}; s_{d2}; ...; s_{dn}; following *default* are executed. As *default* is the last option in the domain of the *switch* statement, no *break* statement is required in default. We have, however, used break as it will not do any harm. If we sometime want to add another case, the presence of break will prevent us from making an accidental error. Constant 1, constant 2, constant n should be integers. They should all be distinct. In other words, they should not have the same value. If *break* is omitted in any of the cases, execution continues with the statements of the following case until the closing brace } of the switch statement is reached. If a *break* is encountered before the closing brace } the statements following the *break* are not executed and control leaves the domain of the *switch* statement.

We give below some legal *switch* statements:

```
int i, h
```

(i) switch (i * i + 4)

```
    {
        case 5 :
            ++k ;
            break ;
        case 8 :
            k += 8 ;
            break ;
    }
```

If i = 2 and k = 4 then i * i + 4 = 8. The program branches to case 8 : k is set to 12 and control passes to the statement following *switch*.

If i = 3 the expression i * i + 4 = 13. None of the constants in this case match. Thus control goes to the statement following switch doing nothing. If default action is specified it would have carried it out.

(ii) int i, k ;

```
    i = 2 ; k = 3 ;
    switch (i - k)
        {
            case 1:
                ++i ;
                ++k ;
                /* WRONG missing break */
            case 2:
                --i ;
                ++k ;
                /* WRONG missing break */
```

```
            default:
                i += 3 ;
                k += i ;
    }
```

This is a legal *switch* statement syntactically. In this case (i − k) when evaluated gives − 1. Thus case 1 is satisfied. A negative constant is legal. The integers *i* and *k* are incremented. *i* becomes 3 and *k* become 4. As there is no *break* the following statements are executed including those following default. Thus finally *i* becomes 5 and *k* becomes 10. Semantically this is a wrong *switch* statement as the programmer possibly wanted to distinguish between cases with (i − k) = −1 and 2.

```
(iii) int i, j, k ;
        scanf("%d%d%d", &i, &j, &k) ;
        switch (i + j − k)
            {
                case 0 : case 2: case 4 :
                    ++i ;
                    k += j ;
                    break ;
                case 1 : case 3 : case 5 :
                    −− i ;
                    k −= j ;
                    break ;
                default :
                    i += j ;
                    break ;
            }
```

Observe that in the above *switch* statement a set of statements are to be executed in many cases. This is allowed by C.

The following are some illegal *switch* statements.

```
(i)    float a ;
        switch (a)
            {
                case 2.5 :
                    b += 2.3 ;
                    break ;
                case 3.2 :
                    b −= 2.8 ;
            }       break ;
        (A floating point constant in this case not allowed.)
```

(ii)   int i, j ;
       switch (i – j + 3)
          {
              case 2 : 3 :
                 j += 6 ;
                 break ;
              case 4 :
                 i –= 4 ;
                 break ;
          }
(only one constant allowed in this case)

It should be written as:
       case 2 : case 3 :
          j += 6 ;
          break ;

(iii) int i, j ;
       switch (i + j) ;
          {
              case 2 :
                 i += 4 ;
                 break ;
              case 4 :
                 i –= 4 ;
                 break ;
          }
(Semicolon after *switch* statement is illegal.)

(iv) int i, j ;
       switch (i + j + 6)
          {
              case 2 :
                 i += 4 ;
                 break ; }
              case 3 :
                 i –= 4 ;
          }
Illegal closing braces } after break

EXAMPLE 14.9   In Chapter 11 we gave a program (Example Program 11.4) to solve a quadratic equation:

$$ax^2 + bx + c = 0$$

We identified three cases, namely, the discriminant $(b^2 – 4ac) < 0$, $(b^2 – 4ac) = 0$ and $(b^2 – 4ac) > 0$. We used *logical if* statements in that example to write the program. We now rewrite the program (as Example Program 14.7) using the *switch* statement. We first assign a value 1, 2 or 3 to an index i depending on the value of (b^2 − 4ac). This index is used in a *switch* statement to branch to the appropriate compound statement. This program is clearer compared to Example Program 11.4. This program will work for any set of values of (a, b, c).

```
/* Example Program 14.7 */
/* Quadratic Equation Solution */
#include <stdio.h>
#include <math.h>
main()
{
    float a, b , c, discrmnt , x_mag_1, x_mag_2,
    x_real_1, x_real_2, temp;
    int i;
    while(scanf("%f %f %f", &a, &b, &c) != EOF)
        {
            printf("a = %f, b = %f, c = %f\n", a, b, c);
            discrmnt = b * b - 4.0 * a * c;
            if (discrmnt < 0)
            i = 1;
            else
                {
                    if (discrmnt == 0)
                        i = 2;
                    else
                        i = 3;
                }
            switch (i)
                {
                case 1:
                    discrmnt = -discrmnt;
                    x_imag_1 = sqrt(discrmnt) / (2.0 * a);
                    x_imag_2 = -x_imag_1;
                    x_real_1 = -b / (2.0 * a);
                    printf("Complex conjugate roots\n");
                    printf("real part = %16.8e\n", x_real_1);
                    printf("imaginary part = %16.8e\n", x_imag_1);
                    break;
                case 2:
                    x_real_1 = -b / (2.0 * a);
                    printf("Repeated roots\n");
                    printf("Real roots = %16.8e\n", x_real_1);
                    break;
                case 3:
                    temp = sqrt (discrmnt);
                    x_real_1 = (-b + temp) / (2.0 * a);
                    x_real_2 = (-b - temp) / (2.0 * a);
                    printf("Real roots\n");
                    printf("real root_1 = %16.8e\n", x_real_1);
                    printf("real root_2 = %16.8e\n", x_real_2);
                    break;
                } /* End switch */
        } /* End while */
}   /* End of main */
```

g a   1 .   Solving quadratic equation—use of switch statement.

EXAMPLE 14.10 Suppose the rates of tax on gross income are as shown in Table 14.8.

Table 1 . Table of tax rates

Income	Tax
< Rs. 10,000	Nil
Rs. 10,000 to Rs. 19,999	10 percent
Rs. 20,000 to Rs. 29,999	15 percent
Rs. 30,000 to Rs. 49,999	20 percent
> Rs. 50,000	25 percent

A program is required to compute the tax. A simple programming technique may be used to code the slab in which a particular income is to be placed. Suppose we divide the income by 10000 as shown below:

$$\text{slab code} = \text{income} / 10000$$

Then for Income < 10000, slab code = 0,

    for 20000 > Income >= 10000, slab code = 1
    for 30000 > Income >= 20000, slab code = 2
    for 50000 > Income >= 30000, slab code = 3 or 4
and   for Income >= 50000, slab code > 5

Observe that if the income > 50000 then slab code > 5. Thus if we want to use a switch statement with slab-code as case index then we should map these values to one index. This is done in Example Program 14.8.

Observe that the two cases slab code = 3 and slab code = 4 in which the action is identical can be put together and this is done in Example Program 14.8.

14.6 THE *break* STATEMENT

We have used a statement called *break* in a *switch* statement to skip statements within the domain of the *switch* statement. This statement can also be used within *while, for* and *do while* loops to abandon processing and leave the loop. We will illustrate this with an example.

EXAMPLE 14.11 We are given a set of *n* numbers, a[0], a[l], a[2], a[3], ..., a[n – 1]. It is stated that they are in strictly ascending order. A program is to be written to check this.

If the numbers are in strictly ascending order then a[i + 1] > a[i] for i = 0 to (n – 2). If for any *i* this is not true we should give a message and stop further checking. This procedure is coded as Example Program 14.9. In the following *for* loop

```
/* Example Program 14.8 */
/* Illustrating the use of switch statements */
#include <stdio.h>
main()
{
    int slab_code, income, account_no;
    float tax_rate, tax ;
    printf("Account No.   Income      Tax\n");
    while(scanf("%d %d", &account_no, &income) != EOF)
        {
            slab_code = income / 10000;
            if (slab_code >= 5)
                slab_code = 5;
            switch(slab_code)
                {
                case 0:
                    tax_rate = 0;
                    break;
                case 1:
                    tax_rate = 0.1;
                    break;
                case 2:
                    tax_rate = 0.15;
                    break;
                case 3:
                case 4:
                    tax_rate = 0.2;
                    break;
                case 5:
                    tax_rate = 0.25;
                    break;
                } /* End of switch */
            tax = (float)income * tax_rate;
            printf ("%10d %10d %10.2f\n", account_no, income, tax);
        }  /* End of while */
    printf("end of input data\n");
}   /* End of main */
```

g a   1 .   Tax calculation.

```
for (i = 0; i <= n - 2; ++i)
    {
        if (a[i + 1] > a[i])
            ascending = 1 ;
        else {ascendmg = 0 ;
            break ;}
    }
```

if for any *i*, a[i + 1] <= a[i] the numbers are not in ascending order. The *break* statement in the *if* statement of the loop commands control to leave the loop. When control leaves the loop

```
/* Example Program 14.9 */
/* Program checks whether a set of numbers are in ascending order */
#include <stdio.h>

main()
{
    int a[10], i, n, ascending;
    scanf("%d", &n);
    for(i = 0; i <= n - 1; ++i)
        scanf ("%d", &a[i]);
    for (i = 0; i <= n - 2; ++i)
        {
        if (a[i+1] > a[i])
            ascending = 1;
        else
            {
            ascending = 0;
            break;
            }
        }
    if (ascending)
        printf("Numbers in ascending order\n");
    else
        printf("Numbers not in ascending order\n");
}   /* End of main */
```

g a   1 .   Checking ascending order of numbers.

it reaches the statement following the loop statement. This statement prints the appropriate message.

We can similarly leave a *while* loop. The most common use of break, however, is in switch statement.

14.7   THE *continue* STATEMENT

There is a statement in C called *continue* which is used to skip executing statements in a loop following it. A *break* abandons processing in a loop and gets out of it. *Continue* statement, however, continues processing the loop from the next iteration. We will illustrate the use of *continue* statement with an example.

We wrote a program (Example Program 14.7) to solve the quadratic equation

$$ax^2 + bx + c = 0$$

We assumed that the coefficient a is not equal to zero. If a equals zero then the equation is a linear equation and Example Program 14.7 will not work. We will now generalize the program to include the possibility of a = 0. This program is given as Example Program 14.10. If a = 0 the equation is linear and the solution is x = – c / b. Once this solution is found

```
/* Example Program 14.10 */
/* Quadratic Equation Solution—Use of continue */
#include <stdio.h>
#include <math.h>
main()
{
    float a, b, c, discrmnt, x_imag_1, x_imag_2,
    x_real_1, x_real_2, temp, x;
    int i;
    while(scanf("%f %f %f", &a, &b, &c) != EOF)
        {
        printf("a = %f, b = %f, c = %f\n", a, b, c);
        if (a == 0.0)
            {
            printf("a = 0, Equation is linear\n");
            x = -c/b;
            printf("Solution is : x = %f\n", x);
            continue;
            }
        discrmnt = b*b - 4.0*a*c;
        if (discrmnt < 0)
            i = 1;
        else
            {
            if (discrmnt == 0)
                i = 2;
            else
                i = 3;
            }
        switch (i)
            {
            case 1:
                discrmnt = -discrmnt;
                x_imag_1 = sqrt(discrmnt) / (2.0 * a);
                x_imag_2 = -x_imag_1;
                x_real_1 = -b / (2.0 * a);

                printf("Complex conjugate roots\n");
                printf("real part = %16.8e\n", x_real_1);
                printf("imaginary part = %16.8e\n", x_imag_1);
                break;
            case 2:
                x_real_1 = -b / (2.0 * a);
                printf("Repeated roots\n");
                printf("Real roots = %16.8e\n", x_real_1);
                break;
            case 3:
                temp = sqrt(discrmnt);
                x_real_1 = (-b + temp) / (2.0 * a);
                x_real_2 = (-b - temp) / (2.0 * a);
                printf("Real roots\n");
```

```
        printf("real root_1 = %16.8e\n"; x_real_1);
        printf("real root_2 = %16.8e\n", x_real_2);
        break;
   } /* End switch */
  } /* End while */
} /* End of main */
```

ga 1 .1 Quadratic equation solution—use of continue.

continue is used to skip the rest of the processing in the loop. Control returns to the *while* statement to process the next set of values.

Continue statement may also be used in a *for* loop. The effect of using *continue* in a *for* loop is illustrated in Example Program 14.11. In this program *continue* is used to prevent division by zero. Observe that the loop is carried out 4 times as the index *i* is incremented and checked for termination condition after each looping by the *for* statement.

```
/* Example Program 14.11 */

#include <stdio.h>
main()
{
    int i, k, p;

    for(i = 0, i <= 4; ++i)
      {
          scanf("%d", &p);
          if (p == 0)
             continue;
          k = 1/p;
          printf("k = %d i = %d p = %d\n", k, i, p);
      }
    printf("out of loop\n");
}
```

ga 1 .11 Illustrates the use of continue in a for loop.

EXERCISES

14.1 The policy followed by a company to process customer orders is given by the following rules:

   (i) If a customer order is less than or equal to that in stock and his credit is OK, supply his requirement.
   (ii) If his credit is not OK do not supply. Send him an intimation.
   (iii) If his credit is OK but the item in stock is less than his order, supply what is in stock. Intimate to him the date the balance will be shipped.

   Obtain a decision table corresponding to these rules. Write a C Program to implement the decision table.

14.2 Obtain a decision table corresponding to Exercise 11.10. If a set of data is given with each data having a customer account number, amount of deposit and period of deposit, write a program which will give as output customer's account number, amount of deposit, period of deposit, interest accrued to the account and total amount in the customer's account.

14.3 Given the date an employee joined a job in the firm: Day/Month/Year and given today's date, write a program to find out whether the given joining date of an employee is a legal date. For example a date such such as 10/14/81 is illegal as the month cannot exceed 12. If the today's date is 17/5/82, an year such as 95 or 30 would be illegal. Further, depending on the month, the range of valid days may be determined.

14.4 In Chapter 5 a decision table was to be developed for Exercise 5.13. Write a program to implement this decision table.

14.5 A certain steel is graded according to the results of three tests. The tests are:

   (i) Carbon content < 0.7 percent
   (ii) Rockwell hardness > 50
   (iii) Tensile strength > 30,000 kilo/cm^2

The steel is graded 10 if it passes all three tests, 9 if it passes only tests 1 and 2, 8 if it passes only test 1, and 7 if it passes none of the tests. Obtain a flow chart corresponding to this statement of the problem. Write a program corresponding to this flow chart.

Obtain a decision table corresponding to this problem. Is an action specified for all the eight possible rules corresponding to the outcomes of the three condition tests? Discuss the difference between the flow chart and decision table formulations. Write a C program corresponding to the decision table.

14.6 Obtain decision tables for simulating an automatic stamp vending machine with the following specifications:

   (i)   It should dispense 25, 15 and 10 paise stamps.
   (ii) It should accept 50, 25, 10 and 5 paise coins.
   (iii) It can accept not more than one coin for each transaction.
   (iv) If more than one coin of the same denomination is to be returned as change after dispensing the stamp, the machine cannot do it. Instead the coin should be returned and a 'no change' signal turned on.
   (v)   The machine should dispense the stamp and the right change and must indicate exceptional cases such as 'insufficient amount tendered', 'no stamp available', 'no change available', etc.

Write a program to simulate the machine. The input to the program would be: Amount tendered and the stamp requested. The output of the program should be: whether stamp is dispensed or not, the value of the stamp dispensed, the denomination of the coins returned (if any) and no change signal if no change is returned and no stamp if the stamp is not available.

14.7 Write a program corresponding to Exercise 5.11.

14.8 A set of rules in a government service for promotion is as follows:

The service has six salary points. Provided a candidate's conduct, diligence and efficiency are considered satisfactory, and he has spent one year as a Class I officer, and has passed satisfactorily the departmental test he advances to the next higher salary point from points 1 or 2. If he is in a higher salary point, then if his conduct, diligence and efficiency are considered satisfactory, and one year has elapsed since his last increment and he has satisfactorily completed a departmental course then he advances to the next higher salary point. Analyse the above statement and find out the input data necessary to decide whether a candidate is to be promoted or not. Write a program to implement the rules.

14.9 The offshore gas company bills its customers according to the following rate schedule:

First	50 m^3	Rs. 40 (flat rate)
Next	300 m^3	Rs. 1.25 per 10 m^3
Next	3000 m^3	Rs. 1.20 per 10 m^3
Next	2500 m^3	Rs. 1.10 per 10 m^3
Next	2500 m^3	Re. 0.90 per 10 m^3

Above this Re. 0.80 per 10 m^3

Given an input for each customer in the format:
Customer number, Previous meter reading, New meter reading.
Write a program to output the following:
Customer number, Previous reading, New reading, Gas used, Total bill.

14.10 An electricity company has three categories of customers: Industrial, Bulk Institutional and Domestic. The rates for these are tabulated below:

Industrial

Minimum up to 5000 units	Rs. 1500
Next 5000 units	Rs. 2.50 per unit
Next 10000 units	Rs. 2.75 per unit
Above this	Rs. 3.00 per unit

Bulk institutional

Minimum up to 5000	Rs. 1800
Next 5000 units	Rs. 2.25 per unit
Next 10000 units	Rs. 2.50 per unit
Above this	Rs. 2.75 per unit

Domestic

Minimum up to 100 units	Rs. 50
Next 100 units	Rs. 2.5 per unit
Next 200 units	Rs. 2.75 per unit
Above this	Rs. 3.00 per unit

Given the customer number, the category of customer, the previous meter reading and the current reading, write a program to output along with the input data, the charges for use of electricity.

15

C Program Examples

LEARNING OBJECTIVES

In this chapter we will learn:

1. How to simulate a small computer.
2. How to write complete programs.

Many important features of C have now been discussed and it will be worthwhile to write complete programs to solve some interesting problems. We will consider three examples in this chapter.

15.1 DESCRIPTION OF A SMALL COMPUTER

In this section we will write a C program to simulate the detailed working of a small hypothetical digital computer. The program is called a simulator program for SMAC (SMALL Computer). This technique of simulating the function of a computer on an already existing computer is widely used for developing software for new computers. Further, this example will illustrate the internal structure and functioning of a typical digital computer.

SMAC has the following specifications:

(i)   1000 memory locations.
(ii) Each memory location can accommodate 5 digits and a sign. We will call a sequence of 5 digits of the form   XXXXX, which can be stored in one location in memory, a *word*.
(iii) Each *word* in the memory can be an instruction or a data.
(iv) An instruction for this machine consists of two parts. One part gives the code for the operation to be performed and the other part gives the location in memory where the operand will be found. The sign is assumed to be positive in an instruction when not explicitly shown. Figure 15.1 illustrates this. As the memory has a total of 1000 locations, three digits (000 to 999) are needed to address all the locations. The remaining 2 digits in the *word* may be used to code the various operations to be performed by the computer. Theoretically 100 operations may be coded with two digits. We will, however, have a much smaller number of operation codes.

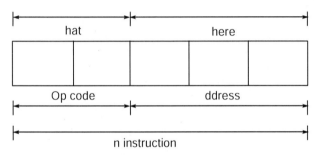

Fig. 1 .1   Instruction format of S   C.

(v) SMAC has an arithmetic logic unit (abbreviated ALU) where all arithmetic operations are performed. The ALU has a one word length (5 digits) register called an accumulator register where the results of arithmetic operations are temporarily stored. It is also used as an implied operand in arithmetic operations.

(vi) The ALU also decodes instructions and supervises execution of programs. It has an instruction register where the operation code and the address part of an instruction are stored and an instruction counter which stores the address of the next instruction to be executed. The first two digits of the instruction register contain the OP code and the last 3 digits the address of the operand to be accessed.

(vii) It has an input unit which reads data from a terminal and has an output unit which prints the results.

A block diagram of the computer with all the registers used in it is shown in Fig. 15.2.

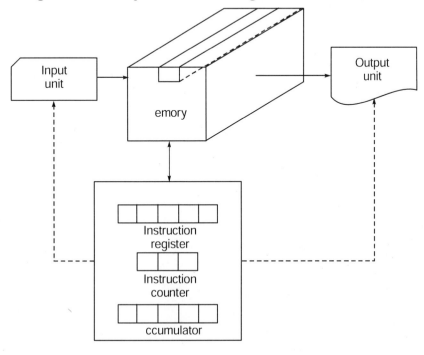

Fig. 1 .2   loc   diagram of S   C.

A program for SMAC consists of a set of machine instructions followed by data. Each data (or operand) can have at most 5 digits and a sign.

The computer operates in two phases. In the first phase the list of instructions is read and stored in the memory starting from address 000. The end of the list of instructions is signaled by a specially coded line. Data follow this line and are not read during this phase.

In the second phase the instruction counter in the control units is set to 000 and the instruction stored in memory location 000 is transferred to the instruction register. The instruction counter is incremented by one to point to the next instruction to be executed.

The operation code (abbreviated OP code) is retrieved from the instruction register and decoded. The ALU activates the appropriate part of the computer for executing the instruction. For example, data will be brought in and stored in memory if the instruction is an input instruction. If the instruction is a branch instruction the content of the instruction counter is determined by the executed instruction. If it is not a branch instruction the order given by the current OP code is executed. The instruction counter gives the address of the next instruction in sequence. The list of OP codes and their purpose is given in Table 15.1. The following abbreviations are used:

Table 1 .1   he meaning of operation codes of S   C

OP code	Instruction format	Meaning	Status of registers
01	01XXX	Clear accumulator and transfer C(XXX) to accumulator	OP = 01 ADDR = XXX C(ACC) = C(XXX)
02	02XXX	Add C(XXX) to accumulator	OP = 02 ADDR = XXX C(ACC) = C(XXX) + C(ACC)
03	03XXX	Subtract C(XXX) from C(ACC)	OP = 03 ADDR = XXX C(ACC) = C(ACC) – C(XXX)
04	04XXX	Multiply C(XXX) by C(ACC)	OP = 04 ADDR = XXX C(ACC) = C(ACC) * C(XXX)
05	05XXX	Divide C(ACC) by C(XXX) (only quotient available)	OP = 05 ADDR = XXX C(ACC) = C(ACC) / C(XXX)
06	06XXX	Store C(ACC) in address XXX	OP = 06 ADDR = XXX C(XXX) = C(ACC)
07	07XXX	Take next instruction from location XXX	OP = 07 ADDR = XXX INCTR = ADDR

(contd.)

Table 1 .1   he   eaning of Operation Codes of S   C   o   d.

OP code	Instruction format	Meaning	Status of registers
08	08XXX	Transfer to location XXX if accumulator contents are negative, otherwise go to the next instruction in sequence	OP = 08 ADDR = XXX IF(C(ACC) < 0) *then* INCTR = ADDR
09	09XXX	Take data from standard input and store in memory address XXX	OP = 09 ADDR = XXX
10	10XXX	Display the contents of location XXX in the VDU	OP = 10 ADDR = XXX
11	11XXX	Stop executing program Address part not used	OP = 11

ACC: Accumulator
INCTR: Instruction counter
ADDR: Address part of an instruction
OP: Operation code part of an instruction
OP code 01: Instruction Form: 01XXX where XXX is the address part of the instruction.
Meaning: Clear the accumulator register and enter the contents of memory location XXX
in it.

In working with machine instructions it is very important to distinguish between the address of a word in memory and the actual contents of the word. We will use the notation C(XXX) to denote the contents of address XXX. An equal to symbol (=) will be used to denote "replaces".

15.2   A MACHINE LANGUAGE PROGRAM

We will now write a small program in the machine language of this machine to compare the magnitudes of two numbers and output the larger of the two. The program is given as Table 15.2. In the program of Table 15.2, columns 2 and 3 contain the machine instruction executed by the machine. Column 1 tells where this instruction is stored in memory. This information is required to write the program. For instance in the program of Table 15.2, the instruction 08 007 commands that if the contents of the accumulator are negative the next instruction to be executed should be taken from location 007. A programmer should thus know the instruction stored in location 007.

The last column in Table 15.2 contains comments to enable a reader to understand the program.

The machine language program is typed with the location of the instruction in the first

Table 1 .2   machine language program to find the larger of t o numbers

Memory location where machine code is stored	Machine code		Explanation of machine instruction
	OP code	Address	
000	09	100	Read from input a number and store it in 100, C(100) = I
001	09	110	Read from input unit a number and store in 110, C(110) = J
002	01	100	ACC = C(100) = I
003	03	110	ACC = ACC – C(110) = I – J
004	08	007	If ACC < 0 take the next instruction from 007
005	10	100	Print C(100) (If I > J Print I)
006	11	000	Stop
007	10	110	Print C(110) (If J > I Print J)
008	11	000	Stop
– 000	00	000	End of machine language program

three columns followed by a blank column, the operation code in the next two columns, a blank column and the operand address in the last three columns.

The machine loads the program in memory starting from location 000. The programmer has to remember this in writing this program and start his first instruction from location 000. He has to know, besides, exactly where each one of the machine instructions is stored in memory. The end of the machine language program is indicated by a data line with a negative number. The loading of the program is stopped when this data line is encountered.

15.3   AN ALGORITHM TO SIMULATE THE SMALL COMPUTER

An algorithm to simulate the operation of the computer is given as Algorithm 15.1. The algorithm is divided into two phases, namely, storing instructions in Phase I and interpreting and executing instructions in Phase II.

Algorithm 15.1   Algorithm to simulate SMAC

Phase I: Storing machine language instructions in memory

Instruction counter = 0.
Read a machine instruction
while end of machine language is not reached
    {Store machine instruction in memory address given by instruction counter;
    ++Insttuction counter;
    Read a machine instruction; }
/*Control will reach this point as soon as all machine language instructions are stored*/

Phase II: *Interpreting and executing machine language instructions*

Instruction counter = 0. /* First instruction is in location 0 */
Repeat the following steps until the stop instruction of a machine language program is reached.

Step 2.1: Retrieve machine instruction from location given by instruction counter.
Step 2.2: ++Instruction counter.
Step 2.3: Branch to actions depending on operation code.

OP code 1: C(ACC) = C(ADDR)
OP code 2: C(ACC) = C(ACC) + C(ADDR)
OP code 3: C(ACC) = C(ACC) – C(ADDR)
OP code 4: C(ACC) = C(ACC) * C(ADDR)
OP code 5: C(ACC) = C(ACC) / C(ADDR)
OP code 6: C(ADDR) = C(ACC)
OP code 7: Instruction counter = ADDR
OP code 8: *if* C(ACC) < 0 *then* Instruction counter = ADDR
OP code 9: Read data and store in specified ADDR
OP code 10: Print the contents of specified ADDR
OP code 11: Stop execution.

end of algorithm.

15.4   A SIMULATION PROGRAM FOR THE SMALL COMPUTER

A simulation program will now be written to simulate SMAC. The composition of the complete program is shown in Fig. 15.3. The program itself is given as Example Program 15.1. This program is essentially Algorithm 15.1 rewritten using C.

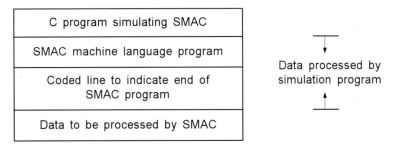

Fig. 1 .3   Composition of program and data to use S   C simulator.

Example Program 15.1 implements the two phases specified in the simulation algorithm (Algorithm 15.1). In phase I the machine language program is read and stored in memory starting from location 0. In phase II machine language instructions are retrieved from memory starting from location 0, the operation code is decoded and the specified operation performed. A *while* loop is used to read and store the machine language in the simulated memory. The end of machine language program is indicated by a dummy instruction with a negative number in its location field. Observe that as a data with a negative number in its location field is not a machine instruction it should not be stored in the simulated memory. Thus when we read such a data we should exit from the loop. Thus a *while* loop is useful in this case. Another *while* loop simulates the execution of machine instructions.

It is a good programming practice to introduce in the program statements to check when values assigned to variables go outside the specified range. When such an error is detected, informative messages should be printed along with the status of the important registers in the simulated computer. This has been done in the simulation program. If the address part of the instruction or the OP code or the instruction counter assume values outside the specified range then an appropriate message is printed and the program unconditionally jumps to the end of the program stopping further execution. A switch statement is ideally suited to decode an operation code and perform different actions depending on this code. This is done in the program. When the operation code for stopping the execution of SMAC is encountered the variable stop is made 1 which terminates the machine language program.

The status of all the important registers of SMAC in each execution cycle may be printed by inserting the statement:

printf ("%d%d%d%d\n", inst counter, op code, address, acc);

before the statement, namely, ++inst counter in the *while* loop. This would give what is known as the *execution trace* of the machine language program. This is very useful in debugging the machine language program. It is shown as a comment in Example Program 15.1.

In Program 15.1 we have used a statement goto abort program. This is called an unconditional jump. When this statement is executed the control jumps to a statement with label abort program. Such an unconditional jump is used only when an abnormal situation is encountered and a program has to halt. The goto statement is rarely used in C. Observe that in Example Program 15.1 the label abort program transfers control to the end of the program and no action is carried out.

```
/* Example Program 15.1 */
/* Simulation of a small computer SMAC */

#include <stdio.h>
main()
{
    int inst_counter = 0, address, op_code, instrn,
    ins_reg, stop = 0, acc = 0, location, memory[1000];

    /* The following loop reads SMAC machine language program given as data to
       this simulator and stores it in SMAC's memory */

    scanf("%d %d %d", &location, &op_code, &address);
    while(location >= 0)
        {
        instrn = op_code * 1000 + address;
        memory[inst_counter] = instrn;
        ++inst_counter;
        if (inst_counter > 999)
```

```
      {
        printf ("Program overflows memory\n");
        goto abort_program;
      }
    scanf ("%d %d %d", &location, &op_code, &address);
  } /* storing of SMAC program in memory over */
/* The machine language instruction is retrieved one by one from SMAC's
    memory, interpreted and executed by the following part of the simulator
    program */
inst_counter = 0;
while (stop == 0)    /* Observe that stop is initialized to 0 */
  {
    ins_reg = memory[inst_counter];
    op_code = ins_reg / 1000;
    if ((op_code <= 0) || (op_code) > 11))
      {
        printf ("Illegal op_code\n");
        printf ("Inst_counter = %d, op_code = %d\n", inst_counter, op_code);
        goto abort_program;
      }
    address = ins_reg % 1000;
  /* printf ("%d %d %d %d\n", inst_counter, op_code, address, acc); */
    ++inst_counter;

    switch (op_code)
      {
      case 01:
        /* Move contents of specified address in memory to accumulator */
        acc = memory[address];
        break;
      case 02:
        /* Add contents of specified address in memory to accumulator */
        acc += memory[address];
        break;
      case 3:
        /* Subtract from accumulator */
        acc -= memory[address];
        break;
      case 4:
        /* Multiply contents of accumulator */
          acc *= memory[address];
          break;
      case 5:
        /* Divide contents of accumulator before dividing check if denominator
           is zero */
        if (memory[address] == 0)
          {
            printf ("Attempt to divide by zero\n");
            printf ("Ins = %d, op = %d, add = %d\n",
              --inst_counter, op_code, address);
            goto abort_program;
          }
```

```
            else
               acc /= memory[address];
            break;
         case 6:
            /* Store accumulator in memory */
            memory[address] = acc;
            break;
         case 7:
            /* Unconditional jump */
            inst_counter = address;
            break;
         case 8:
            /* Conditional jump */
            if (acc < 0)
               inst_counter = address;
               break;
         case 9:
            /* Read data into memory of SMAC */
            scanf("%d", &memory[address]);
            break;
         case 10:
            /* Result stored in memory is displayed in VDU */
            printf("%d\n", memory[address]);
            break;
         case 11:
            /* Machine language stop statement */
            stop = 1;
            break;
      } /* Closing braces of switch statement */
   } /* Closing braces of while loop */

   printf("Program has normal ending instruction\n");
   printf("Inst counter = %d\n", --inst_counter);
   abort_program: ; /* Null statement. No action carried out */
} /* End of main */
```

g a 1 .1 Simulation of a small computer.

15.5 A STATISTICAL DATA PROCESSING PROGRAM

We will consider in this section a typical statistical data processing problem. In this problem a table of the marks obtained by each student in a class along with his/her average marks and division is required. Besides this, the average performance of the class in each subject and some statistical measures relating the performance of the class in different subjects are required. A program for obtaining these will be developed in this section.

The problem specifications are given below:

(i) The class has 100 or less students.
(ii) Each student takes 6 subjects, namely, Physics, Chemistry, Mathematics, Engineering Science, Technical Arts and Humanities.

(iii) The maximum marks in each subject is 100.
(iv) A student passes in the first division if he or she gets an average of more than 60 marks, in the second division if he or she gets an average between 50 and 59, in the third division if he or she gets between 40 and 49, and fails if his or her average is below 40.
(v) The program should compute the average marks and the division of each student.
(vi) It is required to find the performance of the class as a whole in each subject. This is indicated by the class average and the standard deviation of the marks in each subject.
(vii) It is also required to correlate the performance of the class in different subjects.

One wants to draw conclusious such as "if a class does well in Mathematics it also does well in Physics", "the performance of a class in Humanities is uncorrelated with its performance in Mathematics". To draw such conclusions a statistical measure called the correlation coefficient is used. The program should compute the matrix of correlation coefficients relating the performance of students in various subjects. The class average, the standard deviation, the covariance and the correlation coefficient are given by the following equations:

The class average in a subject is given by

$$\bar{m}_i = \frac{1}{N} \left(\Sigma \, m_{ik} \right) \qquad \text{k varying from 1 to N} \tag{15.1}$$

where m_{ik} is the marks obtained by the kth student in the ith subject and N is the total number of students in the class.

The standard deviation of the marks obtained by students in subject i is given by

$$s_i = \frac{1}{N} \left(\Sigma \, (m_{ik} - \bar{m}_i)^2 \right)^{0.5} \qquad \text{k varying from 1 to N} \tag{15.2}$$

The covariance between the marks obtained by students in subject i and subject j is defined by the equation

$$c_{ij} = \frac{1}{N} \Sigma \, (m_{ik} - \bar{m}_i)(m_{jk} - \bar{m}_j) \qquad \text{k varying from 1 to N}$$

$$= \frac{1}{N} \Sigma \, (m_{ik} m_{jk} - \bar{m}_i \bar{m}_j) \tag{15.3}$$

From Eq. (15.3), it is seen that

$$c_{ii} = \frac{1}{N} \left(\Sigma (m_{ik})^2 - (\bar{m}_i)^2 \right) \qquad \text{k varying from 1 to N} \tag{15.4}$$

The quantity c_{ii} is called the variance of the marks in subject i and is the square of the standard deviation. In the computer c_{ij} will be computed and c_{ii} obtained as a by-product by setting $j = i$.

The gross structure of the procedure may be stated as in Algorithm 15.2 below.

Algorithm 15.2 *Procedure to compute class statistics*

while student records are not yet over do

{ Read a student record
   Accumulate count of students
   Find total marks of the student
   Find average marks of the student
   Find the division of the student based on the average marks
   Accumulate marks of students in each subject
   Accumulate products of marks in pairs of subject.
   Print Roll no., marks in each subject, total marks,
   average marks and division of the student }

Calculate class average marks for each subject based on accumulated totals and student count.
Calculate covariance of marks in pairs of subjects based on accumulated cross products.
Calculate standard deviation and correlation coefficients

Print all the calculated values

end of algorithm

This algorithm is implemented as a C program of Example Program 15.2. The program is a straightforward implementation of the algorithm. It has a series of printf statements after the main computation is performed. These statements are needed to present the output in a "good looking" format. Developing these printf statements mainly requires proper counting of columns and attention to detail.

A sample output of Example Program 15.2 is shown below the program to enable the reader to correlate the printf statements with the printed output.

```
/* Example Program 15.2 */
/* Processing of students results */
#include <stdio.h>
#include <math.h>
main()
{
    int total_stud = 0, marks_total, i, j, division,
    roll_no, avge_marks, marks [6], subj _avge [6],
    total_subj [6], std_dev[6], cross_product[6][6], covnce[6][6];
    while(scanf("%d", &roll_no) != EOF)
        {
        for(i = 0; i <= 5; ++i)
            scanf("%d", &marks [i]);
        ++total_stud;
        marks_total = 0;
        for(i = 0; i <= 5; ++i)
            marks_total += marks[i];
        avge_marks = (float)marks_total/6.0 + 0.5;
        if (avge_marks >= 60)
            division = 1;
        else
```

```
      {
        if (avge_marks >= 50)
          division = 2;
        else
          {
            if (avge_marks >= 40)
              division = 3;
            else
              division = 0;
          }
      }
      printf ("%d", roll_no);
      for(i = 0; i <= 5; ++i)
        printf ("%d", marks[i]);
      if (division == 0)
        printf ("%d Failed\n", avge_marks);
      else
        printf ("%d Passed in Division %d\n",
                avge_marks, division);
      /* Initialisation of arrays */
      for (i = 0; i <= 5; ++i)
        {
          total_subj[i] = 0;
          for(j = 0; j <= 5; ++j)
          cross_product[i][j] = 0;
        }
      for (i = 0; i <= 5; ++i)
        {
          total_subj[i] += marks[i];
          for (j = 0; j <=5; ++j)
            cross_product [i][j] +=
              marks[i] * marks[j] ;
        }
    } /* End of while loop */ ,
printf ("\n                Class Averages\n\n");
for (i = 0; i <= 5; ++i)
  subj_avge[i] = total_subj[i]/total_stud;
printf ("                 Phys   Chem    Math");
printf ("    T.A.   E.S.   H.S.\n");
print (" Averages");
printf ("       %4d %5d %5d %5d %5d %5d\n",
      subj_avge[0], subj_avge[1],
      subj_avge[2], subj_avge[3],
      subj_avge[4], subj_avge[5]);
for(i = 0; i <= 5; ++i)
  for(j = 0; j <= 5; ++j)
    covnce[i][j] = cross_product[i][j] /
      total_stud-subj_avge[i]*subj_avge[j];

  for(i = 0; i <=5; ++i)
    std_dev[i] = sqrt((float)covnce[i][i]) + 0.5;
  printf (" Std. Dev.");
```

```
    printf("     %4d %5d %5d %5d %5d %5d\n",
       std_dev[0], std_dev[1],
       std_dev[2], std_dev[3],
       std_dev[4], std_dev[5]);
    printf("\n          The Variance Covariance ");
    printf(" Matrix\n\n");
    printf("    Phys    Chem    Math    T.A.");
    printf("    E.S.    H.S.\n");
    printf("Phys ");
    for (j = 0; j <=5; ++j)
       printf("%-8d", covnce[0][j]);
    printf("\n");
    printf("Chem ");
    for (j = 0; j <=5; ++j)
       printf("%-8d", covnce[1][j]);
    printf("\n");
    printf("Math ");
    for (j = 0; j <=5; ++j)
       printf("%-8d", covnce[2][j]);
    printf("\n") ;
    printf("T.A. ");
    for (j = 0; j <=5; ++j)
       printf("%-8d", covnce[3][j]);
    printf("\n");
    printf("E.S. ");
    for (j = 0; j <=5; ++j)
       printf("%-8d", covnce[4][j]);
    printf("\n");
    printf("H.S. ");
    for (j = 0; j <=5; ++j)
       printf("%-8d", covnce[5][j]);
    printf("\n");
} /* End of main */

Input :
1234 30 40 50 60 70 80
1235 40 30 40 30 40 34
1236 70 60 60 50 60 65
1238 50 35 45 35 40 40
1246 40 60 50 70 60 80
1254 30 30 60 50 35 45

output :
1234 30 40 50 60 70 80 55 Passed in Division 2
1235 40 30 40 30 40 34 36 Failed
1236 70 60 60 50 60 65 61 Passed in Division 1
1238 50 35 45 35 40 40 41 Passed in Division 3
1246 40 60 50 70 60 80 60 Passed in Division 1
1254 30 30 60 50 35 45 42 Passed in Division 3
```

Class Averages

	Phys	Chem	Math	T.A.	E.S.	H.S.
Averages	43	42	50	49	50	57
Std. Dev.	15	14	12	14	16	20

The Variance Covariance Matrix

	Phys	Chem	Math	T.A.	E.S.	H.S.
Phys	217	135	75	-16	75	25
Chem	135	206	95	146	175	217
Math	75	95	137	95	100	110
T.A.	-16	146	95	203	175	260
E.S.	75	175	100	175	254	289
H.S.	25	217	110	260	289	385

g a   1 .2   rocessing students results.

15.6 PROCESSING SURVEY DATA WITH COMPUTERS

A frequent use of digital computers is in the tabulation of the results of surveys. The general principles involved in planning the collection of survey data which are to be ultimately processed by digital computers and the programming aspects may be illustrated by considering an example. The example chosen is the processing of questionnaires (distributed to the participants of a short course on computers) shown as Table 15.3.

The objectives of the survey are to obtain the following tables:

(i)   The distribution of participants by sex
(ii) The average age of the participants
(iii) The distribution of the participants by institutional affiliation
(iv) The distribution of the participants as a function of their primary interest
(v)   The distribution of the participants as a function of their educational background
(vi) A table giving the number of participants with specified interests from different types of institutions.

After deciding the number of groups of each type into which the participants are to be divided it is necessary to uniquely code each group. The division into groups is obvious if sex is the distinguishing characteristic. In this case there are two groups and each one is given a code number. A code 0 is assigned to males and 1 to females. As our aim is to count the number of males and females respectively among the participants it is conveniently done by taking the participants' sex as an array with two components. The first component corresponds to males and the second to females. If the participants are to be grouped using another chracteristic, say their educational background, then this information may be coded into a set of integers. These codes may be thought of as subscripts which group the participants into distinct classes.

The main idea used in processing survey questionnaires may be illustrated by considering the following example in which the participants are grouped into two groups, males and females. Assume that one data is typed per participant and that it has a serial number in

Table 1 .3 sample uestionnaire

Please record the answers to the following questions by entering the code number corresponding to your choice in the box on the right of each question.

Serial number		Column number
(For Office use only)		1
		2
		3
1. What is your sex? Male = 0 Female = 1		4
2. Age: What was your age at the last birthday?		
If it is, say, 25 enter it as:		
	2	5
	5	6
3. What is your institutional affiliation?		7
Private Sector	0	
Educational Institution	1	
Government Office	2	
Public Sector Firm	3	
Research Laboratory	4	
Unemployed	5	
4. What is your primary interest?		8
Science	0	
Engineering	1	
Mathematics	2	
Social Sciences	3	
Business Data Processing	4	
5. What is the highest degree obtained by you?		9
High School	0	
Intermediate	1	
Bachelor's	2	
Master's	3	
Doctor's	4	

columns 1 to 3 and the sex code (0 or 1) in column 4. The program to divide the participants into two groups (namely, males and females) is given as Example Program 15.3. In this program the "bin" sex[0] is set up to count data lines which have sex code = 0 and "bin" sex[1] to count those with sex code = 1. After clearing sex[0] and sex[1] to zeros a data is read. If the code is less than 0 or greater than 2 then it is illegal. In other words, the data has been wrongly typed. This is indicated in the program and the number of such bad data are counted. For correct data if sex code = 0, sex[0] is incremented by 1 and if sex code = 1 then sex[1] is incremented by 1. Thus the value of the sex code "sorts" the data into appropriate "bins". Extension of this technique to the case when the number of groups is greater than 2

```
/* Example Program 15.3 */
/* questionnaire tabulation—Program Development */
#include <stdio.h>

main()
{
    int sex[2], sex_code, ser_no, bad_data = 0, no_quest = 0;
    sex[0] = sex[1] = 0;
    while(scanf("%d %d", &ser_no, &sex_code) != EOF)
        {
        if ((sex_code < 0) || (sex_code > 1))
            {
            ++bad_data;
            printf("Error in Sex code Ser no = %d\n", ser_no);
            }
        else
            {
            ++sex [sex_code];
            ++no_quest;
            }
        } /* End while */
    prlntf("No. of questionnaires tabulated = %d\n", no_quest);
    printf("No. of invalid data = %d\n", bad_data);
    prlntf("No of Males = %d, No. of Females = %d\n",
            sex[0], sex[1]);
}   /* End of main */
```

g a   1 .3   uestionnaire program development.

is obvious. A program to process the questionnaire given at the beginning of this section is given as Example Program 15.4. The student is urged to study this carefully. It will be observed that the programming job by itself is very simple. Most of the work is in obtaining proper formats for spacing, headings, etc.

```
/* Example Program 15.4 */
/* Questionnaire tabulation—one and two way tables */

#include <stdio.h>
main()
{
    int sex_code, inst_code, intrt_code, degree_code,
    age, sex[2], degree[5], institution[6],
    interest[5], inst_vs_intrt[6][5], sum_age = 0,
    avg_age, serial_no, bad_data = 0, no_quest = 0, i, j,
    inp_error;
    /* Initialize all arrays to 0 */
    sex[0] = sex[l] = 0;
    for (i = 0; i <= 4; ++i)
        degree[i] = interest[i] = 0;
```

```
for(i = 0; i <= 5; ++i)
   {
      institution[i] = 0;
      for (j = 0; j <= 4; ++j)
         inst_vs_intrt[i][j] = 0;
   }
printf("Output Tables\n");
while(scanf("%d %d %d %d %d %d", &serial_no,
            &sex_code, &age, &inst_code,
            &intrt_code, &degree_code) != EOF)
   {
      inp_error = 0;
      if ((sex_code < 0) || (sex_code > 1))
         {
            inp_error = 1;
            printf("Error in sex_code Ser no = %d\n" serial_no);
         }
      if ((age < 0) || (age > 99))
         {
            inp_error = 1;
            printf("Error in age Ser no = %d\n", serial_no);
         }
      if ((inst_code < 0) || (inst_code > 5))
         {
            inp_error = 1;
            printf("Error in inst_code Ser no = %d\n", serial_no);
         }
      if ((intrt_code < 0) || (intrt_code > 4))
         {
            inp_error = 1;
            printf("Error in intrt_code Ser no = %d\n", serial_no);
         }
      if ((degree_code < 0) || (degree_code > 4))
         {
            inp_error = 1;
            printf("Error in degree_code Ser no = %d\n", serial_no);
         }
      if (inp_error == 1)
         ++bad_data;
      else
         {
            ++sex[sex_code];
            ++institution[inst_code];
            ++interest[intrt_code];
            ++degree[degree_code];
            sum_age += age;
            ++no_quest;
            ++inst_vs_intrt[inst_code][intrt_code];
         }
   } /* End of while loop */
```

```
avg_age = sum_age/no_quest;
printf("No. of valid Questionnaires = %d\n", no_quest);
printf("No. of invalid Questionnaires = %d\n", bad_data);
printf("Average Age of Participants = %d\n", avg_age);
printf("Distribution of Participants by Sex\n");
printf("Males = %d, Females = %d\n", sex[0], sex[1]);
/* The notation within printf has been split on two lines so that the program
   width does not exceed the page width of this book */

printf("Distribution of Participants by");
printf(" Institutional\nAffiliation\n");
printf("    Pvt.    Edn.    Govt    PubS    Res.    Unemp\n");
printf("    ");
for (i = 0; i <= 5; ++i)
  printf("%-6d", institution[i]);
printf("\n");
printf("Distribution of Participants by");
printf(" Interest\n");
printf("    Sci.    Engg    Math    Soc.    B.D.P.\n");
printf("    ");
for (i = 0; i <= 4; ++i)
  printf("%-6d", interest[i]);
printf("\n");
printf("Distribution of Participants by");
printf(" Qualifications\n");
printf(" H.Sc    Int.    Bach    Mas.    Ph.D\n");
printf("    ");
for (i = 0; i <= 4; ++i)
  printf("%-6d", degree[i]);
printf("\n");
printf("Institutional Affiliation Vs. interest\n");
printf(" Pvt.    Edn.    Govt    PubS    Res.    Unemp\n");
printf("Science     ");
for (j = 0; j <= 5; ++j)
  printf("%-6d", inst_vs_intrt[0][j]);
printf("\n");
printf("Engineer    ");
for (j = 0; j <= 5; ++j)
  printf("%-6d", inst_vs_intrt[1][j]);
printf("\n");
printf("Math        ");
for (j = 0; j <= 5; ++j)
  printf("%-6d", inst_vs_intrt[2][j]);
printf("\n");
printf("Soc.Sc.     ");
for (j = 0; j <= 5; ++j)
  printf("%-6d", inst_vs_intrt[3][j]);
printf("\n");
printf("B.D.P.      ");
for (j = 0; j <= 5; ++j)
  printf("%-6d", inst_vs_intrt[4][j]);
```

```
      printf ("\n") ;
      printf ("-- End of Tables --\n");
}     /* End of main */
```

Input:
```
124   0   25    3   4   3
128   1   35    4   6   3
129   1   45    2   1   2
130   0   38    3   2   1
131   1   28    1   1   0
132   0   30    0   0   0
133   1   45    1   2   3
134   1   45    6   5   4
140   1   35    4   5   4
141   0   65    5   4   4
142   0   102   3   3   4
```

Output:
Output Tables
Error in intrt_code Ser no = 128
Error in inst_code Ser no = 134
Error in intrt_code Ser no = 134
Error in intrt_code Ser no = 140
Error in age Ser no = 142
No. of valid Questionnaires = 7
No. of invalid Questionnaires = 4
Average Age of Participants = 39
Distribution of Participants by Sex
Males = 4, Females = 3
Distribution of Participants by Institutional
Affiliation

Pvt.	Edn.	Govt	PubS	Res.	Unemp
1	2	1	2	0	1

Distribution of Participants by Interest

Sci.	Engg	Math	Soc.	B.D.P.
1	2	2	0	2

Distribution of Participants by Qualifications

H.Sc	Int.	Bach	Mas.	Ph.D
2	1	1	2	1

Institutional Affiliation Vs. interest

	Pvt.	Edn.	Govt	PubS	Res.	Unemp
Science	1	0	0	0	0	0
Engineer	0	1	1	0	0	0
Math	0	1	0	0	0	0
Soc.Sc.	0	0	1	0	1	0
B.D.P.	0	0	0	0	0	0

-- End of Tables --

g a   1 .   uestionnaire tabulation.

EXERCISES

15.1 Write a machine language program for SMAC which will pick the largest of 10 numbers. Test this program with the simulator.

15.2 Write a machine language program for SMAC which will add two 10 component vectors.

15.3 It is desired to add more instructions to SMAC. Some of the machine instructions and their meanings are given below. Rewrite SMAC with these additions and test it.

OP code: 21   Instruction form: 21XXX
                Meaning: C(ACC) = C(ACC) + XXX
OP code: 22   Instruction form: 22XXX
                Meaning: C(ACC) = C(ACC) − XXX
OP code: 31   Instruction form: 31XXX
                Meaning: Shift C(ACC) right by XXX positions.

15.4 Income-tax rules define three categories of persons for tax computation:

   (i) Residents
  (ii) Resident but not ordinarily resident
 (iii) Non-resident.

Definition of Resident:

If a person satisfies any one of the following rules he is considered a resident during a specified year.

   (i) He lived in India for at least 182 days during the year.
  (ii) He maintained a home in India for at least 182 days and lived for at least 30 days in India during the year.
 (iii) He lived in India in the four preceding years for at least 365 days and lived in India for 60 days during the given year.

Definition of Resident but not ordinarily resident:

A person is considered ordinarily resident in India during a year if he satisfies both the conditions given below in addition to being a resident during the year.

   (i) If during preceding 10 years he is a resident of India for at least 9 years.
  (ii) If during preceding seven years he lived in India for a total of 760 days or more.

If he does not satisfy any one of the conditions above, he is considered a resident but not ordinarily resident.

Non-resident

A person who is not resident in India is called non-resident.

   (i) Obtain decision tables to decide into which category a person falls given the required data.
  (ii) How many previous years' data are required to decide about the status of a person in a given year?
 (iii) Write a computer program which prints out the category to which a person belongs given the required data.

15.5 A sociologist conducts a survey among college students and collects the following data:

1. Age
2. Sex
3. Marital status
4. No. of years in college
5. Percentage marks obtained in the last examination
6. Time spent in studies per week
7. Time spent in extra-curricular activities per week
8. Financial support (Parents/guardian/government/charitable organization/others). (Here the student may get support from more than one source.)
9. No. of films seen per month
10. Opinion about usefulness of education (very useful/doubtful/useless).

   (i) Prepare a code to convert the information to one which would be suitable for processing on a computer.
   (ii) Write a program to tabulate the results.

15.6 A hospital keeps a file of blood donors in which each record has the format:

Name   : 20 columns
Address   : 40 columns
Age   : 2 columns
Blood Type : 1 column (Type 1, 2, 3 or 4)

Write a program to print out all blood donors whose age is below 25 and blood is type 2.

15.7 Simulate a simple calculator to perform the following: Add, subtract, multiply, divide, find percentage, find square root. Assume that the input is given as you would do in a hand-held calculator.

15.8 Write a program to generate as monthly sales report of a shop which sells 50 items. The printout should have the item code, the sales during the month, the total sales during the financial year and given the target of monthly sales whether the actual sales are above or below the target.

16

Functions

```
                    LEARNING OBJECTIVES
```

In this chapter we will learn:
1. The need to break up a large program into a number of functions.
2. Defining functions in C language.
3. How functions are called from other functions.
4. Use of arrays as arguments in functions.
5. The concept of local and global variables.

16.1 INTRODUCTION

Functions are subprograms which perform well defined tasks. They may be developed separately and tested. We may then name each such subprogram and specify the method of sending data to each of them and getting processed results from them. Once this is done these subprograms may be linked together to do a given task. The primary merits of this approach to program development are:

(i) It is a good idea to break up a big job into a number of smaller sub-jobs. Divide and conquer, namely, breaking up a complicated problem into smaller parts and solving each separately is a well known problem solving method.

(ii) A program written as a sequence of functions with each function carrying out a specified task, is easy to understand. An understandable program can be modified easily.

(iii) It is easy to test small compact functions.

(iv) Commonly used functions may be generalized, tested thoroughly and kept in a library for future use.

(v) Functions developed by others may be used. For example, a large number of efficient, well tested programs for common problems in string manipulation and numerical computation, are available as libraries usable by C programmers.

(vi) In languages other than C, particularly FORTRAN, many good program libraries are universally available. For instance IMSL (International Mathematical and Statistical Library) and NAG (Numerical Algorithm Group) are well known libraries. Many C compiler implementations permit declaration of FORTRAN programs as external procedures and use them in C programs. Recently, many of the commonly available libraries in FORTRAN are being rewritten in C.

A C language program consists of a collection of functions. The programs written so far define a single function main(). We can break up a program into many functions. The single function main() can use all these functions to carry out the required processing. We will illustrate the definition and use of functions with simple examples in the next section.

16.2   DEFINING AND USING FUNCTIONS

A *function* is defined in Example Program 16.1 to reverse a given integer. Given an integer 4578 the reverse of this integer is 8754. This *function* is:

int reverse of (int n)

```
/* Example Program 16.1 */
/* Illustrates defining a function */
int reverse_of(int n)
{
    int digit, rev_of_n = 0;       /* Local Variables */
    while(n != 0)
       {
          digit = n % 10;
          rev_of_n = rev_of_n * 10 + digit;
          n = n/10;
       }
    return(rev_of_n);
}
```

g a   1 .1   efining a function.

The *name* of the *function* is reverse of. The rules to name a *function* are the same as those used to name an identifier.This *function* is declared to be of type *int*. This says that the result which will be computed and returned by the *function* when it is invoked will be an integer. The variable name inside the parentheses is known as a *formal argument* or *formal parameter* of the *function*. This argument is used by the *function* as input for processing. The type of this variable name should be specified. Observe that no semicolon is used after the function declaration. The statements to be executed by the function *defines* the *function* and is specified next. The *function* definition is enclosed within braces { } and is known as the body of the *function*. The *function* definition begins with the declaration of the variables and their types which will be used in the *function*. These variables are *local* to the *function*. They have no meaning outside the *function* body. This implies that the same names may be used by other *functions* in their definition without any conflict. This is essential as *functions* may be defined and written by different programmers and they should be able to write their programs independently. The local nature of these variables also implies that outside the function their contents cannot be used.

After the declaration a sequence of statements are written which defines the task carried out by the *function*. After the task is carried out the result is sent back by the statement

$$return \ (expression) \ ;$$

where in this statement, *expression* is any legal C expression.

Referring again to Example Program 16.1 the local variables of the *function* reverse of are: digit and rev of n which are both integers. Observe that rev of n is initialized to 0. The *while* loop forms the rev of n. Outside the *while* loop the statement

$$return \ (rev \ of \ n) \ ;$$

sends back the calculated integer to the *function*

$$int \ reverse \ of \ (int \ n);$$

In Example Program 16.2 we illustrate how the *function* is *invoked* or *called* by main. Observe that in the listing of Example Program 16.2 after #include <stdio.h> we have written

$$int \ reverse \ of \ (int \ number);$$

which is called a *function prototype* and is required in ANSI C. The prototype tells the C compiler that a *function* named *reverse_of* of *type* integer which has one argument which is also of type integer will be later defined in the program. This information will be used to check both the definition of the *function* and when the *function* is actually called. The specification that the *function* is of type integer tells that the value returned by the *function* will be of *type* integer. The function prototype must be terminated by a semicolon.

The *main function* is now defined. It reads an integer and stores it in variable name p. In the next statement q = reverse of (p); the appearance of the *function* name reverse of *invokes* or *calls* the *function* reverse of with actual argument p and the value returned by the *function* is stored in q. When *function* reverse of is called with actual argument p the value of p is *copied* into the *formal argument* n of the *function*, the original value stored in p is unaffected. The *function* now uses the value of p and does the computations. Observe that if $p = 2578$, n is assigned the value 2578. Observe that the *function* destroys the value of n in the process of reversing it and n ultimately becomes zero. This does not affect the value of p in the calling function, namely, main(). This fact is very important to remember.

At the end of the *function* reverse of the value of reverse of n is returned by it to the calling *function*, namely, main(). The returned value is stored in q by the statement

$$q = reverse \ of \ (p);$$

in main().

Finally the values of p and its reverse q are printed. The input and output of this program are also shown along with Example Program 16.2.

```
/* Example Program 16.2 */
# include <stdio.h>
/* Function Prototype */
int reverse_of (int number);

main()
{
    int p, q;
    scanf("%d", &p);
    q = reverse_of(p);    /* Function called here */
                          /* p is the actual argument */
    printf("Reverse of %d is %d\n", p, q);
}

int reverse_of(int n)
{
    int digit, rev_of_n = 0;

    while(n != 0)
        {
            digit = n % 10;
            rev_of_n = rev_of_n * 10 + digit;
            n = n/10;
        }
    return(rev_of_n);
}

Input:
47632

Output:
Reverse of 47632 is 23674
```

g a   1 .2   eversing an integer.

In this program the *function* has one formal argument of type int and an integer value was returned by the *function*. In general a *function* may have any number of formal arguments of any type, e.g. float, unsigned int, etc. A *function* may have no argument. For example, main() has no arguments in all the programs we have written so far.

A *function* may return *at most one result*. Thus a *function* may either return no value or return one value. The value returned may be of any type int, float, unsigned int, etc. A *function* which returns no value is defined as

void function name (*type* formal arguments)

where *void* is a key word indicating that no value is returned. Similarly if a *function* has no formal arguments it will have the word *void* within parentheses as shown below:

type function name(*void*)

In Example Program 16.3 we illustrate the use of *functions* with *void* for type names and int for formal argument. Observe that the function

void print palindrome (int k)

```c
/* Example Program 16.3 */
#include <stdio.h>
int reverse_of(int number);
void print_palindrome(int x);
void print_not_palindrome(int x);
main()
    int p;
    while (scanf("%d", &p) != EOF)
       {
          if (p == reverse_of(p))
             print_palindrome(p),
          else
             print_not_palindrome(p);
       }
}    /* End of main */

int reverse_of(int n)
{
    int digit, rev_of_n = 0;
    while(n != 0)
       {
          digit = n % 10;
          rev_of_n = rev_of_n * 10 + digit;
          n = n/10;
       }
    return(rev_of_n);
}

void print_palindrome(int k)
{
    printf("Given number %d is a Palindrome\n", k);
}

void print_not_palindrome(int k)
{
    printf("Given number %d is not a Palindrome\n", k);
}
```

g a   1 .3   Chec ing if an integer is a palindrome.

does not return a value. It merely uses the value passed on to it by the actual argument to print a message.

We give next some more examples.

EXAMPLE 16.1 The definition and use of a *function* to add the digits of an integer is given as Example Program 16.4. Observe that the *function* prototype is given first. The *function* main() reads a number *p* and calls the *function* sum digits with *p* as actual argument. The *function* sum digits is defined next after main(). This *function* uses *n* as the formal argument. It has two *int* variables sum and digit used locally within the *function*. In the body of the *function* sum digits is calculated and returned as sum. This returned value is assigned to the variable *s* in the *function* main(). The main() *function* then prints the value of the actual argument communicated to sum digits (namely, *p*) and the value returned by the function (namely, *s*).

```
/* Example Program 16.4 */
/* Defining and using a function to add digits of a number */
#include <stdio.h>
int sum_digit(int number);

main()
{
    int p, s;
    scanf("%d", &p);
    s = sum_digits(p);
    printf("Sum of digits of %d is %d\n", p, s);
}

/* Function defining sum of digits */
int sum_digits(int n)
{
    int sum = 0, digit;
    if (n < 0)
        n = -n;
    while (n != 0)
        {
            digit = n % 10;
            sum += digit;
            n = n/10;
        }
    return(sum);
}
```

g a   1 .   dding digits of an integer.

EXAMPLE 16.2 Consider the *function* defined below:

$$\text{limiter } (x) = \text{bound} \qquad\qquad x \geq \text{bound}$$
$$\text{limiter } (x) = x \qquad\qquad \text{bound} > x > - \text{bound} \qquad\qquad (16.1)$$
$$\text{limiter } (x) = - \text{bound} \qquad\qquad x \leq - \text{bound}$$

This *function* is defined in Example Program 16.5 as

float limiter (float x, float bound)

```
/* Example Program 16.5 */
/* Defining and using a function limiter */
#include <stdio.h>
float limiter(float p, float q);

main()
{
    float a, b, c, z;
    scanf("%f %f %f" &a, &b, &c);
    z = (limiter(a, c) + limiter(b, c))/
        limiter(a+b, c);
    printf("value of a = %f b = %f c = %f z = %f\n", a, b, c, z);
}

float limiter(float x, float bound)
{
    if (x < -bound)
        return(-bound);
    else
        {
            if (x > bound)
                return(bound);
            else
                return(x);
        }
}   /* End of function limiter (x, bound) */
```

g a   1 .   Simulating a limiter.

Observe that this *function* has two arguments which are both of *type float*. The *function* also returns a result of *type float*. The *function* has more than one *return* statement. This is necessary in this example and is allowed in C.

Before main( ) there is a function prototype defining *limiter*. Observe that the *main function* calls the *function limiter* thrice to compute.

z = (limiter(a, c) + limiter(b, c)) / limiter (a + b, c);

Observe that we have used an expression a + b as one of the arguments. This is allowed.

EXAMPLE 16.3 A bank gives simple interest at *r* percent per year if the balance in one's account is Rs. 1000 or more. No interest is given on balance less than Rs. 1000. It is required to find the balance in a customer's account at the end of *x* years.

The independent variables in this example are interest rate, balance in one's account and the number of years of deposit. The quantity to be calculated based on these independent variables is the total interest amount.

Thus the *function* in this case is the interest and the formal arguments are:

Interest rate, the balance in one's account and the number of years of deposit.

A *function* which calculates the interest is given as Example Program 16.6.

```
/* Example Program 16.6 */
/* Function to calculate interest */

float interest(float rate, float balance, int years)
{
    float calc_int;
    if (balance > 1000.0)
      calc_int = (balance * rate/100.0)*(float)years;
    else
      calc_int = 0.0,
    return(calc_int) ;
}
```

g a   1 .   Interest calculation.

The *function* defined in Example Program 16.6 uses the specified value of Rs. 1000 of minimum balance within the code. It can be generalized if the minimum balance is also taken as a formal argument in the definition of the *function*. As the purpose of a *function* is to allow its flexible use by a class of users it is worthwhile to make it as general as possible. The generalized *function* and its use by a *main function* is illustrated in Example Program 16.7.

```
/* Example Program 16.7 */
/* Generalized function to calculate interest */
#include <stdio.h>
float interest(float rate, float balance, int main_bal, int years);
/* Function prototype defined above */

main()
{
    int min_bal, yrs, acct_no;
    float bal, rate, int_calc, new_balance;

    printf("Acc.   no.   old balance   interest");
    printf("   new balance\n");
    while(scanf ("%d %f %f %d %d", &acct_no, &rate, &bal, &yrs, &min_bal) != EOF)
      {
          int_calc = interest(rate, bal, min_bal, yrs);
          new_balance = bal + int_calc;
          printf (" %5d %12.2f %12.2f %12.2f\n",
                   acct_no, bal, int_calc, new_balance);
      } /* End of while */
} /* End of main */

float interest(float rate, float balance, int min_balance, int years)
{
    int calc_int;
    if (balance > min_balance)
          calc_int = (balance * rate/100.0) *
          (float)years;
    else
      calc_int = 0.0;
    return(calc_int);
}
```

g a   1 .   eneralising interest calculation.

Observe in Example Program 16.7 the definition of *function* prototype is at the beginning. The main *function* calls interest in a *while* loop to calculate the interest of many account holders of the bank. The local variables are declared within main() as required.

16.3 SYNTAX RULES FOR FUNCTION DECLARATION

The general form of a *function* declaration is given below:

type function name(type a_1, type a_2, ..., type a_n)
    { type v_1, v_2, ... , v_n; /* local variables */
       (one or more statements to compute the function)
       return (*expression*);
    }

The first statement is the *function* declaration and defines the name of the *function* and the list of formal arguments. This statement must *not* be terminated by a semicolon. The type of the value returned by the *function* is given as *type function*. The type of each of the formal arguments is also defined. A *function* may not return any value. In such a case the word *void* is used instead of type. If a function has no formal arguments then the word *void* is used instead. Following this the beginning of the *function* definition is indicated by left braces {. Next the local variables used by the *function* are declared.

The *body* of the *function* defines the computations to be carried out by the *function*. The *function* body may contain one or more *return* statements. A *return* statement returns a value to the calling *function*. A *return* statement may not be present if no value is returned. A closing brace } is used to indicate the end of the function definition.

The following rules must be remembered while defining functions:

(i) A *function* prototype declaration must appear at the beginning of the program following #include statement. In a *function* prototype the type of the *function* and the type of each formal argument must be specified. The variable names used for formal arguments in a *function* prototype are arbitrary; they may even be blanks. Each function prototype declaration is terminated by a semicolon.

(ii) A *function* name may be any valid identifier. The *type* of the *function* specifies the *type* of quantity which will be returned to the calling program.

(iii) The formal arguments used in defining a *function* may be scalars or arrays. Each *formal* argument *type* must be specified.

(iv) Within a *function* definition other variables may be declared and used. Such variables are *private* or *local* to the *function* and are not known outside the body of the function. These variables are known as *local* variables. Their values are undefined outside the function.

(v) Within a function definition, one may *not define* another function.

A *function* is called by a program by the appearance of the function name in a statement. The rules to be remembered while calling a *function* are:

(i) The actual arguments in the calling *function* must agree in number, order and *type* with the formal arguments in the *function* declaration.

(ii) Copies of the values of actual arguments are sent to the formal arguments and the *function* is computed. Thus the actual arguments remain intact.

(iii) If the formal argument is an array name the corresponding actual argument in the calling *function* must also be an array name of the same *type*.

(iv) A *return* statement in the body of the *function* returns a value to the calling *function*. The *type* of expression used in return statement must match with the type of the *function* declared. There may be functions without a *return* statement. In such a case the *function* must be declared as *void*.

(v) If type of *function* is omitted it is taken by default as int.

(vi) A function can return *only one* value.

The concept of calling a *function* is summarized in Fig. 16.1.

```
type function name (type a,  type b,  type c)
/* Function prototype */

main ( )
{   /* Beginning of main function */

    Main function body

/* Calling a function */
variable name = function name (x,  y,  z);
        or
function name (x,  y,  z);
x,  y,  z actual parameters
} /* End of main function */


type function name (type p,  type q,  type r)
{ /* Beginning of function */
    type s,  t,  u; /* Local variables */

    Body of function

    return (expression);
/* Value of expression returned to function name */
}   /* End of function */
```

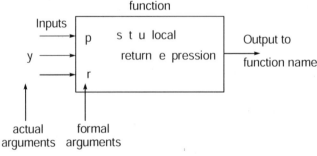

Fig. 1 .1   Illustrating definition and calling of a function.

A function can be written separately and kept in a library for use by a class of users. With this facility a large program may be divided into a number of subprograms and then linked together.

Functions are employed in applications where one needs them in computing expressions. As function name returns a value it may be used as parts of expressions. Functions may also perform operations without returning any value.

We will close this section with two examples in which functions are declared and used.

EXAMPLE 16.4 Suppose the frictional force acting on a particle is given by the equations:

$$f(y) = 0 \qquad \text{for } |y| \leq 0.5 \tag{16.3}$$
$$= 2y^2 \qquad \text{for } |y| > 0.5$$

It is required to use this function in Eq. (16.4)

$$g = (mv/t) - f(v^2) + at \tag{16.4}$$

A small program to do this is written as Example Program 16.8. It is seen from this example that

(i) When the function is called the actual argument may be an expression. This is valid provided it is of the same type as the formal argument.

```c
/* Example Program 16.8 */
/* Function definition and use */
#include <stdio.h>
float friction(float a);
float abs(float p);

main()
{
    float g, m, v, a, t;
    scanf("%f %f %f %f", &m, &v, &a, &t);
    g = (m * v/t) - friction(v*v) + a*t;
    printf("g = %f\n", g);
}

float friction(float y)
{
    if (abs(y) <= 0.5)
        return(0.0);
    else
        return(2.0 * y * y);
}

float abs(float x)
{
    if(x < 0)
        x = -x;
    return(x);
}   /* End of abs(x) */
```

g a   1 .   Function to simulate friction.

(ii) A float arithmetic expression is returned in the body of the subprogram. The value returned to the main program will thus be of type float.

(iii) Observe that the function friction calls another function float abs(x).

EXAMPLE 16.5 A *function* may call another *function* which may in turn call a third *function*. The sequence of calls and returns is illustrated in Example Program 16.9. Observe that when a *function* f calls a *function* g from f, g will do its task and return to the statement calling g. The printed output of the program is shown below the program.

The student should examine the output along with the program to understand the flow of control from calling *function* to the called *function* and back from the called to the calling *function*.

16.4   ARRAYS IN FUNCTIONS

So far we have considered examples where the formal arguments of *functions* are scalars. There are many applications where an entire array has to be used as an argument. We will consider such applications in this section.

We will consider the problem of picking the highest and the second highest marks in a class which was discussed in Chapter 13. We revise Example Program 13.2 and rewrite it using functions.

EXAMPLE 16.6   Example Program 13.2 is written using functions as Example Program 16.10. The *function* first mark has as formal arguments marks[ ] and size. Observe that the *function* is of type *int* indicating that a single value of type *int* will be returned. The first argument of first mark is *int* marks[ ]. The square brackets indicates that marks is an array. The size of the array is specified by the formal parameter *int* size. As the size may vary, the actual argument will send the size when the *function* is called.

The *function* second mark has two formal arguments. The argument *int* marks [ ] is an array and the second formal argument is *int* dim which corresponds to the size of the array marks [ ].

The definitions of the *functions* are straightforward. The body of the function is based on the program given in Example Program 13.2.

The main() *function* defines an array "score" of maximum size 50. The array size is also declared. The actual value of array size should be less than 50. The rest of the main function is self-explanatory. Observe that the *functions* first mark and second mark are called in the printf statement. Calling a function in a printf statement is allowed. Single values returned by the two functions are printed by the printf statement.

In this example we have an array as an argument and the function returns only a single value. If a function is to return multiple values then we have to use a different technique. We will illustrate this in the following example.

EXAMPLE 16.7   In the last example we found the first and second marks in a class. If we want to arrange the marks in descending order we can follow a similar idea. The algorithm

```
/* Example Program 16.9 */
/* Illustrating calls and returns from function */
#include <stdio.h>
/* Definition of function prototypes */
void f(void);
void g(void);
void h(void);
main()
{
    printf("Call to f from main\n");
    f(); /* Call to f */
    printf("Control has returned to main\n");
}   /* End of main */

vold f (void) /* function f defined */
{
    printf("Control now in f\n");
    printf("Call to g from f\n");
    g(); /* End of f */
    printf("Control has returned to f from g\n");
} /* end of f */

void g(void) /* function g defined */
{
    printf("Control now in g\n");
    printf("Call to h from g\n");
    h(); /* Call to h */
    printf("Control has returned to g from h\n");
} /* End of g */

void h(void) /* function h defined */
{
    printf("Control now in h\n");
    prlntf("Return control to g\n");
} /* End of h */
```

Output of Example Program 16.9

```
Call to f from main
Control now in f
Call to g from f
Control now in g
Call to h from g
Control now in h
Return control to g
Control has returned to g from h
Control has returned to f from g
Control has returned to main
```

g a   1 .   Calls and returns from functions.

```
/* Example Program 16.10 */
#include <stdio.h>
/* Function prototype definitions */
int first_marks(int marks[], int size);
int second_marks(int marks[], int size);
main()
{
    int array_size, score[50], i;
    scanf("%d", &array_size);
    for (i = 0; i <= array_size -1; ++i)
        scanf("%d", &score[i]);
    printf("First Marks = %d Second Marks = %d\n",
            first_mark(score, array_size),
            second_mark(score, array_size));
} /* End of main */

int first_mark(int marks[], int size)
{
    int first = 0, i;
    for (i = 0; i <= (size -1); ++i)
        if (marks[i] > first)
            first = marks [i];
    return(first);
} /* End of first mark */

int second_mark(int mks[], int dim)
{
    int second = 0, i;
    for (i = 0; i <= (dim -1); ++i)
        if (mks[i] != first_mark(mks, dim))
            if (mks[i] > second)
                second = mks[i];
    return(second);
} /* End of second mark */
```

g a   1 .1   rray as argument in a function.

we will use is called a *bubble sort*. The way we will implement it is quite inefficient but it illustrates the use of arrays and the method of getting more than one value as output from a function.

The method we follow is to use two *for* loops (see the *function* definition in Example Program 16.11). In the body of the *for* loop we compare marks [1] with marks [0] and interchange them if marks [1] > marks [0]. Now marks [0] will contain the higher marks. We next compare marks [2] with marks [0] and interchange them if marks [2] > marks [0]. This procedure is repeated successively comparing marks [0] with marks [3], etc. till marks [class size]. At the end of this loop marks [0] will contain the highest marks.

Having placed the highest marks in marks [0], the procedure is repeated starting with marks [1] and comparing it with marks [2], marks [3], ..., marks[class size]. The second

```
/* Example Program 16.11 */
/* Sorting Marks */
#include<stdio.h>
void sort_marks(int marks[], int no_of_students);

main()
{
    int i, no_students, score[50];
    scanf("%d", &no_students);
    for (i = 0; i <= no_students -1; ++i)
       scanf ("%d", &score[i]);
    sort_marks(score, no_students);
    printf("Sorted marks", score[i]);
    for (i = 0; i <= no_students - 1; ++i)
        printf("%d ", score[i]);
    printf("\n");
}   /* End of Main */

void sort_marks(int marks[], int class_size)
{
    int i, j, temp;

    for (i =0; i <= class_size-2; ++i)
       for(j = i+1; j <= class_size -1; ++j)
         if (marks[j] > marks[i])
            {
               temp = marks[i];
               marks[i] = marks[j];
               marks[j] = temp;
            }
} /* End of sort marks */
```

g a   1 .11   Sorting mar s.

highest marks will now be in marks [1]. Continuing along the same lines the two loops in the *function* arrange the marks in descending order. The sorted marks are in marks [0], marks [1], ..., marks [class size] within the *function* sort marks.

The question is how to *return* these sorted marks to the calling main *function*. The *return* statement of a *function* can only return one value. The way C programming language solves the problem is to treat arrays, appearing in formal argument list in a different manner. We saw that normally when a *function* calls another *function* the actual argument value is *copied* into the formal argument name and the called *function* uses it in processing. The value of the actual argument in the calling function is unaltered. When an argument is an array, however, a copy of the array elements *is not made* and sent to the formal array. Instead, the address, in memory where the array is stored is made known to the called *function*. In other words the actual array in the calling *function* and the formal array in the called *function occupy the same locations in memory.* Thus the values stored in the formal array are accessible to the calling *functions.* Even though the name of the actual array used as an argument of the calling *function* and the name of the formal array used as an argument in the called function may be different, they are allocated the same locations in memory and thus their contents are identical.

An array processed by a *function* is thus available to the calling *function* which can print it out or do further processing as necessary. In Example Program 16.11 the main function declares score as an array which can store 50 elements. It would have been nice to declare it as score [no students]. This is however not allowed in C. We must use only a constant in array size declaration. If the program is to be used in many instances with varying values of no students the array size should be set to the maximum expected value of no students. After the declaration the main *function* reads the value of no students. This is used in the next *for* loop to read marks from the input and store them in score [i]. After storing the marks, main calls the *function* sort marks with formal arguments score and no students. Observe that while calling, score appears without square brackets. The fact that score is an array is known from the declaration in main. When main calls sort marks the address of the locations in memory where the actual array argument score is stored is passed to the formal array argument marks. Thus score and marks now become synonyms occupying the same locations in memory. The *function* sort marks now sorts score (which is the same as marks). The sorted values are thus available to main in the array score. The last statement in main (which is a *for* loop) prints the value of the sorted marks stored in score. As no value is returned the function sort marks is declared void in the main program.

The method of passing a scalar argument in which a copy of the value of the actual argument of the calling *function* is made and given to the formal argument of the called *function* is known as *call by value.*

The method of passing an array argument in which the *address* of the actual array argument of the calling *function* is given to the formal array argument of the called *function* is known as *call by reference.* (It is better to say "call function giving address of argument".)

In call by *value what* is stored as an argument in memory is sent. In call by *reference* the *address where an argument is stored* is sent. We will now write another program to illustrate the use of arrays in functions.

EXAMPLE 16.8 Given an array a[0], a[1], ... , a[length – 1] it is required to reverse it, interchange a[0] and a[length – 1], a[1] and a[length – 2], and so on. At the end of the operation the original array is destroyed and in its place an array whose elements are interchanged remains.

To solve this problem we have written in Example Program 16.12 a *function* reverse array whose formal arguments are *int* a[ ] and *int* length. As the subscript begins with zero the maximum subscript is (length – 1). If the length of the array is even then a pair of elements are interchanged. If the length is odd the element at the centre remains undisturbed. This idea is implemented in the *for* loop. (length/2) – 1 is used as final index as subscripting starts with zero.

In this problem too, the array is transmitted to main by reference and is thus available to main. The function reverse array is declared void.

We have written Example Program 16.13 using a *function* interchange to interchange two values. This program does not work. This is due to the fact that the individual elements of arrays are *copied* and sent to x and y respectively. The values of x and y are swapped by the function interchange. The swapped values are not returned to the calling function as the

```
/* Example Program 16.12 */
/* Illustrating use of array argument */
#include <stdio.h>
void reverse_array(int p[], int length);

main()
{
    int array_length, i, b[10];
    scanf("%d", &array_length) ;
    printf("Input array\n");
    for(i = 0; i <= array_length -1; ++i)
        scanf("%d", &b[i]);
    reverse_array(b, array_length -1) ;
    printf("Reversed array\n");
    for(i = 0; i <= array_length -1; ++i)
        printf ("%d", b[i]);
} /* End of Main */

void reverse_array(int a[], int length)
    {
        int i, temp = 0, len;
        len = (length/2) - 1;
        for(i = 0; i <= len; ++i)
            {
                temp = a[i];
                a[i] = a[length -i];
                a[length -i] = temp;
            }
    } /* End of function reverse array */
```

g a   1 .12   eversing an array.

```
/* Example Program 16.13 */
/* illustrates mistake in calling a function */

void reverse_array(int a[], int length)
{
    int i;
    for (i = 0; i <= (length/2 - 1); ++i)
        interchange(a[i], a[length - i]); /* Error */
} /* End of function reverse array */

void interchange(int x, int y)
{
    int temp;
    temp = x;
    x = y;
    y = temp;
} /* End of function interchange */
```

g a   1 .13 Illustrating error in calling a function.

calling function does not know the addresses of *x* and *y*. Only *entire arrays* are transmitted *by reference*, i.e. by sending array address to the called function's formal array argument. Array elements are transmitted only *as values*.

EXAMPLE 16.9 Two-dimensional arrays or matrices are also treated just like arrays. To illustrate this we give Example Program 16.14 which sorts the rows of a matrix. This program uses a function sort which is similar to the sort marks function given in Example Program 16.11. Observe that the *function* row sort has as one formal argument, a two-dimensional

```c
/* Example Program 16.14 */
/* This function uses the sort-marks function given in Example Program 16.11 */
#include <stdio.h>
void sort(int row[], int no_cols);
void row_sort(int a[][] , int r_length, int c_length);
main()
{
    int matrix[3][4], row_size, col_size, i, j;
    scanf("%d %d", &row_size, &col_size);
    for (i = 0; i <= row_size-1; ++i)
      for (j = 0; j <= col_size-1; ++j)
          scanf("%d", &matrix[i][j]);
    row_sort(matrix, row_size-1, col_size-1);
    for (i = 0; i <= row_size-1; ++i)
      {
          for (j = 0; j <= col_size-1; ++j)
          printf("%d", matrix[i][j]);
          printf("\n");
      }
}
void row_sort(int a[3][4], int row_dim, int col_dim)
{
    int r;
    for (r = 0; r <= row_dim; ++r)
      sort(&a[r][0], col_dim);
} /* End of row sort */
void sort (int b[], int size)
{
    int i, j, temp;
    for (i = 0; i <= size; ++i)
      for (j = 0; j <= size; ++j)
          if (b[j] < b[i])
              {
                  temp = b[i];
                  b[i] = b[j];
                  b[j] = temp;
              }
} /* End of sort */
```

g a   1 .1   Sorting ro s of a matri .

array, and the others are scalar arguments. Observe that the formal argument, namely matrix a, *must* have its dimensions specified. This is necessary for correct indexing. When row sort calls sort, observe that it specifies the starting address of the array for row 0, row 1 etc. The & operator is used to give the address. The address of the (0, 0) element of the matrix a is transmitted to sort which takes number of elements in one row of matrix a[ ] [ ] each time it is called and sorts this row. The function sort is called once for each row of a[ ][ ]. The rest of the program is self-explanatory. (The address of an array element a[i][j] is given by

$$\text{Address of a}[0][0] + (\text{col.dimension} * i + j))$$

EXAMPLE 16.10 We now consider another example of using a two-dimensional array. We develop a function to transpose a square matrix, i.e. a matrix with number of rows = number of columns. The matrix A is

$$A = \begin{bmatrix} 1 & 4 & 5 \\ 3 & 2 & -5 \\ 4 & 6 & 8 \end{bmatrix}$$

The transposed matrix is

$$A^T = \begin{bmatrix} 1 & 3 & 4 \\ 4 & 2 & 6 \\ 5 & -5 & 8 \end{bmatrix}$$

The (i, j)th element of the transposed matrix A^T is the (j, i)th element of the given matrix A.

The function

$$\text{void transpose (int a[5][5], int dim)}$$

given in Example Program 16.15 transposes the given square matrix. Observe the indexing of the two *for* loops which is important in this program.

We conclude this section with an example which uses three functions.

EXAMPLE 16.11 A program which determines the number of data points in each one of a set of assigned intervals will now be developed. Such a grouping of data into intervals is known as a frequency table and is used extensively in statistics.

The strategy we will adopt to develop the program is as follows:

(1) Given the data array to be grouped in a frequency table find the maximum and minimum values of data in the array.
(2) Given the maximum and minimum values of data and the interval size the number of intervals in which data is to be grouped, is found by dividing the maximum data minus minimum data by the size of the interval and rounding it to the next higher integer value.

```
/* Example Program 16.15 */
/* Maximum size of matrix is 5 x 5 in this program */
#include <stdio.h>
void transpose(int matrix[][], int dim);
main()
{
    int i, j, size, matrix[5][5];
    scanf("%d", &size);
    for (i = 1; i <= size; ++i)
        {
            for (j = 1; j <= size; ++i)
                scanf("%d", &matrix[i][j]);
        }
    transpose(matrix, size);
    for (i = 1; i <= size; ++i)
        {
            {
                for (j = 1; j <= size; ++j)
                    printf("%d", matrix[i][j]);
            }
            printf("\n");
        }
}

void transpose(int a[5][5], int dim)
{
    int i, j, temp;
    for i = 1; i <= dim; ++i)
        {
            for(j = i+1; j <= dim; ++j)
                {
                    temp = a[i][j];
                    a[i][j] = a[j][i];
                    a[j][i] = temp;
                }
        }
}
```

                        g a   1 .1   ransposing a matri .

(3) Having found the number of intervals, a data item is taken and the interval in which
   it is to be placed is determined by a *while* loop. This loop also counts the number of
   data items in each interval.

   The program is structured with three functions. One function is used to find the maximum
data value in the data array, the second one is used to find the minimum data. The third
function counts the number of data items in each interval. The function to find the maximum
data value has the data array and its size as the inputs and returns the maximum value as the
output. Similarly the function to find the minimum accepts the data array and its size and

returns the minimum data value. The function for obtaining the frequency table accepts the data array, its size, interval width, minimum and maximum data of data array and the number of intervals as inputs. It gives as output, the frequency table giving the number of data points in each interval. The program is given as Example Program 16.16.

```c
/* Example Program 16.16 */
#include <stdio.h>
/* Function prototype */
int max_data(int data[], int no_data);
int min_data(int data[], int no_data);
void freq_table(int data[], int no_data, int width,
                int low, int high, int slots, int table [i]);

main( )
{
    int no_of_data, slot_width, in_data[100], max,
    min, i, no_of_intervals, out_table[20];
    scanf("%d %d", &no_of_data, &slot_width);
    for (i = 0; i <= no_of_data-1; ++i)
      scanf("%d", &in_data[i]);
    max = max_data(in_data, no_of_data-1);
    min = min_data(in_data, no_of_data-1);
    printf("Min data = %d, Max data = %d\n", min, max);
    printf("Interval width = %d\n", slot_width);
    no_of_intervals = (max - min) / slot_width + 1;
    printf("No of intervals = %d\n", no_of_intervals);
    freq_table(in_data, no_of_data-1, slot_width,
               min, max, no_of_intervals, out_table);
    printf("Frequency Table \n");
    for (i = 0; i < no_of_intervals; ++i)
      printf("Slot %d = number of data = %d\n", i, out_table[i]);
}   /* End of main program */

int max_data(int data_in[], int no_data)
{
    int i, temp;
    temp = data_in[0];
    for (i = 1; i <= no_data; ++i)
      if (data_in[i] > temp)
        temp = data_in[i];
      return(temp);
} /* End of max data */

int min_data(int data_in[], int no_data)
{
    int i, temp;
    temp = data_in[0];
    for (i = 1; i <= no_data; ++i)
      if (data_in[i] < temp)
        temp = data_in[i];
    return(temp);
} /* End of function min data */
```

```
void freq_table(int data_in[], int no_data,
                int interval_width, int min,
                int max, int no_intervals,
                int tab_freq[])
{
    int i, slot_found, k, limit;
    for (i = 0; i <= no_data; ++i)
    {
        slot_found = 0;
        k = 0;
        limit = min + interval_width;
        while (slot_found == 0)
        {
            if (data_in[i] < limit)
            {
                ++tab_freq[k];
                slot_found = 1;
            }
            else
            {
                limit += interval_width;
                ++k;
            }
        } /* End of while */
    } /* End of for loop */
} /* End of function freq_table */
```

g a   1 .1   Fre uency table.

16.5   GLOBAL, LOCAL AND STATIC VARIABLES

We saw that *functions* return only one value in C. If a number of values are to be returned by a function we have three ways of doing it. One method is to use an array as an argument. The problem with this is that all the array elements should be homogeneous. A second method is to place the values to be returned in variables accessible to *all* functions and the main program. Such variables are called *global variables* in C. In this section we will describe how to declare and use global variables. A third method is to declare formal arguments in *functions* as addresses instead of as variable names. In other words formal arguments are specified as the addresses of variable names.

We will take as an example the solution of a quadratic equation for which a program was developed in Chapter 11 (Example Program 11.4). If we want to write a *function* to solve the quadratic equation then we should get the results, namely, x real 1, x real 2, x imag 1, x imag 2 returned. As a *function* cannot return more than one value, to obtain these values we must find some other way. We solve it by declaring x real 1, x real 2, x imag 1 and x imag 2 as global variables. The program using a function solve quadratic is given as Example Program 16.17. Observe that global values are used inside the function body.

```
/* Example Program 16.17 */
/* Function solve_quadratic solves quadratic equations */
#include <stdio.h>
#include <math.h>
/* Function Prototype */
void solve_quadratic(float p, float q, float r);
/* global variables defined below */
float x_real_1, x_real_2, x_imag_1, x_imag_2;

main()
{
    float x, y, z;
    while(scanf("%f %f %f", &x, &y, &z) != EOF)
        {
            x_real_1 = x_real_2 = x_imag_1 = x_imag_2 = 0;
            printf("Coefficients of the quadratic equation");
            printf(" (a*x*x + b*x + c) are:\n");
            printf("a = %f, b = %f, c = %f\n", x, y, z);
            printf ("Solution of Quadratic equation\n");
            solve_quadratic(x, y, z);
            printf("x_real_1 = %f, x_real_2 = %f\n",
                    x_real_1, x_real_2);
            printf("x_imag_1 = %f, x_imag_2 = %f\n\n",
                    x_imag_1, x_imag_2);
        }
} /* End of main */

vold solve_quadratic(float a, float b, float c)
{
    float discrmnt,
    float temp;
    if (a == 0)
        {
            printf("Linear equation, Only one root\n");
            x_real_1 = -c/b,
            return;
        }
    discrmnt = b+b - 4.0*a*c;
    if (discrmnt > 0)
        {
            printf("Real roots\n");
            temp = sqrt(discrmnt);
            x_real_1 = (-b + temp)/(2.0 * a);
            x_real_2 = (-b - temp)/(2.0 * a);
            return;
        }

    if (discrmnt < 0)
        {
            printf("Complex Conjugate roots\n");
            discrmnt = -discrmnt;
            x_imag_1 = sqrt(discrmnt)/(2.0 * a);
```

```
        x_imag_2 = -x_imag_1;
        x_real_1 = -b/(2.0 *a);
        x_real_2 = x_real_1;
        return;
    }

  if (discrmnt == 0)
    {
        printf("Repeated roots\n");
        x_real_1 = -b/(2.0 * a);
        x_real_2 = x_real_1;
        return;
    }
} /* End of function solve-quadratic */
```

ga   1 .1   Solving uadratic e uation.

The structure of a C program we have written so far is shown in Table 16.1.

Table 1 .1   Structure of a C   rogram

File inclusion statements	#include <stdio.h> #include <math.h> #include ....
Function prototypes	Definition of function prototypes Declaration of global variables. main ()

Body of main	{ Declaration of local variables.
	    Statements in the body main ()
	    including calls to *functions*.
	
	} /* End of main */

Body of fun 1	Void fun 1(int p[ ], float q, int r)
	{ Declaration of local variables.
	    Statements in the body of fun 1()
	    including calls to other functions.
	} /* End of fun 1 */

Body of fun 2	int fun 2 (float a, int z[ ])
	{ Declaration of local variables.
	    Statements in body of fun 2
	    including calls to other functions.
	} /* End of fun 2 */

Variables declared outside the body of all functions (including main) are known as global variables or external variables. Normally in practice they are defined after function prototype definitions and main() as shown in Table 16.2.

Table 1 .2   Illustrating declaration of global variables

```
# include statements
Function prototypes
Declaration of Global Variables
main()
{
 ...
} /* End of main() */
Definition of functions
```

The rules for declaration of global variables are the same as for local variables in functions. Global variables may be accessed by their declared name by any *function* and changed. The latest value will be stored in them. Global variables are initialized automatically to zero by the compiler.

A global variable name should not be declared again in a function. If it is done the value stored in the global variable is not accessible in the function body.

The main disadvantage of global variables are:

1. When functions are developed by different programmers they should know the names of global variables and use the same names. Thus strict coordination between members of the programming team is essential.
2. If the declaration of the global variable is changed, then all functions using these variables must be changed.
3. As many functions can alter the contents of global variables there is always a danger of unintentional change of stored data leading to errors. Such changes are known as "side effects" and are difficult to detect.
4. Normally a programmer must make it a practice to clearly specify the inputs and outputs of functions and use them as formal parameters. All other variables required in the function must be declared as local. Global variables must not be used unless they are essential to solve the problem and there is no simple way of avoiding them.

Referring to Table 16.1 we see that within the body of *functions* we define local variables. As we explained earlier memory locations are allocated to the local variables when a *function* is called. The variables are not automatically initialized. They should be initialized by the programmer. They are available only within the *function*. When control leaves the function the memory locations reserved for local variables are released. Their contents are thus lost and not available to any other *function*. Thus local variables have no meaning outside the *function*. If a *function* is called again, new memory locations are allocated again to the local variables. The old values are lost. The variables should thus be initialized again. Such local variables are also known as *automatic variables* as memory is allocated to them when the *function* is entered. One may declare such variables as:

auto type <variable name>

Normally the key word auto is omitted as by default all local variables declared in a *function* are *auto*. If the value of a local variable in a function is to be preserved and not lost when a *function* is exited then such a variable is declared *static*.

Thus if we write

static int k ;

then the value of *k* will not be lost when control leaves a *function*. Example Program 16.18 illustrated the use of *static* variables.

```
/* Example Program 16.18 */
/* A program to find average age of a group */
#include <stdio.h>
int sum_good_age(int b);
int data_ok(int p);
main()
{
    int s, serial_no, age, no_of_data = 0, good_data = 0, avge_age;
    while(scanf("%d %d", a serial_no, &age) != EOF)
        {
            ++no_of_data;
            s = sum_good_age(age);
            good_data += data_ok(age);

        }
    if (((float)good_data/(float)no_of_data) < 0.90)
        printf("Too many bad data - Result not given\n");
    printf("Good data = %d, No of data = %d\n", good_data, no_of_data);
    else
        {
            avge_age = s/good_data;
            printf("Good data = %d, Average Age = %d\n",good_data, avge_age);
        }
    }
int data_ok(int p)
{
    if ((p < 0) || (p > 100))
        return(0),
    else
        return (1);
}
int sum_good_age(int x)
{
    static int sum = 0;
    if (data_ok(x))
        sum += x;
    return(sum);
} /* End of sum good age */
```

g a   1 .1   verage age of a group.

In this Example Program sum is declared *static* in the function. First time this function is called sum is initialized and used by the function sum good age. When the function is exited, sum is saved as it is declared *static*. Each time the function is entered the earlier value stored is used. The initialization given in static is *valid only the first time* the function is entered. Thus when all data have been read by the *while* loop in main (), sum good age has the final value of sum returned.

This example is cooked up to illustrate the use of static declaration.

There are some more questions on functions we have not answered in this chapter. These are:

   (i) Can *functions* be defined within other *functions* in C language? The answer is NO. Pascal allows this and there is the so called block structure in Pascal which is not available in C.
   (ii) Can a *function* call itself? The answer is Yes. This is called *recursion*. We will discuss this in a later chapter.
   (iii) Can a *function* be made a formal argument of another *function*? The answer is NO.
   (iv) Can a C program invoke programs written in another language such as Fortran? If yes, how? The answer is Yes.

For writing a number of useful C programs it is not necessary to know the answers to these questions. Only after using *functions* in many applications would a programmer reach a level of maturity needing such facilities. We thus postpone answering some of these questions to later chapters in this book.

EXERCISES

16.1 Write a C program for the function f(x) defined below:

$$f(x) = 2x^2 + 3x + 4 \qquad \text{for } x < 2$$
$$f(x) = 0 \qquad \text{for } x = 2$$
$$f(x) = -2x^2 + 3x - 4 \qquad \text{for } x > 2$$

16.2 Write a C function to evaluate the series

$$f(x) = 1 + \frac{x^2}{2!} - \frac{x^4}{4!} + \frac{x^6}{6!} - \frac{x^8}{8!} + \frac{x^{10}}{10!} - \frac{x^{12}}{12!}$$

16.3 Write a C function to evaluate the series

$$\sin(x) = x - \frac{x^3}{3!} + \frac{x^5}{5!} - \ldots$$

    to five significant digits

16.4 Write a function to multiply a square-matrix by a vector. Assume a $n \times n$ matrix and a n component vector. The call would give the size of the matrix and the names of the matrix and a vector.

16.5 Use the function of Exercise 16.4 to generate a 6×6 matrix whose elements are given by

$$a_{ij} = 2^{-(i-j)}$$

16.6 Write a function to find the trace of a matrix. The trace is defined as the sum of the diagonal elements of the matrix. How would this routine be called?

16.7 Write a function to multiply two $n \times n$ matrices.

16.8 Write a function to find the norm of a matrix. The norm is defined as the square root of the sum of the squares of all elements in the matrix.

16.9 Write a function to sort a set on n numbers in ascending order of magnitude. How would this routine be called?

16.10 Write functions to add, subtract, multiply and divide two complex numbers (x + iy) and (a + ib).

16.11 Rewrite Example Program 15.1 using separate functions to
(i) read a SMAC program into memory,
(ii) check op code and address, and
(iii) execute the machine language program.

16.12 Rewrite Example Program 15.2 using functions for
(i) initialization,
(ii) reading a student's marks and validating it,
(iii) finding the average marks and class of a student, and
(iv) determining class average, covariance etc.

16.13 Rewrite Example Program 15.4 using appropriate functions.

16.14 Write a function to validate the elements of a matrix of size n × n. The validation rules are:
(i) All diagonal entries should be positive.
(ii) The matrix should be symmetric.
(iii) All the non-diagonal elements should be negative or zero.

16.15 Write a function to validate data input having an inventory list in the following format:

Column numbers	Information	Valid range
1 to 5	Item number	1 to 99999
6 to 8	Supplier code	222 to 888
7 to 10	Quantity	1 to 9999
11 to 16	Cost/unit	≥ 5.0 and ≤ 500.0

Invalid data should be written out with an appropriate message.

17

Processing Character Strings

┌───┐
│   **LEARNING OBJECTIVES**   │

In this chapter we will learn:

1. How to declare, read, and write characters.
2. How to declare and manipulate strings of characters.
3. How to develop general purpose functions to manipulate strings and how they are used.
└───┘

So far we have considered only the simplest data types available in C. These data types are sufficient for numeric applications. The greatest strength of C is the rich data types and data structures provided by the language. This enables easy development of programs in many application areas such as manipulation of strings of character, lists, records and files. These applications are primarily non-numeric. We will introduce in this chapter a data type called char for characters and illustrate operations on strings of characters.

17.1 THE CHARACTER DATA TYPE

Individual characters such as a, b, c, etc. can be stored in variable names. If a variable name is to store a character then it is declared to be of type char. For example, if we declare

char letter;

then the variable name letter may store any character available in the character set of the computer installation. Character sets are not, unfortunately, standardized. They vary from machine to machine. There is a trend towards standardization using the character set suggested by the American National Standards Institute (ASCII character set). A programmer in an installation should find out what is implemented in the particular C system.

When a variable is declared as char, only a single character can be stored in it. For example, we may write:

letter = 'y';

The character to be stored in the variable name is enclosed by apostrophes (single quotes). A declaration as char implies that the variable name is a scalar data type which can store only one character and not a string of characters. Thus:

char letter ;

letter = "xyz"

is illegal as letter is a scalar. A string is written in C as "xyz". We will describe later how such strings are treated.

Characters are stored internally in a computer as a coded set of binary digits which have positive decimal integer equivalents. These codes can be ordered in ascending sequence called collating sequence. The ASCII collating sequence and codes are given in Table 17.1.

Table 1 .1   ASCII codes for characters

Left Digits	Right Digit → 0	1	2	3	4	5	6	7	8	9
3					!	"	#	$	%	&	'
4	(	)	*	+	,	–	.	/	0	1
5	2	3	4	5	6	7	8	9	:	;
6	<	=	>	?	@	A	B	C	D	E
7	F	G	H	I	J	K	L	M	N	O
8	P	Q	R	S	T	U	V	W	X	Y
9	Z	[	\	]	^	–	'	a	b	c
10	d	e	f	g	h	i	j	k	l	m
11	n	o	p	q	r	s	t	u	v	w
12	x	y	z	{			}	~			

Observe that the codes for upper- and lower-case letters are different. Thus A is different from a. Note also that there are two representations for digits. If a digit 4 is stored in a variable name of type integer then it is converted to binary and can be used in arithmetic expressions. If it is stored in a variable name of type char then it is coded as an ASCII character and has the code 52. It can be used in arithmetic expressions but will be taken as 52.

Codes 00 to 31 and code 127 represent special control characters which cannot be printed. Code 00 represents null and code 32 represents a blank character. The code for Z, for example, is 90 (in decimal) and its binary representation in the computer would be 1011010.

In C language the ASCII equivalent of characters is stored as an integer. We can manipulate these integers using arithmetic operations. We can find out the ASCII equivalent of a character by printing its value as shown below:

```
char letter;
int p;
letter = 'a';
p - letter ;
printf("%d/n", p);
```

The value printed will be 97.

17.2 MANIPULATING STRINGS OF CHARACTERS

In most applications a string of characters rather than a single character is necessary. As an individual variable name can store only one character we need an array to store strings of characters. For example, the declaration

char name[6];

declares name as an array of length 6 where each element of name stores a character. If we write

for (i = 0, i < = 5, i ++)

scanf("%c", &name[i]);

and the data input from the keyboard is

LADDUS

then we will have the following stored:

name[0] = 'L', name [1] = 'A', name[2] = 'D', name [3] = 'D', name[4] = 'U', and name[5] = 'S'

In the format string in scanf, %c is used to specify a character. The letter c in %c is lower-case c.

The string LADDUS can also be read using the statement

scanf("%s", name);

where name should be declared an array. In the format string %s is used to specify a string. Observe that before name the ampersand & is not written as name itself is the address of the element name [0]. The specification %s in the format, states that a string is stored in the array name.

If data input from the keyboard is

LADDUS \n (\n is carriage return)

then we will have as before name [0] = 'L'; name [1] = 'A', name [2] = 'D', name [3] = 'D', name [4] = 'U' and name [5] = 'S'.

There is one danger in using %s specification. If the string being read has a blank then scanf assumes that the string is terminated and stops reading.

Thus if we write

scanf("%s", buffer);

and the input string is

HE CAME

then buffer[0] = 'H' and buffer[1] = 'E'. The string CAME will not be read by the statement. If we write

scanf("%s%s", buff 1, buff 2);

then HE will be stored in array buff 1 and CAME in array buff 2.

Strings may be displayed by using a printf function with %s specification. Thus if we write

printf("name displayed is :%s \n", name);

then the display will be:

name displayed is : LADDUS

If a string HE CAME HOME is stored in the array buff 3 the statement

printf("Display of buff 3:%s\n", buff 3);

will display it. Observe that blanks within a string do not upset the printf function.

In C an individual character is represented by using a pair of single quote marks to enclose the character. If we write

s[l] = 'P';

then the character P is stored in s[1]. If we write

s[1] = "P"; /* This is wrong */

then the right-hand side is taken as a string. A string is a sequence of characters and is automatically terminated by the end of string character '\0' by the C translator. Thus we require two elements in an array to store a string. (Even though \0 looks like two characters, a back slash and a 0, C language treats it as a single end of string character.)

To illustrate the use of character data type, Example Program 17.1 gives a small program to count the number of 'A's in a name. Observe in this program that name is declared as an array with 20 characters. These 20 characters should include the end of line character '\n'.

```
/* Example Program 17.1 */
/* Program to count number of A's in a set of names */
#include (stdio.h)

main()
{
    char name[20];
    int i, countA=0;
    for (i = 0; i < 20; ++i)
      {
        scanf("%c", &name[i]);
        printf("%c", name[i]);
        if (name[i] == '\n' )
          break;
        else
          if (name[i] == 'A' )
             ++countA;
      } /* End of for loop */
    printf("Number of A's in name = %d\n", countA);
} /* End of Main */
```

g a   1 .1 Number of 'A's in a name.

When a name is typed on the terminal we do not type \0 at the end of the name. A carriage return is taken as end of line. If we do not press carriage return after typing the name then the program will continue in the for loop 20 times and will read the blanks, if any, at the end of the name as well. A blank (or white space as it is sometimes called) is also a character (A null character is "absence of a character" and is represented by '\0' which is also used as end of string character.)

Returning to Example Program 17.1, in the for loop scanf reads one character at a time from the standard input and stores it in name [0], name[1] ... etc. up to name [19]. It is printed by printf which is the next statement. The if statement following printf checks if the character read is an end of line character. If it is, then it executes break and leaves the loop. Otherwise it checks if the character is an 'A'. If it is 'A' then it increments the count of A.

C language also provides some library functions to read characters from a terminal and display them on a terminal. These functions are:

int getchar(void)

This function reads a character from the input and returns it. Observe that the returned value is of type int even though a character is read. This need not concern us. If we write

char in char ;

in char = getchar( );

then a character read from input will be stored in the character variable in char.

The companion function to display a character on the terminal is

void putchar(char p);

If we write

char out char;

putchar (out char);

then a character stored in out char will be displayed on the terminal.

We show the use of these functions in Example Program 17.2.

We will now develop a few routines to illustrate basic operations with strings. The routines are:

1. Read a string and store it.
2. Find the length of a string (i.e. the number of characters in a string).
3. Copy a specified portion of a string.
4. Delete the specified characters from a string.
5. Concatenate a string at the left of a given string.
6. Concatenate a string at the right of a given string.
7. Delete the occurrence of a substring from a string
8. Insert a string in a specified position of a given string.

These functions are useful in many complex string processing problems.

As C does not provide a dynamically changing array size we will provide 81 characters as maximum length of a string. This choice is based on the fact that most terminals have 80

```
/* Example Program 17.2 */
/* Illustrating using getchar() and putchar() */
#include <stdio.h>

main()
{
    char name [20];
    int i, countA = 0;
    for (i = 0; i < 20; ++i)
      {
        name[i] = getchar();
        putchar(name[i]);
        if (name[i] == '\n' )
          break,
        else
           if (name[i] == 'A')
             ++countA;
      } /* End of for loop */
    printf("\nNumber of A's in name = %d\n", countA);
}   /* End of main */
```

g a   1 .2   Use of getchar( ) and putchar( ).

characters per line. The 81st character could be the character equivalent of the code when the return key of a terminal is pressed.

Example Program 17.3 reads a line from a terminal and stores it in an array named buffer. If there is an attempt to read an empty line an appropriate message is given by the function. Examining the function read line (char string[ ]) we see that in its body we initialize i to 0, get a character from the standard input unit and store it in string[0]. In the while loop this character is checked and if it is '\n' the while loop is exited and a message printed. If the character is not '\n' the body of the while loop is repeated. The next character is read from the input and assigned to string[1]. Reading a character and storing it in string[i] is repeated until the end of line is encountered. (End of line is indicated by the character corresponding to return key on the terminal which is pressed after typing a line.) When the end of line is encountered, control leaves the while loop.

Observe that if the input string is empty then the first character itself will be '\n'. Control leaves the loop and an error message is printed. If i > 0 then the statements in the body of the loop would have been executed at least once. Control leaves the while loop when it reads a '\n' character. We replace '\n' character by the end of string character '\0' using the statement string [i] = '\0'. Control now leaves the function.

The function print line (char out string[ ]) displays the given string.

Observe the while loop in the function body. It displays characters one after one until the end of string character is encountered.

Example Program 17.4 is a function to find the length of a string. The program is quite simple to understand.

```
/* Example Program 17.3 */
/* A function to read a line and store it in a buffer. Another function to print
   a line is also given */
#include <stdio.h>
void read_line(char s[]);
void print_line(char s[]);
main()
{
    char buffer[81];
    read_line(buffer);
    print_line(buffer);
} /* End of main */
void read_line(char string[])
{
    int i = 0;
    string[i] = getchar();
    while(string[i] != '\n')
        {
            string[++i] = getchar();
        } /* End of while */
    if (i == 0)
        {
            printf("Empty string\n");
            return;
        }
    string[i] = '\0'; /* Overwrites '\n' character */
    return;
} /* End of read_line */
void print_line(char out_string[])
{
    int i = 0;
    while(out_string[i] != '\0')
        {
            putchar(out_string[i]);
            ++i;
        } /* End while */
} /* End of print_line */
```

g a   1 .3 Function to read a line.

```
/* Example Program 17.4 */
/* A function to find the length of a string */
/* length of string does not include '\0' character */
int length(char string[])
{
    int i = 0, len;
    while(string[i] != '\0')
        ++i;
    if (i == 0)
        len = 0;
    else
        len = i;
    return(len);
} /* End of function length */
```

g a   1 .   Finding length of a string.

Example Program 17.5 is a function which copies a specified number of characters from a given position of a string and places it in another string. Example Program 17.6 is a function to delete all the occurrences of a specified character from a string and store the compressed string back in the given string.

```
/* Example Program 17.5 */
/* Copy into new_string, substring of given_string from (from_posn) the given
   number of characters */

void copy_substring(char given_string[],
                    int from_posn,
                    int no_char, char new_string[])
{
    int i;
    for (i = 0; i < no_char, ++i)
       new_string[i] = given_string[from_posn -1 + i];
    /* [from_posn -1 + i] is used as given_string index starts with 0 */
    new_string[i] = '\0';
} /* End of copy_substring */
```

g a   1 .   Copying substring into a string.

Referring to Example 17.6 we see that in the first for loop in the function a character in the given string is copied to the temp string only if it is not to be deleted. If it is to be deleted it is not copied in the temp string. Index i is incremented to read the next character in given string. The index used for temp string is j and it is incremented within the loop. After creating this temporary string it is written back in the given string. At the end of the compressed string the '\0' character is placed. Observe how the program is written using all the functions developed so far in this chapter.

```
/* Example Program 17.6 */
/* Deleting specified characters in a string and compressing it */
#include <stdio.h>
void read_line(char s[]);
void print_line(char s[]);
int length(char s[]);
void delete_compress_str(char s[], char deleted);
main()
{
    char d, string[81];
    /* d is the character to be deleted */
    read_line(string);
    d = getchar();
    delete_compress_str(string, d);
    print_line(string);
    printf("\n");
} /* End of main */
```

```
/* Insert functions read-line, print-line and length here */
void delete_compress_str(char given_string[], char given_char)
{
    int i = 0, j = 0, len, g_length;
    char temp_string[81];
    g_length = length(given_string);
    for(i = 0; i <= g_length; ++i)
      if (given_string[i] != given_char)
          {
              temp_string[j] = given_string[i];
              ++j;
          }
    temp_string[j] = '\0';
    len = length(temp_string);
    for(i = 0; i <= len; ++i)
      given_string[i] = temp_string[i];
    given_string[i + 1] = '\0';
} /* End of compress_string */
```

g a   1 .   Deleting characters from a string.

Example Program 17.7 concatenates (i.e. appends) a string to the right of a given string and prints the concatenated string: Observe that this program uses the functions already developed. The function concatenate right is traced in Table 17.2.

```
/* Example Program 17.7 */
/* Concatenating a string to the right of the given string */
#include <stdio.h>
void read_line(char s[]);
void print_line(char s[]);
int length(char s[]);
void concatenate_right(char s[], char r[]);

main()
{
    char given_string[81], new_string[81];
    read_line(given_string);
    read_line(new_string);
    concatenate_right(given_string, new_string);
    print_line(given_string);
    printf("\n");
} /* End of main */

void concatenate_right(char g_str[], char str[])
    /* Concatenate a string to the right of the given string */
{
    int i, given_length, str_length;
    given_length = length(g_str);
    str_length = length(str);
    for (i = given_length;
         i <= given_length + str_length; ++i)
       g_str[i] = str[i - given_length];
} /* End of concatenate right */

/* Functions read_line, print_line and length are included here */
```

g a   1 .   Concatenating a string to the right.

Table 1 .2 Trace of function concatenate_right

i	0 1 2 3 4	
g string	a b c d \0	given length = 4(\0 not counted)
str	x y z \0	str length = 3(\0 not counted)
for(i = 4;i <= 7; ++i)		
g string[i] = str[i – given length];		
i	0 1 2 3 4 5 6 7	
g string	a b c d x y z \0	
str	x y z \0	

Example Program 17.8 concatenates a string to the left of a given string. This function is more tricky as we have to move the given string right a number of positions equal to the string which is to come on its left. We cannot write given string [i + 1] = given string[i] to

```
/* Example Program 17.8 */
/* Program to concatenate a string to the left of a given string */
#include <stdio.h>
void read_line(char s[]);
void print_line(char s[]);
int length(char s[]);
void left_concatenate(char s[], char r[]);

main()
{
    char given_string[81], conc_string[81];
    read_line(given_string);
    read_line(conc_string);
    left_concatenate(given_string, conc_string);
    print_line(given_string);
    printf ("\n");
} /* End of Main */

/* Place read_line, print_line and length functions here */

/* Concatenate string to the left of given_string */
void left_concatenate(char g_str[], char str[])
{
    int i, g_length, str_length;
    char temp[81];
    g_length = length(g_str);
    str_length = length(str);
    for (i = 0; i < str_length; ++i)
       temp[i] = str[i];
    for (i = 0; i <= g_length; ++i)
       temp[str_length + i] = g_str[i];
    for (i = 0; i < str_length + g_length; ++i)
       g_str[i] = temp[i];
} /* End of concatenate */
```

g a 1 .   Concatenating a string to the left.

shift the given string right as what was originally in given string [i + 1] will be over-written. Table 17.3 is a trace of this function which the student is urged to study carefully.

Table 1 .3   Trace of function left_concatenate

i	0 1 2 3 4								
g string	a b c d \0							g length = 4	
str	x y \0							str length = 2	
for (i = 0; i < 2; ++i)									
temp[i] = str[i];									
	0 1 2								
temp	x y \0								
for (i = 0; i <= 4; ++i)									
temp[str length + i] = g str[i]									
i	0 1 2 3 4 5 6								
g str	a b c d \0								
temp	x y a b c d \0								
for (i = 0; i < 6, ++i)									
g str[i] = temp[i];									
i	0 1 2 3 4 5 6								
g str	x y a b c d \0								
str	x y \0								

Example Program 17.9 is to delete a specified number of characters from a given string from a specified position. After deletion the given string is shortened and the rest of the string to its end is filled with null characters.

The last program in this section is to insert a string in a given string from a specified position. We would demonstrate how to use the previously developed functions to do this job. The strategy we will use is given in Algorithm 17.1. This algorithm is written as a C program in Example Program 17.10.

Algorithm 17.1:   Insert string in a given string
Given: given string, insertion string, position from which to insert the insertion string in given string.

Procedure
    Step 1: Copy the given string from beginning to (insert pos) to a temp string
    Step 2: Delete the copied part of the given string from the given string and compress the given string
    Step 3: Right concatenate the insertion string to temp string
    Step 4: Right concatenate the given string (as at end of step 2) to temp string
    Step 5: Store back the temp string in the given string

```
/* Example Program 17.9 */
/* Function to delete characters from specified position */
#include <stdio.h>
void read_line(char s[]);
void print_line(char s[]);
int length(char s[]);
void delete_chars(char s[], int from, int no_of_char);
main()
{
    char given_string[81];
    int from_position, no_of_chars;
    read_line(given_string);
    scanf("%d %d", &from_position, &no_of_chars);
    delete_chars(given_string, from_position, no_of_chars);
    print_line(given_string);
    printf("\n");
} /* End of main */
/* Place read_line, print_line, length functions here */

void delete_chars(char given_string[], int from_pos, int no_char)
{
    int g_length, i;
    g_length = length(given_string);
    if ((no_char > g_length) || (from_pos > g_length))
       {
          printf("Error in input parameters\n");
          return;
       }
    for (i = from_pos; i <= g_length - no_char; ++i)
       given_string[i] = given_string[i + no_char];
/* This for loop puts null characters to end of given string */
    for (i = g_length - no_char + 1; i <= g_length; ++i)
       given_string [i] = '\0';
} /* End of delete chars */
```

g a 1 . Deleting characters from a specified position.

17.3 SOME STRING PROCESSING EXAMPLES

EXAMPLE 17.1 As the first example we will write a program to rearrange a set of names with last name first. We assume that the names are given in one of the following forms:

First name blank or . Middle name blank or . Last name
First name blank or . Last name
First name
First name blank or . Middle initial blank or . Last name
First initial blank or . Middle name blank or . Last name
First initial blank or . Middle initial blank or . Last name etc.

```
/* Example Program 17.10 */
/* Function to insert string */
#include <stdio.h>
int length(char s[]);
void read_line(char string[]);
void print_line(char out_string[]);
void copy_substring(char s[], int a, int p, char temp[]);
void delete_chars(char s[], int from, int to);
void concatenate_right(char s[], char ins []);
void insert_string(char s[], char ins[], int from);

main()
{
    char given_string[81], insertion_string[81];
    int from;

    read_line(given_string);
    read_line(insertion_string);
    scanf("%d", &from);
    insert_string(given_string, insertion_string, from);
    print_line(given_string); printf("\n");
} /* End of main */

void insert_string(char given_string[], char insertion_string[],
                int insert_position)
{
    int len;
    char temp_string[81];
    /* Copy to temp_string position 0 to (insert_position - 1) of given string */
    copy_substring(given_string, 1, insert_position - 1, temp_string);
    delete_chars(given_string, 0, insert_position - 1);
    concatenate_right(temp_string, insertion_string);
    concatenate_right(temp_string, given_string);
    len = length(temp_string);
    copy_substring(temp_string, 1, len, given_string);
} /* End of insert_string */
```

                    g a   1 .1   Inserting a string.

For example:

Given names	Rearranged names
RAM KUMAR GUPTA	GUPTA RAM KUMAR
S. RAJU	RAJU S.
ARVIND	ARVIND
RAM K. VEPA	VEPA RAM K.
V. RAM KUMAR	KUMAR V. RAM
A.V. GANESH	GANESH A.V.
V.K.R.V. RAO	RAO V.K.R.V.

The strategy of the algorithm is given as Algorithm 17.2.

Algorithm 17.2: Algorithm to rearrange a name

Step 1: Read name string
Step 2: Scan name string from right to left and find the number of characters from end
of name to the first occurrence a '.' or blank. Call it j.
Step 3: Copy these j characters to a temp string
Step 4: Concatenate (length of name – j) characters of name string to the right of temp string.
Step 5: Copy temp string to name string
Step 6: Print name string

This algorithm is implemented as Example Program 17.11. Observe the use of functions
developed earlier in the program. Observe the use of the function exit () provided by C
language. This function returns control to main ().

```
/* Example Program 17.11 */
/* Rearranging names */
#include <stdio.h>
void read_line(char s[]);
void print_line(char s[]);
void copy_substring(char g_s[], int f_p, int no_ch, char s[]);
void delete_chars(char g_s[], int f_p, int no_ch);
void concatenate_left(char g_s[], char s[]);
void concatenate_right(char g_s[], char s[]);
int length(char s[]);

main()
{
    char name_string[81], temp_string[81];
    int i, p, j=0, n_length;
    read_line(name_string);
    print_line(name_string);
    printf("\n");
    n_length = length(name_string);
    /* This for loop scans name from right to left and stops when a blank or a
       '.' is encountered or string ends. It counts the number of characters
       scanned */
    for (i = n_length; (i != 0) &&
        (name_string[i] != ' ') &&
        (name_string[i] != '.'); --i)
      ++j ;
    /* At the end of the for loop j contains the number of characters from the
       end of name to the first occurrence of a '.' or a blank */
    p = n_length - j;
    /* p is the number of characters in name_string from the beginning to the
       last blank or a '.' */
    if (p == 0)
```

```
      {
        print_line(name_string);
        exit(0);
      }
   /* print name and exit if the person has no more initials or first name.
      Otherwise copy into temp_string j characters from position p */
   copy_substring(name_string, p + 2, n_length, temp_string);
   delete_chars(name_string, p + 2, n_length - p);
   concatenate_left(name_string, " ");
   concatenate_right(temp_string, name_string);
   copy_substring(temp_string, 1, n_length + 1, name_string);
   name_string[n_length + 2] = '\0';
   print_line(name_string);
   printf("\n");
} /* End main */
/* Insert functions length, read_line, print_line, copy_substring, delete_chars,
   concatenate_right, concatenate_left */
```

g a   1 .11   Rearranging names.

EXAMPLE 17.2   An identifier in a language is defined as a string with 8 or less characters. Any character beyond 8 are ignored. It must start with an uppercase letter. All other characters in the string should be either an uppercase letter or a digit. A function is to be developed which returns a 1 if it is a legal identifier and a 0 if it is not legal. An appropriate error message should be printed.

The function is given in Example Program 17.12. Observe the use of character class tests isupper and isdigit which are available as a library in C. The character class tests are defined in the library <ctype.h>. The tests available in this library are given in Appendix V.

```
/* Example Program 17.12 */
/* Checking whether an identifier is syntactically correct */
#include <stdio.h>
#include <ctype.h>
int check_identifier(char name[]);
main()
{
    char n[20];
    scanf("%s", n);
    if (check_identifier(n))
       printf("Identifier legal\n");
    else
       printf("Identifier illegal\n");
} /* End of main */

int check_identifier(char name[])
{
    int i, ok;
    if (!(isupper(name[0])))
```

```
    {
        printf ("First Character not an uppercase letter\n");
        return (0),
    }
    for (i = 1, (i <= 7) && (name[i] != '\0'); ++i)
    {
        if (isupper (name[i]))
            ok = 1;
        else
            if (isdigit (name[i]))
                ok = 1;
            else
                {
                    printf ("%dth character illegal\n", i);
                    ok = 0;
                    break;
                }
    }
    return (ok);
} /* End of check_identifier */
```

g a   1 .12   Checking identifier syntax.

EXAMPLE 17.3   A paragraph is given which has more than one line. Each line may have up to 80 characters and is terminated by an end of line character '\n'. It is required to find the number of words in the paragraph. A word is not split between adjacent lines. Words are separated by one blank space or a full stop. The average number of letters per word is also to be computed. Algorithm 17.3 is developed to do this task.

Example Program 17.13 implements the following algorithm.

Algorithm 17.3:   Finding the average number of letters per word

Read a line from the input into a buffer;
While there are more lines in input do
begin
   number of lines = no. of lines + 1;
   repeat
      Scan buffer from left to right till a blank or
      a . is encountered
      Increment word count
      Accumulate the number of characters per word
   until end of buffer is reached
   Read a line
end

Find the average number of characters per word.

```
/* Example Program 17.13 */
/* Counting words in sentences. Finding average length of words */
#include <stdio.h>
void read_line(char s[]);
int length(char s[]);
void print_line(char out_string[]);
main()
{
    int i, letters, count_word = 0, sum_length = 0,
    average_word_length, no_of_lines = 0;
    char buffer[81];
    read_line(buffer);
    print_line(buffer); printf("\n");
    /* while lines remain in input */
    while(length(buffer) != 0)
       {
        ++no_of_lines;
        printf("no lines %d\n", no_of_lines);
        i = 0;
        letters = 0;
        /* while end of line is not reached */
        while (buffer[i] != '\0')
           {
            /* while end of word is not reached */
            if ((buffer[i] == ' ') ||
                (buffer[i] == '.'))
            {
                ++count_word;
                sum_length += letters;
                letters = 0;
            }
            else
               ++letters;
            ++i;
           }
        /* last word in a line counted */
        ++count_word;
        sum_length += letters;
        printf("Count wd = %d, sum_len = %d\n",
                count_word, sum_length);
        read_line(buffer);
        printf("buf_len = %d\n", length(buffer));
        print_line(buffer); printf("\n");
    } /* end of outer-most while loop */

    printf("The number of lines = %d\n",no_of_lines);
    printf("Total number of words = %d\n", count_word);
    average_word_length = sum_length / count_word;
    printf("Average length of a word = %d\n", average_word_length);
}   /* End of main */
/* Place functions length, read_line, print_line here */
```

g a 1 .13 Finding the average word length.

EXAMPLE 17.4 We will now develop a program to convert a Roman numeral to its decimal equivalent. A set of Roman numerals is given one per line. End of the set is indicated by a line with '\n' character only. Assume that the length of a Roman numeral is less than 10. Table 17.4 gives the Roman symbols and their decimal equivalents.

Table 1 . Roman and decimal numerals

Roman	M	C	L	X	V	I
Decimal	1000	100	50	10	5	1

Algorithm 17.4 gives the method of converting a Roman numeral string R_1, R_2, R_3, ..., R_n to decimal.

Algorithm 17.4: Roman to decimal conversion

Decimal equivalent = 0;
Read a character from the input string into R_1;
V_1 = Value of R_1

    Read next character into R_2;

while (R_2 is not end of line character) do
    V_2 = Value of R_2;
    if ($V_1 > V_2$)
       Add V_1 to decimal equivalent;
    else
       { Subtract V_1 from decimal equivalent;
       Replace R_1 by R_2;
       Replace V_1 by V_2; }
    Read next character into R_2;
end while
Print decimal equivalent;

    Example Program 17.14 is traced with the input string CMXXIV. The trace is given in Table 17.5.

```
/* Example Program 17.14 */
/* Program follows algorithm given in text */
#include <stdio.h>
int value(char roman);
main()
{
    int decimal_equivalent = 0, dec_1, dec_2;
    char rom_1, rom_2;
    rom_1 = getchar();
    dec_1 = value(rom_1);
    ram_2 = getchar();
    while ((rom_2 != '\n'))
```

```
    {
        dec_2 = value(rom_2);
        if (dec_1 >= dec_2)
            decimal_equivalent += dec_1;
        else
            decimal_equivalent -= dec_1;
        dec_1 = dec_2;
        rom_2 = getchar();
    } /* End of while */
    decimal_equivalent += dec_1;
    printf ("Decimal equivalent = %d\n", decimal_equivalent);
} /* End of main */

int value(char roman)
{
    switch(roman)
    {
    case 'M': return(1000); break;
    case 'C': return(100); break;
    case 'L': return(50); break;
    case 'X': return(10); break;
    case 'V': return(5); break;
    case 'I': return(1); break;
    default: printf("Error in roman numeral\n"); break;
    } /* End of switch */
}
```

g a   1 .1   Conversion roman to decimal.

Table 1 .   Trace of Example Program 17.14

Input string CMXXIV				
rom-1	dec-1	rom-2	dec-2	decimal equivalent
C	100	M	1000	−100
M	1000	X	10	900
X	10	X	10	910
X	10	I	1	920
I	1	V	5	919
V	5	'\n'		924

17.4 INPUT AND OUTPUT OF STRINGS

We saw that strings may be input using a scanf function. In this case the input string must not have a blank character. Thus we cannot read the string such as "Ram Kumar" and store it in an array using scanf function. This string can be read by using the getchar () function. It is, however, cumbersome to do so as we have to write an explicit loop. C provides a function gets () to read a string. For reading a string we write:

char buffer[80];

gets(buffer);

The gets function reads a string terminated by the end of line (carriage return) character '\n' and stores it in buffer. When it stores the string in a buffer it replaces the '\n' character by the end of string character '\0'. If the gets function reads a NULL string (just a carriage return without any character in the string) it returns NULL. If it encounters an error then also it returns NULL.

The companion function puts (buffer) writes the contents of buffer up to '\0' on to the standard output unit. We illustrate the use of these functions in Example Program 17.15. This program reads a string and prints it as it is and also with all blanks in the string removed. This program reads one string after another from the input till it encounters a carriage return with no characters.

```
/* Example Program 17.15 */
/* Illustrates use of gets and puts functions */
#include <stdio.h>

main()
{
    char buffer[80], n_buffer[80];
    int i, j;
    while(gets(buffer) != NULL)
        {
        printf("String read is :\n");
        puts(buffer);
        i = 0; j = 0;
        while(buffer[i] != '\0')
            {
            if (buffer[i] != ' ')
                {
                n_buffer[j] = buffer[i];
                ++j;
                }
            ++i;
            n_buffer[j] = '\0';
            printf("String with blanks squeezed out\n");
            puts(n_buffer);
        } /* End of while */
} /* End of main */
```

g a   1 .1   Use of e   and   functions.

C language provides in a library many useful functions for manipulating strings. These functions are given in Appendix IV with an explanation of their formal arguments and what computation they carry out.

EXERCISES

17.1 Write a program to find whether a character string is a Palindrome. A Palindrome reads the same whether it is read from left to right or right to left. (ABBA is a Palindrome).

17.2 Write a program to delete all vowels from a sentence. Assume that the sentence is not more than 80 characters long.

17.3 Write a program to count the number of words in a sentence.

17.4 Write a program which will read a line and squeeze out all vowels from it and output the line with no vowels.

17.5 Write a program which will read a line and delete from it all occurrences of the word 'the'.

17.6 Write a program to encrypt a sentence using the strategy of replacing a letter by the next letter in its collating sequence. Thus every A will be replaced by B, every B by C and so on and finally Z will be replaced by A. Blanks are left undisturbed.

17.7 Write a program which takes a set of names of individuals and abbreviates the first, middle and other names except the last name by their first letter. For example: RAMA RAO would become R. RAO. SURESH KUMAR SHARMA would become S.K. SHARMA.

17.8 Write a program to read a sentence and substitute every occurrence of the word 'POST' by the word 'DAK'. Use the following sentence to test your program.

Input line: "The postman came from the post office bringing post"
Output line: "The dakman came from the dak office bringing dak"

17.9 Write a program to convert a hexadecimal number to decimal. For example the decimal equivalent of

$$AC8D = A * 16^3 + C * 16^2 + 8 * 16^1 + D * 16^0$$
$$= 10 * 16^3 + 12 * 16^2 + 8 * 16 + 13$$
$$= 44173$$

17.10 Write a program to convert decimal numbers to hexadecimal. For example the hexadecimal equivalent of 43919 is AB8F.

17.11 Write a program to count the number of occurrences of any two vowels in succession in a line of text. For example, in the following sentence:

"Please allow a studious girl to read behavioural science"

such occurrences are:

ea, io, ou, ea, io, ou, ie.

Observe that in a word such as studious we have counted "io" and "ou" as two separate occurrences of two consecutive vowels.

17.12 Write a program to arrange a set of names in alphabetic order. The sorting is to be on the first two characters of the last name. For example, given the list:

Ramaswamy R.
Arumugam B.
Agarwal K.
Sarma A.B.
Bagchi D.R.

the sorted list should be

Agarwal K.
Arumugam B.
Bagchi D.R.
Ramaswamy R.
Sarma A.B.

18

Enumerated Data Types and Stacks

LEARNING OBJECTIVES

In this chapter we will learn:

1. The definition and use of a data type called enumerated data type.
2. How new data type names can be obtained by using a feature called typedef.
3. The use of typedef to create a data type named Boolean which is very useful in programming.
4. How to create a data structure called stack and define operations necessary to use a stack effectively.

C provides a number of data types and structures which are normally not provided in other programming languages such as Fortran and Cobol. The motivation for providing these is to ease program development and readability.

The standard scalar data types provided by C are integer, real and character. In this chapter we will first consider another scalar data type known as enumerated scalar data type. The primary use of this data type is to enhance program understandability. A subsidiary advantage is the possibility of automatic checking of input data at execution time.

By a data structure we mean a collection of similar types of data making up a composite. Such a composite or structure has some special properties which make it easy to develop algorithms. The only data structure we have encountered so far is the array structure. We have used arrays to store vectors, strings of characters, tables of values, etc. In this chapter we will introduce a data structure known as a *stack* which has a number of applications in programming. C does not provide this data structure as a standard type. We will simulate this structure with an array structure and define procedures for operations relevant to this structure.

18.1 ENUMERATED DATA TYPE

A variable declared as an enumerated data type can assume a value defined by a set of identifiers. For example, one may define

enum subject {math, phy, chem, ta, esc, hss};

which defines a new data type named *subject* which can assume one of the six values specified within braces. The word *enum* is a keyword and is an abbreviation of enumerated. In order to declare a variable name *course* to be of the enumerated *type subject* we write:

enum subject course;

Observe that we again use the keyword *enum* to specify that the variable name *course* is an enumerated type. The type itself is then stated as *subject*. The identifier *course* cannot assume any value other than that within the enumeration. If it does, an error message is given by the C compiler. There must be a blank space between *enum* and *subject* and another blank between *subject* and *course*. The rules for forming type name and the enumerated identifiers are the same as for any identifier.

Some more examples of enumerated data types are given below:

```
enum card suit {clubs, diamonds, hearts, spades};
enum card suit given card;
enum day of week {mon, tue, wed, thu, fri, sat, sun};
enum day of week week day, holiday;
enum colour {violet, indigo, blue, green, yellow, orange, red};
enum colour paint, tile;
enum designation {ldc, udc, asst, suptd};
enum designation employee, staff;
```

We can use the enumerated variable in any statement. For example if there is a variable name *course* of enumerated type *subject* then:

if (course==chem)

credit = 15;

will assign 15 to credit if the course happens to be chem. An enumerated variable can also be used in a switch statement as shown below:

```
switch (course)
    {   case math : credit = 20; break;
        case chem : credit = 15; break;
        case phy : credit = 18; break;
        case ta : credit = 10; break;
        case esc : credit = 16; break;
        case hss : credit = 9; break;
        default : printf ("error in course value \n");
        break;
    }  /* End switch */
```

The enumerated data types are not part of what the hardware provides in a computer such as integers and reals. C includes a set of routines to implement these types. The implementation details need not concern a programmer. The primary idea used in implementation is to assign integer values starting from 0 to the successive components of the enumerated type. Thus, for example, in enum day of week {mon, tue, wed, thu, fri, sat, sun};

0 will be assigned to mon, 1 to tue, 2 to wed, 3 to thu, 4 to fri, 5 to sat and 6 to sun. This fact allows the use of enumerated variables in statements such as in *switch*, *if* and *for*.

We could declare a variable name such as day of week as integer and use 0, 1, 2 etc. for the different days of the week. However, the use of enumerated type and assignment of meaningful name enhances the understandability of C programs.

We will now illustrate the use of enumerated type with an example.

EXAMPLE 18.1   A college requires a student to take five subjects each semester. The subjects are: mathematics, physics, chemistry, computing and english. Each subject has a specified weightage. At the end of the semester, letter grades are assigned to each subject for each student. The letter grades are: A, B, C, D, F and I. It is required to find at the end of each semester the Grade Point Average (GPA) for each student using the following definition:

GPA = Sum of (Points corresponding to letter grade obtained by student * Course weight)/ Sum of (course weight)

The points for grades A, B, C, D, F are respectively 10, 8, 6, 4 and 2. The point for grade I is 0. This grade is given to a student who has not completed the course. Thus when an I grade is encountered this course should be ignored in GPA calculation, that is, the weight of this course is not added.

We design the program as follows. We first decide how to represent data. As there are a finite number of grades and subjects, we choose enumerated data types to represent these. Thus we define:

enum grade {A, B, C, D, F, I};
enum subject {math, phy, chem, comp, english};
enum grade student grade;
enum subject course;

The weights for each subject and the points for each letter grade are stored in two arrays. An array is convenient to use as a summation and this with subject as index is needed to find GPA. The values for weights for each subject and points for each letter grade are read as data. This allows the program to accommodate any changes in these values if required.

Each student's performance is given in the form:

roll no, grades in math, phy, chem, comp and english.

The order of these grades is to be *strictly* followed. One line per student is used in the input. The end of students is indicated by a line with 000 for roll no. An example data is the following:

3385BACFI
5452ABICD
......   ← other data

Last line   0000XXXXX

The strategy used is given in Algorithm 18.1.

Algorithm 18.1

Algorithm to compute student grade

1. Store course weights in an array
2. Store points for grades in another array
3. Read a student's record
4. While student's records remain do
   { if (grade != I)
       {total points = total points + points for grade * weight of course;
       total weight = total weight + course weight;
   }
5. GPA of student = total points/total weight

This algorithm is converted to Example Program 18.1. In Example Program 18.1, observe that an enumerated variable name is used as the index in a *for* loop. This is allowed as enumerated types are internally represented by the C compiler as integers.

```
/* Example Program 18.1 */
/* Student grade example—Use of enumerated data-type */
#include <stdio.h>
main()
{
    enum grade {A, B, C, D, F, I};
    enum subject {phy, chem, math, comp, english};
    enum subject course;
    enum grade stud_grade;
    int roll_no, total_points = 0, total_weight = 0,
    weight[5], points[6], error_code;
    float grade_point_avge;
    char temp;
    for (course = phy; course <= english; ++course)
       scanf("%d", &weight[course]);
    for (stud_grade = A; stud_grade <= I; ++stud_grade)
       scanf("%d", &points[stud_grade]);
    /* A typical student record is 3683ABDIC */
    scanf("%d", &roll_no);
    printf("%d ", roll_no);
    while(roll_no != 0)
       {
           for (course = phy; course <= english; ++course)
               {
                   temp = getchar();
                   putchar(temp);
                   switch(temp)
                       {
                           case 'A': stud_grade = A; break;
                           case 'B': stud_grade = B; break;
                           case 'C': stud_grade = C; break;
                           case 'D': stud_grade = D; break;
```

```
            case 'F': stud_grade = F; break;
            case 'I': stud_grade = I; break;
                default : printf("Error in grade\n");
                error_code = 1; break;
            } /* End of switch */
      /* If there is error in input goto next record */
      if (error_code == 1)
          continue;
      if (stud_grade != I)
          {
              total_points += points[stud_grade] *
              weight[course];
              total_weight += weight[course];

          }
      } /* End of for loop which processes one student's grade */

      grade_point_avge = (float)total_points /
          (float)total_weight;
      printf("GPA = %4.2f\n", grade_point_avge);
      /* end of processing one student's record */
      scanf("%d" , &roll_no);
      printf("%d ", roll_no);
      total_points = 0; total_weight = 0;
    } /* End of while */
  printf("End of Processing all student records\n");
} /* End of main */
```

g a   1 .1   Students grade calculation.

Observe that a data record is typed in the form

3683ABDIC

No blank should separate 3683 from ABDIC. There are no blanks separating A from B, B from D, etc.

When the record is read by the statement:

scanf("%d", &roll no);

the integer 3683 is stored in roll no and the scanning of input line stops. The next statement in the *for* loop

temp = getchar ( ) ;

reads the first character from the input, A in this case and stores it in temp. It is important to understand that getchar( ) stores A as a character in temp. In other words temp now contains 'A'. The symbol A in the enumerated data type grade is not to be confused with the character 'A'. A in the enumerated type is a code for 0. Thus we need the *switch* statement to assign the enumerated data type values to stud grade. It would be an *error* to write:

stud grade = temp ;

as temp is of type *char* and stud grade is an enumerated type.

The *for* loop

$$\text{for (course} = \text{phy; course} <= \text{english; ++course)}$$

first starts with course = phy, finds the grade obtained by the student in this course, calculates the points obtained by the student by multiplying the points for the course by the weight of the course and adds it to total points. It then accumulates the weights of course. This is repeated for the other courses taken by the student. Observe that the order in which the grades are typed in the input line must strictly follow the order phy, chem, math, comp and english which is the order used in enumeration.

After the *for* loop is complete, the next student's record is read and processed. This is repeated till the last record is reached. The last record has 000 as roll no which is used as the termination condition in the while loop.

18.2   CREATING NEW DATA TYPE NAMES

We can create new data type names in C language using a facility called *typedef.* For example, the declaration

$$\text{typedef int Boolean ;}$$

makes the name Boolean a synonym of int. The type Boolean can be used in declarations in exactly the same way as int. If we declare

$$\text{Boolean end of file, error found ;}$$

then end of file and error found are actually int.

Similarly the declaration

$$\text{typedef char Letter ;}$$

makes Letter a new type name.

We will use typedef later in the book to define more complex data types. Observe that we have used capital letter as the first letter of data type name declared using typedef to distinguish it from built-in types.

It must be understood that typedef declaration does not add any new data type; it merely renames an existing data type which is useful in program understanding and in program portability.

We will illustrate the use of typedef in Example Program 18.2.

EXAMPLE 18.2   Given the date of birth of an undergraduate student in the form

$$\text{day   month   year}$$

for example, 250370,

a program is required to check if the date is a "reasonable" date and if it is so, then write the date in the expanded form:

$$\text{Day   Name of the month   Year}$$

For example, write 25 MARCH 1970 corresponding to the input date 250370. We will use the following criteria to determine "reasonableness":

1. If the month is January, March, May, July, August, October or December then $1 \leq$ day ≤ 31.
2. If the month is April, June, September or November then $1 \leq$ day ≤ 30.
3. If the month is February then $1 \leq$ day ≤ 29 if the year is a leap year. If the year is divisible by 100 then it should be divisible by 400 for it to be a leap year. For example the year 1900 is *not* a leap year but the year 2000 is a leap year.

```c
/* Example Program 18.2 */
#include <stdio.h>
#define TRUE 1
#define FALSE 0
typedef int Boolean;
Boolean leap_year(int year);
Boolean day_ok_for_month(int day, int month, int year);
void print_date(int day, int month, int year);
int day_for_month[12] = {31, 28, 31, 30, 31, 30, 31, 31, 30, 31, 30, 31};

main()
{
    int date, day, month, year, approx_age, current_year, roll_no, upper_age,
    lower_age;
    Boolean error_found;
    scanf("%d %d %d", &current_year, &upper_age, &lower_age);
    while(scanf("%d %d", &roll_no, &date) != EOF)
      /* date in the form ddmmyy e.g. 050791 */
      {
        year = date % 100;
        month = (date/100) % 100;
        day = date/10000;
        approx_age = current_year - year;
        if ((approx_age > upper_age) ||
            (approx_age < lower_age))
          {
            error_found = TRUE;
            printf("Error in age, roll_no = %d\n", roll_no);
            continue;
          }
        if ((month > 12) || (month < 1))
          {
            error_found = TRUE;
            printf("Error in month, roll_no = %d\n", roll_no);
            continue,
          }
        if ((day <= 31) && (day >= 1))
          day_ok_for_month(day, month, year);
        else
```

```
            {
               error_found = TRUE;
               printf("Error in day of month, roll %d\n",
                     roll_no);
        .      continue;
             }
        if (! day_ok_for_month)
             {
               error_found = TRUE;
               printf("Error in day of month, roll_no = %d\n",
                     roll_no);
               continue;
             }
        printf("%d ", roll_no);
        print_date(day, month, year);
    } /* End of while */
} /* End of main */
Boolean day_ok_for_month(int day, int month, int year)
{
    if (day <= day_for_month[month])
      return(TRUE);
    else
      if ((month == 2) && leap_year(year) && (day <= 29))
         return(TRUE);
      else
         return(FALSE);
} /* End of day_ok_for_month */
Boolean leap_year(int year)
{
    if ((year % 100 == 0) && (year % 400 == 0))
      return(TRUE); /* it is a leap year */
    else
      if (year % 4 == 0)
         return(TRUE); /* it is a leap year */
      else
         return(FALSE); /* it is not a leap year */
} /* End of leap-year */
void print_date(int day, int month, int year)
{
    printf("%2d ", day);
    switch(month)
      {
      case 1:
        printf("January"); break;
      case 2:
        printf("February"); break;
      case 3:
        printf("March"); break;
      case 4:
        printf("April"); break;
```

```
     case 5:
       printf("May"); break;
     case 6:
       printf("June"); break;
     case 7:
       printf("July"); break;
     case 8:
       printf("August"); break;
     case 9:
       printf("September"); break;
     case 10:
       printf("October"); break;
     case 11:
       printf("November"); break;
     case 12:
       printf("December"); break;
   } /* End of switch */
   printf("%d\n", year);
} /* End of print_date */
```

g a 1 .2 Chec ing date of birth of a student.

Example Program 18.2 implements the date checking program. Observe that the input data is typed in the form

4642 250370

with a blank between roll no and date.

The program first reads the current year which is given as data. It then reads the first student record. The end of student records is indicated when the end of file is reached.

The *while* loop does the processing of one record. The first *if* statement in the *while* loop checks whether the year of birth of student is reasonable. The criterion used is that a student in a college must be between the upper and lower age limits set by the college authorities. If the student's age is not within these bounds then the Boolean variable error found is set to TRUE and an error message is printed. As a *continue* statement is the next one, the rest of the statements are not executed and control returns to *while* to process the next record.

After this, the value given for month is checked. If it is not correct an error message is again given and control returns to process the next record. The checking of day value is a little more complicated as the day value depends on the month and the year. The rules given in the statement of the problem are used in the function day ok for month (day, month, year). Observe that this function uses another function for finding if the year is a leap year. The maximum days in each month is stored in the global array day for month. As this data is invariant it is initialized and stored as a global array. This may is used by the function day ok for month to check whether the day exceeds the maximum allowed days for a month. If the month is February, then the leap year function is invoked to check if day < 28 for a non-leap year. Finally the function print date is invoked to print the date in the format required in the problem specification.

18.3 A STACK

In an array structure any element may be retrieved by specifying the appropriate subscript. We may also store an element anywhere in the array. As opposed to this, *a stack* is a structure with a group of cells in which only the top cell is accessible. Thus only the element at the top of the stack may be retrieved. Any new element to be stored in the stack is also stored at the top. Figure 18.1 illustrates this.

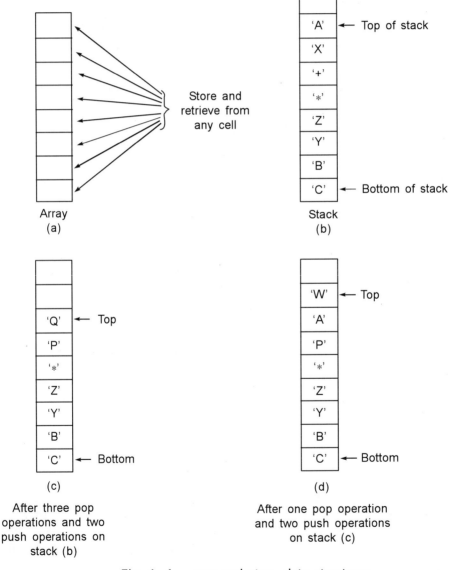

Fig. 1 .1   rray and stac data structures.

The store operation is called *Push* and the retrieve operation *Pop*. Because of the nature of storing and retrieving elements at the same end of the stack the element accessed is the last one stored. Hence a stack is also known as a *last-in-first-out(LIFO)* store.

One may visualize the operation of a stack with the following analogy. Imagine a dish washer in a hotel washing plates and stacking, that is, placing them one on top of another. When a waiter wants to take a plate to serve a customer he will take a plate from the top of the stack. This plate is the most recently washed plate. When the cleaner washes another plate he will place it on top of the stack.

Given the stack of Fig. 18.l(b) if we execute three Pop operations the elements will be retrieved (removed) from the stack in the order 'A', 'X' and '+'. If we now Push ('P'), then Push ('Q') the element 'Q' will be on top of the stack as in Fig. 18.1(c). A Pop will now remove 'Q'. This last-in-first-out retrieval property of a stack is extremely useful in a number of programming situations. These situations arise in programming language translation such as evaluating arithmetic expressions using arithmetic operator precedence rules, implementing procedure calls and returns, etc.

18.4   SIMULATION OF A STACK

In C the operations on a stack can be simulated using an array. In this section we will develop declarations to implement a stack and functions to simulate the operations Push and Pop on a stack.

A stack is declared as an array with an index which will point to the top of the stack. We will assume that each cell of the stack stores a character. (In general a cell can store anything that can be stored in a cell of an array). We will also declare variables of type Boolean to indicate whether the stack is full or empty. The declarations are given as Example Program 18.3 and, are global.

We will simulate the operation Push by the function push. The input to the function is the pushed character. The current index giving top of stack and status of stack, namely, whether it is full or empty are available through global variables. The function first checks if the stack is already full. If it is full it gives a message that the pushed character cannot be stored and aborts the procedure. If the stack is not full then it increments the top of the stack index by 1 and stores the pushed character at the top of the stack. As the stack now contains a character, stack empty is assigned a value FALSE. The pointer value is now compared with its maximum allowed value determined by the stack size. If it is above this value then the variable stack full is assigned a TRUE value.

The operation Pop from a stack is simulated by function pop. The popped character is the output of this function. The function first checks if the stack is empty. If it is empty then nothing can be retrieved. A message is given and the function is aborted. If the stack is not empty then a character from the top of the stack is popped. The index top of stack is decreased by 1 to point to the 'new' top element in the stack.

As a character has been popped the stack can be empty. The index value is compared with its minimum allowed value which is one. The minimum value is 1 because a push increments top of stack before storing data in stack. If it is below 1 then the variable stack empty is assigned a TRUE value.

```
/* Example Program 18.3 */
/* These are defined as global outside main() */
#define STACK_SIZE   80
#define FALSE        0
#define TRUE         1
char stack[STACK_SIZE];
typedef int Boolean;
Boolean stack_empty, stack_full;
int top_of_stack;

/* top_of_stack is the array index of stack[]. It specifies
    from where a data can be stored or retrieved */

/* Functions defining push and pop operations for a stack */

void push (char pushed_char)
{
    if (stack_full)
       {
          printf("Error-Stack is full\n");
          return;
       }
    else
       {
          ++top_of_stack;
          stack[top_of_stack] = pushed_char;
          stack_empty = FALSE;
       }

    if (top_of_stack == STACK_SIZE)
       stack_full = TRUE;
} /* End of push */
char pop()
{
    char temp;

    if (stack_empty)
       {
          printf("Error-Stack is empty\n");
          return(' '),
       }
    else
       {
          temp = stack[top_of_stack];
          --top_of_stack;
          if (top_of_stack <= 0)
             stack_empty = TRUE;
          return(temp);
       }
}   /* End of pop */
```

g a   1 .3   Stac   declaration and operations.

EXERCISES

18.1 Rewrite Example Program 15.3 (which illustrates a tabulation technique) using enumerated scalar data type.

18.2 Rewrite Example Program 15.4 using enumerated scalar data types to represent various responses to questions. Discuss the advantages and disadvantages of this approach compared to the approach used in Chapter 15.

18.3 A Company pays normal wage for work during week days from Monday to Friday and 1.5 times wage for work on Saturday and Sunday. Given data in the following form:

Employee Number, Wage/hour, hours worked on Monday, hours on Tuesday, ..., hours on Sunday.

Write a program to write out the Employee number and weekly wage. Use enumerated data type in your program.

18.4 Write a program to check whether a given string is a valid real number. Use the syntax rules for real numbers given in Chapter 8.

18.5 In the Fortran 77 language variable names are defined as follows:

Integer variable name: A string of up to 6 alphanumeric characters. The first character must be I, J, K, L, M or N. The other characters may be either letters or digits.

Real variable name: A string of up to 6 alphanumeric characters. The first character may be any letter except I, J, K, L, M, N. The other characters may be any of the 26 letters or digits. Write a program to check whether a given string is a valid integer variable name, real variable name or valid as a variable name.

18.6 Write a program to read a line of text and delete all the vowels from it.

18.7 Write a program to determine if an input character string is of the form XaY. X is a string of arbitrary length using only the characters A and B. For example, X may be ABBAB. Y is a string which is the reverse of X. Thus for the string X given above, Y is BABBA. a is any arbitrary character which is not A or B. For example, given ABAACABAB the program should write a message that this string is invalid. For the string ABBABCBABBA the program should write a message that it is valid. Use a stack.

18.8 Use the Push and Pop operations on a stack to do the following:

  (i) Assign to a variable name Y the value of the third element from the top of the stack and keep the stack undisturbed.
  (ii) Given an arbitrary integer n pop out the top n elements. A message should be given if an unusual condition is encountered.
  (iii) Assign to a variable name Y the value of the third element from the bottom of the stack and keep the stack undisturbed.
       (*Hint:* You may use a temporary stack in this case)

18.9 A queue is a data structure in which a new element is inserted at the back of the queue and an element is retrieved from the front (the other end) of the queue. For example, given a queue,

ABCDEFXYZ

back   front

a retrieval operation will retrieve Z. An insert operation will insert an element behind A. Write a program to:

(i) Define a data structure for a queue of characters using an array.
(ii) Write functions to add an element to a queue and to retrieve an element from the queue.

The functions must have parameters to indicate queue full, queue empty conditions and set pointers for adding and retrieving elements.

18.10 A *dequeue* is an ordered set of elements in which elements may be inserted or retrieved from either end. Using an array, simulate a *dequeue* of characters and the operations *retrieveleft, retrieveright, insertleft, insertright.* Exceptional conditions such as dequeue full or empty should be indicated. Two pointers (namely, left and right) are needed in this simulation.

19

Structures

```
┌─────────────────────────────────────────────────────────────┐
│                    LEARNING OBJECTIVES                        │
│  In this chapter we will learn:                               │
│    1. Representation of related data items as a structure.    │
│    2. Applications of structures.                             │
│    3. Use of arrays in structures.                            │
└─────────────────────────────────────────────────────────────┘
```

There are many applications where it is convenient to treat related data items as one entity. Individual components of such an entity would usually be of different data types. Such an entity is called a *structure* and the related data items used in it are called its *components*. For example, consider several items in a store. Each item in the store may be described by its code, current stock and its price. Each item can thus be described by the definition

```
struct item in store
{    int item code;
     int qty in stock;
     float price;
};
```

The above definition is called a *structure definition*. In this definition a name is given to the structure. The name of the above structure is item in store. It is similar to the name we gave to enumerated scalar data type in Chapter 18. The name tells the compiler that three locations in memory should be reserved for each data of *type* item in store. The first location will store an integer, the second location also an integer and the third a floating point number.

The following declaration declares soap and hair oil to be of *type*: item in store.

```
struct item in store soap, hair oil;
```

We can use typedef to give a name to a structure. For example,

```
typedef struct date
   { int day;
     int month;
     int year;
   } Date;
Date birth day, marriage day;
```

The use of typedef names the structure as Date and declares birth day and marriage day as the structure specified. Observe that date and Date are different names as C distinguishes between upper- and lower-case letters. Observe that in the name of structure given by typedef we use an uppercase letter as the first letter. This is a good practice to distinguish it as a structure name.

```
typedef struct comp no
   {    float real part;
        float imag part;
   } Complex number;
Complex number x, y;
```

We have defined above a structure Complex number which has two components, one called real part and the other imag part. It declares the variable names *x* and *y* to be of *type* Complex number.

```
typedef struct isbn code
   {    int country code;
        int publisher code;
        int serial no;
        char check char;
   } ISBN;
ISBN pascal book, fortran book;
```

The above definition defines structure isbn code as one which has four components, three of which are of *type int* and the fourth of *type char*. It names the structure ISBN.

The variable names pascal book, fortran book are declared to be type ISBN.

The general syntax of structure definition is:

```
struct <structure identifie>
   { type name <identifie>;
     type name <identifier>;
     :
     type name <identifier>;
   };
```

Observe that semicolons must terminate the definition of each component identifier of the structure. A semicolon *must* also be present after the right braces which closes the struct definition.

The syntax of declaration of a variable name as of *type* structure is:

struct <structure identifier> <variable identifier>;

The syntax rules for structure identifier and variable identifier are the same as for any identifier. The types used within a structure definition may be any *type*: int, float, char, array, enum, and even struct.

19.1 USING STRUCTURES

Let us consider the variable name soap which is declared to be of *type* struct item in store. If we want to find the price of soap we use the notation: soap.price. Similarly the item code and qty in stock of soap may be found by using the notation soap.item code, soap.qty in stock. In fact the storage assignment for storing information about soap is shown in Table 19.1.

Table 1 .1 Storage of struct soap item in store.

	soap.item code	2542 int
soap	soap.qty in stock	95 int
	soap.price	3.50 float

In general the syntax is:

struct variable name.struct component identifier

No blank should be left before and after the .(dot) which is used between the variable name and its component identifier. For example:

soap. item code

is an *error* as blank spaces are there. The correct specification is:

soap.item code

If suppose a shop stocks a number of brands of soap and we want to find the number of different brands of soaps and the total value of soaps stored in the shop, it is done by Example Program 19.1.

```
/* Example Program 19.1 */
/* Illustrates use of struct declaration and use */
#include <stdio.h>
typedef struct item_in_store
{
    int item_code;
    int qty_in_stock;
    float price,
} Item;
```

```
main()
{
    Item soap;
    int no_of_brands = 0;
    float total_soap_value = 0;
      while (scanf("%d %d %f", &soap.item_code,
          &soap.qty_in_stock,
          &soap.price) != EOF)
      {
          total_soap_value += soap.qty_in_stock * soap.price;
          ++no_of_brands;
      } /* End of while */

    printf("Number of brands of soap in store = %d\n", no_of_brands);
    printf("Total value of soaps stocked = Rs %f\n", total_soap_value);
}   /* end of main */
```

g a   1 .1   Structure definition and use.

Observe in Example Program 19.1 that the structure definition follows #include and before main(). As the structure definition is a *type* definition it is usually global. In the main program we declare soap as of *type* Item. Remember that Item is a synonym for struct item in store. Observe that we read each component of the structure soap in the scanf statement with appropriate format declaration. The *while* loop is self-explanatory.

We can use structures in functions. We illustrate this in Example Program 19.2. These functions are implemented to perform the operations of addition, multiplication, and division of complex numbers. The definition of these operations are:

Given a complex number a + ib ; *a* is called the real part, and *b* the imaginary part; *i* represents square root of –1.

Given two complex numbers a + ib and c + id the definitions of sum, product and quotient are:

sum: $(a + ib) + (c + id) = (a + c) + i(b + d)$
product: $(a + ib) * (c + id) = (ac - bd) + i(ad + bc)$
quotient: $(a + ib) / (c + id) = \{ac + bd / (c^2 + d^2)\} + i\{bc - ad / (c^2 + d^2)\}$

```
/* Example Program 19.2 */
/* Defining a structure for complex numbers */
#Include <stdio.h>
typedef struct complex_number
{
    float real;
    float imag;
}   Complex;
Complex sum(Complex m, Complex n);
Complex product(Complex m, Complex n);
Complex quotient(Complex m, Complex n);
```

```
main()
{
    Complex x, y, z, p, q, r, d, e, f;
    scanf("%f %f %f %f", &x.real, &x.imag, &y.real, &y.imag);
/* Sum of Complex numbers x and y */
z = sum(x, y);
printf("Sum of complex numbers x and y \n");
printf("%f + i%f\n", z.real, z.imag);
scanf("%f %f %f %f", &p.real, &p.imag, &q.real, &q.imag);
/* Product of complex numbers p and q */
r = product(p, q);
printf("Product of complex numbers p and q\n");
printf("%f + i%f\n", r.real, r.imag);
scanf("%f %f %f %f", &d.real, &d.imag, &e.real, &e.imag);
/* Quotient of complex numbers d and e */
f = quotient(d, e);
printf("Quotient of complex numbers d and e \n");
printf("%f + i%f\n", f.real, f.imag);
} /* End of main */

Complex sum(Complex m, Complex n)
{
    Complex p;
    p.real = m.real + &real;
    p.imag = m.imag + n.imag;
    return(p);
} /* End of sum */
    Complex product(Complex m, Complex n)
    {
        Complex p;
        p.real = m.real * n.real - m.imag * n.imag;
        p.imag = m.real * n.imag + m.imag * n.real;
        return(p);
    } /* End of product */

Complex quotient(Complex m, Complex n)
{
    Complex p;
    float denom;
    denom = n.real*n.real + n.imag*n.imag;
    p.real = (m.real*n.real + m.imag*n.imag)/denom;
    p.imag = (m.imag*n.real - m.real*n.imag)/denom;
    return(p);
} /* End of quotient */
```

g a 1 .2 Comple numbers and operations.

Example Program 19.2 implements the sum, product and quotient functions for complex numbers. Observe that each function has structure variable names as formal arguments. The function *type* is defined as a structure and thus the result returned to the function name is the specified structure. Observe that in the body of the function we have declared a variable *p* as a structure and assigned calculated values to p.real and p.imag. Having found the two component values, the structure *p* is returned to the function name. We could have attempted to write

sum(Complex m, Complex n, Complex p)

with the intention of getting the result back in the structure *p*. This is not allowed. The result cannot be returned to a structure name used as a formal argument.

As the last example in this section, we will reconsider the example given in Chapter 14 (Example 14.7). The problem is: given the today's date and the date an employee joined a job to find if he/she has completed one year service. We will now use a structure and a function to solve the problem.

The structure used is Date which is defined in Example Program 19.3. The main advantage of using a structure in this case is a uniform data type definition of the two dates of relevance in this problem. The rest of Example Program 19.3 is self-explanatory.

```
/* Example Program 19.3 */
/* Illustrates use of structure in function */
#include <stdio.h>
#define TRUE 1
#define FALSE 0
typedef struct date
{
    int day;
    int month;
    int year;
} Date;
typedef int Boolean;
Boolean one_year_service(Date today, Date joining_day);

main()
{
    Date today, join;
    int emp_no;
    scanf("%d %d %d", &today.day, & today.month, &today.year);
    while(scanf("%d %d %d %d", &emp_no, &join.day,
            &join.month, &join.year) != EOF)
        {
        if (one_year_service(today, join))
            printf("Emp No = %d Completed one year service\n", emp_no);
        else
            printf("Emp No = %d Not completed one year service\n", emp_no);
        } /* End while */
} /* End of main */

Boolean one_year_service(Date today, Date joining_date)
{
    int diff_day, diff_month, diff_year;
    diff_day = today.day - joining_date.day;
```

```
    diff_month = today.month - joining_date.month;
       diff_year = today.year - joining_date.year;
    if ((diff_year > 1) || (diff_year == 1) &&
          (diff_month > 0) ||
          ((diff_year == 1) && (diff_month == 0) &&
          (diff_day >= 0)))
       return(TRUE);
    else
       return(FALSE);
} /* End one_year_service */
```

g a   1 .3   se of structure in function.

19.2   USE OF STRUCTURES IN ARRAYS AND ARRAYS IN STRUCTURES

So far we have considered arrays in which the individual elements were scalars. Elements of an array can also be structures. Consider the structure item in store described at the beginning of the chapter. The structure is

typedef struct item in store
{   int item code;
     int qty in stock;
     float price;
} Item;
Item inventory [l00];

The above declaration states that the array inventory has 100 components each of which is a structure. The storage will be as shown in Table 19.2.

Table 1 .2   Illustrates an array   hose elements are structures

	int item code	int qty in stock	float price
inventory [0]			
inventory [l]			
⋮			
inventory [99]			

An individual element is referred to as

inventory[2].price

which gives the price of inventory[2].

We illustrate the use of this array in Example Program 19.4 which lists items out of stock in the store and computes the total value of inventory kept in the store.

Observe in Example Program 19.4 the definition of struct as global (i.e. outside main). The maximum size of inventory is declared as 100. The actual number of items in the inventory is read in as data. The *for* loop reads one record corresponding to one inventory item and processes it. If an item is out of stock (that is, if inventory[i].qty in stock == 0) its code is printed out. It is not included in calculating the inventory value. The inventory value is accumulated in the *for* loop. Finally the inventory value is rounded to the nearest rupee and printed out.

It is possible to have arrays as components of structures. For example, if we want the name of items besides their item code we may define a structure.

```
typedef struct item in store
{   int item code;
    char item name[20];
    int qty in stock;
    float price;
} Item;
```

```
/* Example Program 19.4 */
/* Illustrates use of structures as array elements */
#include <stdio.h>
typedef struct item_in_store
{
    int item_code;
    int qty_in_stock;
    float price;
} Item;

main()
{
    Item inventory[100];
    int i, no_of_items, value_of_inventory;
    float inv_value = 0;
    scanf("%d", &no_of_items);
    /* No_of_items in store. It must be less than
       100 the maximum size of inventory */
    for (i = 0; i < no_of_items; ++i)
        {
            scanf("%d %d %f", &inventory[i].item_code,
                    &inventory [i].qty_in_stock,
                    &inventory [i].price);
            if (inventory [i].qty_in_stock == 0)
                printf("Item number = %d out of stock\n",
                        inventory[i].item_code);
            else
                inv_value += inventory[i].qty_in_stock*
                    inventory [i].price;
        } /* End of reading all inventory records */
    value_of_inventory = inv_value + 0.5; /* rounding */
    printf("Inventory value to nearest rupee = %d\n", value_of_inventory);
}   /* End of main */
```

g a   1 .   se of structure as array element.

If in Example Program 19.4 we want to print the name of inventory items which are out of stock we may modify the *if* statement in the program. This is given in Fig. 19.1.

```
if ( inventory[i].qty_in_stock == 0 )
{
    printf ("The following item is out of stock\n");
    printf ("Item code is %d\n", inventory[i].item_code);
    puts ( inventory[i].item_name );
    printf ( "\n" );
}
else
    inv_value += inventory[i].qty_in_stock
    *inventory[i].price;
```

Fig. 1 .1   se of an array in a structure.

(We have assumed that the name of the inventory item has already been read in by a scanf statement.)

It is also possible to define structures within structures. We illustrate this with an example. Suppose it is required to describe suppliers who supply items to a store. This may be described by the structure:

```
typedef struct supp record
    {  int supp code;
       char supp name[20];
       struct supp address
           {  char street[30];
              char city [20];
              int pin code;
           }
    } Supplier rec; /*End of structure supplier */
Supplier rec supplier[100];
```

Observe that the address of the supplier is declared as a structure within the structure supp record. We will now write an instruction to illustrate how such a structure can be used. This instruction is to find out the name of all suppliers whose address has the Pin Code 560001 and is given in Fig. 19.2.

```
for ( i = 0; i < no_of_suppliers; ++i )
    {
        if ( supplier[i].supp_address.pin_code == 560001 )
            {
                puts ( supplier[I].supp_name );
                printf ( "\n" ) ;
            }
    }
```

Fig. 1 .2   se of structure   ithin a structure.

We have specified two structures in this section. One of them describes item in an inventory and the other suppliers. We will now see how they can be used together in a program. Suppose it is required to find out the address of all suppliers who supply a particular item to a store. In the current structure describing an item in store there is no reference to who supplies the item. Similarly there is no information in supp record about what items the supplier is capable of supplying. Thus it is not possible to find out who could supply an item which is out of stock in a store. We will alter the item in store structure to include the supp code of all suppliers who supply this item. The altered item in store structure is shown below:

```
typedef struct item in store
   {  int item code;
      char item name[20];
      int qty in stock;
      float price;
      int supp code[3];
   } Item;
```

In the above structure we have allowed for three suppliers for each item in store. An array with three components stores these three suppliers' codes.

We now give a program segment in Fig. 19.3 to print the name and address of all suppliers who can supply individual items which are out of stock in the store. Observe in this program that if inventory item 4, for example, is out of stock, then search key [1], [2] and [3] will store the codes of the three suppliers for item 4. Using these three codes we now search all the supplier records to find the three suppliers who have these codes and immediately print their names and addresses.

```
Item inventory[100];
for ( i = 0; i < no_of_items; ++i )
    {
       if ( inventory[i].qty_in_stock == 0 )
          {
             for ( j = 0; j < 3; ++j )
                 search_key[j] == inventory[i].supp_code[j];
             for ( k = 0; k < no_of_suppliers; ++k )
                 for ( m = 0; m < 3; ++m )
                     if ( supplier[k].supp_code == search_key[m] )
                         print_supplier_address ( supplier, k ) ;
          } /* End of finding suppliers for inventory[i] */
    } /* End of search of all items in inventory */
```

Fig. 1 .3   rinting names and addresses of all suppliers   ho can supply a specified out of
            stoc   item.

The function which prints the address of a supplier is given in Fig. 19.4. Observe that to access an array of a structure within a structure, we write

supplier[k].supp address.street

```
        void print_supplier_address ( Supplier_rec  supplier[ ], int k )
        {
            puts ( supplier[k].supp_name ) ;
            printf( "\n" ) ;
            puts ( supplier[k] .supp_address.street ) ;
            printf( "\n" ) ;
            puts ( supplier[k].supp_address.city ) ;
            printf ( "\n %d \n", supplier[k].supp_address.pin_code ) ;
        } /* end of function print_supplier_address */
```

Fig. 1 .   rinting the name and address of a supplier from a given supplier structure.

This will find the street name in the supplier address of the kth supplier. Observe that the identifier supp code is used in two structures item in store and supp record. This is allowed as these names by themselves have no meaning unless qualified by the structure identifier.

Structures are used in files and have many applications. We will return to this topic after we discuss what are known as *pointers* in the next chapter.

EXERCISES

19.1 Create a structure to specify data on students given below:

Roll no., Name, Department, Course, Year of joining

A typical student's data will be

1456 S. Raghavan C.S. B.E. 1991

Assume that there are not more than 500 students in the college.

 (i) Write a function to print names of all students who joined in a particular year.
(ii) Write a function to print the data on a student whose roll number is given.

19.2 Create a structure to specify data on customers in a bank. The data to be stored is:

Acct. no, Name, Balance in account.

Assume maximum of 200 customers in the bank.

 (i) Write a function to print the Acct. no and name of each customer with balance below Rs. 100.

If a customer gives a request for withdrawal or deposit it is given in the form:

Acct. no, amount, (1 for deposit, 2 for withdrawal)

 (ii) Write a program to give a message, "the balance is insufficient for the specified withdrawal".

19.3 Create a structure for items in a store with the following data.

Part no., Part name, Qty on hand, Re-order level, Re-order quantity, Supplier code.

Assume there are 100 items in the store:

(i) Write a program to print details of items whose stock is below the re-order level.

(ii) Write a function to automatically re-order items whose stock is below the re-order level.

19.4 Create a structure to store employee's data with the following information:

Employee's no., Employee's name, Employee's pay, date of joining (which is itself a structure)

(i) It is decided to increase the pay as per the following rules:

Pay <= Rs. 2000   : 15 % increase
Pay <= Rs. 5000 but > Rs. 2000   : 10 % increase
Pay > Rs. 5000   : no increase

Write a program to do this. (Assume there are 200 employees.)

(ii) Write a program to print details of employees who have completed 20 years service.

19.5 A scooter company has serial numbers of scooters starting from AA0 to FF9. The other characteristics of scooters to be specified in a structure are:

Year of manufacture, Colour, Horsepower.

(i) Specify a structure to store information corresponding to a scooter.

(ii) Write a program to retrieve information on scooters with serial numbers between BB0 and CC9.

20

Pointer Data Type and its Applications

LEARNING OBJECTIVES

In this chapter we will learn:

1. The distinction between the contents of a variable and the address of a variable.
2. How to declare variable names to store addresses also known as pointers.
3. The use of the operator & to find the address of a variable name.
4. The use of operator * to retrieve contents of a variable, given its address.
5. Calling functions by passing addresses of formal arguments to it.
6. The use of an array name as a pointer.

Pointer data type is an important data type in C as it is used extensively by professional C programmers. Beginners find it difficult to understand what is a pointer data type and how it is used. We will explain these ideas first.

20.1 POINTER DATA TYPE

When we declare a variable name x as type integer we tell the compiler that a location in memory where an integer can be stored should be found and it should be given a name x.
  Thus writing

$$\text{int } x \text{ ;}$$

will pick a memory box (i.e. a location in memory) and give it a name x. The variable name is a symbolic name for the address of the memory box. This is shown in Fig. 20.1. The

	Variable name	address	contents
Memory box	x	2568	

Fig. 2 .1   ffect of declaring a variable name.

numeric value of the address corresponding to x is shown as 2568 in Fig. 20.1. If we write $x = 32$ then the integer 32 is stored as contents of x as shown in Fig. 20.2.

Variable

name	address	contents
x	2568	32

Fig. 2 .2   variable name   ith a value assigned to it.

We have already encountered the operator & which was used in scanf function. The operator & is called an address operator. If we write:

$$\&x$$

the operator & tells the compiler to find the numeric value of the address of a memory box whose symbolic name is x. We see from Fig. 20.2 that the address corresponding to x is 2568. Thus $\&x$ is 2568. If we write

$$y = \&x \ ;$$

then 2568 which is an *address* is stored in y. When a variable stores an address we declare that variable as a *pointer data type*.

Thus y is declared as:

$$\text{int } ^*y \ ;$$

This declaration says that y will store the address of an integer variable name.

In this case y is the address of the integer variable name x. Figure 20.3 shows what happens when we write

$$y = \&x \ ;$$

Variable

name	address	contents
y	8468	2568

Fig. 2 .3   ffect of   riting

The address allocated by the compiler to store y is shown in Fig. 20.3 as 8468 (observe that it has no relation to 2568 which is the address of x).

If we write

$$z = ^*y \ ;$$

* is taken as an operator which is called an *indirection operator*.

The indirection operator * asks the compiler to:

1. Read the contents of y. (As y is declared as of *type* pointer its contents will be an address.)

2. Go to the address found in Step 1 and retrieve its contents
3. Store the value retrieved in Step 2 in z.

From Fig. 20.3 we see that 2568 is stored in *y*. It is interpreted as an address. The contents of this address are 32 as shown in Fig. 20.2. Thus 32 will be stored in *z*. This is shown in Fig. 20.4.

Variable
name   address   contents

| z | 6426 | 32 |

Fig. 2 .   ffect of assignment

Pictorially we have shown the sequence of operations described in Fig. 20.5.

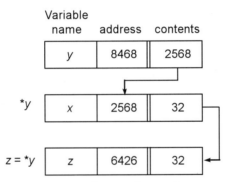

Fig. 2 .   Se uence of operations   hen   e   rite

Observe that in a statement * is taken as an indirection operator. The indirection operator can operate only on addresses. Thus the operand of an indirection operation should be declared to be a pointer data type. The symbol * used in the *declaration* has a different meaning from the * used in a *statement*. In the declaration it only gives information that *y* will store an address whereas in a statement it is an operator commanding that the address stored in *y* should be retrieved and used.

We illustrate in Example Program 20.1 the use of the indirection operator * and pointer type data declaration.

The sequence of operations *(&x) is meaningful. However, the sequence &(*x) is meaningless. *x commands that the address of *x* should be found and contents of that address which will be a value is to be retrieved. & is a command to find the address of a value. This is meaningless. Address is meaningful only for a variable name.

```
/* Example Program 20.1 */
/* Illustrating pointer data type */
#include <stdio.h>

main()
{
    char p, z , w;
    char *address_of_p;
    p = ' A ' ;
    address_of_p = &p;
    z = *address_of_p;
    /* Look up address of p find contents and assign to z */
    w = *(&p);
    putchar(p);
    putchar(z);
    putchar(w);
} /* End of main */

output:
AAA
```

g a   2 .1   Illustrating pointer data type.

20.2 POINTERS AND ARRAYS

An array in C is declared as

$$int\ a[5] = \{8, 6, 4, 9, 11\}\ ;$$

which states that *a* is an array of integers and that the array has 5 components a[0], a[l], a[2], a[3] and a[4]. The array is stored in consecutive addresses in memory as shown in Table 20.1.

Table 2 .1   Illustrating storage of an array

name	address	contents
a[0]	2688	8
a[l]	.2689	6
a[2]	2690	4
a[3]	2691	9
a[4]	2692	11

If we write

$$int\ *x\ ;$$

$$x = \&a[0]\ ;$$

it will result in

$$x = 2688\ ;$$

If we write instead

$$x = a ;$$

then also x will be 2688. The reason is that in the C language the *name* of an array variable is taken as the *address* of its zeroth component. Thus a is the pointer to the array a[5]. Using this fact we can write Example Program 20.2 to store characters in an array and display them.

```
/* Example Program 20.2 */
/* Storing characters in an array & displaying them */
#include <stdio.h>

maln()
{
    char *ptr;
    char b[5];
    for (ptr = b; ptr < b+5; ++ptr)
        {
            *ptr = getchar();
            putchar(*ptr);
        }
    putchar('\n');
}
```

g a   2 .2   Illustrating that array name is pointer.

We could have done this also by using subscripts. What we have done above is only as an illustration.

Example Program 20.3 reverses a character string and prints it.

```
/* Example Program 20.3 */
/* Use of array name as pointer */
#include <stdio.h>
main()
{
    char magic[] = "ABRACADABRA";
    char *addr;
    addr = magic + 11;
    while (--addr >= magic)
        putchar(*addr);
    putchar('\n');
}
```

g a   2 .3   eversing string.

In Example Program 20.3 the variable name magic stores the starting address of the string magic. One is added to the address of the *last* character in the array magic and stored in addr. The *while* loop prints the characters in reverse. Observe the use of – – addr for comparison in the *while* loop.

20.3 POINTERS AND FUNCTIONS

Pointers can be passed as arguments to a function and can also be returned to the name of the function. We will show a small application of this with an example. The problem is to write a function to interchange values of two integers a and b. In other words if a = 25 and b = 38 the function should, after doing its work, give a = 38 and b = 25.

We now write a function:

void interchange (int x, int y)

with x and y as formal arguments. The function is shown below:

```
void interchange (int x, int y)
{   int temp;
    temp = x;
    x = y;
    y = temp;
} /* End of interchange (x, y) */
```

If we now write in the main program

```
a = 25; b = 38;
interchange (a, b);
```

then 25 is copied into x and 38 to y which are the formal arguments of the function interchange. The function interchanges the values of x and y. However, a and b will *not* be interchanged as the values interchanged by the function are not sent back to the locations where a and b are stored. The statement interchange (a, b) does not get them back. This is illustrated in Fig. 20.6. Observe that the address of x and y are not known outside the function in which x and y are used.

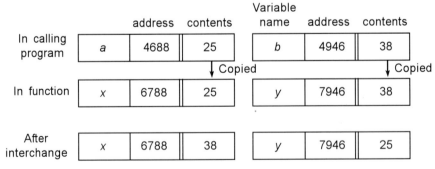

Fig. 2 .   elation bet een calling and called functions.

We can circumvent this problem by using an array as the formal argument in the *function* interchange. We have seen in Chapter 16 that values computed in functions can be returned to its formal arguments only if they are arrays. We rewrite the *function* interchange as follows:

```
void interchange (int x [ ]);
    {  int temp;
       temp = x[0];
       x[0] = x[1];
       x[1] = temp;
    } /* End of interchange */
```

We can call the function with another array *a*

interchange (a) ;

where *a* is declared as: int a[2]

Remember that the argument *a* in interchange(a) is in fact a pointer (i.e. an address) and not a value. Thus when interchange is called with *a*, its *address* is taken as the address of *x*. In other words, array *a* and array *x* occupy the *same locations in memory*. They have different symbolic names which are in fact synonyms. Thus when x[0] and x[1] are interchanged by the *function* interchange, a[0] and a[1] also get automatically interchanged. This is illustrated in Fig. 20.7.

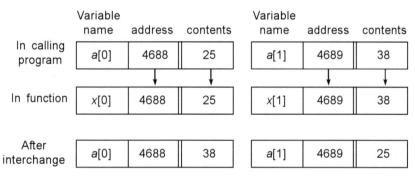

Fig. 2 .   Illustrating the fact that addresses of the actual argument are passed to the formal argument   hen the argument is an array.

We can use this idea of sending addresses rather than values to the formal arguments of the *function*. The *function* interchange is redefined as shown in Example Program 20.4. In this program the function interchange has as its formal arguments two pointer variables, ptr x, ptr y respectively. In the body of the function in the statement

temp = *ptr x ;

the operator * commands that the address contained in ptr x (namely address of *a*) should be referred and the contents of this address read and stored in temp. Thus this statement is equivalent to writing

temp = *(&a) = a;

The next statement

*ptr x = *ptr y;

is equivalent to writing

a = b;

```
/* Example Program 20.4 */
/* Interchanging Numbers */
#include <stdio.h>
void interchange(int *ptr_x, int *ptr_y);
main()
{
    int a, b;
    scanf("%d %d", &a, &b);
    printf("a = %d, b = %d\n", a, b);
    interchange(&a, &b);
    printf("a = %d, b = %d\n", a, b);
}

void interchange(int *ptr_x, int *ptr_y)
{
    int temp;
    temp = *ptr_x;
    *ptr_x = *ptr_y;
    *ptr_y = temp;
} /* End of interchange */
```

g a   2 .   Interchanging numbers.

The statement

$$*ptr\ y = temp;$$

is equivalent to

$$b = temp;$$

Thus the values of *a* and *b* in the calling program are interchanged. This is illustrated in Fig. 20.8.

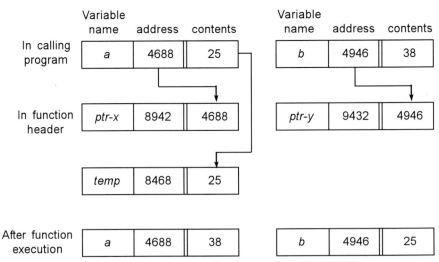

Fig. 2 .   assing pointers as arguments to functions.

In summary when addresses of variables are passed to the formal arguments (which should be of type pointer) of a function, the formal and actual arguments occupy the same locations in memory. Thus the values of the formal variables of function are changed by operations within the function. Figure 20.9 illustrates what happens when the formal parameters of a function are a mixture of normal variables and pointer variables.

Function definition

Int f_name(int x, float y, char *ptr)
{
....
....
return( ) ;
....
....
return( ) ;
} /* End of functlon */

Calling function

int a; float b; char c;
f_name(a, b, &c);

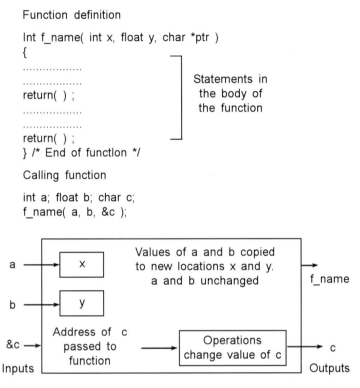

Fig. 2 .   ffect of using pointer variable as an argument of function.

EXERCISES

20.1 Given the following information, answer the questions which follow:

Variable name	Address	Contents
p	2568	425
q	4284	2568
r	6242	4284
a[0]	8468	232
a[10]	8478	2568

(i) &p = ?
(ii) *q = ?
(iii) **r = ?

(iv) &q = ?
(v) *(&q) = ?
(vi) &(*r) = ?
(vii) &a[0] = ?
(viii) a = ?
(ix) a[0] = ?
(x) &a[5] = ?
(xi) a[10] = ?
(xii) *a[10] = ?

20.2 Given three variables x, y, z, write a function to circularly shift right their values. In other words if $x = 5$, $y = 8$, $z = 10$ after circular shift $y = 5$, $z = 8$ and $x = 10$. Call the function with variables a, b, c to circularly shift their values.

20.3 Given an array p of size 5, write a function to shift it circularly left by two positions. Thus p[0] = 5, p[1] = 3, p[2] = 8, p[3] = 9, p[4] = 6 then after the shift p[0] = 8, p[1] = 9, p[2] = 6, p[3] = 5 and p[4] = 3. Call this function with a (3×5) matrix and get its rows left shifted.

20.4 Write a function to solve a quadratic equation $ax^2 + bx + c = 0$. The input to the function are the values a, b, c and the outputs of the function should be stored in variable names p, q appropriately declared.

20.5 Write a function which will take as its input a matrix mat of size ($m \times n$) ($m < 10$, $n < 5$) and return the same matrix with all its elements replaced by absolute values.

21

Lists and Trees

LEARNING OBJECTIVES

In this chapter we will learn:
1. How to create a list data structure.
2. Applications in which such structures are useful.
3. Operations on list data structures.
4. How to create a tree data structure.
5. Applications of tree data structures.

21.1 LIST DATA STRUCTURE

The two data structures we have encountered so far for representing collections of data items are arrays and structures. Retrieval of information from any array is simple. It is, however, necessary to specify the size of the array before it is used. Thus situations could arise where the specified storage is too much or too little. For example, we used arrays to represent strings of characters in Chapter 17. When characters were to be inserted in the string then we had to move to the right all the characters appearing after the insertion point. The array size should be sufficient to accommodate the expanded string. If a substring is to be deleted from a string then again characters on the right of deleted substring have to be moved left. The string would now become smaller and part of the array would thus be unused and wasted. The procedures to delete and insert would also involve fair amount of bookkeeping of array index to move characters. Thus in applications which require frequent editing of strings of characters it would be useful to have a data structure in which we can dynamically allocate space as needed and also release unused space. Further, operations of insertion and deletion should be simplified.

There are also other applications of computers in which it is necessary to have dynamically changing data structures. For example, a list of books issued from a library would grow as new books are issued and shrink when books are returned. Besides this there are applications in which flexible links between data items are necessary. For example, in a lending library it may be necessary to find out the list of books issued to each member and overdue books. In such a case a link should be established between a membership list and the book issue list. Writing programs for such applications is facilitated by using a data structure known as a *list structure*. We will now define this data structure and explain how operations are carried out on data organized as a list structure.

A linear linked list consists of a number of elements called *nodes*. A node consists of two fields, a field called the *information field* and a field called the *next address field*. The information field holds the actual information in a list element. The next address field holds the address of the next node in the list. In other words it establishes a link to the next element in the list. The next address which is used to access the next node is known as *pointer*. The entire linear linked list is referred to and accessed by a *pointer* which points to (i.e. it contains the address of) the first node of the list. This pointer is external to the list and is a *list identifier* which contains the address of the first element of the list. The last node of the list is specified by storing a special symbol known as NULL in its next address field. The structure of a list is shown in Fig. 21.1.

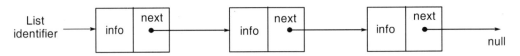

Fig. 21.1 A list structure.

C provides a method of creating a list with a structure and a *pointer data type*. For example, if a node of a list is to be defined in C it may be done by the following declaration:

```
typedef struct node
    {   char info;
        struct node *next node;
    }   List node;
List node *list of char, n1;
```

The declaration defines a structure named node. This structure has two components. The first is of type char. It tells that info will store a character. The next component is a structure of type node. Observe that we have defined a structure (which refers to itself) within a structure. This is allowed in C. This declaration states that a pointer (namely, an address) named next node will point to another structure of the type node. Following this we have declared list of char as a pointer which will point to (i.e. contain the address of) a data of type List node. A node named n1 is also declared as of type List node. If we write the following statement

$$*\text{list of char} = \&n1;$$

$$n1.info = 'X';$$

the effect will be to create a node n1 pointed to by list of char. This is shown in Fig. 21.2. We will now create a list of three nodes shown in Fig. 21.3. We have named the nodes n1, n2 and n3.

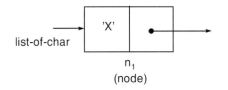

Fig. 21.2   Creating a node in a list-of-char.

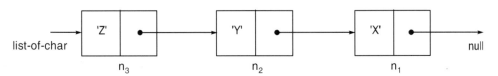

Fig. 21.3   A list with three nodes to be created.

A program for doing this is given as Example Program 21.1. Examining this program we see that we declare list of char as a pointer to List node and n1, n2, n3 as of type List node. We store in n1.info 'X' and store NULL in its address field. NULL is a symbol defined in <stdio.h> and is used to indicate the end of a list. Thus we now have a list with one node. We now take node n2 and store in its information field 'Y'. In its next address field we store the address of n1 (&n1), thereby linking n2 to n1. Finally in n3 we store 'Z'. Its next node pointer is set to &n2. To identify the list, we call it list of char and store the address of n3 in it. Observe that n3 is the node added last to the list (see Fig. 21.3).

The printf statement prints the character stored and the next node address of each of the three nodes.

The problem with Example Program 21.1 is the need to declare all the nodes nl, n2, n3 at the beginning. As the main purpose of lists is to store variable number of nodes we must find a better method of creating a list without having to name and declare nodes before creating the list. We will do this next.

In order to do this we need a C function provided in the C library. This function is called *malloc* (which is an abbreviation for memory allocate). We will also use the unary operator *sizeof*. We will define these next.

The function *malloc* allocates at run time the number of bytes needed to store a node. It has one argument which specifies the number of bytes to be allocated. If the function successfully allocates the requested storage it will return the address of the requested storage. If it is unable to provide the requested storage (e.g. when there is no space left in memory), it will return NULL. As *malloc* returns an address, this address must be cast to the type of data structure it must point to. For example, if we want to allocate one int cell and set a pointer to this address we do the following:

$$\text{int *ptr;}$$

$$\text{ptr = (int *) malloc (sizeof(int));}$$

The argument of malloc is sizeof (int). The operator *sizeof* returns the number of bytes

```
/* Example Program 21.1 */
/* Creation of a list */
#include <stdio.h>
typedef struct node
{
    char info;
    struct node *next_node;
}   List_node;

main()
{
    List_node *list_of_char, n1, n2, n3;
    /* Store ' X ' in n1 */
    n1.info = ' X ';
    n1.next_node = NULL;
    /* n1 is the only node in the list now */
    n2.info = 'Y';
    n2.next_node = &n1;
    /* Node n2 is created and linked to n1 */
    n3.info = ' Z ' ;
    n3.next_node = &n2;
    list_of_char = &n3;
    /* End of creation of list */
    printf("node3 = %c %x, node2 = %c %x\n",
            n3.info, n3.next_node, n2.info,
            n2.next_node);
    printf("node1 = %c %x, header addr = %x\n",
            n1.info, n1.next_node, list_of_char);
} /* End of main */
```

Output of Example Program 21.1:

```
node3 = Z 7fffe080, node2 = Y 7fffe088
node1 = X 0, header addr = 7fffe078
```

g a   21.1   Creation of a list with three nodes.

needed to store a data of the *type* specified. The function malloc now returns the address where these bytes can be stored. (int *) casts this address to be of *type* pointer to an integer. ptr is declared to be an address for storing a data of type int by the declaration int *ptr. Thus, we now set ptr to point to the address of the correct type of argument needed.

If we want to allocate a location in memory to store a data of *type* struct node, we do the following:

struct node *ptr;

ptr = (struct node *) malloc(sizeof(struct node));

The function *malloc* provides the address of locations in the memory to store ptr. Thus by using malloc we can create lists of indefinite length.

We will now rewrite Example Program 21.1 as Example Program 21.2 using *malloc* function. In Example Program 21.2, temp and list of char are declared as pointers to struct node.

```
/* Example Program 21.2 */
/* Allocate memory for a list and creating it */
#include <stdio.h>
typedef struct node
{
    char info;
    struct node *next_node;
} List_node;
List_node *temp, *list_of_char, *print_node;

main()
{
    char a_char;
    temp = (List_node *)malloc(sizeof(List_node));
    a_char = getchar();
    (*temp).info = a_char;
    /* The symbol (*temp).info has another notation
       temp->info where -> is a minus sign followed
       by a > sign. This symbol is a shorthand
       notation and is extensively used */
    temp->next_node = NULL;
    list_of_char = temp;
    while ((a_char = getchar()) != '\n')
        {
            temp = (List_node *)malloc(sizeof(List_node));
            temp->info = a_char;
            temp->next_node = list_of_char;
            list_of_char = temp;
        } /* End of while */
    print_node = list_of_char;
    while (print_node != NULL)
        {
            printf("Char = %c, Link Address = %x\n",
                    print_node->info,
                    print_node->next_node);
            print_node = print_node->next_node;
        } /* End of while */
} /* End of main */

Output of Example Program 21.2:

Char = P, Link Address = 1834
Char = W, Link Address = 1824
Char = Z, Link Address = 1814
Char = Y, Link Address = 1804
Char = X, Link Address = 0
```

g a   21.2   Creating a list using malloc function.

In the main program an address is allocated to temp by the function *malloc*. A character is read by the getchar () function. It is stored in the char field of the structure whose address is temp by the statement

$$(*temp).info = a\ char;$$

As statements of the type (*ptr).info occur very often in C a shorter notation is provided. This notation is ptr –> info which is identical in its effect to (*ptr).info. Thus the statement (*temp).info may be written as: temp –> info. The symbol –> is a minus sign followed by the greater than symbol. The next node field of temp is made NULL. We have now created a list with one node. To add more nodes to the list we first store the address of temp in list of char; read another character from input and enter the *while* loop. In the *while* loop a new node address is obtained using malloc function and is stored in temp. The character read is stored in this node and the node is linked to the existing list by the statement

$$temp–>next\ node = list\ of\ char;$$

The new node address is stored in list of char, another character is read and the *while* loop is re-entered. This procedure is repeated till the end of input is reached. Outside the loop the list is printed. The steps in creating the linked list are shown in Fig. 21.4.

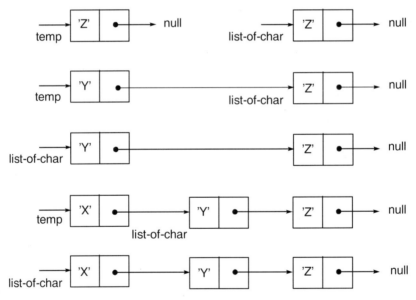

Fig. 21.   Steps in creation of a linked list.

21.2 MANIPULATION OF A LINEARLY LINKED LIST

In this section we will illustrate with a running example various manipulations which may be performed on lists. The program is briefly described in what follows.

EXAMPLE 21.1   A lending library keeps a list of issued books. Each item in the issue list has the following information. Accession number of the book, issue code which is either I, B or L and the identification code of the member to whom issued. The issue code I is used if issued to an individual member, B if sent for binding and L if issued to another library. As the number of books issued will be continuously changing we will use a list structure for issued books.

In Example Program 21.3 we will create a list of issued books. The following operations have to be normally performed on this list:

1. If a member asks for a book it is necessary to search the list of issued books to find its status.
2. When a book is issued to a member this should be added to the list of issued books.
3. When a book is returned by a member it should be deleted from the list of issued books.

```c
/* Example Program 21.3 */
/* Function to create a book list */
#include <stdio.h>
typedef struct book
{
    int acc_no;
    char issue_code;
    struct book *next_book;
} Book;
Book * add_book(int book_no, char code, Book *list_of_books);

main()
{
    int no_of_book;
    char code_of_book;
    Book *book_list = NULL;
    scanf("%d %c", &no_of_book, &code_of_book);
    while (no_of_book != 0)
        {
            book_list = add_book(no_of_book, code_of_book, book_list);
            scanf("%d %c", &no_of_book, &code_of_book);
        }
} /* End of main */

Book * add_book(int book_no, char code, Book *list_of_books)
{
    Book *new_book;
    new_book = (Book *)malloc(sizeof(Book));
    new_book->acc_no = book_no;
    new_book->issue_code = code;
    new_book->next_book = list_of_books;
    list_of_books = new_book;
    return(list_of_books);
}
```

g a   21.3   Creating a list of books.

In Example Program 21.3 the function add book appends an issued book to an existing list of books. An integer variable book no, a character variable code and a pointer variable list of books are formal arguments of the function add book. In the function, a node to add a new book to be issued is allocated by the function malloc. In this node called new book the book number and issue code are stored. The next book address is made list of books and this address is returned to add book function. As *list of books is initialized to NULL when add book is called the first time next node address will be NULL. The next time the function is invoked the address returned will be used thereby linking this new book node to the existing list.

Observe that add book function is a pointer type. This is necessary as a pointer is returned to the function name. Example Program 21.4 is a function to search the list of issued books to locate a book with specified accession number. In this function the *while* loop follows the pointers in the list until the specified book is found or the end of the list is reached. The address of the header list of books is assumed available from Example Program 21.3.

```
/* Example Program 21.4 */
/* Function to search a list for a book */
/* List of books created by Example Program 21.3
   and address list_of_books is assumed available */
#include <stdio.h>
#define TRUE  1
#define FALSE 0
typedef struct book
{
    int acc_no;
    char issue_code;
    struct book *next_book;
} Book;
typedef int Boolean;

Boolean found_book(int book_no, Book *list_of_books)
{
    Book *temp;
    temp = list_of_books;
    while (temp != NULL)
      {
          if (temp->act_no == book_no)
             return(TRUE);
          else
             temp = temp->next_book;
      } /* End of while */
return(FALSE);
} /* end of found_book */
```

g a   21.   Searching a list of books.

Example Program 21.5 is a function to delete a book from the list. When a book is deleted from the list then the node corresponding to the book should be removed from the list.

Assuming that the node marked current node in Fig. 21.5 is to be removed then the link address of the previous node should be replaced by the link address of the current node. This will make the previous node point to the next node "short circuiting" the current node. After this operation the link address field of the current node may be set to NULL. Further, the library function *free* may be used to free the pointer to the node so that it maybe reused. The library function *free* takes as its formal argument a pointer and releases that pointer. An exception to this strategy occurs if the very first node (namely, the header node) is to be removed. In this case there is no "previous" node. Thus the header pointer is moved to point to the next node.

```
/* Example Program 21.5 */
/* Function delete_book */
typedef struct book
{
    int acc_no;
    char issue_code;
    struct book next_book;
} Book;
Book *list_of_books;

Book *delete_book(int no_of_book, Book *list_of_books)
{
    Book *prev_book, *current_book;
    if (list_of_books->acc_no == no_of_book)
        {
            list_of_books = list_of_books->next_book;
            return(list_of_books);
        }
    prev_book = list_of_books;
    current_book = prev_book->next_book;
    while (current_book != NULL)
        {
            if (current_book->acc_no == no_of_book)
                {
                    prev_book->next_book = current_book->next_book;
                    free(current_book);
                    return(list_of_books);
                }
            else
                {
                    prev_book = current_book;
                    current_book = current_book->next_book;
                }
        } /* End of while */
    printf("Book not in list\n");
    return(list_of_books);
} /* end of delete_book */
```

g a   21.   Deleting a book from list-of-books.

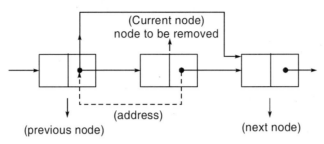

Fig. 21.   Deletion of a node from a list.

21.3   CIRCULAR AND DOUBLY LINKED LISTS

One of the shortcomings of a linear linked list is that having reached a node in the list we cannot go back to preceding nodes unless their addresses are stored. Suppose we make a small change in the structure of a list so that the next address field of the last node in the list is not NULL but is the address of the first node of the list, then we have what is called a *circular list* (see Fig. 21.6). In such a structure we can reach any node from any other node in the list. Along with this there is a danger of endlessly looping round the list. To prevent this the

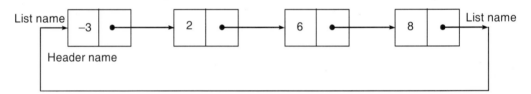

Fig. 21.   A circular list of positive integers.

header node, namely, the first node in the list is made distinct by storing in its information field an element which distinguishes it from the other nodes in the list. Such a node is called a *sentinel node*. A sentinel node of a circular list of positive integers may store a negative integer. A circular list of integers is created by Example Program 21.6. Observe that the function create circ list returns the address of the header of the list to main. The method of creation of the list is illustrated in Fig. 21.7.

We will illustrate the use of circular lists with an example.

EXAMPLE 21.2   Suppose we want to add two long positive integer numbers. The length of each number may vary from case to case. One way of representing a number is by using a list structure. We can store one digit of the number at each node. Minus one may be stored in the header node to indicate that it is the header. The two numbers to be added are stored in two circular lists. The least significant digit of the number is stored in the node next to the header. Thus if we want to add 96784 to 3678 the two numbers would be stored in two lists as shown in Fig. 21.8.

```
/* Example program 21.6 */
#include <stdio.h>
typedef struct dig_node
{
    int number;
    struct dig_node *next_digit;
} Digit_node;
Digit-node *create_circ_list(Digit_node *k);

main()
{
    Digit_node *list_head = NULL;
    list_head = create_circ_list(list_head);
} /* End of main */

    Digit_node *temp, *last_address;
    int digit;
    header = NULL;
    temp = (Digit_node *)malloc(sizeof(Digit_node));
    last_address = temp;
    while (scanf ("%d", &digit) != EOF)
        {
            temp->number = digit;
            temp->next-digit = header;
            header = temp;
            /* If true link header to last_address */
            if (digit < 0)
                last_address->next_digit,= header;
            else
                temp = (Digit_node *)malloc(sizeof(Digit_node));
        } /* End of while */
    return(header);
} /* End of create_circ_list */
```

g a   21.   Creating a circular list.

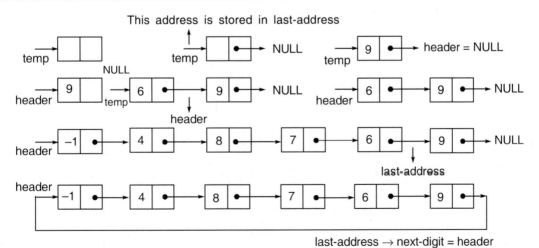

last-address → next-digit = header

Fig. 21.   Steps in creation of a circular list.

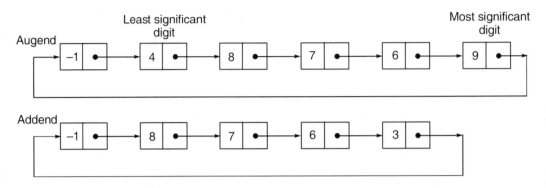

Fig. 21.   Circular lists for augend and addend to be added.

Once the two lists are created the digits in the corresponding nodes (beginning from the least significant digit) of augend and addend are added and stored in a new list named result. The procedure to do this is given in Example Program 21.7. Comments are included to make the program self-explanatory. Observe that by using circular lists we are able to position the pointers of the augend and addend at the header of the respective lists.

```
/* Example Program 21.7 */
/* Program to add two integers */
#include <stdio.h>
typedef struct digit_node
{
    int number;
    struct digit_node *next_digit;
} Digit_node;

Digit_node *create_circ_list(Digit_node *header);
void print_circ_list(Digit_node *header);
Digit_node *Add_numbers(Digit_node *result_addr,
                        Digit_node *addend,
                        Digit_node *augend);
main()
{
    Digit_node *and_head, *aug_head, *result_head;
    and_head = create_circ_list(and_head);
    printf("Printing from main addend list\n");
    print_circ_list(and_head->next_digit);
    aug_head = create_circ_list(aug_head);
    printf("Printing from augend list\n");
    print_circ_list(aug_head->next_digit);
    result_head = Add_numbers(result_head, and_head, aug_head);
    printf("Printing from main result list\n");
    print_circ_list(result_head->next_digit);
} /* End of main */
Digit_node *Add_numbers(Digit_node *result_addr,
                        Digit_node *addend,
                        Digit_node *augend)
```

```
{
    Digit_node *temp, *last_address, *header, *operand;
    int sum, carry;
    /* The following three statements initialize a circular list to store the
       result */
    temp = (Digit_node *)malloc(sizeof(Digit_node));
    last_address = temp;
/* Pointers of augend and addend lists are moved to point to the least significant
    digits */
addend = addend->next_digit;
augend = augend->next_digit;
carry = 0;
while ((addend->number >= 0) && (augend->number >= 0))
    {
        /* Addition of digits of addend and augend begins */
        sum = addend->number + augend->number + carry;
        temp->number = sum % 10;
        carry = sum/10;
        /* After addition the node is linked to the previous node */
        temp->next_digit = header;
        header = temp;
        /* A new node for result is created. Pointers of addend and augend are
           advanced */
        temp = (Digit_node *)malloc(sizeof(Digit_node));
        addend = addend->next_digit;
        augend = augend->next_digit;
    } /* End of while */
/* If end of either addend or augend list is reached then the operand is taken
    from the appropriate list */
if (addend->number < 0)
    operand = augend;
else
    operand = addend;
/* Carry if any is added to the operand and the result is stored in new list */
while (operand->number >= 0)
    {
        sum = operand->number + carry;
        operand = operand->next_digit;
        temp->number = sum % 10;
        carry = sum/10;
        temp->next_digit = header;
        header = temp;
        temp = (Digit_node *)malloc(sizeof(Digit_node));
    } /* End of while */
    /* Carry if any is stored in the result list */
    if (carry == 1)
        {
            temp->number = carry;
            temp->next_digit = header;
            header = temp;
            temp = (Digit_node *)malloc(sizeof(Digit_node));
        }
```

```
      /* -1 is stored in the header node of the result */
      temp->number = -1;
      temp->next-digit = header;
      last_address->next_digit = temp;
      result_addr = temp;
      return(result_addr);
} /* End of function Add_numbers */

Digit_node *create_circ_list(Digit_node *header)
{
      Digit_node *temp, *last_address;
      int digit;
      header = NULL;
      temp = (Digit_node *)malloc(sizeof(Digit_node));
      /* Store address of node created at the beginning */
      last_address = temp;
      while (scanf("%d", &digit) != EOF)
         {
            /* In the following statements read a digit and store it in the node
               already created. Set the next address held of the node = previously
               created node address (namely, header) */
         temp->number = digit;
         temp->next_digit = header;
         header = temp;
         printf("%d %d\n", digit, header);

         /* If digit < 0 link header to last_address */
         if (digit < 0)
            {
               last_address->next_digit = header;
               printf("Last link addr = %d\n", header);
            }
         else
            temp = (Digit_node *)malloc(sizeof(Digit_node));
         if (digit < 0)
            break;
         } /* End of while */
      return(header);
} /* End of create_circ_list */

void print_circ_list(Digit_node *header)
{
      Digit_node *temp;
      int digit;
      temp = header;
      digit = temp->number;
      while (digit >= 0)
         {
           printf("Addr = %d, digit = %d\n", temp, digit);
           temp = temp->next_digit;
           digit = temp->number;
         }
} /* End of print_circ_list */
```

g a   21.   Adding two numbers represented as circular lists.

21.4 A DOUBLY LINKED CIRCULAR LIST

A doubly linked circular list consists of a number of nodes where each node is not only linked to the node to its right but also to the node to its left. In other words a node has a pointer giving the address of the next sequential node and another pointer giving the address of the previous node.

A doubly linked circular list is illustrated in Fig. 21.9. In this example, the information in each node is assumed to be a positive digit. We will identify one node as a header node and store a – 1 in it to distinguish it as the header. A list of this type may be described by the declaration given in Example Program 21.8.

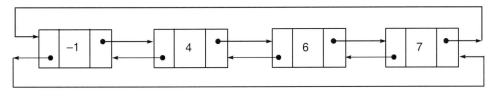

Fig. 21. A doubly linked circular list.

The primary advantage of a doubly linked list is that we can traverse it in both directions. Another advantage is the ease with which an arbitrary node may be deleted. Deletion is easy as links to both the previous node and the next node exist at all nodes.

Example Program 21.8 illustrates the creation of a doubly linked circular list. The sequence of creation of the list is illustrated in Fig. 21.10 with input data 2 4 6 –1. This sequence is obtained by tracing the procedure given in Example Program 21.8 step by step.

Observe that in a doubly linked list the following relation holds for any node pointer

$$p = p\text{->next left->next right} = p\text{->next right->next left};$$

```
/* Example program 21.8 */
/* Function to create a doubly linked list */
#include <stdio.h>
typedef struct node
{
    int info;
    struct node *next_right;
    struct node *next_left;
} Node;
Node *header;

Node *create_doub_link_list(Node *header)
{
    Node *temp, *last_addr;
    int digit;
    header = NULL;
    temp = (Node *)malloc(sizeof(struct node));
    /* Store address of first node created */
    last_addr = temp;
```

```
while (scanf("%d", &digit) != EOF)
    {
        temp->info = digit;
        temp->next_right = header;
        header = temp;
        if (digit < 0)
            /* Link header node to last node and vice versa */
                {
                    header->next_left = temp;
                    last_addr->next_right = header;
                    header->next_left = last_addr;
                }
        else
                {
                    temp = (Node *)malloc(sizeof(struct node));
                    header->next_left = temp;
                }
    } /* End of while */
} /* End of create_doub_link_list */
```

g a   21.   Function to create a circular doubly linked list.

Deletion of a node is quite easy in a doubly linked list as both the left and right pointers of a node are available in the node itself. For example, if a node containing a specified information is to be removed from the list of Fig. 21.10 it may be done by the procedure given as Example Program 21.9.

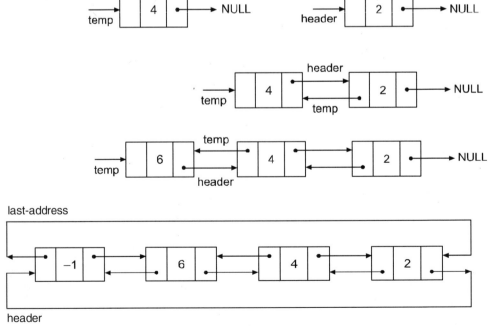

Fig. 21.1   Progressive creation of a doubly linked circular list.

If a node is to be inserted to the right of a specified node *p* it may be done by the following statements:

Statements to insert a node

```
temp = (Node *) malloc(sizeof (Node));
temp->next right = p->next right;
p->next right->next left = temp;
p->next right = temp;
temp->next left = p;
temp->info = digit;
```

```c
/* Example Program 21.9 */
#include <stdio.h>
#define TRUE   1
#define FALSE  0
typedef struct node
{
    int info;
    struct node *next_right;
    struct node *next_left;
}   Node;
Node *header;
typedef unsigned int Boolean;
Node *delete_node(Node *header, int del_digit);
Node *create_doub_link_list(Node *header);
main()
{
    int delete_digit;
    header = create_doub_link_list(header);
    printf("header(create) = %d\n", header);
    scanf("%d", &delete_digit);
    printf("del-digit = %d\n", delete_digit);
    header = delete_node(header, delete_digit);
    printf("header(delete) = %d\n", header);
    header = header->next_right;
    while( header->info >= 0 )
        {
            printf("Header = %d, header_info = %d\n", header, header->info);
            printf("Header_next_right = %d\n", header->next_right);
            header = header->next_right;
        }
} /* End main */
Node *delete_node(Node *header, int del_digit)
{
    Boolean deleted;
    Node *temp;
    deleted = FALSE;
    temp = header->next_right;
    while((!deleted) && (temp->info >= 0))
```

```
      {
         if (temp->info == del_digit)
            {
               temp->next_right->next_left = temp->next_left;
               temp->next_left->next_right = temp->next_right;
               deleted = TRUE;
            }
         else
            temp = temp->next_right;
      }
   if (deleted)
      printf("Node deleted\n");
   else
      printf("Node not found and not deleted\n");
   return(header);
} /* End of delete_node */

/* Include function Node *create_doub_link_list here */
```

g a   21.   Deleting a node from a doubly linked list.

21.5 BINARY TREES

A binary tree is a finite set of elements of which one element is called the *root* of the tree and its remaining elements are partitioned into two disjoint subsets, each of which is itself a binary tree. These two subsets are called the *lefi subtree* and the *right subtree* of the original tree. Each element of a binary tree is called a *node* of the tree.

Figure 21.11 illustrates a binary tree consisting of 9 elements. In this binary tree A is the root of the tree. The left subtree consists of the tree with root B. The right subtree is the tree with root C. B has an empty right subtree and its left subtree has root G. C has a left subtree consisting of the single element D. This element which has no further trees emanating from it is known as a *leaf* node. The right subtree of C has E as its root element. E has an empty right subtree and its left subtree is the leaf node F. The node G has a left subtree with a leaf node H and a right subtree with leaf node J. The binary tree of Fig. 21.11 may be represented using pointers as shown in Fig. 21.12. A node of the tree may be described by the following declaration:

```
            struct node
               {  char info;
                  struct node *left tree;
                  struct node *right tree;
               };
            struct node *tree node;
```

From the given data one may create the binary tree data structure of Fig. 21.12. The procedure becomes a little cumbersome if we use a straightforward brute force method. A more elegant procedure is possible if we use a recursive technique which we will discuss in the next chapter.

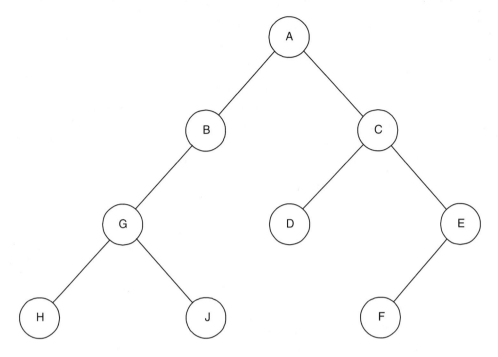

Fig. 21.11   A binary tree.

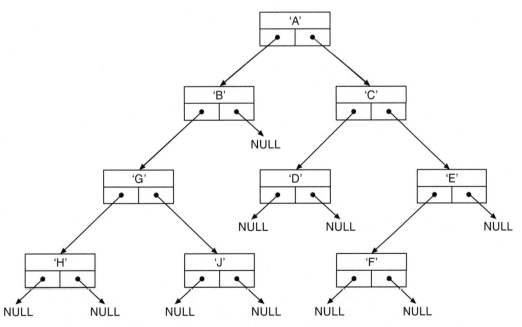

Fig. 21.12   Binary tree representation with pointers.

Binary trees have many applications in programming. They are used to represent arithmetic expressions, moves by opponents in a game, decision sequences, sort strategies, etc. We will conclude this chapter after illustrating the use of a binary tree with an example.

EXAMPLE 21.3   A procedure to pick all duplicate numbers in a set of numbers is to be developed. A straightforward method would be to pick a number and compare it with the rest of the numbers in the list. This, however, needs N^2 comparisons for a set of N numbers. A binary tree based algorithm reduces the number of comparisons to a considerable extent. The algorithm is sketched below:

Algorithm to pick duplicate numbers from a list
```
    Read(number);
    Root node content = number;
    Right subtree = null;
    Left subtree = null;
    while there is data do
       begin
          Read(number);
          Compare number with contents of root node;
       repeat
          if match then
             declare as duplicate and
             set duplicate found as true
          else
             if number < root then
                root = left subtree root;
             else root = right subtree root;
       until duplicate found or (root == NULL);
       if (root == NULL) then place number in root;
    end; /* End of while */
```

This algorithm is developed as Example Program 21.10. The reader should trace this program and check it with a list of input numbers such as:

16 18 3 11 9 18 7 9 3 12

We use – 99999 to indicate the end of input numbers.

```
/* Example Program 21.10 */
/* Storing digits in a tree deleting duplicates */
#include <stdio.h>
typedef struct node
{
    int digit;
    struct node *right_tree;
    struct node *left_tree;
}   T_node;
```

```
T_node *tree_node= NULL, *p = NULL, *q = NULL;
int number;
T_node *make_tree(T_node *tree, int digit);
T_node *set_left_tree(T_node *tree, int digit);
T_node *set_right_tree(T_node *tree, int digit);

main()
{
    /* Read a number and store in root */
    scanf("%d", &number);
    tree_node = make_tree(tree_node, number);
    while(scanf("%d", &number) != EOF)
        {
            q = tree_node;
            p = tree_node;
            while ((number != p->digit) && (q != NULL))
                {
                    p = q;
                    if (number < p->digit)
                        q = p->left_tree;
                    else
                        q = p->right_tree;
                } /* End of inner while */
        if (number == p->digit)
            printf("Number %d is a duplicate\n", number);
        else
            /* Insert number to the right or left of p */
            {
                if (number < p->digit)
                    p = set_left_tree(p, number);
                else
                    p = set_right_tree(p, number);
            } /* End of else clause */
        } /* End of outer while */
} /* End of main */

T_node *make_tree(T_node *tree_node, int info)
{
    tree_node = (T_node *)malloc(sizeof(T_node));
    tree_node->digit = info;
    tree_node->left_tree = NULL;
    tree_node->right_tree = NULL;
    return(tree_node);
} /* End of make_tree */

T_node *set_left_tree(T_node *tree_node, int info)
{
    T_node *temp;
    if (tree_node->left_tree != NULL)
        printf("Illegal set_left_tree function use\n");
    else
```

```
    {
        temp = make_tree(temp, info);
        tree_node->left_tree = temp;
    }
  return(tree_node);
} /* End of set_left_tree */

T_node *set_right_tree(T_node *tree_node, int info)
{
    T_node *temp;
    if (tree_node->right_tree != NULL)
      printf("Illegal set_left_tree function use\n");
    else
      {
        temp = make_tree(temp, info);
        tree_node->right_tree = temp;
      }
  return(tree_node);
} /* End of set_right_tree */
```

g a   21.1   Storing digits in a tree after deleting duplicates.

EXERCISES

21.1 Simulate a stack using a list structure. Write functions to Push and Pop in the stack.

21.2 Simulate a queue data structure with a list structure. A queue is a first-in-first-out data structure. Write procedures to add an element to the queue and retrieve an element from the top of the queue.

21.3 A dequeue is a data structure in which elements may be inserted at either end and removed from either end. The two ends of the dequeue are called left and right. Use a list structure to simulate a dequeue. Write functions to remove elements from left, remove from right, insert at left, insert at right. The functions should take care of operations when the dequeue becomes empty.

21.4 Write routines to do the following in a linear sequential list:
   (i)   Append an element to the tail of the list.
   (ii) Concatenate two lists.
   (iii) Reverse a list so that the last element becomes the first and vice versa.
   (iv) Insert a node as the nth node of the list.
   (v)   Copy a list into another.
   (vi) Count the number of nodes in a list.
   (vii) Delete all even nodes in the list.
   (viii) Interchange the nth and kth nodes of a list.

21.5 Create a data structure which would represent the record of each member of a library. The record should contain membership number, name, borrower category and a part which would contain a list of books borrowed by a member.

21.6 Write a function which would scan the member data structure and print out the books borrowed by a specified member.

21.7 Write a function which would print out the names of all members who have borrowed more than 6 books.

21.8 Write a function to merge two sorted lists.

21.9 Define a list data structure to facilitate the symbolic manipulation of polynomials. For example a term of the polynomial

$$a_n x^n + a_{n-1} x^{n-1} + a_{n-2} x^{n-2} + \ldots + a_1 x^1 + a_0$$

may be represented by the node

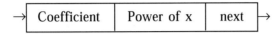

  (i) Write a routine to add two polynomials represented by two lists.
  (ii) Write another routine to symbolically differentiate a polynomial and obtain a list which represents the derivative polynomial.

21.10 A sparse vector is a vector in which more than 80 percent of the components are zero. Represent a sparse vector by a circular list.

21.11 Write a routine to add two sparse vectors represented by two lists.

21.12 Repeat Exercise 21.3 using a doubly linked circular list.

21.13 Design doubly linked circular lists to store the following sparse matrix. Pictorially show the lists to represent this matrix.

$$\begin{matrix} 2 & 0 & 0 & 4 \\ 0 & 0 & 5 & 0 \\ 0 & 7 & 0 & 6 \\ 1 & 4 & 0 & 0 \end{matrix}$$

Each node of the list would have the row and column index of the matrix element and the value of the element.

21.14 Write a program to add two $n \times n$ sparse matrices and store the result in a third matrix.

21.15 Write a program to count the number of nodes in a binary tree.

22

Recursion

LEARNING OBJECTIVES

In this chapter we will learn:
1. The concept of recursion.
2. The advantages and disadvantages of using recursion.
3. Applications of recursion in programming.

In Chapter 16 we asked the question: Can a function call itself? The answer to this question is yes. In this chapter we will discuss when and how this feature, called *recursion,* is to be used in programming. We will also answer some of the other questions raised in Chapter 16 regarding rules which govern the calling of functions by other functions in C language.

22.1 RECURSIVE FUNCTIONS

Recursion is the name given to the technique of defining a function or a process in terms of itself. The best known example of a recursively defined function is the factorial function defined as follows:

Factorial Function:

$$0! = 1$$
$$n! = n(n - 1)!$$

Here n! is defined in terms of $(n - 1)!$, which is in turn defined in terms of $(n - 2)!$ and so on till we reach 0! which is explicitly defined to have a value 1. Any recursive definition must have an explicit definition for some value or values of the argument(s); otherwise the definition would be circular. Some more recursively defined functions are:

Fibonacci Numbers:

(i) $Fib(0) = 0; Fib(1) = 1;$
(ii) $Fib(n + 1) = Fib(n) + Fib(n - 1);$

Arithmetic Expression:

   (i) <Arithmetic Expression>: = <Variable Name>

  (ii) <Arithmetic Expression>: = <Arithmetic Expression> op <Arithmetic Expression>
      where op is an arithmetic operator + – * or /.

A Tree Structure:

   (i) ☐ is a tree

  (ii) If t_1 and t_2 are trees, then

      t_1 t_2

      is a tree.

A List:

   (i) A node is a list

  (ii) A list concatenated to a list is a list.

The power of recursion lies in the possibility of defining an infinite set of objects by finite statements. Similarly a recursive program can define an infinite number of computations even though it may not have any explicit loops. Recursive algorithms are appropriate when the problems to be solved or the data structure to be processed are already defined recursively.

If a function R contains an explicit reference to itself, then it is said to be *directly recursive*. If R contains a reference to another function S which contains a reference to R, then R is said to be *indirectly recursive*.

The following function is a recursive definition of the factorial function.

Algorithm 22.1   *A recursive function for factorial*

```
int factorial(int n)
    {  int result;
          if(n == 0)
              return(1);
          else
              {  result = n * factorial(n – 1);
                 return(result);
              }
    } /* End of factorial */
```

Functions normally have locally defined objects such as variables, constants, types and other functions. These have no existence or meaning outside the function. Each time a function is invoked recursively a new set of objects is created. Although they have the same names, their values have to be preserved till the end of recursion. This puts an extra load on the translator of the language. It is this provision which distinguishes a language that provides recursion from one which does not. For example, the languages Fortran 77 and Cobol do not provide recursion whereas Fortran 90 and Pascal allow recursion. If recursion is required to solve a problem, then it is not necessary to set up the necessary mechanism in C as the provision for the same is already there.

22.2 RECURSION VERSUS ITERATION

As mentioned in the last section recursive algorithms are appropriate when the problem to be solved or the data structure to be processed are defined recursively. This does not mean that in such cases recursive algorithms are necessarily the best way of solving these problems. Let us, for example, consider two algorithms to compute Fibonacci numbers. Fibonacci numbers are recursively defined as follows:

$$fib(0) = 0; fib(1) = 1$$

$$fib(n + 1) = fib(n) + fib(n - 1)$$

A recursive algorithm is given below as Algorithm 22.2.

Algorithm 22.2 *Recursive algorithm to compute Fibonacci numbers*

```
int fib (int n)
    { int result;
        if (n == 0)
            return(0);
        else if(n == 1)
                return(1);
        else
        {
            result = fib(n - 1) + fib(n - 2);
            return(result);
        }
    } /* End of fib */
```

If n = 5 then this algorithm will activate itself 15 times as shown in Fig. 22.1. The value of fib(5) is calculated working backwards starting from the leaf nodes of the tree of Fig. 22.1 and ending at the root node.

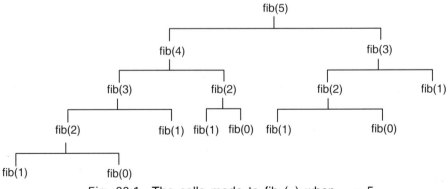

Fig. 22.1 The calls made to fib ( ) when   = 5.

It is clear that the total number of calls to fib and consequently computing it will grow exponentially with *n*. Each call requires reservation of storage for values and links. Such a program to solve the problem needs extra resources. In contrast to this, Fibonacci numbers may be generated iteratively as illustrated in the function of Algorithm 22.3.

Algorithm 22.3 *An iterative algorithm to calculate Fibonacci numbers*

```
int fib(int n)
   { int i, prev, current, next;
      if (n == 0)
        return(0);
      else
        if(n == 1)
           return(1);
        else
           { prev = 0; current = 1;
             for (i = 2, i <= n, ++i)
                { next = prev + current;
                  prev = current;
                  current = next;
                }
           }
        return(current);
   } /* End of fib */
```

In this iterative algorithm the number of computations performed increases linearly with *n*. It is thus much more efficient compared to the recursive program. Observe, however, that the recursive program is concise and "elegant" and closely follows the problem definition.

In spite of the elegance of the recursive methods of programming it is necessary to explore alternative methods based on iteration due to considerations of efficiency. In general a thumb rule one should follow is to use iteration if there is an *obvious* iterative algorithm to solve the problem. If one is forced to mimic recursion by using stacks and operations on stacks then recursion is a better technique to use.

22.3 SOME RECURSIVE ALGORITHMS

As the first example of recursion we will develop a program to find whether a given string is a string representing a valid arithmetic expression. The definition of a valid arithmetic expression may be given recursively as pointed out in the last section and thus a recursive algorithm is appropriate. The definition is given in detail below:

<letter> ← ['A' ... 'Z']   (22.1)

<variable name> ← <letter>   (22.2)

<Arithmetic expression> ← <variable name>   (22.3)

<operator> ← ['+', '–', '/', '*']　　　　　　　　　　　　　　　　　　(22.4)

<Arithmetic expression> ← <Arithmetic expression>

　　<operator> <Arithmetic expression>　　　　　　　　　　　　　　(22.5)

The algorithm faithfully follows the above definition. A symbol is read. We proceed further if it is not the end of line. If it is a letter then the next symbol is read. If it is end of line then we declare the string a valid arithmetic expression as per Eq. (22.2). If the symbol read is not the end of line then the symbol should be an operator as defined by Eq. (22.4). If it is an operator we call arith expn to check if the rest of the string is an arithmetic expression. If it is not an operator then the string is not a valid arithmetic expression. The program is given as Example Program 22.1.

```
/* Example Program 22.1 */
#include <stdio.h>
#define TRUE    1
#define FALSE   0
typedef unsigned int Boolean;
char symbol;
Boolean valid;
void arith_expr(void);
Boolean is_operator(char s);

main()
{
    valid = FALSE;
    arith_expr();
    if (valid)
      printf("Valid arithmetic expression\n");
    else
      printf("Invalid expression\n");
} /* End of main */

void arith_expr(void)
{
    symbol = getchar();
    if ((symbol >= 'A') && (symbol <= 'Z'))
      {
          symbol = getchar();
          if (is_operator(symbol))
            arith_expr();
          else
            {
              if (symbol == '\n')
                valid = TRUE;
              else
                valid = FALSE;

            }
      }
    else
       valid = FALSE;
} /* End of arith_expr */
```

```
Boolean is_operator(char s)
{
    if ((s == '+') || (s == '*') || (s == '-')
        || (s == '/'))
      return(TRUE);
    else
      return(FALSE);
} /* End of is_operator */
```

g a   22.1   Checking validity of arithmetic expression.

As the second example we will consider again the example of picking duplicate numbers from a set of numbers. We solved this problem in the last chapter without using recursion. We will solve it now using recursion.

The strategy we will adopt would be to read each number and place it at an appropriate node of a tree, if it is not already in the tree. A procedure to do this is evolved remembering that the basic definition of a tree data structure is recursive. Thus the tree can be built recursively. This is given as Algorithm 22.4.

Algorithm 22.4   *Building a tree*

Buildtree (struct tree *node, int number);
{   *if* (number > value at node)
        then if right branch of tree is empty
          then {
                    Create a node;
                    Place number in it;
                    Attach node to tree;
                 }
        else Buildtree (right branch, number)
        else if (number < value at node)
          then if leftbranch of tree is empty
            then {
                      Create a node;
                      Place number in it;
                      Attach node to tree;
                   }
          else Buildtree (leftbranch, number)
        else Write ('Number is a duplicate')
} /* End of algorithm 22.4 */

This procedure may be used in a program to detect duplicates as given in Algorithm 22.5.

Algorithm 22.5 *Program to detect duplicates*
Read an input value;
Create a root node for a tree and
place it in the node;
While data remain in input
{   Read(input value);
    Buildtree(rootnode, input value);
}

These algorithms are converted as Example Program 22.2. The program has been traced with the following data to illustrate the way the tree is built.

Input data: 15 25 30 25 12 22 14 28

The trace is shown as Fig. 22.2. The student should trace the program and verify the tree building procedure.

```
/* Example Progrm 22.2 */
/* Traverse a tree in-order left-root-right */
#include <stdio.h>
typedef struct tree
{
    int value;
    struct tree *right;
    struct tree *left;
} Tree;
Tree *root_node;
int inp_value;
void build_tree(Tree *t, int n);
void trav_in_order(Tree *node);
main()
{
    scanf("%d", &inp_value);
    /* Create root of tree and store value read */
    root_node = (Tree *)malloc(sizeof(Tree));
    root_node->value = inp_value;
    root_node->right = NULL;
    root_node->left = NULL;
    while (scanf("%d", &inp_value) != EOF)
        build_tree(root_node, inp_value);
} /* End of main */
void build_tree(Tree *node, int number)
{
    Tree *new_node;
    if (number > node->value)
        {
            if (node->right == NULL)
                /* If terminal node on right branch */
```

```
            {
                /* Create node and link to right */
                new_node = (Tree *)malloc(sizeof(Tree));
                new_node->value = number;
                new_node->left = NULL;
                new_node->right = NULL;
                node->right = new_node;
            }
        else
            build_tree(node->right, number);
        }
    else
        {
            if (number < node->value)
                if (node->left == NULL)
                    /* If terminal node on left branch */
                    {
                        /* Create node and link to left */
                        new_node->value = number;
                        new_node->left = NULL;
                        new_node->right = NULL;
                        node->left = new_node;
                    }
                else
                    build_tree(node->left, number);
            else
                printf("duplicate number = %d\n", number);
        }
} /* End of build_tree */

void trav_in_order(Tree *node)
{
    if (node != NULL)
        {
            /* Visit left node */
            trav_in_order(node->left);
            printf("%d", node->value);
            /* Visit right node */
            trav_in_order_(node->right);
        }
} /* End of trans_in_order */
```

g a   22.2 Building a tree removing duplicate integers.

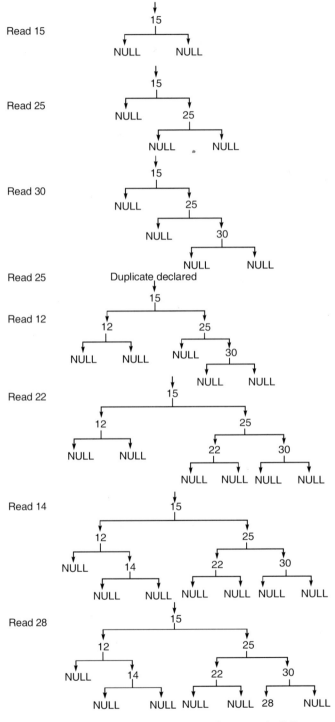

Fig. 22.2   Illustrating recursive tree building.

22.4 TREE TRAVERSAL ALGORITHMS

The tree was generated by Algorithm 22.4 systematically, keeping smaller numbers in a left subtree and larger numbers in a right subtree. This tree has the property that the contents of each node in the left subtree of a node t are less than the contents of t. Thus if we travel through all the nodes of the tree in the order left node, rootnode, rightnode starting from the left most node of the tree, we will pass through the numbers in ascending sequence. This method of travelling through the nodes in the order left, root, right is known as *inorder traversal of the tree*.

We can specify this traversal recursively as:

1. Traverse the left subtree *inorder*
2. Visit the root
3. Traverse the right subtree *inorder*

The above method may be expressed as Algorithm 22.6.

Algorithm 22.6 *Inorder tree traversal to print numbers in ascending order*

```
Travinorder(struct tree *node)
    { if node <> nil then
            {   Travinorder (node->left);
                Write (node->value, ' ');
                Travinorder (node->right)
            }
    }
```

This algorithm is converted to Example Program 22.3.

With the data given for Example Program 22.2, the order in which nodes will be "visited" and values printed is shown in Fig. 22.3. If the numbers in the list are to be printed in descending order then we would again traverse the tree in order but from right to left.

```
/* Example Program 22.3 */
#include <stdio.h>
typedef struct tree
{
    int value;
    struct tree *right;
    struct tree *left;
} Tree;
Tree *root_node;
int inp_value;
void build_tree(Tree *t, int n);
void trav_in_order(Tree *node);
main()
```

```
{
    scanf ("%d", &inp_value);
    /* Create root of tree and store value read */
    root_node = (Tree *)malloc(sizeof(Tree));
    root_node->value = inp_value;
    root_node->right = NULL;
    root_node->left = NULL;
    while (scanf("%d", &inp_value) != EOF)
        build_tree(root_node, inp_value);
    printf("Inorder sequence :");
    trav_in_order(root_node);
    printf ("\n");
} /* End of main */
void trav_in_order(Tree *node)
{
    if (node != NULL)
        {
            /* Visit left node */
            trav_in_order(node->left);
            printf("%d", node->value);
            /* Visit right node */
            trav_in_order(node->right);
        }
} /* End of trav_in_order */

/* Place function build_tree here */
```

g a   22.3   Sorting integers-tree traversal by recursion.

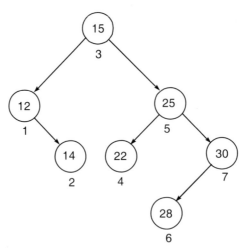

Fig. 22.3   Showing inorder traversal of a tree.

Besides the inorder traversal in which the root is visited in the middle there are two other methods of systematically visiting the nodes of a tree. They are the *preorder* and *postorder* traversals. In preorder we visit the root first and then the left and right subtrees. In postorder we visit the left and right subtrees and the root last. The postorder traversal is useful in converting an *infix* algebraic expression (A + B) * (C − D) to a *postfix* expression AB + CD − *. This is illustrated by Algorithm 22.7. The tree corresponding to an arithmetic expression is shown as Fig. 22.4. The postorder traversal algorithm would print out the answer as:

$$AB + CD - *$$

Algorithm 22.7 *Postorder traversal of tree*

```
Travpostorder
{   If node <> nil then
    {   visit the left subtree
        Travpostorder (node->left);
        /* visit the right subtree */
        Travpostorder (node->right);
        /* Write contents of root */
        Write (node->value, ' ');
    }
}
```

The order in which the nodes are visited by the algorithm is shown by placing numbers below each node in Fig. 22.4.

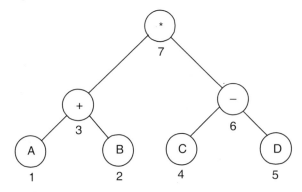

Fig. 22.   Tree representing an arithmetic expression.

The algorithm for preorder traversal is given as Algorithm 22.8. In this case the algorithm would print * + AB − CD for the tree of Fig. 22.4.

Algorithm 22.8 *Preorder traversal of tree*

```
Travpreorder
    {
        if node <> nil then
            {
                /* Visit the root */
                Write (node->value, ' ');
```

```
            Visit the left subtree
            Travpreorder (node -> left);
            /* Visit the right subtree */
            Travpreorder(node -> right);
        }
    }
```

EXERCISES

22.1 The Ackerman's function is defined as follows:

$A(0, n) = n + 1$

$A(m, 0) = A(m - 1, 1)$ $(m > 0)$

$A(m, n) = A(m - 1, A(m, n - 1))$ $(m, n > 0)$

(i) Using the above definitions show that $A(2, 2) = 7$

(ii) Write a C function to compute $A(m, n)$.

22.2 Write a recursive function to compute a^n where a is real and n is an integer. Compare it with an iterative function.

22.3 Let Committee (n, k) be the number of committees of k persons which can be formed from among n persons. For example Committee $(4, 3) = 4$. Given four persons X, Y, Z, W there are 4 committees which can be formed with three persons, the committees being XYZ, XYW, YZW, XZW. Show that

Committee $(n, k) =$ Committee $(n - 1, k) +$ Committee $(n - 1, k - 1)$; $(n, k > 0)$
Committee $(1, 1) = 1$, Committee $(2, 1) = 2$.

Write a recursive C program to compute

Committee (n, k) for $n, k >= 1$.

22.4 Write a recursive algorithm to search for a given key from a list of integer valued keys. [*Hint:* First place the keys in a tree systematically and then search the tree.]

22.5 Write a recursive algorithm to print out all possible character strings of length n by picking characters out of a set of k characters. For example if the given set of characters is 'A', 'B', 'C', then 9 possible strings exist of length n = 2.

22.6 Write a recursive function that accepts a prefix expression consisting of the arithmetic operators +, −, * and / and single digit integer operands and returns the value of the expression.

22.7 A height balanced tree is one in which for each node the number of nodes on its left and on its right differ at most by 1. Modify the tree building procedure, given as Example Program 22.2, to create a height balanced tree. The formal parameters to the buildtree procedure would be pointer to node, value at node and the numher of items in the list.

22.8 Write a recursive algorithm to recognise whether a given string is a valid identifier in C.

22.9 Given a string representing a parentheses-free infix arithmetic expression, write a procedure to place it in a tree in the infix form. Assume that a variable name is a single letter. Traverse the tree to produce an equivalent postfix expression string.

22.10 Write a procedure to count in a binary tree:

 (i) The total number of nodes
 (ii) The number of leaf nodes.

23

Bit Level Operations and Applications

LEARNING OBJECTIVES

In this chapter we will learn:

1. Operations available in C to manipulate the individual bits of numbers stored in variable names.
2. Use of bit level operators to carry out some useful functions in C.

One of the special features of C is the availability of operations on bits and strings of bits. This facility is not available in most high level languages. These operations are primarily useful in simulating digital systems at a low level. Packing bits in a word is possible and useful to minimize storage requirements in some problems. In this chapter we will first define various operations on bits and how they can be applied.

23.1 BIT OPERATORS

In Table 23.1 the symbols used for operations on bits, their types and precedence are given.

Table 23.1   it operators

Operator symbol	Operation	Type of operation	Precedence or rank of operator	
&	Bitwise AND	Binary		3
^	Bitwise Exclusive OR	Binary		4
|	Bitwise OR	Binary	Lowest	5
~	One's complement	Unary	Highest	1
<<	left shift	Binary		2
>>	right shift	Binary		2

Binary operations can be used with variables of type signed or unsigned integer or character but not with floating point. The definition of the operators is given in Table 23.2.

Table 23.2   efinition of bit operations

a	b	a&b	a|b	a ^ b	~a
0	0	0	0	0	1
0	1	0	1	1	1
1	0	0	1	1	0
1	1	1	1	0	0

Observe that for & (AND) operator both operands must be 1 for the result to be 1. For | (OR) operator either operand should be 1 for the result to be 1. For ^(EOR) operator either operand but not both must be 1 for the result to be 1. The ~ (complement) operator is a unary operator. It changes the operand to 1 if it is 0 and to 0 if it is 1. The left and right shift operators are explained in Table 23.3.

Table 23.3   efinition of left and right shift operators

String p	p >> 3	Action
01011010	00001011	p shifted right by 3 positions. Left most bits filled with 0s. Right most 3 bits lost

String q	q << 4	Action
11000110	01100000	q shifted left by 4 positions. Right most bits filled with 0s. Left most 4 bits lost

23.2 SOME APPLICATIONS OF BIT OPERATIONS

EXAMPLE 23.1   As the first example we will write Example Program 23.1 to find out whether a given integer is odd or even. If the least significant bit of a number is 0 it is even, otherwise it is odd. To find the least significant bit we AND bitwise the given number with 1. As 1 is represented in binary as 0001, AND will zero all bits of the given number except the last bit. The last bit will equal the least significant bit of the given number. For example, if the given number = 0011011 then the given number & mask

$$001101 \& 000001 = 1$$

```
/* Example Program 23.1 */
#include <stdio.h>

main()
{
    int given_number, mask = 1;
    while(scanf("%d", &given_number) != EOF)
        {
            if (given_number & mask)
                printf("Given number %d is odd\n", given_number);
            else
                printf("Given number %d is even\n", given_number);

        }
} /* End of main */
```

g a   23.1   as ing a binary string.

EXAMPLE 23.2   The next example is to write a program to divide an unsigned number x by 2^n. Each right shift of a bit string is equivalent to dividing it by 2. Thus to divide by 2^n we shift right n positions the operand. When a string is shifted right its left most bits get filled with 0s. The sign bit should not be normally shifted. It, however, depends on the machine. We have thus decided to use an unsigned integer. Example Program 23.2 illustrates this. Remember that $y >> = n$ is equivalent to $y = y >> n$.

```
/* Example Program 23.2 */
#include <stdio.h>

main()
{
    unsigned int x, two_power_n, n = 0, y;
    while(scanf("%u %u", &x, &two_power_n) != EOF)
        {
            /* The following while loop finds for a power of two number such as
                8 the integer power namely 3 */
            while (two_power_n != 1)
                {
                    two_power_n >>= 1;
                    ++n;
                }
            y = x;      /* x is stored in y */
            y >>= n;    /* y shifted right by n places */
            printf("x = %u divided by 2 power %u is %u\n", x, n, y);
            n = 0;
        } /* End of outer while */
}   End of main */
```

g a   23.2   ividing an integer by an integer   hich is a po er of .

EXAMPLE 23.3   Characters are normally stored in 1 byte of a computer. Only 7 bits are needed to code characters. The eighth bit can be used for a parity. We will now write a program to generate an even parity bit. If the total number of 1's in an eight bit string (including the parity bit) is even then this string satisfies even parity. If the number of 1s in a string is even then the Exclusive OR of the bits taken pairswise should be zero. In other words if the string is

$$a_7 \ a_6 \ a_5 \ a_4 \ a_3 \ a_2 \ a_1 \ a_0$$

then $\qquad\qquad a_0 \wedge a_1 \wedge a_2 \wedge a_3 \wedge a_4 \wedge a_5 \wedge a_6 \wedge a_7 = 0$

This is used to generate the parity bit. Given a string

$$a_6 \ a_5 \ a_4 \ a_3 \ a_2 \ a_1 \ a_0$$

even parity bit $\qquad\qquad p_7 = a_0 \wedge a_1 \wedge a_2 \wedge a_3 \wedge a_4 \wedge a_5 \wedge a_6$

Example Program 23.3 generates this bit. In this program the expression $(x\&1)$ gets the least significant bit of x. The statement parity bit $\wedge = (x\&1)$ exclusive ors the existing parity bit (initialized to 0) with the least significant bit of x. The character read, which is stored in x, is now shifted one bit position to the right. If after shifting one bit x is 0, no further work

```
/* Example Program 23.3 */
#include <stdio.h>

main()
{
    unsigned char ch, x;
    unsigned int parity_bit = 0;
    ch = getchar();
    while (ch != '\n')
        {
        x = ch;
        parity_bit ^= (x & 1);
        /* least significant bit of x is used */
        x = x >> 1;
        while (x != 0)
            /* when x == 0 parity bit does not change */
            {
            /* .parity_bit using next bit of x */
            parity_bit ^= (x & 1);
            x = x >> 1;
            }
        printf("Even parity bit of %c = is %u\n",
                ch, parity_bit);
        parity_bit = 0;
        ch = getchar();
        } /* End while */
} /* End of main */
```

g a   23.3   enerating a parity bit for a character.

need to be done as all bits of *x* would be zero. If *x* is not equal to 0 then the least significant bit of *x* shifted by 1 position is Exclusive ORed with the parity bit. These statements are repeated in the *while* loop until *x* becomes 0. The parity bit is then printed.

EXAMPLE 23.4   As the next example we simulate what is known as a full adder. When a string of bits *x* is added to another string *y* then the sum is obtained by first adding the least significant bits of *x* and *y*. Carry if any is taken and added to the next significant bits of *x* and *y*. This is shown below.

carry	1	1	1	1	1	1	0	
x	0	1	1	1	0	1	0	
y	1	0	1	0	1	1	0	
Sum	0	0	1	0	0	0	0	

Table 23.4 is a table showing the result of addidg three bits.

Table 23.   able to sho   bit addition

x_bit	*y_bit*	*carry_bit*	*sum_bit*	*Carry to next bit position*
0	0	0	0	0
0	0	1	1	0
0	1	0	1	0
0	1	1	0	1
1	0	0	1	0
1	0	1	0	1
1	1	0	0	1
1	1	1	1	1

Using Table 23.4 we can write:

$$\text{sum bit} = \text{carry bit} \verb|^| (\text{x bit} \verb|^| \text{y bit})$$

Carry to next bit position = (x bit & y bit) |
(x bit & carry bit) |
(y bit & carry bit)

The sum for the strings *x* and *y* is obtained by first adding the least significant bits of *x* and *y* with the carry bit if any. This is stored in Sum string. Carry is also stored separately. Next *x* and *y* are shifted one position to the right. The least significant bits of shifted *x* and shifted *y* are added and the carry is added. The next bit of sum is thus obtained. The carry bit is also generated. This procedure is repeated until all bits in *x* and *y* are shifted. The program to implement this procedure is given as Example Program 23.4.

The program closely follows what we have explained that x >> = 1 is equivalent to writing x = x >> 1. Observe that the sum obtained is being shifted left by one bit as we calculate the least significant bit of sum and each new bit should occupy the least significant bit position.

```
/* Example Program 23.4 */
#include <stdio.h>

main()
{
    unsigned int x, y, sum, carry_bit, x_bit, y_bit,
    sum_bit, i;
    while (scanf("%x %x", &x, &y) != EOF)
        {
        sum_bit = 0;
        carry_bit = 0;
        sum = 0;
        printf("x = %x, y = %x\n", x, y);
        printf("Bits printed from LSB to MSB\n");
        for (i = 1; i <= 4; ++i)
            {
            x_bit = (x & 1);
            y_bit = (y & 1);
            sum_bit = carry_bit ^ (x_bit ^ y_bit);
            carry_bit = (x_bit & y_bit) |
                (x_bit & carry_bit) |
                    (y_bit & carry_bit);
            /* Bit placed in least significant position of sum */
            sum |= sum_bit;
            x >>= 1;
            y >>= 1;
            sum << 1;
            printf("sum of x and y = %x, carry = %x\n",
                    sum_bit, carry_bit);
            } /* End of for loop */
        } /* End of while */
} /* End main */
```

g a   23.   Simulating a full adder.

23.3   BIT FIELDS

Bit fields can be packed into an unsigned integer. This is primarily used to save space. We take an example to illustrate this. In Chapter 15 we illustrated a questionnaire format. It is reproduced as Table 23.5.

Assume that there are a large number of questionnaires and the information filled up in them is to be stored for later retrieval. Instead of using one variable name (which will occupy one word in memory) for the answer to each question we can pack the information as shown in Fig. 23.1.

```
typedef struct packed quest
        {   unsigned int sex: 1 ;
            unsigned int age: 6 ;
            unsigned int institution: 3 ;
            unsigned int interest: 3 ;
            unsigned int education: 3 ;
        }  Quest ;
```

Questionnaire information may now be defined as Quest participant data[1000];

Table 23.   sample   uestionnaire

Record the answers to the following questions by entering the code number corresponding to your choice in the box on the right of each question.

		Column Number
Serial Number		1
For Office use only		2
		3
1. What is your sex? Male = 0 Female = 1		4
2. Age: What was your age on the last birthday?		
If it is, say, 25 enter it as:		
	2	5
	5	6
3. What is your institutional affiliation?		7
Private Sector	0	
Educational Institution	1	
Government Office	2	
Public Sector Firm	3	
Research Laboratory	4	
Unemployed	5	
4. What is your primary interest?		8
Science	0	
Engineering	1	
Mathematics	2	
Social Sciences	3	
Business Data Processing	4	
5. What is the highest degree obtained by you?		9
High School	0	
Intermediate	1	
Bachelor's	2	
Master's	3	
Doctor's	4	

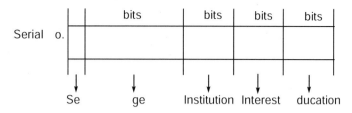

Fig. 23.1   ac ing information in an unsigned int using bit fields.

The serial number is used as the array index in the above definition. In order to find the age of participant with serial number 285 we write:

participant data [285].age

Observe that with 6 bits we can represent maximum age of 63. We thus have to assume that the age of participants is within this. In a similar way the education may be found by writing

participant data [285].education

Example Program 23.5 illustrates how one can retrieve the required infomation from packed data.

```
/* Example program 23.5 */
#include <stdio.h>

main()
{
    typedef struct packed_quest
        {
            unsigned int sex : 1;
            unsigned int age : 6;
            unsigned int institution : 3;
            unsigned int interest : 3;
            unsigned int education : 3;
        } Quest;
    Quest participant_data[100];
    int i, no_quest;
    unsigned int serial_no, s, a, ins, intr, edu;
    scanf("%d", &no_quest);
    for (i = 1; i <= no_quest; ++i)
        {
            scanf("%u %u %u %u %u", &s, &a, &ins, &intr, &edu);
            participant_data[i].sex = s;
            participant_data[i].age = a;
            participant_data[i].institution = ins;
            participant_data[i].interest = intr;
            participant_data[i].education = edu;
            printf("address of participant[%d] = %x\n", i, participant_data[i]);
        }
```

```
    printf("Find the age of participant with Ser No = ");
    scanf("%u", &serial_no);
    printf("Age in record is %u\n", participant_data[serial_no].age);
    printf("Find education of participant with Ser No = ");
    scanf("%u", &serial_no);
    printf("Education in record is %u\n", participant.dataserial_no].education);
} /* End of main */
```

g a   23.   ac ing bits in a   ord.

The bit fields structure is machine and computer implementation dependent. Whether the fields are assigned in a word left to right or vice versa varies from machine to machine. In our Example we assumed that the first field defined in the structure occupies the most significant bit. This may not be so in all machines. The individual fields cannot be pointers or arrays. Use of bit fields should be done with extreme caution. Avoid it if you can.

EXERCISES

23.1 Two's complement of a number is obtained by scanning it from right to left and complementing all bits after the first appearance of a 1. Thus two's complement of 11100 is 00100. Write a function to find the two's complement of a binary number.

23.2 Write a function to find the binary equivalent of a given decimal integer and display it.

23.3 Write a function to find the decimal equivalent of a binary number.

23.4 Write a program to subtract a positive binary number b from another positive binary number a.

23.5 Write a program to multiply a signed 4-bit binary number a by another signed 4-bit binary number b.

23.6 Write a program to construct a single error correcting code called Hamming Code. For a 4 bit number, Hamming Code appends 3 more parity bits making it a seven bit code. The seven bits are labelled P_1, P_2, I_3, P_4, I_5, I_6, I_7.

P_1 satisfies even parity on bits P_1, I_3, I_5, I_7.

P_2 is even parity for bits P_2, I_3, I_6, I_7 and bit P_4 is even for parity bit for bits P_4, I_5, I_6, I_7.

23.7 Write a simulator for a small computer with the following characteristics:
8 bit word, 3 bit op code. The operations are read, write, AND, OR, NOT, shift accumulator, load accumulator, store accumulator.
    Write a program for this simulated computer to add two 4 bit numbers.

23.8 Write a program to search whether a given bit string pattern appears in a 16 bit number. The inputs to the program are

(a) the given number, and
(b) the given pattern.

For example, the pattern 101 appears three times in the 16 bit number 0010100101101001.

24

Files in C

LEARNING OBJECTIVES

In this chapter we will learn:

1. How to create and store files on a disk using C language.
2. How to create, update, and retrieve information from sequential files.
2. The available features in C language to retrieve information directly from a file stored on disk using the direct access feature.

So far we assumed that all data input to a program originate from the standard input device, namely, the keyboard of a video terminal. We have also assumed that all output information is displayed on the standard output device, namely, the screen of a video terminal. Thus we do not know at this time how data can be read from a device such as a disk and how results can be stored in a disk. The operating system under which the C programs run do provide facilities for reading data from disk or writing on disk. The C programming language by itself does not provide any input/output functions. These are provided either by the operating system or by standard libraries which can be accessed by a C programmer. We have so far been using the standard input/output library <stdio.h>. This library also provides facilities to store data in other devices such as disks and read data from other devices. In this chapter we will describe how data stored on *files* can be read.

24.1 CREATING AND STORING DATA IN A FILE

C assumes that input data appears as a sequence called *stream* which can be stored in one or more devices connected to the computer. There are two types of streams: a stream of ASCII characters or a stream of bits. We will be mostly concerned with character streams.

We have so far used *scanf* statement to read data from the standard input. The equivalent statement for data to be read from a file is *fscanf*. Similarly corresponding to *printf* we have *fprintf*. There are equivalents also for *getchar* and *putchar*. We will discuss in this section how a name is given to a file, how it is made ready to store data, how data is stored in it and how it is closed when the job of storing data is over.

The first thing which is done is to declare a data type called FILE and a pointer to that file. We then give a name to the file and open it. This is shown below:

FILE *address of file;

address of file = fopen("sample.dat", "w");

The function fopen specifies that a file named "sample.dat" has been *opened* on the disk. The string "w" states that it will be used for *writing* data. The function fopen returns a pointer to a structure of type FILE. We have named this pointer address of file. If the function fopen is unable to return an address (i.e. a pointer) to store the file then it returns NULL as the address. The function fopen may not be able to provide an address, for example, if the disk is full and no space is left in it. When an address is returned by fopen it means that the file named sample.dat may be stored starting at that address.

If the string "This is a sample string \n" is to be written in sample.dat, one way of doing it is to use the function fprintf. The statement used is:

fprintf(address of file, "This is a sample string \n");

The above statement will write in the file whose pointer is address of file the given string. "This is a sample string" and place an end of line marker \n at its end. If this is the only data to be written then we close the file with the statement:

fclose(address of file);

Gathering all the statements, Example Program 24.1(a) is written. There is only one defect in this program. When fopen returns NULL then the program must give a message and stop. This is shown in Example Program 24.1(b).

```
/* Example Program 24.1a */
#include <stdio.h>

main()
{
    FILE *file_ptr;
    file_ptr = fopen("sample.dat", "w");
    fprintf(file_ptr, "This is a sample string\n");
    fclose(file_ptr);
} /* End of main */
```

g a   2 .1 a   Creation and storing information in a file.

If we want to read the file sample.dat and display its contents on the standard output device we write Example Program 24.2. In this program we define type FILE and a pointer named pointer to file. Observe that in the fopen function we use a string "r". This specifies that the file is opened for reading. The fopen function returns the address of the file and stores it in pointer to file. If the file cannot be opened a message is given. If the file is successfully opened the function fgets is used to read the string stored in the file. fgets is similar to gets.

```
/* Example Program 24.1b */
#include <stdio.h>

main()
{
    FILE *address_of_file;
    address_of_file = fopen("sample.dat", "w");
    if (address_of_file == NULL)
        {
            print("cannot open file to write sample.dat\n");
            return(0);
        }
    fprintf(address_of_file, "This is a sample string\n");
    fclose(address_of_file);
} /* End of file */
```

g a   2 .1 b   iving message if a file cannot be opened.

```
/* Example Program 24.2 */
#include <stdio.h>
#define ARRAY_SIZE 80
main()
{
    FILE *pointer_to_file;
    char temp [ARRAY_SIZE];
    pointer_to_file = fopen("sample.dat", "r");
    if (pointer_to_file == NULL)
        {
            printf("Cannot open sample file to read\n");
            return(0);
        }
    fgets(temp, 81, pointer_to_file);
    if (temp == NULL)
        {
            printf("Error in reading file sample.dat\n");
            return(0);
        }
    printf("%s", temp);
    fclose(pointer_to_file);
} /* End of main */
```

g a   2 .2   rinting contents of a file.

The only difference is that in fgets we specify the pointer to the file from where data is to be read. In gets function that we used in previous chapters, no pointer to file is specified as standard input is assumed. In Example Program 24.2 the statement used is:

fgets(temp, 81, pointer to file);

temp is an array with maximum 81 characters into which the data is read from the file.

If for some reason fgets is not able to access the file (may be it has been erased) then pointer to file will be NULL. In this case a message is displayed and main is exited. If the file is successfully read then the string is displayed by the printf function. After displaying the contents of the file, the file is closed.

The general form of fopen function is fopen (string giving the file name, string giving options). The options available are given in Table 24.1.

Table 2 .1   Options in fopen

File opening option	Action carried out	Does the file exist?
"w"	opens new file for writing	No. Newfile is created
"r"	opens file for reading	Yes. If no, it is an error
"a"	opens file for appending	Yes. If no, it is not an error File is created
"r+"	opens file for reading and/or writing	Yes. If no, it is an error
"w+"	opens file for reading and for writing at the end of the file	Yes

EXAMPLE 24.1   We will now write programs to solve the following problem. A list of names of students in a class is given, one name per line as shown below:

AGARWAL, P.R.
ARUN, R.S.
BHASKAR, A.V.
CHANDRU, K.
GANDHI, S.K.
RAJU, P.
SANTHANAM, R.
SUNANDA, A.
SURESH, P.
TATA, P.
USHA, R.
VASU, P.
ZAIDI, B.S.

The names do not have any embedded blanks. They are already sorted in alphabetical order. It is required to:

1. Store the names in a file on disk.
2. Display the nth name in the list (n is data to be read)
3. Display all names starting with S.

In Example Program 24.3 we first define a data type FILE and f ptr as a pointer to a file. We then declare name as an array with at most 30 characters. We have thus assumed that no name can be longer than 30 characters. Next we open a file called name.dat with the option of reading or writing in it. The beginning of the file is pointed to by f ptr. After doing this we read names from the standard input, namely, the keyboard and write them in the disk file using the function fprintf(f ptr,"%s\n", name). After writing all the names in the file it is closed. We now have the names stored in a disk file name.dat whose pointer is f ptr.

```c
/* Example Program 24.3 */
#include <stdio.h>
#define NAME_SIZE   30

main()
{
    FILE *f_ptr;
    char name[NAME_SIZE];
    int i, n;

    f_ptr = fopen("name.dat", "w+");
    if (f_ptr == NULL)
        {
            printf("File name.dat cannot be opened\n");
            return(0);
        }
    scanf("%d", &n); /* nth name to be displayed */
        /* read name from keyboard input */
    while(scanf("%s", name) != EOF)
        /* store in name.dat */
            fprintf(f_ptr, "%s\n", name);

        /* The names have now been stored in a disk file
           'name.dat' whose pointer is f_ptr */
        rewind(f_ptr);

        /* The following statement reads and skips the first.(n - 1) names */

        /* This is done to get and print the nth name */
        for (i = 1; i < n; ++i)
            fscanf(f_ptr, "%s", name);
        /* The file pointer is now pointing to the nth name in file */
        /* Get nth name in file */
        fscanf(f_ptr, "%s", name);
        printf("%dth name = %s\n", n, name);
        /* The pointer pointing to name is */
        /* reset to point to the first name */
        rewind(f_ptr);
        while (fscanf(f_ptr, "%s", name) != EOF)
            {
                if (name[0] < 'S')
                    continue;
                if (name[0] == 'S')
                    printf("Names starting with S = %s\n", name);
                else
                    break;
            }
    fclose(f_ptr);
} /* End of main */
```

g a   2 .3   rinting the nth name and the names starting   ith S from a file of names.

The problem given is to display the nth name. The names will be stored in name.dat as shown in Fig. 24.1 with the file pointer as shown. Each time we read a name in the file the file pointer will advance by one position.

Top_of_file	→ AGARWAL.P.R.	AGARWAL.P.R.	AGARWAL.P.R.
f_ptr	ARUN.R.S.	ARUN.R.S.	ARUN.R.S.
	- - - - - -	BHASKAR.A.V.	- - - - - - -
	- - - - - -	→ CHANDRU.K.	- - - - - - -
	- - - - - -	- - - - - - - -	- - - - - - -
End of	- - - - - -	- - - - - - - -	- - - - - - -
file	ZAIDI. B.S.	ZAIDI. B.S.	→ ZAIDI. B.S.
	Pointer at	Pointer after	Pointer after
	file	reading 3	reading all
	beginning	names	names

Fig. 2 .1   Illustrating position of file pointer.

Thus in order to read the nth name in the list we have to skip the first $(n - 1)$ names. This is achieved by the *for* statement for $(i = 1; i < n; ++i)$. After skipping $(n - 1)$ names the pointer is positioned at the nth name. This is read by the function fscanf (f ptr, "%s", name). Observe that fscanf is similar to scanf. The only difference is that in scanf we do not specify a file pointer as it is assumed to be the standard input from keyboard. In fscanf we specify the pointer to the file from which data is to be read. Having read the nth record it is displayed using the printf function. We take the pointer back to the top of the file by using the function *rewind (f_ptr)*.

The third problem posed is to display all names starting with S. We are given that the names are in alphabetical order. Thus in the *while* loop we read a name and if its first character   is < S (i.e. A to R) we go back and advance the pointer to the next name. This is achieved by the continue statement which returns control to *while*. If the first letter in name is S we display the name. Thus all names starting with S will be displayed one by one. When the first letter is > 'S' we leave the *while* loop using the break statement. Finally, we close the file.

We summarize in Table 24.2 the file functions that we have used so far. A large number of useful programs can be written using only these functions.

24.2   SEQUENTIAL FILES

A sequential file is a data structure which consists of a sequence of records of the same type and size. The records in the file can be read only sequentially, that is, one after the other starting from the beginning of the file. An array in contrast to a sequential file has a fixed predetermined number of components. Any arbitrary component of an array may be accessed using an index. The primary advantage of a sequential file compared to an array is that it can grow or shrink dynamically. The disadvantage is sequential access. If the tenth record of a sequential file is to be read the first nine records must be passed over before reaching the tenth record.

Table 2 .2   Important File Functions

Function	Use of function	Syntax
fopen	To open a file	fopen ("file name string", "option"); Example: fopen("Sample.dat", "r+"); Returns pointer to file "Sample.dat"
fclose	To close file. Clean up buffers used by it Reposition pointer to beginning of file	fclose (pointer to file); Example: fclose(f ptr);
fscanf	Read from specified file formatted data	fscanf(file pointer, "format string", address of identifiers); Example: fscanf(f ptr, "%c, %d, %s", &a char, &number, string); (string is name of array)
fprintf	Write in specified file formatted data	fprintf(file pointer, "format string", names of identifiers); Example: fprintf(f ptr, "%c, %d, %s", a char, number, string); (String is name of array where a character string is stored)
rewind	Repositions file pointer to the start of the file	rewind (file pointer); Example rewind(f ptr);

EXAMPLE 24.2   We will now illustrate the creation of a sequential file in C. We will assume that the structure of each record is as shown below:

Roll No.	Name	Marks 1	Marks 2	Marks 3
integer >0	25 chars	integer >=0	integer >=0	integer >=0

As records in a sequential file can be retrieved only in a rigid order it is necessary to arrange them systematically using one of the unique fields in the record as a key. Usually the records in the file are arranged in ascending or descending order of this *key field*. In this example Roll Number is the appropriate field to be used as the key field as it is unique to each student. We will assume that the records are arranged in ascending order of this key. The file we will create will be a sequential file with records arranged in ascending order of roll number. Before creating a file it is given a name. This file which we will call infile.dat should be initialized ready for writing by the statement:

fopen("infile.dat", w+);

After this a record is read from the standard input and put in infile.dat. The read and store operations are repeated till no data is left in the input. This method is illustrated as Example Program 24.4. This program is developed using five functions. We first declare a global struct stud record and a global FILE *infile ptr. In the function create file we first open a file infile.dat whose pointer is infile ptr. We then read one record after another and store it in the file using function store in file. The end of input records is signalled by an end of file record which has a 0 stored in roll no field. The function print file record opens the file in which data has been written. Each record is read by the function read file record. After reading a record it is displayed by a series of printf statements in the function print file record. The function feof(infile ptr) returns 0 as long as the end of infile.dat is not reached. This is used in a while loop to display records. When all records have been displayed the file is closed. The display of stored records is done to check whether data read has been correctly recorded in the file.

```
/* Example Program 24.4 */
#include <stdio.h>
struct stud_record
{
    unsigned int roll_no;
    char name[25];
    unsigned int marks[6];
};
struct stud_record temp;

FILE *infile_ptr;
void read_record(void);
void store_in_file(void);
void create_file(void);
void read_file_record(void);
void print_file_records(void);

main()
{
    create_file();
    print_file_records();
} /* End of main */

void read_record(void)
{
    scanf("%d %s %d %d %d", &temp.roll_no, temp.name,
          &temp.marks[1], &temp.marks[2], &temp.marks[3]);
} /* end of read_record */
```

```
void store_in_file(void)
{
    fprintf(infile_ptr, "%d %s %d %d %d\n", temp.roll_no,
            temp.name, temp.marks[1], temp.marks[2],
            temp.marks[3]);
} /* End of store_in_file */

void create_file(void)
{
    infile_ptr = fopen("infile.dat", "w+");
    if (infile_ptr == NULL)
        {
        printf("Error in opening infile.dat while creating\n");
        return;
        }
    read_record();
    while(temp.roll_no != 0)
        {
        store_in_file();
        read_record();
        }
    fclose(infile_ptr);
} /* End of create_file */

void read_file_record(void)
{
    fscanf(infile_ptr,"%d %s %d %d %d", &temp.roll_no, temp.name, &temp.marks[1],
            &temp.marks[2], &temp.marks[3]);
} /* End read_file_records */

void print_file_records(void)
{
    int i;
    infile_ptr = fopen("infile.dat", "r");
    if (infile_ptr == NULL)
        {
        printf("Error in opening infile.dat for printing\n");
        return;
        }
    read_file_record();
    while(!feof(infile_ptr))
        {
        printf ("%d %s", temp.roll_no, temp.name);
        for (i = 1; i <= 3; ++i)
            printf("%d", temp.marks[i]);
        printf("\n");
        read_file_record();
        }
    fclose(infile_ptr);
} /* End of print_file records */
```

g a 2 .   Creating a se uential file of student records.

EXAMPLE 24.3 (SEARCHING A SEQUENTIAL FILE). We will now develop a function to retrieve a record with a specified key from a file. We will assume that the file is arranged in ascending order of the key field which is the roll number. A procedure to do this is given as Example Program 24.5. The key of the record to be retrieved is passed as the actual argument sr no to the function search. In the *while* loop a record is read from infile.dat. The key of this record is compared with the key of the record to be retrieved (which is in desired roll no). If they match no further search is needed (as the key is assumed unique). The control leaves the function search after details of the retrieved record are printed and the file is closed. If the key field read from the sequential file becomes greater than the search key without the two being equal at any point during search it means that the key being searched is not in the file. We can come to this conclusion as the file is arranged in ascending order of keys. When such a condition is detected, further search is abandoned and an appropriate message is printed.

```
/* Example Program 24.5 */
/* Searching a sequential file */
/* The same global declarations as in Example program 24.4 are assumed. It is
    assumed that infile.dat is created as shown in Example program 24.4 */
#include <stdio.h>

struct stud_record
{
    unsigned int roll_no;
    char name[25];
    unsigned int marks [6];
};
struct stud_record temp;

FILE *infile_ptr;
void read_file_record(void);
int search(int desired_roll_no);

main()
{
    int sr_no;
    scanf ("%d", &sr_no);
    search(sr_no);
} */ End of main */

int search(int desired_roll_no)
{
    int i;
    infile_ptr = fopen("infile.dat", "r");
    if (infile_ptr == NULL)
       {
         printf("Error in opening infile.dat for searching\n");
         return(0);
       }
```

```
    read_file_record();
    while(!foeof(infile_ptr))
        {
            if (temp.roll_no == desired_roll_no)
                {
                    printf("%d %s", temp.roll_no, temp.name);
                    for (i = 1; i <= 3; ++i)
                        printf("%d", temp.marks[i]);
                    printf("\n");

                    fclose(infile_ptr);
                    return(0);
                }
            else
                read_file_record();
        }
    printf("Roll no = %d not in file\n", desired_roll_no);
} /* End of search */

void read_file_record(void)
{
    fscanf(infile_ptr,"%d %s %d %d %d",
        &temp.roll_no,
        temp.name,
        &temp.marks [1],
        &temp.marks [2],
        &temp.marks [3]);
} /* End of read_file_record */
```

g a   2 .   etrieving information from a se uential file.

It should now be evident why sequential files are arranged strictly in ascending or descending order of the key.

EXAMPLE 24.4   (UPDATING A SEQUENTIAL FILE).   In Example Program 24.2 each student's record had marks in three subjects. Suppose the marks in a fourth subject become available. A program is required to do the following:

(i) Include the marks in a fourth subject in each student's record in infile.dat
(ii) Compute the total marks in four subjects and include it in each student's record in the file
(iii) Print each student's record

We will assume that the marks in the fourth subject are input using a keyboard in ascending order of roll numbers.

The program to be written is known in computer jargon as updating the records in a master file with new information from a transaction file and creating a new master file. The updating program is given as Example Program 24.6. At the beginning of the function update file the master file, namely, infile.dat is opened. A file named outfile.dat is made ready to be written into by opening it. A record from infile.dat is now read.

A *while* loop is initiated in which records from infile.dat are read and processed until the end of the file infile.dat is reached. The function feof(infile.ptr) returns 0 when the end of the file infile.dat (pointed to by infile.ptr) is reached. After reading a record from infile.dat the roll no and marks in the fourth subject of a candidate are read. The roll no of the record read from infile.dat is compared with the roll no read from terminal. If the two match the total marks are computed by adding marks[l], marks[2], marks[3] and marks[4] and storing the result in marks[5]. The updated record consisting of roll no, name and marks[l] to marks[5] are written in the structure struct stud record temp which is declared as global in Example Program 24.6. If roll no read from terminal does not match that read from infile.dat, no updating is done and no record is written in outfile.dat. An appropriate message is written.

```c
/* Example Program 24.6 */
/* Updating a file which is already created */
#include <stdio.h>

struct stud_record
{
    unsigned int roll_no;
    char name[25];
    unsigned int marks[6];
};
struct stud_record temp;

FILE *infile_ptr;
FILE *outfile_ptr; /* This is a new declaration */
void read_file_record(void);
void update_file(void);

main()
{
    update_file();
} /* End of main */

void read_file_record(void)
{
    fscanf(infile_ptr,"%d %s %d %d %d",
        &temp.roll_no,
        temp.name,
        &temp.marks[1],
        &temp.marks[2],
        &temp.marks[3];
} /* End of read_file_record */

    void update.file(void)
    {
        int i, fourth_mark, roll_no;
        infile_ptr = fopen("infile.dat", "r");
        if (infile_ptr == NULL)
```

```
    {
        printf("Error in opening infile.dat for updating\n");
        return;
    }
outfile_ptr = fopen("outfile.dat", "w");
if (outfile_ptr == NULL)
    {
        printf ("Error in opening outfile.dat for updating\n");
        return;
    }
read_file_record();
while (!feof(infile_ptr))
    {
    /* marks[5] has sum of marks[1] to marks[4] */
        temp marks[5] = 0;
    scanf("%d %d", &roll_no, &fourth_mark);
    if (temp.roll_no == roll_no)
    /* Add marks in 4 subjects and find total */
    {
        temp.marks[4] = fourth_mark;
        for (i = 1; i <= 4; ++i)
            temp.marks[5] += temp.marks[i];
        /* Write new record in outfile.dat */
        fprintf(outfile_ptr, "%d %s", temp.roll_no, temp.name);
        for(i = 1; i <= 5; ++i)
            fprintf(outfile_ptr, "%d", temp.marks[i]);
        fprintf(outfile_ptr, "\n");
    /* Writing of one record in outfile.dat complete */
    }
    else
        {
            printf("Transaction roll_no does not match\n");
            printf("Transaction roll_no = %d,
            File roll_no = %d\n", roll_no, temp roll_no);
        }
    read_file_record();
    } /* End of while */

    fclose(infile_ptr);
    fclose(outfile_ptr);
} /* End of update file */
```

g a 2 . pdating a file.

The next record is now read from infile.dat and the while loop is repeated. Finally, both infile.dat and outfile.dat are closed. Observe that struct stud record has already been defined globally with the array variable name having six components 0, 1, 2, 3, 4, 5. This will thus suffice to store outfile.dat.

24.3 UNFORMATTED FILES

In the last section we discussed how files may be created with a format specification. Formatting is mainly needed for convenience of reading data from terminal and printing results on a printer or displaying on video display units. Data from main memory may be stored in binary form in disk files as exact replicas of how they are found in memory. Similarly unformatted binary data may be stored in memory from files. The operation of reading data from main memory and writing in a file in binary form is performed by a function *fwrite*. Reading binary stream of data from a file and storing in memory is performed by a function *fread*.

The format of the fwrite function is:

fwrite (address of structure or array in memory from where data is to be read,
      size of structure or array,
      Number of items to be read,
      pointer of the file where data is to be written)

For example, if we want to read an array called buffer of size SIZE and write in file whose pointer is f ptr, we write:

fwrite(buffer, SIZE, 1, f ptr);

(Remember that buffer is an array and thus its name itself is a pointer).

The format for the fread function is:

fread (address of structure or array in memory where data is to be stored,
      size of structure or array,
      number of items to be stored,
      pointer of the file from which data is to be read)

For example, if we want to store in a structure named cust record data from file whose pointer is a ptr, we write:

fread(&cust record, sizeof(cust record), 1, a ptr);

Disk is an addressable storage device. Thus files stored in a disk are addressable. C language has recognized this and has provided a function called *fseek* to directly access a record in a file. *fseek* assumes that the file is a binary file created by *fread*. It will not work with a formatted file. We will now illustrate the use of *fread*, *fwrite* and *fieek* functions by rewriting Example Program 24.3 using *fread* and *fwrite*. Example Program 24.7 illustrates retrieving the nth record directly, using the *fseek* function.

The general form of the fseek function is:

fseek(pointer to file, number of bytes to be skipped from the position x of the file, k);

when $k = 0$ position x is taken as the beginning
when $k = 1$ position x is current position
when $k = 2$ position x is end of file

```
/* Example Program 24.7 */
/* Use of fread, fwrite, fseek illustration */

#include <stdio.h>
#define NAME_SIZE 30

main()
{
    FILE *f_ptr;
    char name[NAME_SIZE];
    int n;

    f_ptr = fopen("name.dat", "w+");
    if (f_ptr == NULL)
      {
        printf("File name.dat cannot be opened\n");
        return(0);
      }
    scanf("%d", &n); /* nth name to be displayed */
/* read name from keyboard input */
    while(gets(name) != NULL)
       fwrite(name, NAME_SIZE, 1, f_ptr);
/* The names have now been stored in a disk file 'name.dat' whose pointer is
    f_ptr */
    rewind(f_ptr);

    fseek(f_ptr, (long)(NAME_SIZE * n), 0);
    fread(name, NAME_SIZE, 1, f_ptr);
    puts(name);
    fclose(f_ptr);
} /* End of main */
```

g a   2 .   irect access of information from a dis file.

EXAMPLE 24.5   A bank gives account numbers in serial order starting with serial number 1. The structure of a customer record is:

Account No. 4 digits
Balance in acct : XXXXX.XX (Rs & ps)
Account active or closed : 1 digit (1 for active 0 for closed)

We will write a program to

1. Store customer records in a file.
2. Retrieve the record of a customer with a specified account number and display it. Update it (if required) and store it back in file.
3. Append a new customer record to the file.

Example Programs 24.8, 24.9 and 24.10 are written to do this.

```
/* Example Program 24.8 */
/* Creates an account file */
#include <stdio.h>
struct cust_record
{
    unsigned int acct_no;
    float balance;
    unsigned short int status;
};
/* Customer accts record declaration */
struct cust_record cust_acct;
FILE *afil_ptr;
void create_accounts_file(void);

main()
{
    create_accounts_file(),
}

void create_accounts_file(void)
{
    /* A file "accts.dat" opened to store customer accounts */
    afil_ptr = fopen("accts.dat", "w+");
    if (afil_ptr == NULL)
        {
        printf("error in opening accts.dat file \n");
        return;
        }
    /* Customer record is read and stored in file */
    while(scanf("%u %f %hu", &cust_acct.acct_no,
            &cust_acct.balance, &cust_acct.status) != EOF)
        fwrite(&cust_acct, sizeof(struct cust_record), 1, afil_ptr);
    /* The file is rewound to point at the beginning */
    rewind(afil_ptr);
}
```

g a   2 .   Creating a file of customer accounts.

In Example Program 24.8, we first define a structure to store customer records and declare globally cust acct and *afil ptr. We open the file accts.dat and store customer records in it in binary form and rewind it.

In Example Program 24.9 we read from the terminal the account no of the customer whose record is to be read. The statement:

$$\text{fseek(afil ptr, (long)((acct no} - 1)\text{*s size), 0);}$$

advanced the file pointer[(acct no – 1)*sizeof (struct cust record)] bytes from the beginning of the file (s size = sizeof(sruct customer record)). We have assumed that account numbers are in strict serial order. The number of bytes in each customer record is obtained by using

```
/* Example Program 24.9 */
/* Illustrating direct access to records in a file */
#include <stdio.h>
struct cust_record
{
    unsigned int acct_no;
    float balance;
    unsigned short int status;
};
struct cust_record cust_acct;
FILE *afil_ptr;
/* Use 'accts.dat' created in Example Program 24.8 */
main()
{
    unsigned int account_no;
    float amount;
    unsigned short int trans_type;
    int s_size;

    scanf("%u %f %hu", &account_no, &amount, &trans_type);
    s_size = sizeof(struct cust_record);
    afil_ptr = fopen("accts.dat", "r");
    if (afil_ptr == NULL)
        {
            printf("Error in accts.dat file\n");
            exit(1);
        }
    printf("record of customer with acct.no = %u\n", account_no);
    /* The file pointer moved to record with specified acct.no */
    fseek(afil_ptr, (long)((account_no - 1) * s_size), 0);
    /* Read and display record */
    fread(&cust_acct, s_size, 1, afil_ptr);
    printf ("Account no = %u, Balance = Rs %.2f", cust_acct.acct_no, cust_acct.
            balance);
    if (cust_acct.status)
      printf ("  Active account\n");
    else
      printf ("  Account closed\n");
      /* End of displaying customer account details */
      /* Updating the account of a customer record */
      /* trans_type = 1 is for deposit, trans_type = 0 for withdraw */
    if (cust_acct.status) /* If account is active */
        {
            printf("Customer Acct.No = %u is being updated\n", cust_acct.acct_no);
            if (trans_type)
              cust_acct.balance += amount; /* if deposit */
            else
              {
              cust_acct balance -= amount; /* if withdrawal */
              if (cust_acct.balance < 0)
```

```
                {
                    printf("Balance negative, withdrawal not allowed\n");
                    cust_acct.balance += amount;
                }
            }
        printf("New balance in acct = Rs %.2f\n", cust_acct.balance);
        }
    else
        printf("Customer account closed - No transactions allowed\n");
    /* Updated record is stored back in the file by the following statement */

    fwrite (&cust_acct, s_size, 1, afil_ptr);
    fclose(afil_ptr);
} /* End of main */
```

g a   2 .   irectly accessing a customer accounts record and updating it.

the *sizeof* operator. The multiplying factor is (acct no – 1) because when acct no = 1, (acct no – 1) = 0 and the file pointer points to the first record in the file. Thus to point to the kth record the number of bytes to be skipped = (k – 1) * no. of bytes in each record. Now that the file pointer points to the record with the specified acct no we read the record from the file and print it. We also give a message if the account is closed. Having displayed the account details if a deposit or a withdrawal is specified this is carried out as shown in the program. The updated record is stored back in the file and the file is closed.

Next we see in Example Program 24.10 how a new record is appended to the file. The file accts.dat is opened with the option to read and append (String "r+" in open specifies this). We use the function *fseek* to go to the end of the file. The argument 2 in fseek specifies that the pointer should advance to the end. To find out the last account number assigned we take the pointer backwards by one record length as specified by s size from the current position. We read the last record stored in the file and display it. We add 1 to the customer acct no to get the next customer acct no to be assigned. We feed from the terminal the deposit made by the customer and store it as the appended record in the file. The file is then closed.

```
/* Example Program 24.10 */
/* Adding a new customer account at the end of file */
#include <stdio.h>

struct cust_record
{
    unsigned int acct_no;
    float balance;
    unsigned short int status;
};

/* Customer accts record declaration */
struct cust_record cust_acct;
FILE *afil_ptr;
```

```
main()
{
    int s_size, items;
    /* File acct.dat opened for apppending at end */
    afil_ptr = fopen("accts.dat", "r+");
    if (afil_ptr == NULL)
        {
            printf("File 'accts.dat' cannot be opened\n");
            return;
        }
    s_size = sizeof(struct cust_record);
    printf("s_size = %d\n", s_size);

    /* Position the file pointer to end of file */
    /* This is done using 2 for the last field of fseek */
    fseek(afil_ptr, (long)(-s_size), 2);
    /* This puts pointer to point to the last record */
    items = fread(&cust_acct, s_size, 1, afil_ptr);
    printf("Items read = %d\n", items);
    printf("Last account number = %u\n", cust_acct.acct_no);
    /* Next account no = current no + 1 */
    cust_acct.acct_no ++;
    printf("New customer account being appended = %u\n", cust_acct.acct_no);
    scanf("%f", &cust_acct.balance); /* Real deposit made */
    cust_acct.status = 1;
    fwrite(&cust_acct, s_size, 1, afil_ptr);
    close(afil_ptr);
}
```

g a   2 .1   ppending a ne   record to a file.

24.4   TEXT FILES

A file which is a string of characters is known as a text file. There are simple functions available to:

1. Read characters from a file
2. Write characters in a file
3. Read a string of characters from a file
4. Write a string of characters in a file

We will illustrate the use of some of these functions in this section.

EXAMPLE 24.6   A text file is stored in a file infile.txt. It is to be copied to another file outfile.txt after squeezing out all blanks in infile.txt. A program to do this is written as Example Program 24.11. Observe the use of functions fgetc and fputc in the program. The program is self-explanatory. There are many more functions to handle input/output of files.

```
/* Example Program 24.11 */
#include <stdio.h>
FILE *in_ptr, *out_ptr;
main()
{
    char temp;
    in_ptr = fopen("infile.txt", "r");
    if (in_ptr == NULL)
        {
            printf("infile.txt cannot be opened\n");
            return(0);
        }
    out_ptr = fopen("outfil.txt", "w");
    if (out_ptr == NULL)
        {
            printf("outfil.txt cannot be opened\n");
            return(0);
        }
    /* Read a character from "infile.txt" into temp */
    temp = fgetc(in_ptr);
    while(temp != EOF)
        {
            if (temp != ' ')
                /* store temp in outfil.txt if it is not a blank character */
                fputc(temp, out_ptr);
            temp = fgetc(in_ptr);
        }
    rewind(in_ptr);
    rewind(out_ptr);
    close(in_ptr);
    close(out_ptr);
} /* End of main */
```

g a   2 .11   eading a te t file and manipulating it.

We will now discuss reading unformatted text files and writing unformatted text files. We will illustrate the use of *fread* and *fwrite* functions by showing how to copy a file to another file. Example Program 24.12 illustrates this. This program defines a function copy with two arguments. The two arguments are pointers to two files. We define a character buffer which can store 80 characters. The two files are opened. *fread* reads 80 characters into the buffer from the file pointed to by a fil and *fwrite* writes the characters stored in buffer to the file pointed to by b fil. When end of file a.txt is reached the two files are closed.

There are many more functions to manipulate files in C. We will not discuss them in detail. They are listed in an Appendix.

```
/* Example Program 24.12 */
#include <stdio.h>
#define ARRAY_SIZE   79

main()
{
   copy ("a.txt", "b.txt");
}/* End of main */

void copy(char *a_f_name, char *b_f_name)
{
   int bytes_read;
   char buffer [ARRAY_SIZE];
   FILE *a_fil, *b_fil;
   a_fil = fopen(a_f_name, "r");
   if (a_fil == NULL)
      {
         printf("cannot open a.txt file\n");
         return;
      }
   b_fil = fopen(b_f_name, "w");
   if(b_fil == NULL)
      {
         printf("cannot open b.txt file\n");
         return;
      }
   while((bytes_read = fread(buffer, sizeof(char),
         sizeof(buffer), a_fil)) != 0)
     fwrite(buffer, sizeof (char), bytes_read, b_fil);
   close(a_fil);
   close(b_fil);
}
```

g a   2 .12 Copying a te t file.

EXERCISES

24.1 A structure item in store was defined in Section 19.1. Create an INVENTORY.FILE with these records. Write a procedure to find the total value of the inventory in the store.

24.2 Suppose a store has a number of items in their inventory and that each item is supplied by at most two suppliers. Create the inventory and supplier files. Find the addresses of all suppliers who supply more than 10 different items. Discuss any changes in data structure you would suggest to simplify solving this problem.

24.3 A student master file was created in Example 24.3. Wriie a program which will read this file and print out a list of students who have failed in one or more subjects. Assume 40 percent as pass marks.

24.4 An updated record was created in Example 24.4. Using this file compute for each student his average marks and class. (Assume that 40 to 49 percent is III class, 50 to 59 is II class and above 60 is I class.) Update the file and create a new master file with this additional information.

24.5 Arrange the master file in descending order of average marks and create a new file.

24.6 Assume that at the end of the year a set of students join the class and another set leaves. Using the roll number and an appropriate code to add or delete a student, update the master file. The updated file should be in ascending order of the roll numbers.

24.7 In Exercise 24.4 a master file was created with average marks and class, in addition to other information. Using this file create another file which has only ROLL NO., average marks and class. At the end of the file add a last record which has the total number of records in the file, the number passing in I class, II class, III class and the overall class average. Print this summary information.

24.8 Assume that there are two sections of students who took the same examination and their Roll No. and total marks obtained are recorded in two sequential files.
    (i) Write a program to merge the two sequential files assuming that the two files are arranged in strict ascending order of their Roll No.
   (ii) Modify the program to reject records which are out of sequence (that is, not in strict ascending order) and print an appropriate error message.

24.9 In a small firm, employee numbers are given in serial numerical order, that is, 1, 2, 3 etc.
    (i) Create an unformatted file of employee data with the following information: employee no, name, sex, gross salary
   (ii) If more employees join, append their data to the file.
  (iii) If an employee with serial no. 25 (say) leaves, delete it by making gross salary 0.
  (iv) If some employee's gross salary is increased by 15 percent, write a program to retrieve the records and arrange them. For example, if the salaries of employees with serial numbers 15, 23, 28, 42 are increased, the new file must have the new salaries.
   (v) The company has two sections. The sections are expected to give distinct employee serial numbers and create files with serial number and gross salary. Merge the two files. If there are duplicates, appropriate error messages should be printed.

24.10 Write a program corresponding to Exercise 24.1 with an unformatted file.

24.11 Given a text file, create another text file deleting all the vowels (a, e, i, o, u).

24.12 Given a text file, create another text file deleting the words *a, the, an* and replacing each one of them with a blank space.

25

Miscellaneous Features of C

LEARNING OBJECTIVES

In this chapter we will learn:

1. Some shorthand notations available in C to write concise C programs. In particular we will discuss the use of conditional and comma operators.
2. We will see how macros can be written in C.
3. Finally we will discuss the use of command line arguments to run C programs with many data sets and parameter sets.

In this chapter we will present a variety of features available in C which we have not discussed so far in this book. Some are shorthand notations for operations we could do using the features of C we already know. Others are useful for writing large programs or for combining programs written by a team of programmers.

25.1 CONDITIONAL OPERATOR

We have been using the conditional statement

> if (expression 1)
>   (expression 2);
> else
>   (expression 3);

If (expression 1) is true then (expression 2) is executed, *else* (expression 3) is executed. The statement can be written in an alternative form (which is less readable) using as a *conditional operator*.

> (expression 1) ? (expression 2): (expression 3) ;

The above statement is interpreted as:

$$\text{if (expression 1)} \neq 0 \text{ then}$$
$$\text{perform (expression 2)}$$
$$\text{else}$$
$$\text{perform (expression 3)}$$

If we write

$$\text{max} = (x > y) ? x : y ;$$

max has the larger of x and y when the above statement is executed. The following statement finds whether an integer x is odd or even.

$$(x\%2) ? \text{printf}(\text{“x=\%d is odd\textbackslash n”, x}):\text{printf}(\text{“x =\%d is even \textbackslash n”, x}) ;$$

25.2 COMMA OPERATOR

A new expression may be formed from a sequence of other expressions by separating them by a comma , . The expressions in the sequence are evaluated from left to right. If one is interested in knowing the value of the whole expression it is that of the rightmost in the sequence. In the following example:

$$q = 4; r = 7;$$

$$p = q + 2, r + 1, q + r;$$

As $q + 2 = 6$ and $r + 1 = 8$, $q + r = 6 + 8 = 14$. This value is assigned to p. The comma operator is most often used in *for* loop expressions. For example,

$$\text{for (i} = 1, \text{sum} = 1 ; \text{i} <= 4 ; \text{sum} += \text{i, i} += 2)$$

$$\text{/* NULL statement */ ;}$$

is equivalent to

$$\text{sum} = 1;$$
$$\text{for (i} = 1 ; \text{i} <= 4; \text{i} += 2)$$
$$\text{sum} += \text{i};$$

Observe that in the version of *for* using comma operator all the work needed in the looping is done in the *for* statement itself with no other statement in the domain of the loop. As a *for* loop requires a statement we put a semicolon to indicate the termination of the loop. This is called a NULL statement.

In Example Program 25.1 we illustrate the use of conditional operator and comma operator. The function palindrome checks whether a string reads the same whether read from left to right or right to left (ABBA is, for example, a palindrome). In the *for* loop we compare pairwise the left and right most characters in the given string. As soon as one mismatch occurs, control leaves the loop and FALSE is returned. Observe how the left and right indices are simultaneously set. Also the left index is incremented and the right index decremented simultaneously in the *for* loop. This program is concise but not easy to understand. This style is not recommended for beginners.

25.3 MACRO DEFINITION

C provides a pre-processor which processes the source code file before it is compiled. The instructions to the preprocessor which are placed before the program are known as preprocessor directives. We have already been using two such directives. Examples of these are:

#include <stdio.h>

and

#define TRUE 1

A directive starts with the symbol #. Only one directive is allowed per line. The directive is *not* terminated by a semicolon.

The #define directive we have used so far is of the type

#define identifier constant

The #define directive is in fact more general. For instance if a message is to be printed often, we can write:

#define ASK ROLL NO printf("\n Type your Roll no\n")

```
/* Example Program 25.1 */
/* Check if a string is a palindrome */
#include <stdio.h>
#include <string.h>
#define TRUE    1
#define FALSE   0
#define EQUALS  ==
typedef unsigned int Boolean;
Boolean palindrome(char str[]);

main()
{
   char given_string[80];
   /* Given string should not have any blanks */
   while (scanf ("%s", given_string) != EOF)
     palindrome(given_string) ?
         printf("Given string is a palindrome\n"):
         printf("Given string is not a palindrome\n");
} /* End of main */

Boolean palindrome(char str[])
{
   Boolean match_till_now = TRUE;
   int left, right;
   for (left = 0, right = strlen(str) -1;
        (left < right) && match_till_now; left++, right--);
     match_till_now = (str[left] EQUALS str[right]);
   return(match_till_now);
} /* End of palindrome */
```

g a   2 .1   se of conditional and comma operators.

In a program we can then write

```
main()
{

    ASK ROLL NO; /* a MACRO */

}
```

This definition is called a *macro*. Macros can also have parameters. For example,

#define ABS(x) x < 0 ? – (x) : x

Observe that we have used –(x) instead of –x as when an argument is substituted the text of the argument is substituted. Thus if x = 4 – y if we had written

x < 0 ? – x : x

the answer would be – 4 – y instead of – 4 + y. Observe that x can be of any type.

Another macro is

#define SQUARE(x) (x) * (x)

Again parentheses around x in the macro definition are required. If we had written x*x without parentheses then if x = p + 2 the SQUARE(x) would be computed as

p + 2 * p + 2 which is not the same as (p + 2) * (p + 2)

Observe that in macros, textual substitution is done. If this fact is forgotten the result will be wrong. It is very difficult to detect such an error. Thus MACROS should be used with care.

25.4   UNION

There is a declaration called union in C which is used when, for example, one would like to store different data types in a variable or an array. The use of union saves storage space but should be used with care. An example of union declaration is:

```
union any type
{   int i ;
    char c ;
    float f ;
};
```

Observe that the declaration is somewhat like the definition of struct. Unlike a struct, no space is reserved for the three variables declared within union. If we declare a variable x as union any type x then x can store only one variable of any of the three types at a time. If we write

x.i = 4;

printf("%d\n", x.i);

the value printed will be the integer 4.

On the other hand if we write

$$x.c = `P';$$

$$putchar (x.c);$$

the value printed will be P.
    If we write

$$x.c = `P';$$

$$x.f = 22.4678 ;$$

then x will contain the number 22.46778 and not 'P'.

25.5 COMBINING C PROGRAMS IN DIFFERENT FILES

So far we have assumed that an entire C program is written and stored in one file which is then compiled and executed. If a program is large it would be preferable to store functions in different files, compile them and test them separately and then combine these files. Such a method is also necessary if a large C program is developed by different programmers in a team and they are to be combined.

Assume that a program consists of part 1, and part 2 and these are stored in files part1.c and part2.c. If they are to be compiled separately using the UNIX operating system then the UNIX command

cc part1.c part2.c

will do the job. Error messages, if any, for part1.c and part2.c will be separately given. If part1.c compiles without any error and part2.c has errors then part2.c file could be corrected and only part2.c may be recompiled using the command:

cc part1.o part2.c

Observe that the object file created for part1.c is being used without any change. It is reiterated that the two parts are compiled *independently*. One of these parts *must* contain a main. Both, of course, should not have main. Independent compilation is possible if the two parts are self-contained. In general, however, one part may refer to functions defined in the other part. Many questions arise. They are:

1. Can the same variable names be used in part1.c and part2.c without confusion?
2. Can the same function names be used in part1.c and part2.c without confusion?
3. Can the values stored in a variable name in part1.c be used in part2.c. If yes, how?
4. Can the functions defined in part1.c be used in part2.c?

The answer to question 1 is yes, provided

* The variable names are defined within function blocks.
* If the variable names are outside function blocks they must have a prefix static. In such a case the scope of the variable name is within the individual files part1.c and part2.c.

The following example clarifies this:

part1.c

```
#include <stdio.h>
static int p; /* static prefix restricts scope to part1.c p */
main ()
    {   int i; /* i's scope is main */
        for( i = 0; i <= 4; i++)
            p += i ;
        printf ( "%d\n", x(p));
    }
int x (int i)
    {   int y ; /* y's scope is the function x */
        y += i; /* i's scope is function x */
        return(y);
    }
```

part2.c

```
    static int p = 2;
    int y (int j)
        {   int i ; /* i's scope is function y */
            for (i = 0; i <= 6; ++i)
                j *= (i + p); /* j's scope is function y */
            return (j) ;
        }
```

The variable name *p* appearing in both part1.c and part2.c are declared static to restrict their scope.

The answer to question 2 is : No.

The answer to question 3 is yes. If a variable defined in part1.c is to be used by part2.c then prefix *extern* is placed in the declaration of the variable name in part2.c. This is shown in the example below:

part1.c

```
#include <stdio.h>
    int p = 8 ;
main ()
    {   int k, x = 3;
        printf("p = %d\n", p) ;
        k= f(x) ;
        printf ("k = %d\n", k);
    }
```

part2.c

```
extern int p;
int f (int a)
    { int i, k ;
      i = p - 5 ;
      k = a + 2 * i * p ;
      return (k) ;
    }
```

Observe that p is defined (given a value) in part1.c and declared extern and used in part2.c. Definition of a variable should be done where the variable is not declared extern. These two files if compiled, separately, combined and executed will give

$$p = 8$$
$$k = 51$$

The answer to question 4 is yes. In fact functions defined in any of the files can be used in other files. There is no need to define functions as *extern*. When functions are defined they are by default *extern*. If it is required to make a function private to a file and not accessible in other files, we declare it as *static*. Table 25.1 summarizes these rules.

Table 2 .1   Summary of e tern and static

Objective	How achieved
To access variable x external to all functions and defined in file i from file j	declare x as extern x in file j
To make a variable x external to all functions and defined in file i *not* accessible to any other file	declare x as static x in file i
To use a function $f(x)$ defined in file i in file j	No special declaration needed
To make a function float(float x) defined in file i inaccessible to all other files	declare $f(x)$ as: static float f(float x);

25.6   COMMAND LINE ARGUMENTS AND THEIR USE

There are many situations when after a program is written, checked out and compiled one would like to execute it with:

(i) data stored in different data files
(ii) different values of a parameter. For example, a different starting value in iterations.

This should be done automatically without recompilation. Information about the names of the data files to be used or values of parameters should be given to the program. This information is given as part of the command used at execution time. For example, if UNIX is the operating system used to run the C program the steps used to compile and run the program contained in a file prog.c are:

cc prog.c   (compilation step)

The compiled executable code is stored by default in a file named a.out. If we write

a.out   (execution step)

the program is executed. If instead of using the default name a.out we want to give another name to the executable file we write

cc prog.c –o test   (compilation step)

In this case the executable code is stored in test. If we want to execute the program we write

test   (execution step)

and the program test is executed.
If instead of just writing test we write

test fl.dat f2.dat   (execution step)

the strings fl.dat and f2.dat can be read by the C program for appropriate use by specifying two arguments in the main () function. These two arguments are, by convention, known as argc and argv. The main is written as:

main (int argc, char **argv[ ])

The argument argc gives how many arguments are there in the execution command line. *argv[ ] gives the addresses where the strings read from the command line are stored. If the command line is

test fl.dat f2.dat

then
argc   =3;
argv[0] = test;
argv[1] = fl.dat;
argv[2] = f2.dat;
argv[3] = NULL;

Example Program 25.2 is a program to read and display a file named sample.dat. The main () function has no arguments in it. If we want Example Program 25.2 to read a file f1.dat first and display it and repeat the program with another file f2.dat we can modify it using command line arguments. This is done in Example Program 25.2. The main function has two arguments int argc and char ** argv[ ]. The file names f1.dat and f2.dat are read into argv[1] and argv[2] at execution time from the command line. As we intend to read and display more than one file FILE * pointer to file is declared to be an array to accommodate more than one file. In the *for* loop we start with i = 1 as argv[0] stores the name of the program. fopen has argv[i] as the file name. As the array pointer to file starts with 0 we have used pointer to file [i – 1]. The rest of the program is self-explanatory.

```
/* Example Program 25.2 */
/* Reading and displaying two files */
#include <stdio.h>
#define ARRAY_SIZE 80
#define NO_FILES   3

main(int argc, char **argv[])
{
    FILE *pointer_to_file[NO_FILES];
    char temp[ARRAY_SIZE];
    int i;
    for (i = 1; i < argc; ++i)
      {
        pointer_to_file[i-1] = fopen(argv[i], "r");
        if (pointer_to_file[i-1] == NULL)
          {
            printf("Cannot open file %s to read\n", argv[i]);
            return(0);
          }
        fscanf(pointer_to_file[i-1], "%s", temp);
        if (temp == NULL)
          {
            printf("Error in reading file %s\n", argv[i]);
            return(0);
          }
        printf("%s", temp);
        fclose(pointer_to_file[i-1]);
      } /* End of for */
} /* End of main */
```

g a   2 .2   se of command line arguments to read and display different files.

We give as another example the use of command line arguments to read values. In Example Program 25.3 we have written a program to sum the series

$$\text{sum } (x^i/i!) \qquad \text{for } i = 1 \text{ to } n$$

The recurrence relation is

$$\text{term } (i + 1) = \text{term } (i) * (x/i)$$

$$\text{sum} = \text{sum of term } (i) \qquad \text{for } i = 1 \text{ to } n$$

The value of x and n are read using command line arguments. The core of the program is contained in the *for* loop:

```
for (i - 1; i <= n; ++i)
    {   term *= x/(float)i ;
        sum += term ;
    }
```

```
/* Example Program 25.3 */
/* Illustrating use of values from command line arguments */
#include <stdio.h>

main(int argc, char **argv [])
{
    int i, n;
    float sum, x, term = 1.0;
    sscanf(argv[1], "%f", &x);
    sscanf(argv[2], "%d", &n);
    for (i = 1; i <= n; ++i)
        {
            term *= x/(float)i;
            sum += term;
        }
    printf("x = %f, n = %d, sum = %f\n", x, n, sum);
    /* End of main */

/* If the name of the program is 'series' then the UNIX commands to compile and
   run are
   cc series.c-o series
   series
*/
```

g a   2 .3   se of command line arguments to read parameters for a program.

If the name of the program is series the UNIX commands to compile and run it are:

> cc series.c–o series   (compile and store object program)
> series 0.3 10   (execute)

> argc = 3, argv[0] = series, argv[1] = 0.3, argv[2] = 10

The main function now has argument argc; argv[0], argv[1] and argv[2] are character strings. They have to be converted to numbers and stored in x and n. This is done by the scanf function. The general form of scanf function is sscanf(string1, format string, pointers to variables). It reads string 1, converts it using format string and stores the values in the specified variable names.

We could have done the same job in a simpler way by writing without command line arguments the statement:

> scanf("%f%d", &x, &n);

Example Program 25.3 is cooked up to show the use of integer and real values as command line arguments and the use of scanf function.

25.7   CONDITIONAL COMPILATION

Besides providing means of defining constants and macros the C preprocessor also has a feature known as conditional compilation. Conditional compilation is useful in the following situations:

1. When a program has to be run on different machines which have slightly different characteristics such as word length, memory size, etc.
2. When a program is to be run in two modes—a debugging mode in which a number of printf statements are included to help in debugging and a normal mode in which all the printf statements are to be omitted.

Assume that the maximum size of an array which can be stored in a IBMPC is 5000 whereas it is 50000 in another machine, say VAX 8810. We can then use the preprocessor statements:

```
#ifdef IBMPC
#define ARRAY SIZE 5000
#else
#define ARRAY SIZE 50000
#endif
```

If a program test.c is to be compiled for IBMPC, we write in UNIX

cc –D IBMPC test.c

The option – D IBMPC defines IBMPC to the operating system and it takes ARRAY SIZE as 5000.

If we write

cc –D VAX8810 test.c

then ARRAY SIZE is taken as 50000 as IBMPC is not defined and the false branch of the preprocessor statements is taken. If we have a third computer for which ARRAY SIZE is 10000 we can modify the preprocessor statements to:

```
#ifdef IBMPC
#define ARRAY SIZE 5000
#elif VAX8810
#define ARRAY SIZE 50000
#else
#define ARRAY SIZE 10000
#endif
```

In this case if we write

cc –D XYZ test.c

the ARRAY SIZE will be taken as 10000 for XYZ computer.

For debugging a program one normally places printf statements at crucial places in the program to display values of variables. When debugging is over and the program is to be executed these debug lines may be removed by editing the source file and recompiling the code. The preprocessor allows a simpler way. The debug statements may be written as follows:

```
        scanf("%d%f%c\n", &x, &y, &p) ;
#ifdef DEBUG
        printf( "Echoing input data \n") ;
        printf("x =%d, y = %f, z = %c\n", x, y, z) ;
#endif
```

If the program is compiled under UNIX with DEBUG option as shown below:

cc –D DEBUG test.c

then all statements enclosed by #ifdef DEBUG and #endif are compiled and thus the printf statements print values needed. If we compile without DEBUG, that is, give the command

cc test.c

then the statements with #ifdef DEBUG and #endif are not compiled. The executable code will thus become shorter when used for production runs. Another method of including commands for debugging is to write a preprocessor statement

#define	DEBUG 1

and to write

#define	DEBUG 0

for production runs.
we may also write

#define	DEBUG 1

for debugging and

#undef	DEBUG

for production runs.

EXERCISES

25.1 Write a conditional expression to:

    (i) Find the absolute value of a variable
    (ii) Find min of two variables
    (iii) Find min(a, b, c, d, e, f)
    (iv) Find if a variable is a power of 2.

25.2 Use a comma operator in a *for* loop to add all integers < 25 divisible by 3.

25.3 Use a *for* loop with comma operator to find e^{-x} for $x = 0.2$.

25.4 Define a macro called half(x). Use it to find $(ax + b)/2$.

25.5 Define a macro to display an appropriate message on a video screen whenever an integer is to be entered.

25.6   (i) Use command line to find e^{-x} for $x = 0.3$ till the last term added becomes less than 0.00005.

    (ii) If $x = 0.15$ and the last term added is < 0.0005, how would you change the command line?

Appendix I

Compiling and Running C Programs under UNIX

Suppose we have the following C program to compile and execute

```
#include <stdio.h>
main ()
   {   int a, b, c ;
        a = 4 ;
        b = 8 ;
        c = a + b ;
     printf("Answer is c = %d \n", c);
}
```

A file is opened and the code is entered and edited. Let us name this file test 1.c.

The extension .c is used for the file. This is the convention used to indicate that it is a C program and is essential. To compile this program in UNIX environment we type cc test 1.c after a system prompt (we assume it is $) appears as shown below and press the return key.

$cc test 1.c

This is a command to compile test 1.c and generate a *loadable object module* which can be executed. This object code is not stored.

If the compilation has proceeded smoothly and there are no errors then a system prompt ($) appears at the beginning of the next line. If we now type a.out as shown below

$a.out

the computer executes the program and displays the answer:

Answer is c = 12

The UNIX C compiler always puts a *loddable object module* in the file a.out. (The name of the file may be changed if you want.) A load module is directly executable. If we want to just obtain a compiled code and not a loadable executable code, then we give the command

$cc −c test 1.c

Here –c is called a *compile only flag*. In this case an object code is produced and stored in file which is given the name

$$\text{test 1.o}$$

by the UNIX system.

If three different files of C programs named main.c, t.c and p.c are created and are to be compiled one by one, we use the commands

$cc – c main.c
$cc – c t.c.
$cc – c p.c

The object codes created are main.o, t.o and p.o. If there is an error in t but main and p are correct then we can correct t and recompile using the command

$$\text{\$cc –c t.c}$$

The load module is automatically named a.out which can be executed when the $ prompt appears by typing

$$\text{\$a.out}$$

If we want to give a different name, say, example.out to the load module we use the option

$$\text{\$cc – o example.out main.o t.o p.o}$$

The load module is now called example.out and may be executed using the command

$$\text{\$example.out}$$

Appendix II

Reserved Words in C

auto	double	int	struct
break	else	long	switch
case	enum	register	typedef
char	extern	return	union
const	float	short	unsigned
continue	for	signed	void
default	goto	sizeof	volatile
do	if	static	while

Appendix III

Mathematical Functions

The following mathematical functions are defined in <math.h>
    In all the functions given below the arguments are of type *double* and result in also of type *double*

Name	Description
sin(x)	sine of x
cos(x)	cosine of x
tan(x)	tangent of x
asin(x)	arc sin(x). x in range $[-\pi/2, \pi/2]$ and x in range $[-1, 1]$
acos(x)	arc cos(x). x in range $[0, \pi]$ and x in range $[-1, 1]$
atan(x)	arc tan(x). x in range $[-\pi/2, \pi/2]$
atan2(y, x)	arc tan(y/x) in range $[-\pi, \pi]$
sinh(x)	hyperbolic sine of x
cosh(x)	hyperbolic cosine of x
tanh(x)	hyperbolic tangent of x
exp(x)	exponential of x
log(x)	natural logarithm of x (ln x), $x > 0$
$\log_{10}$(x)	logarithm to base 10 of x. $x > 0$
pow(x, y)	x raised to power y. Error indication if $x = 0$ and $y <= 0$ or if $x < 0$ and y is an integer
sqrt(x)	$x^{0.5}$, $x >$ or $= 0$
fabs(x)	absolute value of x
fmod(x,y)	floating point remainder of x/y with the same sign of x. If $y = 0$ the result is implementation dependent.
ceil(x)	Smallest integer $< x$. Returned as double
floor(x)	Largest integer not greater than x. Returned as double

Appendix IV
String Functions

The following functions are some of the functions defined in <string.h>

In the following description sd, sc, s3 are pointers to null-terminated character strings. A single character is represented by c and an integer by n.

char *strcpy(sd, sc)
> Copy string sc to sd including '\0' ; return sd

char *strncpy (sd, sc, n)
> Copy at most n characters of sc to sd; return sd. If sc has less than n characters pad the rest with '\0'.

char *strcat (sd, sc)
> Concatenate string sc at the end of string sd; return sd.

char *strncat (sd, sc, n)
> Concatenate at most n characters of sc to sd and terminate sd with '\0' ; return sd.

char *strchr (sd, c)
> Compare characters of sd with character c starting at the head of the string sd. Return pointer to the first occurrence of c in sd. If c is not present in sd return NULL.

char *strrchr (sd, c)
> Compare characters of sd with character c starting at the tail of the string sd. Return pointer to the first match of c in sd. If c is not present in sd return NULL.

char *strpbrk (sd, sc)
> Return pointer to first occurrence in string sd of *any* character of string sc or NULL if no character of sc is present in sd.

char *strstr (sd, sc)
> Return pointer to first occurrence of the *whole* string sc in sd. If string sc is not present in sd then return NULL.

unsigned int strlen (sd)
> Return length of sd (excluding end of string character '\0').

int strcmp (sd, sc)
> Compare strings sd and sc. Return a value < 0 if sd is lexicographically less than sc, a value $= 0$ if sd $==$ sc and > 0 if sd is lexicographically $>$ sc.

int strncmp (sd, sc, n)
> Compare at most n characters of sd and sc. Return < 0 if sd $<$ sc, $= 0$ if sd $==$ sc, > 0 if sd $>$ sc.

Appendix V

Character Class Tests

Character class tests are defined in <ctype.h>. The argument must be representable as a single character. The functions return non-zero (*true*) if the argument c satisfies the condition described. Otherwise it returns a zero (*false*).

Name	Description	Example
isdigit(c)	If c stores a digit it returns *true*	if c = 8 isdigit(c) = 1
islower(c)	If c stores a lowercase letter it returns *true*	if c = 'x' islower(c) = 1 if c = 'A' islower(x) = *false* = 0
isupper(c)	If c stores an uppercase letter it returns *true*	if c = 'P' isupper(c) = 1
isalpha(c)	isalpha(c) is *true* if isupper(c) or islower(c) is *true*	if c = 'X' isalpha(c) = 1 if c = 'y' isalpha(c) = 1 if c = 9 isalpha(c) = 0
isalnum(c)	if isalpha(c) is *true* or if isdigit(c) is *true* it returns *true*	
isspace(c)	if c is space, form feed, newline, carriage return, tab or vertical tab it returns *true*	if c = '\n' isspace(c) = 1 if c = 'z' isspace(c) = 0
ispunct(c)	if c is a printable character other than space, or digit it returns *true*	if c = ',' ispunct(c) = 1
iscntrl(c)	if c is a control character it returns *true*	if c = 0 iscntrl(c) = 1
isprint(c)	if c is a printable character including space it returns *true*	
isgraph(c)	if c is a printable character except space it returns *true*	
isxdigit(c)	if c is a hexadecimal digit it returns *true*	if c = A isxdigit(c) = 1

Functions to convert case of letters

tolower(c)	returns lowercase letter if c is uppercase else there is no change in c	
toupper(c)	returns uppercase letter if c is lowercase else there is no change in c	

Appendix VI

File Manipulation Functions

Some of the common file manipulation functions available in the C library <stdio.h> are given below. The definitions of EOF, NULL, stdin, stdout, stderr and FILE are included in <stdio.h>. In the following description file name, access mode and format are pointers to strings (terminated by NULL), *buffer* is a pointer to a character array, file pointer is a pointer to a FILE structure, *n* and *size* are positive integers and *c* is a character.

FILE *fopen (*file_name, access_mode*)
  Opens the specified file with the indicated access mode. Valid modes are "r" for reading, "w" for writing, "a" for appending to the end of an existing file, "r+" for read/write access starting at the beginning of an existing file, "w+" for read/write access (and the previous contents of the file, if any are lost), and "a+" for read/write access with all writes going to the end of the file. If the file to be opened does not exist, then it will be created if the *access mode* is write ("w", "w+"), or append ("a", "a+"). If a file is opened in append mode ("a" or "a+"), then it is not possible to overwrite existing data in the file. If the fopen call is successful, then a FILE pointer will be returned to be used to identify the file in subsequent I/O operations; otherwise, the value NULL is returned.

FILE *freopen (*file_name, access_mode, file_pointer*)
  Closes the file associated with *file_pointer*, and opens the file *file_name* with the specified *access_mode* (see the fopen function). The file that is opened is subsequently associated with *file_pointer*. If the freopen call is successful, then *file_pointer* will be returned; otherwise, the value NULL will be returned. The freopen function is frequently used to reassign stdin, stdout or stderr in the program. For example, the call

freopen ("output data", "w", stdout)

will have the effect of reassigning stdout to the file output data, which will be opened in write mode. Subsequent I/O operations performed with stdout will be performed with the file output data, as if stdout had been redirected to this file when the program was executed.

int fscanf (*file_pointer, format, arg1, arg2, ..., argn*)
  Data items are read from the file identified by *file_pointer*, according to the format specified by the character string *format*. The values that are read are stored into the arguments specified after *format*, each of which must be a pointer. The *format* characters

that are allowed in *format* are the same as those for the scanf function. The fscanf function returns the number of items successfully read and assigned or the value EOF if end of file is reached before the first item is read.

int fseek (*file_pointer, offset, mode*)

Positions the indicated file to apoint that is *offset* (a long integer) bytes from the beginning of the file, from the current position in the file, or from the end of the file, depending upon the value of *mode* (an integer). If *mode* equals 0, then positioning is relative to the beginning of the file. If *mode* equals 1, then positioning is relative to the current position in the file. If *mode* equals 2, then positioning is relative to the end of the file. If the fseek call is successful, then a non zero value is returned; otherwise, zero is returned.

long ftell (*file_pointer*)

Returns the relative offset in bytes of the current position in the file identified by *file_pointer,* or −1 on error.

int fwrite (*buffer, size, n, file_pointer*)

Writes *n* items of data from *buffer* into the specified file. Each item of data is *size* bytes in length. Returns the number of items successfully written.

int getc (*file_pointer*)

Reads and returns the next character from the indicated file. The value EOF is returned if an error occurs or if the end of the file is reached.

int putc (*c, file_pointer*)

Writes the character *c* to the indicated file. On success, *c* is returned; otherwise, EOF is returned.

FILE *tmpfile( )

Creates and opens a temporary file in write update mode, returning a FILE pointer identifying the file, or NULL if an error occurs. The temporary file is automatically removed when the program terminates. (Functions called **tmpnam** and **tempnam** are also available for creating temporary file names.)

int ungetc (*c, file_pointer)*

Effectively "puts back" a character to the indicated file. The character is not actually written to the file but is placed in a buffer associated with the file. The next call to getc will return this character. The ungetc function can only be called to "put back" one character to a file at a time; that is, a read operation must be performed on the file before another call to ungetc can be made. The function returns *c* if the character is successfully "put back" or the value EOF otherwise.

int fprintf (*file_pointer, format, arg1, arg2, ..., argn*)

Writes the specified arguments to the file identified by *file_pointer,* according to the format specified by the character string *format.* Format characters are the same as for the printf function (see Chapter 19). The number of characters written is returned.

int fputc (*c, file_pointer*)

Writes the character *c* to the file identified by *file_pointer,* returning *c* if the write is successful, and the value EOF otherwise.

int fputs (*buffer, file_pointer*)

Writes the characters in the array pointed to by *buffer* to the indicated file until the terminating null character in *buffer* is reached. *A* newline character is not automatically written to the file by this function. On failure, the value EOF is returned.

int fread (*buffer, size, n, file_pointer*)

Reads *n* items of data from the identified file into *buffer*. Each item of data is *size* bytes in length. For example, the call

fread (text, sizeof (char), 80, in file)

reads 80 characters from the file identified by in file, and stores them into the array pointed to by text. The function returns the number of characters that are successfully read.

int fflush (*file_pointer*)

Flushes (writes) any data from internal buffers to the indicated file, returning zero on success and the value EOF if an error occurs.

int fgetc (*file_pointer*)

Returns the next character from the file identified by *file_pointer,* or the value EOF if an end of file condition occurs (remember that this function returns an int).

char *fgets (*buffer, n, file_pointer*)

Reads characters from the indicated file, until either n – 1 character are read or until a newline character is read, whichever occurs first. Characters that are read are stored into the character array pointed to by *buffer*. If a newline character is read, then it will be stored in the array. If an end of file is reached or an error occurs, then the value NULL is returned; otherwise, buffer is returned.

int fclose (*file_pointer*)

Closes the file identified by *file_pointer,* and returns zero if the close is successful, EOF if an error occurs.

int feof (*file_pointer*)

Returns nonzero if the identified file has reached the end of the file and zero otherwise.

int ferror (*file_pointer*)

Checks for an error condition on the indicated file and returns zero if an error exists, and nonzero otherwise. (There is a related function **clearerr**, which can be used to reset an error condition on a file.)

void rewind (*file_pointer*)

Resets the indicated file back to the beginning of the file.

The functions **sprintf** and **sscanf** are provided for performing data conversion in memory. These functions are analogous to the **fprintf** and **fscanf** functions except a character string replaces the FILE pointer as the first argument.

int sprintf(*buffer, format, arg1, arg2, ..., argn*)

The specified arguments are converted according to the format specified by the character string *format* and are placed into the character array pointed to by *buffer*. The number of characters placed into *buffer* is returned, excluding the terminating null.

int sscanf *(buffer, format, arg1, arg2, ..., argn)*

The values as specified by the character string *format* are "read" from buffer and stored into the corresponding pointer arguments that follow *format*. The number of items successfully assigned is returned by this function.

Appendix VII
Utility Functions

The library <stdlib.h> has a number of functions for number conversion, storage allocation, sorting and a number of useful tasks. We explain some of the more useful ones below.

double atof(*string*)
Converts character *string* to a double precision number.
Example: double atof (char a[ ]);

int atoi (*string*)
Converts character (*string*) to an integer value
Example: int atoi (char a[ ])

long atol (*string*)
Converts character *string* to long integer value

int rand (void)
Returns a pseudo random integer in the range 0 to 32767

void srand (unsigned int seed)
Uses *seed* to produce a new sequence of pseudo random numbers. Initial seed is 1.

void calloc (unsigned int *n*, unsigned int *s*)
Calloc returns space for an array of *n* objects each of size *s* or NULL if the request cannot be satisfied. The space is initialized to 0 bytes.

void *malloc(unsigned int *s*)
malloc returns a pointer to an object of size *s* or NULL if the request cannot be satisfied. The space is uninitialized.

void *realloc (void *p, unsigned int *s*)
realloc changes the size of objects pointed to by *p* to *s*. The contents will be unchanged up to the minimum of the old and new sizes. If the new size is larger, the new space is uninitialized, realloc returns a pointer to the new space, or NULL if the request cannot be satisfied, in which case *p is unchanged.

void free (void *p)
free disallocates the space pointed to by *p*. It does nothing if *p* is NULL. *p* must be a pointer previously allocated by malloc, calloc or realloc.

void abort(void)
abort causes the program to terminate abnormally.

void exit (int status)
exit causes normal program termination.
status = 0 for successful termination.

int abs(int *n*)
abs returns the absolute value of *n*.

long abs (long *n*)
abs returns the absolute value of long argument
div_t div (int num, int denom)

```
    struct div_t
        {  int quot ;
           int rem ;
        };
```

div computes quotient and remainder of num/denom. The results are stored in the struct div_t.

ldiv_t ldiv(long num, long denom)

same as div except that it uses long integer arguments.

Appendix VIII

Applications of MS Office Software

A1. INSTALLING A SOFTWARE PACKAGE

Step 1: Insert the CD and click on the icon (see Fig. A1.1) to begin the installation

Step 2: Once installation is initiated, installation dialog box would appear. Follow the instructions given by the dialog box and you can install the software needed.

Fig.   1.1   Set up icon for installing ne   soft are.

Removing a Software Package

Step 1: Go to Start → Settings → Control Panel. Select the icon Add/Remove. A pop window displays a list of all software installed (see Fig. A1.2). Select the software from the list displayed and click on the button **Change/Remove** (right pointed by arrow). The software will be removed and its description will disappear from the display.

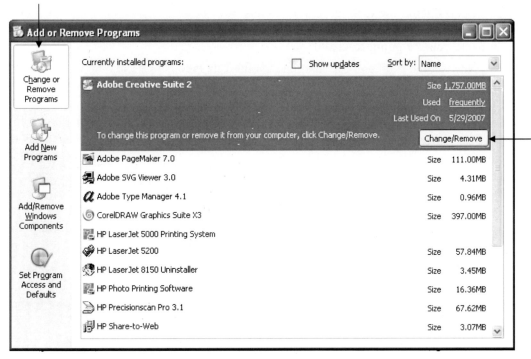

Fig. 1.2 ist of installed soft are.

A2. CREATING A DOCUMENT IN MS WORD

Step 1: Go to START → PROGRAMS → MICROSOFT OFFICE → click Microsoft Word. A Window opens (see Fig. A2.1).

Toolbar containing Options, File, Edit, etc.

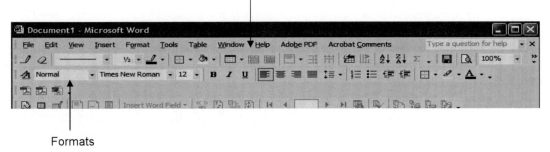

Formats

Fig. 2.1 icrosoft ord menu and tool bars.

Step 2: Click **File** on the tool bar and then click Save in the File Menu. A window opens. Enter the file name in the **File Name** box , e.g.<chapter.doc> and then click save. This saves the file name you are going to create.

Step 3: Now set the right and left margins. On the **File** menu click **Page Setup**. A window pops up. Click **Margins** tab and set the right and left margins to the desired level. Click OK using the left button of the mouse.

Step 4: Start keying in the matter you want to be stored in the file chapter.doc. After entering the matter if you want the title to be bold face, large font and centered, do the following:

1. Select the text to be centered and click ≡ button on the Formatting tool bar

2. Select the text and click **B** button on the Formatting tool bar

3. Select the text and type the font size (e.g. 10 or 12)or click on the drop down list on the Formatting tool bar (see Fig. A2.2).

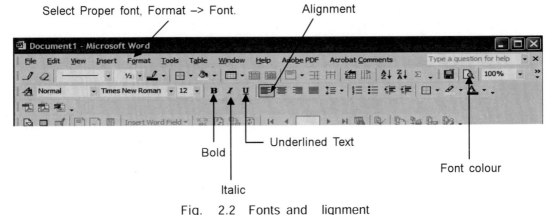

Fig. 2.2 Fonts and lignment

Other basic facilities available on most word processors are:

1. Editing a document which includes correcting typing errors, italicizing, boldfacing and underlining words.
2. Polishing the document by correcting spellings, grammar.
3. Formatting a document by providing appropriate margins proper heading, paragraphing, etc.
4. To add bullets or numbering to the existing text, select the text to be numbered/ bulleted and on the Formatting tool bar, click ⅸ button for numbering and ⅸ button for bulleting. To finish the list press enter twice or give a backspace.

We will now explain how each of these is done.

Editing: The simplest editing is to correct typing errors. To do this select and block the word to be corrected. Delete it and type the new matter. Single letters and a block of letters may also be corrected.

Underlining: Select the word/text to be underlined on the Formatting tool bar. Click $\underline{\textbf{U}}$ button

EXAMPLE: Before entering a text it is given a file name, for example, essay1.doc.

Italicising: Select the word to be italicized and on the Formatting tool bar click $\boxed{\textbf{\textit{I}}}$ button

Spell Check and Corrections

Wrongly spelt words will be underlined by red wavy lines as you type. Select the paragraph to be spell checked. On the Standard tool bar click spelling and grammar and make the changes in the spelling dialog box as shown below (See Fig. A.23).

EXAMPLE:

The softw are is intelligent enough not ot reak a workd arbitrarily in the middle. Instead, an entire word is taken to the next line. Thisis called word wrap-around.

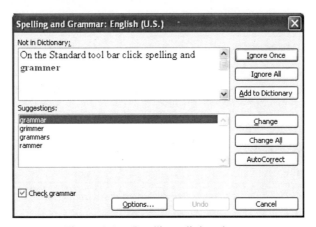

Fig. 2.3 Spelling dialog bo .

Note: If you have mistyped a word but the result is not a misspelling, e.g. dusk and desk the spell checker will not underline the word.

Interchanging paragraphs using cut and paste facility

(i) Select the text (Place the cursor at the beginning of the word, click the right button of the mouse and drag it to the end of the word to be selected).

(ii) Go to **Edit** menu and click **cut**.

(iii) Place the cursor in the active window where you want to paste, go to **Edit** and click paste (see Fig. A2.4).

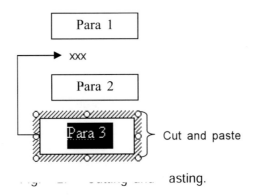

asting.

A3. MAIL MERGE USING MS WORD

What is Mail Merge?

It is an application program available in MS Office to create a set of personalized letters, addresses etc. Consider the following letter which is the main document:

> Dear <name>
>
> A meeting has been arranged in Hotel Rama on October 30, 2007, to discuss our club's activities. We will be very happy if you and your <wife> can attend it.
>
> Looking forward to seeing you,
>
> Yours sincerely,
>
> Ramu

Fig.   3.1   ough model of invitation

Suppose the above invitation is to be sent to several persons. For each letter <name> and <wife> are to be changed. To do this:

- Create a word document with contents of Fig. A3.1.
- A data source has to be specified
- Data source is another word file given in Fig. A3.2 which you should enter and save. Observe that the fields <name> and <wife> are separated by a colon. The values for <name> and <wife> are entered in subsequent lines and should also be separated by colons or other specified delimiters. Each record (i.e. a line) should be separated by

> <name>:<wife>
> Kichu:Kamala
> Gopal:Lakshmi

Fig.   3.2   ata source   ith values.

a delimiter which may be a comma or merely pressing the enter key. (Note: other allowable data sources are a database, address book, excel table etc.).

• In Fig. A3.1 the fields shown in angular brackets < > are to be replaced with fields, in the data source of Fig. A3.2. To do this the following steps are taken:

Step 1: From the Tools Menu point to letter and mailings (See Fig. A3.3) and click Mail Merge Wizard . The mail merge task pane opens. The task buttons steps you through the process. Alternatively, you can use mail merge tool bar which displays instructions to be followed.

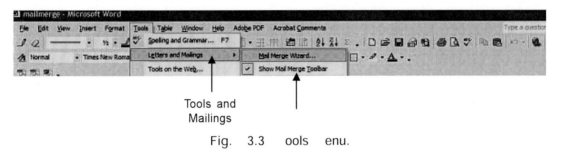

Fig. 3.3 ools enu.

Step 2: Using the mail merge wizard open main document (Fig. A3.1). Select letters from mail merge options (See Fig.A3.4)

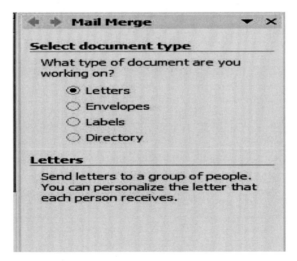

Fig. 3. ail merge options.

Step 3: Follow the instructions on the mail merge wizard to open data source file and view mail recipients.

Step 4: Place the cursor in the documents containing invitation. Click on Insert Merge Fields to match and insert fields where cursor is positioned in the document. The system will now display <<name>> and <<wife>>.

Step 5:   Finally an icon – Insert Merge Fields should be clicked in task pane.

Insert

Fig.   3.   Insert   ail   erge icon.

Step 6:   Now the fields to be merged shown in source document will be inserted in the first letter.

Step 7:   Repeat the above steps record by record as many times as the number of letters to be personalized. Each personalized letter will be on a separate page (file). (*Note:* You can also merge the whole bunch of letters by merge "all" command or "from record to record". However in this case all letters will appear on the same page. You have to now block each letter and store each in a separate file.

Note: You may also merge to each letter an address field by storing the list of addresses in a source document and following the instructions given above for mail merge.

A4. EXCEL (SPREADSHEET PROGRAM)

What is Excel?

Excel is an MS Office application program which allows you to perform various arithmetic and logical operations on numerical entries in a table. It also allows you to draw various charts such as bar chart, pie chart, etc., for display.

Step 1:   Start the Excel application. The Excel window would appear on the screen. A portion of the window is shown as Fig. A4.1.

- A cell is identified by its column and row names, e.g. A2 where A stands for the column and 2 stands for the row.
- A selected cell will be bounded by a bold face rectangle,. See Fig. A4.1 where A2 is selected.
- Once a cell is selected, letters or numbers keyed in will be displayed in that cell.
- Row 1 is usually used for giving headings for columns.
- A selected cell name will appear in the Formula bar at extreme left. In Fig. A4.1 you can see that A2 is selected and it appears at extreme left on the formula bar.

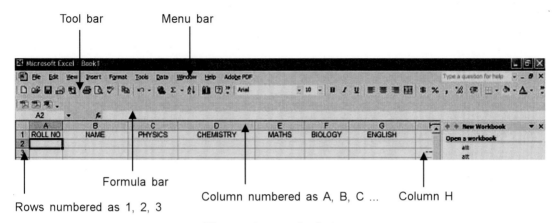

Fig.   .1   cel   indo .

Rows numbered as 1, 2, 3

Menu bar	contains Menu options for selections like file, edit, help etc.
Tool bar	has options like open, save, bold, italics etc., shown in icons.
Formula bar	is the place where you enter the formula to be applied to a cell. The cell would contain the result on the execution of the formula. For example, in Fig. A4.1 if you enter marks of subjects in C2, D2, ..., G2 respectively and you want the average of marks obtained for 5 subjects to appear in H2 then select H2 and write the following formula in the formula bar = (C2+D2+E2+F2+G2)/ 5 or use average function. The function will be listed if you click fx in the formula bar. Pressing enter would leave the average in the cell H2.

The above step can be applied to cells H3, H4, etc. for each student after his marks are entered in the five subjects. (*Note:* To select an entire column you drag the + symbol which appears at the lower right hand corner of H2 by pressing the left mouse button till the end of the column). The appropriate cell values will be automatically set).

Keeping the above in mind let us examine the steps to prepare mark sheet of students and finally draw a bar chart showing the distribution of grades.

Step 2: Applying Step 1 for H2...H3... will fill the cells with corresponding student's average. If you want the respective grades to appear in I2, I3, I4 etc., based on the rule to be used for awarding grades from marks, select I2 and in the formula bar type the formula (see Fig. A4.2) to determine the grade, as shown below:

=IF(AND(H2>=85,H2<=100),"A",IF(AND(H2>=70,H2<=84),"B",IF(AND(H2>=55,H2<=69), "C",IF(AND(H2>=40,H2<=54), "D","F")))

The above formula is applied to cells I2, I3, I4.... By selecting the entire I column as explained earlier. Grade of each student will appear in the column. Having found the grades to get the count of As, Bs, Cs, ... you may select columns J, K, L, M, N to hold the respective counts. Count of As is obtained as follows:

Enter formula = IF(AND (H2>=85,H2<=100), 1, 0) in the formula bar (See Fig. A4.3).

Fig. .2 Formula bar display.

Fig. .3 Counting s.

The above formula is to check whether cell H2 contains a value greater than or equal to 85 and less than or equal to 100. If yes, 1 will be entered in J2 and also in subsequent cells J3, J4 etc. To find counts of B use the formula:

$$=IF\ (AND(H2>=70,H2<=84),\ 1,\ 0)$$

Similar formulae for C, D and F are applied to columns K, L, M and N.

Step 3: This step is in preparation for drawing the bar chart of grades. The following steps will sum the values in columns J, K, L, M and N to find the count of grades, A, B, C, D, F.

- Place labels A, B, C, D, F representing grades, in cells O2....O6 (see Fig. A4.4)
- P2....P6 are to be filled with the counts of A, B, C, D and F

To put the count of grade A in P2 do the following:

- Select the cell P2
- Enter the following formula in the formula bar
  =SUM(J2:J19) as column J contains 1 for each A. The Sum of As, namely, 3 will appear in P2.
  (*Note:* SUM is a predefined function which adds values in the cells given as its argument, namely, J2 to J19)
      The above steps are repeated for cells P3, P4.... in each case varying the argument of function SUM. Thus SUM (K2:K19) will give count of Bs in cell P3 if P3 is selected and the formula applied.
      Repeat the above steps to fill P4, P5 and P6 to fit with corresponding counts of C, D and F respectively.

After the completion of step 3, columns O and P contains values as shown in Fig. A4.4. (Figure A4.4 shows only the first 6 rows and is partial)

	E	F	_G	H	I	J	K	L	M	N	O	P
	MATHS	BIOLOGY	ENGLISH	AVG	GRADE	AGRADE	BGRADE	CGRADE	DGRADE	FGRADE		
1												
2	90	84	85	85.8	A	1	0	0	0	0	A	3
3	86	86	90	85.4	A	1	0	0	0	0	B	5
4	94	90	70	87.8	A	1	0	0	0	0	C	8
5	49	56	91	61.6	C	0	0	1	0	0	D	1
6	65	75	56	69	C	0	0	1	0	0	F	1

P2 =SUM(J2:J19)

Fig. . Count of C F.

Step 4: To plot the graph representing the frequency of grades select columns O and P and select chart graphic icon in the tools bar as pointed by the arrow (see Fig. A4.5).

Graph Icon

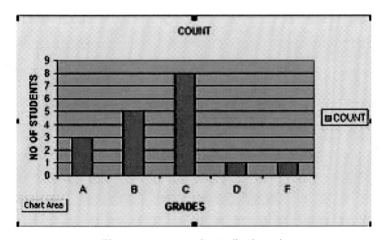

Fig. . ool bar sho ing icon for bar chart.

Step 5: When graphic icon is selected instructions appear on the screen giving you several graph options. Select the option called Column Graph and its parameters. Finally the graph would appear as shown in Fig. A4.6. The appropriate X-axis and Y-axis captions and graph title are to be typed in as required.

Fig. . ar chart displayed.

The graph can be embedded in the same page or placed in the next worksheet. The steps are self explanatory once you click the chart icon

A5. AN INTRODUCTION TO POWERPOINT

What is PowerPoint?

PowerPoint is an application program for designing presentation of lectures, research papers and so on. It involves preparation of slides. These slides can be stored in the hard disk or as CDs and projected or even run on the web.

Starting PowerPoint

Step 1: Start the computer

Step 2: Select Program option from start up menu

Step 3: Select Microsoft PowerPoint. PowerPoint window opens.

As in other Programs the window has many bars containing several options (see Fig. A5.1).

Menu Bar   Tool Bar   Formatting Bar

Fig. .1 o er oint tools.

1. Title bar
2. Menu bar—Shows a list of commands such as File, Edit, View, Slide Show etc.
3. Standard tool bar—This has icons for Open, Save, Print .... etc.
4. Formatting tool bar—Contains buttons for formatting like boldface, italics, underline etc.
5. Slide area—where the contents of the current slide is displayed (see Fig. A5.2)
6. Add notes area—In this area below slide area notes can be added
7. Drawing tool bar—It provides icons for insetting text, drawings, etc.
8. View buttons—This helps in changing the display of the slides
9. Outline Pane—This is used for organizing the presentation

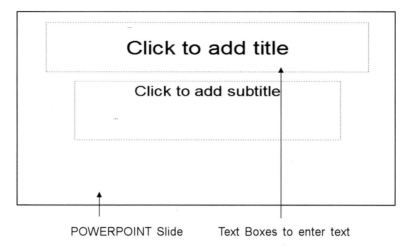

POWERPOINT Slide   Text Boxes to enter text

Fig. A5.2 Blank slides.

Step 4: Creating a Slide
Even though several options are available for preparing slides we will look at the basic steps of creating slides of our choice.

    1. Click with the left button File option after opening the Microsoft PowerPoint program. A drop down menu follows:

Text Boxes

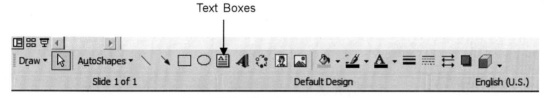

Fig. A5.3 File drop down menu.

    2. Click on the **New** option
    3. A dialog box appears
    4. In that click **Blank Presentation** option
    5. PowerPoint displays several layouts on the side (see Fig. A5.4). Select the layout you desire.

We will now learn the following:

    1. How to Align Text
    2. How to create Bullets in Text
    3. How to apply Footer to all Slides
    4. How to create a new Slide
    5. How to start slide show

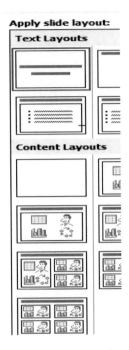

Fig. A5.4 Layout options.

Step 5: Aligning Text

In Fig. A5.5, pointed by Arrows, three Alignment Options are Available

1. Left
2. Center
3. Right

Select the text to be aligned and select any of the Alignment Options

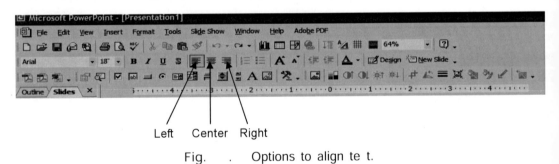

Left   Center   Right

Fig.   .   Options to align te t.

Step 6: Creating bullets in text

- Select the group of text
- From the menu bar choose the option for applying Bullets or Numbers see Fig. A5.6

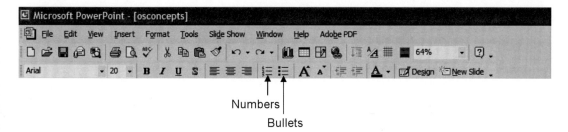

Fig.   .   Choosing numbers or bullets.

- The icons, Numbers, Bullets will get highlighted only when a text is selected and subsequently either bullets or numbers is clicked. The slide entered and formatted is shown in Fig. A5.7.

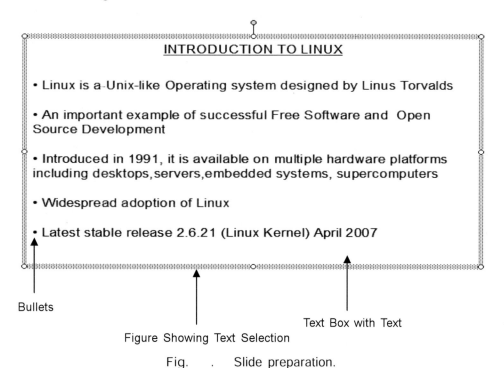

Fig.   .   Slide preparation.

Step 7:   Applying footer for all slides

- Select View -> Header and Footer
- Once Selected, a dialog box will appear, where you can input your text which should appear as footer and Select the **option Apply to all Slides**. See Fig. A5.8. Do the same for header. Save this.

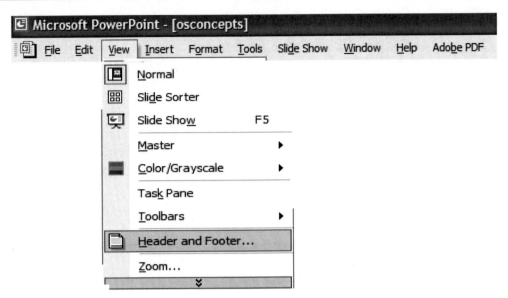

Fig.   .   ic ing header and footer

Step 8:   Creating New Slide
Click on icon New Slide as shown in Fig. A5.9.

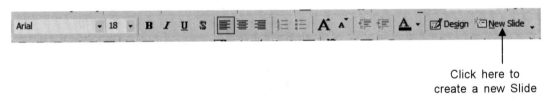

Click here to
create a new Slide

Fig.   .   Creating a ne   slide.

You can create more slides following steps 5 to 7

Step 9:   Starting Slide Show
- After preparing the set of slides we need to start the slide show. This is done by clicking on Slide Show in the menu bar as shown in Fig. A5.10
- While the show is in progress, pressing ESCAPE key would return the control to start.

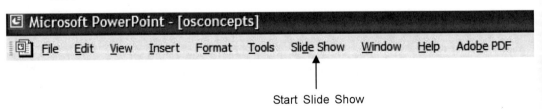

Start Slide Show

Fig.   .1   Starting slide sho   .

Additional Notes

Note 1:   If we want to maintain the format for a set of slides we have an option of creating a "slide master". To to do this click on the view menu, select slide master. With the help of layout and slide area we can create a master slide of our choice. This will apply to the slides which follow.

Note 2:   We can design slides using design templates. These will help us to have animation and colourful slides. To explore one can refer to "help".

Thus the use of power point lies with the creativity of a person keeping clarity of presentation as the key feature.

Bibliography

Brown, D.L., From ascal to , Narosa Publishing House, New Delhi, 1985.

Esakov, J. and Weiss, T.   ata Structures An Advanced Approach sing , Prentice-Hall, Englewood Cliffs, N.J., 1989.

Hancock, L. and Krieger, M., he   rimer McGraw-Hill, New York, 1987.

Holzner, S.,   rogramming Prentice-Hall of India, New Delhi, 1992.

Jhonsonbaugh, R. and Kalin, M., Applications rogramming in , Macmillan Publishing Company, New York, 1990.

Jones, R. and Stewart, I., he Art of   rogramming Narosa Publishing House, New Delhi, 1988.

Kernighan, B.W. and Ritchie, D.M., he   rogramming anguage Prentice-Hall of India, New Delhi, 1989.

Kochan, S.G., rogramming in , CBS Publishers, Delhi, 1987.

Rajaraman, V., omputer rogramming in ascal Prentice-Hall of India, New Delhi, 1991.

Rajaraman, V., Fundamentals of omputers, 4th ed., Prentice-Hall of India, New Delhi, 2005.

Rajaraman, V., Introduction to Information echnolog Prentice-Hall of India, New Delhi, 2007.

Tizzard, K., for rofessional rogrammers Affiliated East-West Press, New Delhi, 1986.

Index

Algorithm, 18, 23, 65, 70
Arithmetic conversion, 120
Arithmetic expressions
    examples of, 116
    floating point, 113
    integer, 113
    use of parenthesis, 115
Arithmetic operators, 112
    precedence of, 114
Array declaration, 169
Array variable, 168
Arrays
    with multiple subscripts, 173
    reading and writing, 174
    syntax rules of, 171
Assembler, 31
Assembly language, 30
Assignment expression, 121
Assignment statements, 118
    explicit type conversion, 120

Binary digits, 6
    counting, 8
Binary trees, 332
    declaration of node, 332
    representation with pointers, 333
    use of, 334
BIOS (Basic Input–Output system), 25
Bit operations, 353
    applications, 353
Bit operators, 352
    definition of, 353
Break statement, 196, 201
Browser, 48
    facilities provided by, 58

C
    history of, 88
    mathematical functions, 398
    reserved words, 397
    string functions, 397
    structure of a program, 252
C program files
    combining, 387
C programs
    compiling, 395
    executing, 396
Character class tests, 401
Character data type, 257
    declaration of, 257
Character strings, 259
    basic operations, 261
Characters
    ASCII code, 12
        for characters, 258
    encoding of, 10
    ISCII code, 13
    unicode, 13
Circular list, 324
    creation of, 325
Collating sequence, 258
Comma operator, 384
    use in *for* statement, 384
Command line arguments, 389
    use of, 390, 391, 392
Comment, 93
Compile time diagnostics, 88
Compiler, 32, 87
Compound statement, 140
Computer
    block diagram of, 16
    characteristics of, 68

data processing using, 17
desktop, 18
   keyboard, 18
   video display unit, 19
features of, 68
hardware, 20, 23
model of, 15
motherboard, 19
operating system, 20, 24
memory
   main, 19
   secondary, 19
network, 38
personal, 19
programs, 17
a simple model, 72, 73
software, 20, 23
Conditional compilation, 392
Conditional operator, 383
   use of, 385
Conditional statement, 138, 141
   example programs, 145
   nested, 143, 144
   programming style, 149
Constants
   defining, 109
   floating, 103, 105
   floating point exponent, 106
   floating point fractional, 105
   hexadecimal, 105
   integer, 103
   octal, 104
Continue statement, 203
   use of, 205

Data structures
   array, 170
   file, 361
   lists, 316
   stack, 288
   tree, 332
Data types
   array, 168
   audio, 5
   character, 257
   creating new names, 284
   enumerated, 279

floating point, 113
image, 5
integer, 113
internal representation, 6
list, 316
logical, 187
pointer, 306
scalar, 107
structure, 293
test, 5
video, 6
Decision tables, 82
Declaration, 94
Defragging, 27
Device driver, 25
Direct access file, 374, 375
   accessing a record, 378
   appending a record, 379
   creating, 376
Domain name system, 46
Domain names, 47
Doubly linked list, 324
   circular list, 324, 329
   creation of, 329, 330
   deleting a node from, 332

e-mail systems, 48
Encoding decimal numbers, 7
End of file (EOF), 135
Ethernet
   CSMA/CD, 41
   message format, 40
Execution time error, 88

File mainipulation functions, 402
File transfer protocol (FTP), 58, 59
Files in C, 361
   creating, 362
   declaraction, 362
   file functions, 367
   opening, 362, 363, 364
   printing, 363
   sequential, 366
Firewall, 42
Firmware, 25

Flow charts, 70
    conventions of, 71
    examples, 64
    tracing of, 76, 77
Function main(), 93
Functions, 229
    arrays in, 240
    call by reference, 244
    call by value, 244
    calls and returns from, 241
    definition and calling, 238
    formal argument, 231
    fread, 374, 380
    fseek, 374
    fwrite, 374, 380
    main, 230
    malloc, 317, 318
        use of, 319
    pointer, 310
    prototype, 231
    recursive, 338
    syntax rules, 237

Hexadecimal digits, 9
Hypertext, 52
Hypertext Markup Language, 51
Hypertext Transfer Protocol, 51

Identifier, 107
Information technology, 3
Input function
    characters in format string, 134
    general format, 133
    scanf, 133
Input statement, 96
Interpreter, 32
Internet, 34, 37, 43
    applications, 47
    downloadable software, 59
Internet Service Provider (ISP), 49, 50
IP address, 43, 45, 46

Library functions
    getchar, 261
    putchar, 261

Linked list, 320
    manipulation of, 320
List creation of, 318, 321
List data structure, 315
    declaration of, 316
List searching of, 322
Local area network, 38
    ethernet, 40
    hub, 39
Logical expressions, 185, 187
    use of, 191
Logical operators, 185, 187
    definition of, 188
    precedence rules, 189
    use of, 188
Loops in programs
    do while loop, 154, 164
    for loop, 154, 159
    while loop, 154

Machine independent language, 87
Machine language, 86
    program, 211
Macro definition, 385
Microsoft Office, 20
Modem, 44
MS Office
    creating a Word document, 409
    Excel, 414
    installing a software, 408
    mail merge, 412
    PowerPoint presentation, 418

Network interface unit (NIU), 38
NULL, 317

Object program, 87
Operating system
    classification of, 29
    functions of, 26
    types of, 27
Operators
    arithmetic, 113
    binary, 125
    bit, 353

decrement, 122, 126
hierarchy of, 125
increment, 122, 126
for pointers, 306
precedence of, 190
relational, 139
shift, 353
sizeof, 317
unary, 125
Output function
conversion specification, 133
printf, 129

Packing bits in a word, 360
Pointer(s), 20
in arrays, 308
data type, 305, 316
declaration of, 306
in functions, 310
interpretation in statements, 307
Preprocessor directive, 93
Programming language, 17, 23, 30, 68
classification of, 33
description of, 90
high level, 31, 86, 87
steps in compilation, 89
semantic rules, 90
syntax rules, 90

Recursive function, 338
algorithm(s), 340, 341–344
definition of, 338
examples of, 338, 339
vs. iteration, 340
tree building, 345, 346
Relational operator, 139
Resource directories, 55
Return statement, 231
Router, 42, 43

Scanner, 20
Search engine, 56
Sequential files, 366
creating of, 367, 369
retrieving, 371

searching 370
updating, 371, 373
Software
application, 24
packaged, 24
system, 24
Source program, 87
Stack, 288
simulation of, 289
Statements in C
arithmetic, 94
assignment, 94, 118
break, 201
continue, 203
do while, 164
for, 159
function, 230
fclose, 367
fopen, 367
fseek, 374
fscanf, 367
fprint, 367
goto, 214
if, 138
if then else, 138, 141
printf, 95, 129
return, 231
rewind, 367
scanf, 96, 133
switch, 193
while, 154
Statistical data processing, 216
String processing, 268
Strings
gets function, 276
puts function, 276
Structures, 293
definition, 293, 296
use in a function, 299
use in arrays, 299
Survey data processing, 221
Switch statement, 193, 283
syntax rules, 196
use of, 200

TCP/IP protocol, 43
Telnet, 58, 60

Text files, 379
   copying, 381
   manipulating, 380
   reading, 380
   writing, 380
Three bit adder, 356
Tree traversal, 347
   inorder traversal, 347
   postorder traversal, 348, 349
   preorder traversal, 348, 349

Union declaration, 386
URL (Universal Resource Locator), 48, 52, 53, 54, 55
Utility functions, 406

Variables
   automatic, 354
   declaring, 108
   defining, 119
   enumerated, 280
   external, 389
   global, 250, 253
   local, 250, 253
   scalar, 107
   static, 250, 254, 389

Wide area network, 38, 41
Word processing, 13
World Wide Web, 48, 51
   information retrieval from, 55